ILLUSTRATED
HANDBOOK
OF THE BIBLE

GEORGE W. KNIGHT

ILLUSTRATED HANDBOOK OF THE BIBLE

A CLEAR, CONCISE REFERENCE FOR EVERYDAY USE

BARBOUR
PUBLISHING

Published by Barbour Publishing, Inc., 1810 Barbour Drive, Uhrichsville, Ohio 44683, www.barbourbooks.com

Our mission is to inspire the world with the life-changing message of the Bible.

 Member of the
Evangelical Christian
Publishers Association

Printed in China.

To all my Bible teachers and students,
past and present,
who have sparked my commitment
to a lifetime study
of God's Word.

Contents

Acknowledgments 11
Introduction 13
A Note on the Notes 14

Part 1: The Old Testament 15

   Chapter 1: Books of the Law .16
      Genesis 17
      Exodus 24
      Leviticus 29
      Numbers 33
      Deuteronomy 39

   Chapter 2: Books of History .44
      Joshua 45
      Judges 49
      Ruth 55
      1 Samuel 57
      2 Samuel 63
      1 Kings 70
      2 Kings 77
      1 Chronicles 84
      2 Chronicles 89

Ezra 97
Nehemiah .100
Esther 104

Chapter 3: Books of Poetry and
Wisdom 108
Job 109
Psalms 113
Proverbs. .124
Ecclesiastes 129
Song of Solomon. 132

Chapter 4: Books of the Major Prophets . . 134
Isaiah 135

Jeremiah. 142
Lamentations. 151
Ezekiel. 153
Daniel 159

Chapter 5: Books of the Minor Prophets . . .163
Hosea. 164
Joel. 166
Amos 168
Obadiah. 170
Jonah 171
Micah 173
Nahum. 175
Habakkuk 177
Zephaniah 179
Haggai. 180
Zechariah. 182
Malachi 185

Part 2: The New Testament 187

Chapter 6: The Gospels 188

Matthew 189

Mark 205

Luke 214

John 229

Chapter 7: Acts, a History of the Early Church 237

Chapter 8: Epistles of the Apostle Paul 250

Romans 251

1 Corinthians 256

2 Corinthians 262

Galatians 265

Ephesians 268

Philippians 270

Colossians 273

1 Thessalonians 275

2 Thessalonians 277

1 Timothy 280

2 Timothy 283

Titus 285

Philemon 286

Chapter 9: The General Epistles . . 287

Hebrews 288

James 293
1 Peter 296
2 Peter 299
1 John 300
2 John 303
3 John 304
Jude 305
Revelation 307
Maps 315
Index 325
Art Credits 347

Acknowledgments

A book like this doesn't happen without the encouragement and support of many people. My special thanks to those who have played a major role in its creation. Paul K. Muckley, senior editor for nonfiction at Barbour Publishing, served as cheerleader and problem-solver for the entire project. He worked under an impossible schedule to make sure all the pieces came together in the right order. My thanks to him for a job well done.

As an editor myself, I realize that behind-the-scenes book publishing professionals seldom get the recognition they deserve. So let me say a special thank you to those creative professionals on the production team who assisted Paul so capably: Jason Rovenstine, design director; Robyn Martins, page designer; Lauren Schneider, proofreader; and others who played smaller but very important roles in the process.

I am also grateful to my late friend and colleague Rayburn Ray, who worked with me several years ago to cowrite *The Layman's Bible Dictionary*, on which this book was based. My thanks for Rayburn's contribution to that project, and his friendship over many years.

Finally, I express the warmest thank you of all to my wife, Dorothy. For more than forty years she encouraged me in my writing efforts. She tolerated my "creative moodiness," never complaining about the hours I spend at the typewriter or word processor. She even went the second mile by helping me with some of the "grunt work" required for the creation of a reference book such as this—checking scripture references, proofreading, and compiling indexes. King Solomon, author of the book of Proverbs, described her well: "She openeth her mouth with wisdom; and in her tongue is the law of kindness. . . . Let her own works praise her in the gates" (Proverbs 31:26, 31).

Introduction

As a regular, everyday student of the Bible, you deserve biblical study tools that are handy, affordable, and easy to understand. And that's exactly what you get in this *Illustrated Handbook of the Bible*.

This book provides an overview and summary of all sixty-six books in the Bible. Nearly two hundred notes on customs of Bible times will help you understand God's Word better, and are placed near the appropriate biblical passages where these customs are described. An extensive map section will help you see the locations of various Bible cities, towns, and regions.

Your study and research will also be enhanced by the drawings and photographs—most of them in full color—of Bible places and personalities throughout the book. These art pieces were specifically selected to make the scriptures come alive for students of God's Word.

You will also enjoy the abundance of scripture references included. These are intended to encourage you to dig deeper in your study of the Bible. The translation on which this book is based is the familiar Authorized, or King James Version. But variant readings are cited from the New International Version and the New Revised Standard Version to clarify obscure words and phrases.

My prayer is that this *Illustrated Handbook of the Bible* will serve as a valuable source of information for all students who, like the citizens of Berea in the New Testament, are eager to learn more about the Bible, studying expectantly and "with all readiness of mind" (Acts 17:11).

GEORGE W. KNIGHT
HARTSELLE, ALABAMA

A Note on the Notes

The Illustrated Bible Handbook gives an overview of the entire Bible by following a book-by-book format. Each of the sixty-six books of the Bible is introduced and summarized in thumbnail fashion to help you gain a "big picture" understanding of God's Word.

Notes on Bible customs and curiosities are scattered as sidebars throughout the handbook text. These notes are designed to help you dig deeper into the customs and practices of Bible times that are puzzling and strange to many modern readers.

For example, the Israelites were commanded by the Lord not to move "thy neighbour's landmark" (Deut. 19:14). These landmarks were actually boundary stones that marked property lines, much as fences do today. The Israelites were not to move these markers over by a few feet to increase their own land holdings. This was a form of stealing from their neighbors. When we understand these facts, we realize why the Lord would issue such a command.

This customs and curiosities note, titled "Boundary Stones," appears as a sidebar close to the summary passage that it clarifies—Deuteronomy 19:14–21 (see p. 42). This is how you will find these illuminating notes scattered throughout the handbook text.

PART 1

THE OLD TESTAMENT

The Bible has two grand divisions—the Old Testament and the New Testament. The Old Testament is the larger of these two divisions, containing more than twice as much material as the New Testament. The thirty-nine individual Old Testament books were written under the inspiration of the Lord across a period of many centuries by several different authors. The Old Testament also contains many different types of literature: law, history, poetry, prophecy, and wisdom writings.

The word *testament* means "covenant." The Old Testament tells how God called a people, the nation of Israel, to live in covenant with Him.

The five major divisions of the Old Testament are (1) books of the Law—Genesis through Deuteronomy; (2) historical books—Joshua through Esther; (3) books of poetry and wisdom—Job through the Song of Solomon; (4) books of the major prophets—Isaiah through Daniel; and (5) books of the minor prophets—Hosea through Malachi. These divisions of the Old Testament are discussed in the following chapters.

CHAPTER 1
BOOKS OF THE LAW

The first five books of the Old Testament are known as the "Books of the Law." This title is appropriate because the laws and commands of God are the central theme of this section of the Old Testament. God revealed to Moses His expectation of the nation of Israel. Moses recorded these commands as laws in the books of Exodus, Leviticus, Numbers, and Deuteronomy. Genesis contains no specific laws, but it does describe the covenant relationship that God established with His people, the Israelites. This covenant relationship demanded loyalty and obedience from God's chosen people.

These first five books of the Old Testament are also known as the Pentateuch, a Greek term meaning "five-volumed." These five books together take us from the creation of the physical world through the formation of the nation of Israel under the leadership of Moses.

OVERVIEW: Creation of humans, animals, and the physical universe and establishment of the covenant relationship between God and His people.

Introduction to Genesis

The word *Genesis* means "creation, origin, source, or the coming into being of something." Thus, Genesis is the Bible's book of beginnings. As the first book in God's Word, it recounts (1) the beginning of the physical world, (2) the beginning of God's plan of sal-vation for the human race, and (3) the beginning of the nation of Israel.

Creation. Genesis gives us a picture of a sovereign, all-powerful God who brought the physical world into being through the power of His spoken word. The words "and God said" appear as an introduction before each of the six days of creation.

The six days of creation also show that God brought the world into existence in an orderly fashion in accordance with His divine plan. The crowning achievement of His creation was man, whom He created in His image.

As the all-powerful Creator, God had the right to set limits and boundaries beyond which man could not go. But man chose to disobey God in the Garden of Eden. This brought about the need for the second major theme of Genesis.

Sin and Salvation. Before his sin, man enjoyed unlimited fellowship with God. But this relationship was marred and broken when Adam and Eve ate the forbidden fruit. They were banished from the garden and from God's presence.

:1–31. "In the beginning, God created the heaven and the earth." God would quickly bathe the new world in light and fill the earth with every sort of living thing.

But in an act of mercy, God killed an animal and made clothes from its hide to cover their nakedness (3:21). This symbolized His commitment to provide salvation for man, to restore the broken relationship between Himself and humankind.

Throughout the Old Testament, the restoration of this relationship depended on man's keeping the law and obeying God's commandments. But in the New Testament, He sent Christ—His own Son—to do away with law keeping as the basis of salvation. Through His death on the cross, Christ paid the penalty for humankind's sin.

Nation of Israel. From the beginning, God was concerned for the salvation of all humanity. But He chose to channel this concern to the world through a people who would belong to Him in a special sense—the nation of Israel.

God began to build this nation when He called Abraham to leave his pagan surroundings and to go to a new land "that I will shew thee" (12:1)—the land of Canaan. God made a covenant with Abraham in which He promised, "I will make of thee a great nation, and I will bless thee, and make thy name great; and thou shalt be a blessing" (12:2).

The book of Genesis shows how this covenant was renewed across several generations with the descendants of Abraham: Isaac, Jacob, and Jacob's twelve sons, particularly Joseph. It was several hundred years before the tribal descendants of Jacob claimed the land of Canaan as their own, but the promise was planted and nourished in the book of Genesis.

Summary of Genesis

1:1–31. God creates the world in six days (Heb. 1:10).

2:1–25. God creates Adam and Eve, the first man and woman.

3:1–24. Adam and Eve disobey God by eating the forbidden fruit and are cast out of the Garden of Eden.

4:1–2. Two sons, Cain and Abel, are born to Adam and Eve.

4:3–15. Cain murders his brother Abel. God punishes Cain by driving him out of his homeland but protects him by placing a mark on him.

4:16–24. Cain's descendants are listed.

> **[4:16–24] THE TERM *FATHER*.** *Jubal...was the father of all such as handle the harp and organ* (Gen. 4:21).
>
> In the ancient Middle East, the originator of any custom was frequently spoken of as the "father" of that custom. Thus, Jubal was called "the father of all such as handle the harp and organ" because he invented those instruments.
>
> In Isaiah 9:6 the Messiah is called "the everlasting Father," meaning He is the giver of eternal life. In 2 Corinthians 1:3, God is called "the Father of mercies," and in Ephesians 1:17, "the Father of glory."

4:25–5:32. Adam's descendants are listed.

6:1–8. Wickedness spreads throughout the earth, and God determines to destroy the world. But Noah is looked upon with favor by the Lord because of his righteousness (see Exod. 33:12).

6:9–22. The Lord tells Noah to build a huge ark, or boat, in which he and his family will be safe from the catastrophe that He plans to send on the earth. Noah does exactly as God commands.

7:1–16. Noah and his family enter the ark, along with pairs of different animals. Rain pounds the earth for forty days and forty nights.

7:17–24. The earth is struck with a great flood, which lasts for 150 days. But Noah and his family and the animals are safe in the ark (2 Pet. 2:5).

7:17–24. Noah's ark was three stories tall with a single door. Eight human beings and countless animals rode out a flood that "prevailed upon the earth an hundred and fifty days" (Genesis 7:24).

8:1–22. The floodwaters recede, and Noah and his family leave the ark. Noah builds an altar and offers sacrifices to the Lord.

9:1–19. God makes a covenant with Noah and causes a rainbow to appear in the sky as a token of His promise.

9:20–27. Noah falls into a drunken stupor and pronounces a curse on Canaan, a descendant of Noah's son Ham.

9:28–29. Noah dies after living for 950 years.

10:1–32. Noah's descendants are listed.

11:1–9. God confuses human languages at the Tower of Babel because of man's pride and arrogance.

11:10–32. Descendants of Noah's son Shem—the ancestors of Abram/Abraham—are listed.

12:1–20. God calls Abram/Abraham to leave his homeland and settle in a new country, Canaan, where He will give him many descendants and make them into a great nation (Heb. 11:8).

13:1–18. Abram/Abraham and his nephew Lot go their separate ways after a disagreement over grazing lands for their livestock.

14:1–24. Abram/Abraham rescues Lot and pays tithes to Melchizedek, a priest and king.

15:1–21. God makes a covenant with Abram/Abraham and renews His promise to give him a land and many descendants (Gen. 12:1–2).

16:1–16. Abram/Abraham fathers a son, Ishmael, by the Egyptian servant of his wife, Sarah.

17:1–27. God renews His covenant with Abram, renames him Abraham, and promises that Sarah will bear a son. All males in Abraham's household are circumcised as a sign and seal of the divine covenant.

18:1–33. Abraham pleads with God to spare the wicked cities of Sodom and Gomorrah.

19:1–29. Lot escapes when Sodom and Gomorrah are destroyed by the Lord (2 Pet. 2:6).

> **[11:1–9] BABYLONION BRICKS.** *They [builders of the tower of Babel] said..., Let us make brick, and burn them throughly. And they had brick for stone, and slime [tar, NIV] had they for mortar* (Gen. 11:3).
>
> Many of the bricks used in Babylonia, where the Tower of Babel was built, were sun-dried, but others were cured by burning, just like those used in this tower. Fire-cured bricks were stronger, so they were sometimes laid next to a wall of sun-dried brick to give it strength and stability.

[15:1–21] A STARTLING SIGN. *And it came to pass, that, when the sun went down, and it was dark, behold a smoking furnace, and a burning lamp that passed between those pieces* (Gen. 15:17).

A few hours before this event, the Lord had made a covenant with Abraham. He promised to bless Abraham with many descendants and make them into a nation devoted to Him.

To seal the covenant, Abraham cut several animals into two pieces and walked between the two sections. This was a solemn declaration of his intention to keep the covenant. Just as the two separate pieces belonged to one animal, so the two people making this agreement were of one mind about the terms of the covenant.

When darkness fell, God caused a burning lamp, signifying His divine presence, to pass between the two sections of the slaughtered animals. This was a bold and startling sign to Abraham that God would keep His promise.

19:30–38. Lot fathers two sons, who become the ancestors of the Moabites and the Ammonites.

20:1–18. Abraham tries to pass off Sarah as his sister in the territory of Abimelech, a Philistine king.

21:1–21. A son, Isaac, is born to Abraham and Sarah; Hagar and Ishmael are banished to the wilderness.

21:22–34. Abraham and Abimelech reach an agreement about a well at Beersheba.

22:1–14. God tests Abraham's faithfulness, but Abraham is prevented from sacrificing his son Isaac.

22:15–19. God renews His promise to make Abraham's descendants into a great nation (Gen. 12:1–2).

22:20–24. Abraham's relatives are listed.

23:1–20. Abraham's wife, Sarah, dies; Abraham buys a cave at Machpelah as a burial site.

[23:1–20] MONEY BY WEIGHT. *Abraham weighed to Ephron the silver... four hundred shekels of silver, current money with the merchant* (Gen. 23:16).

Abraham paid Ephron the Hittite four hundred shekels of silver for a plot of ground as a burial site for his family.

Coins and paper money did not exist in Bible times, so Abraham paid Ephron in silver bullion. This bullion weighed four hundred shekels—the agreed-upon price. Money had to be weighed rather than counted by bills and coins, as we do today.

The exact weight of a shekel is not known. The word *shekel* (from the Hebrew *shakal*, "to weigh") indicated this method of figuring money by weight rather than by number or coins or bills.

The weighing of money is also referred to in Jeremiah 32:9–10 and Zechariah 11:12.

[19:1–29] SITTING AT THE CITY GATE. *And there came two angels to Sodom at even; and Lot sat in the gate of Sodom* (Gen. 19:1).

Cities of the ancient world were surrounded by massive defensive walls made of stone. People gathered at the gateway through the city wall to conduct business, pass the time with friends, catch up on the latest news, or just to watch the passing crowds.

Lot happened to be sitting in the gateway of the city of Sodom, just as evening was falling, when these two angels entered the city.

The Bible refers several times to the city gate as a gathering place (Gen. 23:10; 1 Sam. 4:18; Ps. 127:5; Prov. 1:21).

24:1–67. Abraham's son Isaac is married to Rebekah.

25:1–11. Abraham dies and is buried.

25:12–18. Descendants of Ishmael, Abraham's son by Hagar, are listed.

25:19–26. Twin sons, Jacob and Esau, are born to Isaac and Rebekah.

[26:1–35] CONTROVERSY OVER WELLS. *All the wells which his [Isaac's] father's servants had digged in the days of Abraham his father, the Philistines had stopped them, and filled them with earth* (Gen. 26:15).

Springs and streams are scarce in the hot, dry climate of the ancient Middle East. Shepherds had to dig wells to provide water for their flocks and herds.

The wells that Abraham had dug for his animals years before in the unoccupied territory of southern Canaan had given him and his heirs the right to graze their flocks in this region. But after Abraham died, the Philistines had filled these wells with dirt, denying Isaac the right as Abraham's heir to continue using these pasturelands.

Isaac and the Philistines eventually reached a compromise that allowed him access to the grazing lands around a productive well that he named Sheba ("productive well"). The ancient city of Beersheba ("well of Sheba") took its name from this well (Gen. 26:17–23).

25:27–34. Esau, the older brother, trades his birthright to Jacob for a bowl of stew (1 Chron. 5:1–2).

26:1–35. Isaac digs several wells in the territory of the Philistines; God promises Isaac that the covenant He has made with His father, Abraham, will be continued through him and his descendants.

27:1–46. Jacob tricks his father into blessing him rather than his older son, Esau.

28:1–22. Jacob travels to Haran in search of a wife; God assures him in a dream that His promise to Abraham will be realized through Jacob's descendants (Gen. 15:1–21).

29:1–30. In Haran, Jacob works seven years for the hand of Leah and seven years for Rachel, daughters of Laban.

29:31–30:24. Jacob fathers many sons by several different wives.

30:25–43. Jacob prospers while raising livestock in the household of his father-in-law, Laban.

31:1–32:23. With Laban's blessing, Jacob returns to Canaan with his family, along with presents for his estranged brother, Esau (Gen. 27:41).

32:24–32. Jacob wrestles with an angel; he is renamed Israel and assured of God's blessings.

33:1–20. Jacob is greeted and forgiven by his brother, Esau (Gen. 27:41).

34:1–31. Jacob and his sons avenge the sexual assault of Jacob's daughter Dinah by Shechem.

35:1–15. God renews His covenant with Jacob at Bethel and assures him that his descendants will receive the land promised to Abraham (Gen. 15:1–21).

35:16–20. Rachel dies while giving birth to Jacob's twelfth son, Benjamin.

35:21–26. The twelve sons of Jacob by four different wives are listed.

35:27–29. Jacob's father, Isaac, dies.

[29:1–30] MARRIAGE AMONG RELATIVES. *It is better that I [Laban] give her [Rachel] to thee [Jacob], than that I should give her to another man* (Gen. 29:19).

Laban was the brother of Jacob's mother, Rebekah (Gen. 29:10). This relationship would have made Laban's daughter Rachel—the woman whom Jacob wanted to marry—Jacob's first cousin.

Sometimes the term *brother* was used loosely in Bible times to refer to any male relative such as a nephew or an uncle. So Rachel may have been a distant relative of Jacob.

Marriage among distant relatives from the same tribe or bloodline was common in Old Testament times. Abraham sought a wife for his son Isaac from among his kinsmen in Mesopotamia (Gen. 24:2–4).

[33:1–20] **GIFTS FOR AN ENEMY.** *Jacob said, Nay, I pray thee [Esau], if now I have found grace in thy sight, then receive my present at my hand* (Gen. 33:10).

In Bible times people presented gifts to others for many reasons: to secure a bride through a dowry, or bride price; to seal a friendship, or to show love. In this instance Jacob presented gifts to his estranged brother, Esau, because he had wronged him in the past. He hoped his gifts would appease Esau's anger.

The giving of gifts is mentioned many times in the Bible (Judg. 3:18; 1 Sam. 10:27; Ps. 72:10; Prov. 18:16; Matt. 2:11).

36:1–43. Descendants of Esau, Jacob's brother, are listed.

37:1–36. Jacob's son Joseph is sold into slavery by his brothers and taken into Egypt.

38:1–30. Judah, a son of Jacob, fathers twin sons by his daughter-in-law Tamar.

39:1–23. Joseph is imprisoned in Egypt on a false charge.

40:1–23. Imprisoned with the pharaoh's chief butler and baker, Joseph explains the meaning of their dreams and develops a reputation as an interpreter of dreams.

41:1–43. Joseph is appointed a high official in the Egyptian pharaoh's administration after foretelling a severe famine by interpreting the pharaoh's dream.

41:44–52. Joseph fathers two sons, Manasseh and Ephraim, through his Egyptian wife, Asenath.

41:53–57. The famine that Joseph has foretold strikes Egypt.

42:1–6. Because of the famine, ten of Joseph's brothers come to Egypt to buy grain. Benjamin, Joseph's full brother and youngest son of Jacob (Gen. 35:16–20), does not make the trip. The ten brothers appear before Joseph, now one of Egypt's high officials.

42:7–17. Joseph recognizes his brothers, but they do not recognize him. He has them imprisoned for several days after accusing them of being spies.

42:18–38. Joseph holds his brother Simeon as a hostage. He sends the others back to Jacob with the charge to bring their youngest brother, Benjamin, to him in Egypt. This will prove that they are not spies and result in the release of their brother Simeon.

43:1–34. Joseph's brothers, including Benjamin, return to Egypt to buy grain. Joseph

37:1–36. Young Joseph is forced into a well by his jealous older brothers. They hated him as the favorite of their father, Jacob, and for sharing his dreams that they would bow before him. In time, his dream would prove true.

[37:1–36] JOSEPH'S UNUSUAL COAT. *Israel [Jacob] loved Joseph more than all his children, because he was the son of his old age: and he made him a coat of many colours* (Gen. 37:3).

Joseph's "coat of many colours" has been translated in various ways by modern translations ("richly ornamented robe," NIV; "long robe with sleeves," RSV). The precise meaning of the Hebrew word behind this phrase is uncertain.

This "coat" may have been the long outer robe that was worn by both men and women in Bible times. It was different than the robes worn by Joseph's brothers, thus setting him apart as his father's favorite son.

releases Simeon and invites all of them to a feast at his house. Again, they do not recognize Joseph.

44:1–13. Joseph sends all his brothers back to Jacob with their sacks of grain. But he plants one of his silver cups in Benjamin's sack. Then he sends his soldiers after them to search for stolen merchandise. All the brothers are arrested and returned to Joseph after the soldiers find the silver cup.

[43:1–34] SUPER-FRESH MEAT. *Joseph...said to the ruler of his house, Bring these men [Joseph's brothers] home, and slay, and make ready; for these men shall dine with me at noon* (Gen. 43:16).

The meat that Joseph served his brothers came from a freshly slaughtered animal. In Old Testament times, there was no way to preserve meat. An animal was slaughtered immediately before the meal at which meat was to be served (Gen. 18:7–8; 1 Sam. 28:24).

44:14–34. Judah pleads with Joseph on behalf of his brother Benjamin. He offers to

become a slave of Joseph if he will let Benjamin return to his father.

45:1–28. Overcome with emotion, Joseph finally reveals himself to his brothers. He sends them back to their homeland to tell Jacob that his son Joseph is alive and doing well in Egypt.

46:1–47:31. With the help of Joseph, Jacob and his sons and their families move to Egypt to escape the famine (Acts 7:14–15).

48:1–22. Jacob blesses the two sons of Joseph—Ephraim and Manasseh.

49:1–33. After predicting the future for each of his sons, Jacob dies in Egypt.

[49:1–33] A HAND OF VICTORY. *Judah, thou art he whom thy brethren shall praise: thy hand shall be in the neck of thine enemies* (Gen. 49:8).

Before he died Jacob called his twelve sons together and predicted their future. He foretold the importance of Judah and his descendants—the tribe of Judah—by using the image of Judah's hand on the neck of his enemies. To place one's hand on the neck of another was a symbol of superiority and victory in battle (2 Sam. 22:41; Lam. 5:5).

Judah did become the central tribe in Israel's history. King David was born into this tribe, and it was through David's lineage that the Messiah emerged (Matt. 1:1–17; Judah is spelled *Judas* in the KJV; see Matt. 1:2).

50:1–13. Joseph and his brothers return Jacob's body to Canaan for burial (Acts 7:16).

50:14–21. Joseph assures his brothers of his unconditional forgiveness.

50:22–26. Joseph dies in Egypt.

3:1–22. At the base of Mount Sinai, a monastery marks the spot where an ancient tradition says God talked to Moses from a burning bush, sending him to free the Israelites. Tradition also says that this mountain is where God later gave Moses the Ten Commandments.

OVERVIEW: The Lord delivers His people from enslavement by the Egyptians.

Introduction to Exodus

The book of Exodus begins where the book of Genesis ends—with the descendants of Jacob who settled in Egypt to escape a severe famine in their territory (Gen. 46:1–47:31). This move to Egypt was possible because of the favored status of Joseph—one of Jacob's sons—who rose to a high position in the Egyptian government. For many years the Hebrew people multiplied and prospered with the blessings of the Egyptian pharaoh.

But then the political climate changed: "There arose up a new king over Egypt, which knew not Joseph" (Exod. 1:8). Jacob's descendants were reduced to the status of slaves and forced to work on various Egyptian building projects.

But God did not forget His people. He called Moses to lead His people out of Egypt. With his brother, Aaron, as his helper, Moses confronted the pharaoh of Egypt and insisted that he let the Hebrew people go. God worked many miracles on behalf of His people to win their freedom.

The book of Exodus also tells how God took care of His people while they wandered in the wilderness area around Mount Sinai. Through Moses, God also delivered the Ten Commandments and other laws to guide their lives as His special people.

At God's command through Moses, the people also built a tabernacle in the wilderness. This sacred tent, a central place for sacrifice and worship, traveled with the Hebrew people when they moved from place to place in the wilderness. It symbolized God's presence in the midst of His people.

The dominant personality of the book of Exodus is Moses. God often spoke directly to him and gave him a message to pass on to the people. Moses was responsible for leading the people in their quest for the Promised Land—the territory of the Canaanites that God had promised to Abraham and his descendants many centuries before (Gen. 12:1–5).

Moses continues his leadership of the Hebrew people up through the book of Deuteronomy. Many scholars believe he wrote these four Old Testament books, as well as the book of Genesis. His important role in God's plan for His people makes him one of the central figures of biblical history.

Summary of Exodus

1:1–7. The descendants of Jacob/Israel multiply at an astonishing rate in Egypt.

1:8–14. The pharaoh of Egypt enslaves the Israelites.

1:15–22. The pharaoh orders all male Israelite infants killed to control their population growth.

2:1–4. A baby boy named Moses is hidden in a basket on the Nile River to escape the pharaoh's decree (Heb. 11:23).

1:8–14. Bricks of mud and straw from Morocco. As a race of slave laborers, the Israelites made similar bricks some 3,000 years ago, building cities for Egypt's pharaoh.

[2:1–4] MOSES' PAPER ARK. *She [Moses' mother] took for him an ark of bulrushes [papyrus basket, NIV], and daubed it with slime [tar, NIV] and with pitch and put the child therein* (Exod. 2:3).

Moses was hidden by his mother to protect him from the death order issued by Pharaoh against all male children of the Israelites (Exod. 1:15–16).

The "ark" in which he was hidden was probably a basket woven from leaves of the papyrus plant. This reedlike plant grew in abundance along the banks of the Nile River. The Egyptians used papyrus for making paper, as well as shoes and clothes.

2:5–10. The pharaoh's daughter discovers Moses and adopts him as her son.

2:11–15. After he reaches adulthood, Moses kills an Egyptian official who is abusing an Israelite slave. Moses flees to Midian to escape the pharaoh's wrath.

2:16–25. Moses becomes a shepherd in the household of a Midianite named Reuel (also known as Jethro) and marries his daughter Zipporah.

3:1–22. God appears to Moses in a burning bush and calls him to deliver His people, the Israelites, from enslavement by the Egyptians (Acts 7:30).

4:1–13. God assures Moses through miraculous signs that He will stand with him before the pharaoh.

4:14–31. God deals with Moses' excuses by appointing his brother, Aaron, to serve as Moses' spokesman. Moses returns to Egypt to confront the pharaoh.

> **[5:1–23] EGYPTIAN BRICKS WITH STRAW.** *Ye [Egyptian slave supervisors] shall no more give the people [Israelite slaves] straw to make brick, as heretofore: let them go and gather straw for themselves* (Exod. 5:7).
>
> The bricks used in the building projects of ancient Egypt were molded from mud, then placed in the sun to dry. Over time sun-dried bricks would crumble from exposure to the wind and rain.
>
> To give these bricks greater strength and stability, chopped straw from wheat or barley stalks was sometimes added. Pharaoh added to the hard labor of the Israelite slaves by forcing them to forage for straw to be used in the manufacturing process.
>
> Apparently the Israelites were under a quota system. They were expected to produce so many bricks per day—no excuses accepted (Exod. 5:13–14).

5:1–23. The pharaoh responds to Moses' demands by forcing the Israelite slaves to make bricks without straw.

6:1–13. God assures Moses and the Israelites that the covenant He had made with Abraham over 400 years before (Gen. 15:1–21) is still in force; God will bring the Israelites out of slavery into their own land.

6:14–15. The descendants of Jacob's sons Reuben and Simeon are listed (Num. 26:5–14).

6:16–30. The descendants of Jacob's son Levi (Gen. 29:34), who include Moses and Aaron, are listed.

7:1–13. Aaron's rod turns into a snake, but this miraculous sign fails to impress the Egyptian pharaoh and his court magicians.

7:14–10:29. God sends nine plagues upon the Egyptians to convince the pharaoh to release the Israelite slaves, but he remains stubborn and unmoved.

11:1–10. God announces through Moses the tenth and final plague—the death of all the Egyptian firstborn.

12:1–30. All the Egyptian firstborn are killed. The Israelites are spared because they obey God's command to mark the doorposts of their houses with the blood of sacrificial lambs (Ezek. 9:6).

12:31–51. Crushed by the widespread death of his people, the pharaoh releases the Israelites, who travel into the desert territory east of Egypt.

13:1–20. God directs that the firstborn of both animals and people among the Israelites are to be dedicated to Him.

13:21–22. God leads the Israelites with a cloud by day and a fire by night.

14:1–31. God swallows the pursuing Egyptian army in the Red Sea after the Israelites pass over on dry land (Heb. 11:29).

15:1–22. Through the "Song of Moses," the Israelites celebrate God's miraculous deliverance (Deut. 31:30–32:47).

15:23–27. At Marah, God miraculously turns bad water into good water for the Israelites.

> **[12:1–30] ALL THE GODS OF EGYPT.** *Against all the gods of Egypt I will execute judgment: I am the LORD* (Exod. 12:12).
>
> To be superior to "all the gods of Egypt" was quite a claim, since the Egyptians are known to have worshiped more than thirty pagan deities. These included the bull god Apis, who ensured fertility; Hathor, the goddess of love; and Thoth, the god of wisdom and books.
>
> But God proved, through the death of all the Egyptian firstborn (Exod. 12:29), that He held the power of life and death over the Egyptians and their religious system. Months later, after Moses had led the Israelites out of slavery in Egypt, God declared to him, "I am the LORD thy God, which have brought thee…out of the house of bondage. Thou shalt have no other gods before me" (Exod. 20:2–3).

[16:1–36] **EGYPT AND THE GOOD OLD DAYS.** *Would to God we [Israelites] had died…in the land of Egypt, when we sat by the flesh pots [pots of meat, NIV], and when we did eat bread to the full* (Exod. 16:3).

Soon after leaving Egypt, the Israelites began to whine for the "good old days." They began to think their existence as slaves was preferable to the harsh life of the wilderness.

Flesh pots were three-legged metal containers in which the Egyptians cooked meat over an open fire. But it is likely that meat was a delicacy enjoyed only by the elite of Egyptian society. The Israelites exaggerated when they claimed they had eaten meat regularly from these cooking pots.

That's the problem with nostalgia: Looking back, things always seem better than they actually were.

16:1–36. God miraculously provides manna, a bread substitute, to feed the complaining Israelites in the wilderness.

17:1–7. The Lord produces water from a rock to sustain His people.

17:8–16. God gives the Israelites a victory over the Amalekites.

18:1–27. Taking the advice of his father-in-law, Jethro, Moses delegates some of his burdensome duties on behalf of the people to other Israelite leaders (Deut. 1:1–18).

19:1–25. God reveals Himself in smoke and fire to Moses and the Israelites at Mount Sinai; He promises to make them "a kingdom of priests, and an holy nation" (v. 6).

20:1–17. God reveals the Ten Commandments to Moses (Deut. 5:1–22).

20:18–26. God cautions the Israelites against worshiping false gods.

21:1–23:33. Various laws governing human relationships, property rights, slavery, and treatment of the poor are listed (Deut. 22:1–25:4).

24:1–18. Moses enters the cloud of God's glory and communes with Him for forty days on Mount Sinai.

25:1–27:21. God tells Moses to rally the Israelites to build the tabernacle as a place of worship; He gives Moses a detailed blueprint of the tent and its furnishings.

28:1–29:46. The Lord instructs Moses to appoint and consecrate his brother, Aaron, and Aaron's descendants as the official priesthood for the Israelites (Num. 3:32).

30:1–10. God gives Moses instructions about the altar in the tabernacle on which incense is to be burned as an act of worship.

30:11–16. The Lord directs Moses to collect a half-shekel tax from every male Israelite to support the tabernacle and its services (Matt. 17:24–27).

30:17–38. God specifies that a special anointing oil is to be used by the priests to consecrate the tabernacle's altar and its vessels and furnishings.

31:1–11. God reveals to Moses that He has selected two craftsmen, Bezaleel and Aholiab, to perform the skilled stonecutting, metalwork, and woodworking required for the tabernacle.

[19:1–25] **CLEAN BEFORE THE LORD.** *The Lord said unto Moses, Go unto the people, and sanctify them to day and to morrow, and let them wash their clothes* (Exod. 19:10).

About three months after leaving Egypt, Moses led the Israelites to the base of Mount Sinai in the wilderness (Exod. 19:1–2). Here they would have a dramatic encounter with the living Lord, who had led them out of slavery.

In order to prepare the people for this special revelation of Himself, God commanded that the people be both spiritually ("sanctify them") and physically ("wash their clothes") clean. Such cleanliness was essential for those who would stand in the presence of the holy God.

32:1–35. Moses and Joshua, coming down from Mount Sinai with the Ten Commandments, find the Israelites cavorting around a golden calf idol. In anger Moses throws down the tablets, shattering them.

[32:1–35] **A GOLD-PLATED CALF.** *All the people brake off the golden earrings which were in their ears…and he [Aaron] received them at their hand, and fashioned it with a graving tool, after he had made it a molten calf* (Exod. 32:3–4).

The word *molten* implies that the calf idol that Aaron created in the wilderness was cast from gold. But thousands of melted-down earrings would have been required to produce such an idol.

It is more likely that the calf image was first carved from wood. Then it was plated with a thin layer of gold to produce the final idol worshiped by the people. This method of producing pagan images was described by the prophet Isaiah (Isa. 40:19–20).

31:12–18. God reminds Moses that the Israelites are to observe the seventh day of the week as the Sabbath; they are not to do any work on this day (Exod. 20:8–11).

32:1–35. Aaron and the Israelites sin against God during Moses' absence on Mount Sinai by fashioning a golden calf as an object of worship.

33:1–34:35. Moses pleads for God to forgive the sinful Israelites; the Lord renews His pledge to guide and protect them.

35:1–35. At the urging of Moses, the Israelites contribute the materials needed for the building of the tabernacle.

36:1–38:31. The tabernacle is built according to the specifications issued by the Lord (Exod. 25:1–27:21).

39:1–31. The distinctive styles of dress required for Aaron as the high priest and the other priests of Israel are described.

39:32–43. The features and furnishings of the completed tabernacle are reviewed as they are presented to Moses.

40:1–38. Moses and the Israelites dedicate the tabernacle as they assemble its furnishings; God shows His pleasure by filling the sacred tent with His glory (Neh. 9:12).

[40:1–38] **INCENSE ALTAR.** *Thou [Moses] shalt set the altar of gold for the incense before the ark of the testimony* (Exod. 40:5).

Incense was a sweet-smelling substance burned in the tabernacle as an offering to God. It was offered by a priest on this special altar made of gold. The pleasant aroma symbolized the prayers of the Israelites before the Lord.

Only incense made by using a formula specified by God (Exod. 30:34–38) was to be burned on the incense altar. Two sons of Aaron were destroyed for burning incense by "strange fire" (Lev. 10:1–3). They may have been offering incense not produced by this divine formula.

OVERVIEW: God institutes the ceremonial law to govern the life of His people.

Introduction to Leviticus

In the book of Exodus, God gave His people the moral law—instructions for moral and ethical behavior. The book of Leviticus contains His ceremonial law—how to observe the rituals that were considered important acts of worship for the people of ancient Israel.

Leviticus describes the formal establishment of the priesthood, at God's command, through Aaron, his sons, and their successors. The priests were to preside at the altar in the tabernacle—

1:1–7:38. An artist's conception of Israel's tabernacle shows fire on the altar in front of the holy tent. Unblemished bulls, sheep, goats, and doves were all acceptable burnt offerings. Such offerings are an important element of the book of Leviticus.

later the temple—when people presented their offerings to God. Various types of offerings are described in Leviticus—burnt offerings, grain offerings, peace offerings, sin offerings, and guilt or trespass offerings.

But perhaps the most significant offering in terms of its symbolism for modern believers was the blood offering—presenting the blood of a sacrificial animal to God. New Testament believers taught that Jesus was the ultimate blood sacrifice. He gave His life by shedding His own blood to make atonement for our sins.

In addition to sacrifice, another important theme of Leviticus is holiness. The concept of holiness involves difference or separation. God's people were to be different than, and separate from, the pagan peoples of the surrounding nations. Thus, they were not to eat certain foods that were considered unclean. They were to avoid contact with anything that was considered unclean. Even a house could be made unclean if touched by a person with an infectious skin disease. God was concerned that His people should remain clean and undefiled in the midst of a depraved and corrupt world.

[1:1–7:38] NO YEAST OR HONEY. *Ye [Israelites] shall burn no leaven, nor any honey, in any offering of the LORD made by fire* (Lev. 2:11).

Leaven, or yeast, was mixed with dough to cause bread to rise. Any bread brought to the Lord as an offering was to be baked without leaven. Neither was honey, used as a sweetening agent, to be used in any food items presented to the Lord.

The reason for these prohibitions is that both yeast and honey were associated with offerings presented to pagan gods.

12:1–8. God prescribes the ritual by which a woman may be declared clean after giving birth to a child.

13:1–14:57. God issues regulations for dealing with leprosy—or an infectious skin disease. Even a house or tent that has been exposed to this disease is to be cleansed in accordance with a prescribed ritual.

15:1–33. Procedures are established by which a person who experiences a bodily discharge may be rendered clean again.

16:1–34. God specifies how Aaron, the high priest, is to make atonement for himself and

Summary of Leviticus

1:1–7:38. God prescribes the procedures to be followed by the Israelites and the priests in making various offerings to the Lord (Num. 15:1–31).

8:1–36. Moses consecrates Aaron and his sons as priests in holy service to the Lord and His people.

9:1–24. Aaron and his sons present a sin offering, a burnt offering, and a peace offering on behalf of the people.

10:1–3. Nadab and Abihu, sons of Aaron, are destroyed by fire for using an unauthorized procedure in burning incense at the altar (Num. 16:35).

10:4–20. Moses reminds Aaron and his remaining sons of the responsibility of priests to show reverence and respect toward God and His requirements.

11:1–47. God lists the clean animals that may be eaten by the Israelites, but those considered unclean are not to be eaten or even touched (Deut. 14:1–21).

8:1–36. Israel's priests, from the family of Moses' brother Aaron, wore special clothing and used special tools, all specifically detailed by God Himself.

[13:1–14:57] **REPLASTERING WITH MORTAR.** *They [Israelites] shall take other stones, and put them in the place of those stones; and he shall take other morter [clay, NIV], and shall plaister the house* (Lev. 14:42).

These instructions were intended for the Israelites after they had settled in permanent homes in the land of Canaan. If a plague of mildew or fungus broke out in a house, the owner was to replace the infected stones and replaster the entire dwelling with "morter," or clay.

The mortar of Bible times was made by mixing clay with finely chopped straw. Sometimes sand, ashes, or lime was added to give this substance more body and to make it last longer.

If this renovation of the house with new stones and new mortar did not eliminate the plague, the dwelling was to be torn down. The debris was to be carried outside the city to "an unclean place" (Lev. 14:45)—perhaps a garbage dump designated for this purpose.

all the people on one specific day each year known as the Day of Atonement (Num. 29:7).

17:1–9. God prohibits the Israelites from presenting offerings at any place other than the tabernacle.

17:10–16. God cautions the people not to eat the meat of a slaughtered animal unless the blood has first been drained from the flesh.

18:1–30. God warns the people not to participate in the depraved sexual practices of the surrounding pagan nations.

19:1–21:15. God calls His people to a high moral standard. They are to honor the Lord with their behavior and to treat other people with fairness and justice.

21:16–22:16. God establishes strict physical and moral requirements for Aaron and his descendants who serve as priests among the people.

22:17–33. Animals offered to God as sacrifices are to be healthy and free of physical defects (Mal. 1:8–9).

23:1–44. God cites the special days and religious holidays or festivals that are to be observed by the Israelites: the weekly Sabbath (v. 3), the yearly Passover and Feast of Unleavened Bread (vv. 5–8), the offering of firstfruits (vv. 9–14), the Feast of Pentecost (vv. 15–21), the Feast of Trumpets (vv.

23–25), the Day of Atonement (vv. 27–30), and the Feast of Tabernacles (vv. 33–36) (Deut. 16:1–17).

[23:1–44] **THE DRINK OFFERING.** *They [sacrificial animals] shall be for a burnt offering unto the LORD, with their meat offering, and their drink offerings* (Lev. 23:18).

A drink offering to God was usually given along with other offerings, such as the burnt offering, the sin offering, and the trespass offering. The drink offering was a quantity of wine. It was presented by the worshiper to a priest, who poured it out at the base of the altar of burnt offering.

24:1–4. God directs that the oil-burning lamps before the altar in the tabernacle are to be kept burning continuously.

24:5–9. Twelve loaves of fresh-baked bread, representing the twelve tribes of Israel, are to be placed on a table near the altar in the tabernacle each week to replace the old loaves; the old loaves are then to be eaten by the priests (2 Chron. 2:4).

24:10–23. The people stone a man for blasphemy, or disrespect toward God, at Moses' command.

25:1–7. God directs that the farmland of the Israelites, once they possess it, is to be given a Sabbath of its own; after six consecutive

[26:1–46] PAGAN HIGH PLACES. *I [God] will destroy your [pagan worshipers'] high places* (Lev. 26:30).

A "high place" was generally a mountaintop or a hilltop on which pagan worshipers bowed down before images of their false gods. They believed these elevated sites would put them closer to their gods and increase their chance of being heard.

God made it clear that He would judge the Israelites if they adopted the worship practices of their pagan neighbors.

years of production, it is to remain idle during the seventh year.

25:8–55. God decrees that every fiftieth year (following seven "Sabbaths" of seven years each) is to be a liberating year known as the "jubile." During this year, Israelites who were forced to sell themselves into slavery to pay off a debt are to be set free. Tracts of land that were sold because Israelite families fell upon hard times are to be returned to the original owners.

26:1–46. God declares that His covenant with Israel is conditional. If they obey and worship Him after they possess the land, He will bless and prosper His people. But if they rebel against Him and worship other gods, He will withdraw His presence and visit them with disaster.

27:1–34. If a person has made a voluntary vow to give himself or his property to God, he is allowed to pay a redemption price to the priest in order to "buy back" himself or the property. God establishes guidelines for determining the redemption price to be paid under various circumstances.

Overview: The Israelites wander for many years in the wilderness of Sinai.

Introduction to Numbers

The book of Numbers is so named because of the two "numberings" (censuses) of the Israelites that were commanded by the Lord in chapters 1 and 26. The book traces the aimless wanderings of the Israelites in the wilderness during a period of more than forty years as God was preparing them to enter the Promised Land.

Why this long delay? Why didn't the Israelites proceed immediately to conquer the land of Canaan? The first census counted more than 600,000 able-bodied men above twenty years of age who were ready for military duty (1:18–46). Surely this would have been a potent fighting force against any enemy.

The problem was the people's lack of faith in God and His promises. In preparation for military action, Moses chose twelve scouts—one from each of the tribes—and sent them on a fact-finding mission into Canaan. They returned with good news and bad news. The land was rich and fertile and able to support the Israelites. But it would not be easy to conquer the warlike Canaanites, who seemed invincible behind their walled cities.

Only two of the twelve spies—Joshua and Caleb—recommended that the Israelites proceed immediately to take the land. They believed God's promise that He would lead them to victory. But the majority of the people, paralyzed by fear, refused to move by faith against the enemy. So the Lord sentenced them to forty years of wandering in the wilderness before they could enter the land of promise (14:1–38).

During these years the people also showed their rebellious, faithless spirit in other ways. They complained about Moses and his leadership and about their food and water supply. They grumbled against God and accused Him of abandoning them in the wilderness, even though He provided miraculously for their needs time after time. Some of the Israelite men even worshiped the false gods of the Moabites (25:1–18).

Finally, even Moses lost his patience with the people. At God's command, he struck a rock to provide a miraculous flow of water for the people—but he did so in a fit of anger. God punished Moses by declaring that he would not be allowed to enter the Promised Land (20:1–13).

The book of Numbers shows that the Lord does not hesitate to punish His people for their sin. But He is also a God who keeps His promises. He would ultimately bless His people by bringing them into a land of their own.

Summary of Numbers

1:1–3. God directs Moses to take a census of all able-bodied Israelite men, twenty years old and above, who are able to go to war (2 Sam. 24:2).

[2:1–2] STANDARDS AND BANNERS. *Every man of the children of Israel shall pitch by his own standard, with the ensign [banners, niv] of their father's house* (Num. 2:2).

God directed the twelve tribes of Israel to camp in three-tribe units on the northern, southern, eastern, and western sides of the tabernacle (Num. 2:3–31). Each of these three-tribe units had a distinct sign on a pole, known as a standard, around which they gathered to make sure they followed the camping arrangement specified by the Lord.

These standards may have been similar to those used by the Egyptians as military symbols for different units of their army. Many of these Egyptian standards featured images of their pagan gods. The Bible does not say what symbols were used on the Israelite standards.

The phrase "ensign of their father's house" probably refers to a small flag or banner that was carried by each tribe or even the separate clans that made up each tribe.

1:4–17. Representatives of each tribe are appointed to assist with the census.

1:18–46. Male descendants of twelve Israelite tribes—Reuben, Simeon, Gad, Judah, Issachar, Zebulun, Ephraim, Manasseh, Benjamin, Dan, Asher, and Naphtali —are counted in the census. The total number of males twenty years old and above is 603,550.

1:47–54. The Levites, descendants of the tribe of Levi, are not included in the census because they do not have a military role in the life of Israel. Their function is to take care of the tabernacle and preside over its religious ceremonies (Num. 3:5–10).

2:1–2. God specifies that the tribes of Israel are to camp at a distance all around the tabernacle.

2:3–9. The tribes of Judah, Issachar, and Zebulun will camp east of the tabernacle.

2:10–17. The tribes of Reuben, Simeon, and Gad will camp south of the tabernacle.

2:18–24. The tribes of Ephraim, Manasseh, and Benjamin will camp west of the tabernacle.

2:25–31. The tribes of Dan, Asher, and Naphtali will camp north of the tabernacle.

2:32–34. The tribal census and the camping order of the tribes around the tabernacle are summarized.

3:1–4. Descendants of Aaron are listed (Exod. 28:41).

3:5–13. The Levites, descendants of the tribe of Levi, are set apart and consecrated for their religious duties on behalf of the other tribes of Israel.

3:14–20. God directs Moses to take a census of the tribe of Levi. All male Levites one month old and above are to be counted. Separate counts are to be made for the three divisions of Levi—Gershonites, Kohathites, and Merarites—that sprang from Levi's three sons.

3:21–26. The Gershonites, 7,500 in number, are assigned specific tabernacle duties from their position west of the tabernacle.

3:27–32. The Kohathites, 8,600 in number, are assigned specific tabernacle duties from their position south of the tabernacle.

3:33–37. The Merarites, 6,200 in number, are assigned specific tabernacle duties from their position north of the tabernacle.

3:38–39. Moses, Aaron, and Aaron's sons are to be positioned to the east and directly in front of the tabernacle for its general oversight and protection.

3:40–51. God directs Moses to take a census of all the firstborn males among the Israelites who are one month old and above. God accepts the Levites as a substitute for these firstborn, who are considered the Lord's own. But the census reveals that the number of firstborn Israelite males exceeds the number of Levites by 273. The redemption price paid by the parents of these 273 sons is to be given to Aaron and his sons, the priests.

4:1–49. God gives a more detailed description of

the tabernacle duties required of the three branches of the Levites—Kohathites, Gershonites, and Merarites.

5:1–4. People with an infectious skin disease and other unclean people are to be banished outside the camp (Lev. 13:45–46).

5:5–10. God makes provision for the atonement of sin through the trespass offering.

5:11–31. A woman accused of adultery is to be proven innocent or guilty through an ordeal known as the water of jealousy, or bitter water.

6:1–21. God establishes regulations and procedures to be observed by any person who vows to be especially consecrated to God as a Nazarite (Judg. 13:5).

6:22–27. God issues a benediction with which the Israelites are to be blessed by the priests.

7:1–89. At the dedication of the altar of the tabernacle, representatives of the twelve tribes of Israel present offerings to support the Levites and their priestly service.

8:1–4. The seven-branched candlestick, or menorah, is placed to illuminate the altar of the tabernacle (Exod. 40:25).

8:5–26. The Levites are purified and dedicated to serve at the tabernacle under the direction of Aaron and the priests (Num. 1:47–54).

9:1–14. The Passover is to be observed annually by the Israelites to memorialize their deliverance by the Lord from enslavement by the Egyptians.

9:15–23. God assures Israel of His presence with a cloud over the tabernacle during the daytime and a fire over the tabernacle at night (Exod. 13:21–22). The cloud signals when the people are to camp and when they are to break camp and move on.

10:1–10. Moses makes two silver trumpets to alert the people when to assemble for battle and when it is time to move the camp.

10:11–36. The twelve tribes of Israel move out in orderly fashion when the cloud tells them to leave the wilderness of Sinai and camp in the wilderness of Paran.

11:1–35. The Israelites complain about Moses' leadership and the food they are forced to eat. God sustains them with manna and quail meat (Exod. 16:12–15).

12:1–16. Miriam and Aaron complain about the leadership of their brother, Moses. God punishes Miriam by striking her with leprosy, then heals her at Moses' request.

13:1–16. Moses selects one representative

[11:1–35] FULL TO THE NOSE. *Ye [Israelites] shall not eat one day...nor twenty days; but even a whole month, until it come out at your nostrils* (Num. 11:19–20).

The Israelites complained to Moses that they had no meat to eat—only the bread substitute known as manna, which had been miraculously provided by the Lord (Exod. 16:15, 31). This complaining angered God, and He promised to send them so much meat to eat that it would make them sick. Being filled "to the nose" is a common expression for overeating still heard in many cultures today.

The Lord kept His promise by sending "quails from the sea" (Num. 11:31) to provide meat for the people, accompanied by a plague to punish the complainers.

from each of the twelve tribes of Israel to go into Canaan on a spying and exploration mission.

13:17–33. The scouts explore Canaan and return with good news and bad news: The land is fertile and productive, but it is inhabited and well defended by several strong tribal groups.

14:1–4. The Israelites moan over this bad news, rebel against God, and declare that they should have stayed in Egypt (Deut. 17:16).

14:5–10. Joshua and Caleb, two of the twelve spies, encourage the people to remain faithful to God. They declare that the Israelites can take the land if they follow His guidance.

14:11–19. God declares that He will wipe out the Israelites because of their lack of faith. Moses pleads for God to show them mercy.

14:20–35. God responds by sentencing the Israelites to forty years of wandering in the wilderness before they will be allowed to enter the Promised Land. During this time the older generation of rebellious Israelites will die in the wilderness.

14:36–45. Some of the Israelites attack the residents of Canaan, but they are turned back in defeat.

15:1–31. God establishes regulations and procedures for the various offerings to be presented by the Israelites after they enter the Promised Land (Lev. 1:1–7:38).

15:32–36. A man is stoned to death for desecrating the Sabbath by doing work on this sacred day (Exod. 20:8–11).

15:37–41. God directs the Israelites to put tassels on their clothes to remind them to obey His commandments (Deut. 22:12).

16:1–40. God destroys Korah and a group of his followers, including Dathan and Abiram, because they rebelled against the leadership of Moses and Aaron.

16:41–50. God threatens to destroy all the Israelites by sending a plague upon them because they sympathized with Korah. But Aaron turns back the plague by burning incense among the people to atone for their sin.

17:1–13. God causes Aaron's rod to bloom and produce almonds to demonstrate Aaron's spiritual authority over all the tribes of Israel (Heb. 9:4).

[17:1–13] AARON'S PRIESTHOOD CONFIRMED. *On the morrow Moses went into the tabernacle of witness; and behold, the rod of Aaron for the house of Levi was budded* (Num. 17:8).

Some Israelites questioned Aaron's right to serve as priest and for his descendants to continue his priestly work among the nation (Num. 16:1–3). So Moses conducted a test to determine who should serve in this leadership position.

Moses placed twelve staffs or sticks, representing the twelve tribes of Israel, in the tabernacle overnight. The next morning Aaron's staff had budded and produced almonds. This was undeniable proof that Aaron of the tribe of Levi and his descendants had been selected by the Lord for this ministry.

[20:23–29] **ELEAZAR SUCCEEDS AARON.** *Moses stripped Aaron of his garments, and put them upon Eleazar his son; and Aaron died there in the top of the mount* (Num. 20:28).

At Aaron's death the special clothes that he wore as high priest of Israel (Exod. 40:13) were transferred to his son Eleazar. This showed that Eleazar was the legitimate successor to his father in this role.

Eleazar served as high priest for the rest of Moses' life and also for a time after Joshua succeeded Moses as leader of the Israelites. Eleazar assisted in the division of the land of Canaan among the twelve tribes (Josh. 14:1).

18:1–19. Through the offerings of the people, God provides for the material needs of Aaron and his sons and the priests who will come after them.

18:20–32. Through the tithes of the people, God provides for the material needs of the Levites (Deut. 18:1–8).

19:1–22. Moses and Aaron are instructed to use the ashes of a red heifer to make a solution called the water of separation. People who have been made ritually unclean are to be cleansed when sprinkled by a priest with this special solution.

20:1–13. In anger, Moses strikes a rock at Meribah to produce water for the Israelites. God punishes him and Aaron for disobeying His directions, refusing to let them enter the Promised Land (Num. 27:12–14).

20:14–22. The king of Edom refuses to allow the Israelites to pass through his territory (Deut. 2:8).

20:23–29. Aaron dies on Mount Hor.

21:1–9. God punishes the Israelites for their rebellion by sending poisonous snakes to bite them. Then God delivers the people by means of a brass serpent on a pole erected by Moses (John 12:32).

21:10–20. Several camping sites of the Israelites are listed.

21:21–32. The Israelites defeat Sihon, king of the Amorites.

21:33–35. The Israelites defeat Og, king of Bashan.

22:1–21. Balak, king of Moab, sends messengers to hire Balaam the soothsayer to curse the Israelites.

22:22–35. On his way to meet Balak, Balaam encounters the angel of the Lord, who gets Balaam's attention through his stubborn donkey. The angel tells Balaam to meet Balak but to speak only the words that God will direct him to speak.

22:36–41. Balaam meets Balak and prepares to curse the Israelites.

23:1–24:25. On three separate attempts, Balaam fails to curse the Israelites, blessing them instead.

25:1–18. Some of the Israelites commit idolatry because of the temptations of Moabite women.

26:1–56. All able-bodied Israelite males twenty years old and above are counted again at the end of the forty years of wandering in the wilderness. This census is to be used as the basis for assigning land to the tribes after they conquer the territory of the Canaanites (Num. 1:1–3).

26:57–65. A separate count is made of the tribe of Levi, or the Levites.

27:1–11. The five daughters of Zelophehad are allowed to inherit his property, since he died with no male heirs; principles of inheritance are established.

27:12–14. God reminds Moses that he will not be allowed to enter the Promised Land with the other Israelites (Num. 20:1–13).

27:15–23. Joshua is selected by the Lord as Moses' successor (Deut. 34:9).

28:1–29:40. Regulations and procedures for various types of offerings are prescribed by the Lord.

32:1–42. Sheep graze on a Jordanian hillside. When Israelites of the Exodus arrived in this area just east of the Promised Land, the tribes of Reuben and Gad and half the tribe of Manasseh decided to settle here because of the fertile pastures.

30:1–16. Vows made to the Lord are a serious matter, but people may be excused from their vows in special circumstances (Gen. 28:20–22).

31:1–54. Israel defeats the Midianites, and all the people share in the spoils of war.

32:1–42. Moses allows the tribes of Reuben and Gad and half the tribe of Manasseh to settle on the fertile pasturelands east of the Jordan River across from Canaan (Josh. 12:1–6). In return, these three tribes promise to help the other tribes in their campaign against the Canaanites.

33:1–49. The places where the Israelites camped in the wilderness for forty years after they left Egypt are listed.

33:50–56. God repeats His promise to give the land of Canaan to the Israelites. He urges them to drive out all the pagan Canaanites, lest they become a stumbling block to His people.

34:1–15. God establishes the boundaries of the territory in which the Israelite tribes will settle.

34:16–29. Tribal representatives are selected to serve with Joshua and Eleazar the priest to divide the land among the various tribes.

35:1–34. The tribe of Levi will not receive a specific land inheritance like the other tribes because of their religious function. Rather, Levites are to live among all the other tribes in forty-eight designated cities. Six of these cities are to be known as cities of refuge—places to which a person can go after killing another person to keep from being killed by an avenging relative. In these refuge cities, guilt or innocence of the person accused of murder will be determined through due process (Deut. 19:1–13).

36:1–13. Once the land is divided among the tribes, each tribal allotment is to remain intact. The daughters of Zelophehad (Num. 27:1–11) are to marry within their tribe to ensure that the land they inherited from their father does not pass to another tribe.

OVERVIEW: Moses restates God's law for the Israelites before they enter the Promised Land.

Introduction to Deuteronomy

This book takes its name from the Greek word *Deuteronomion,* which means "second law." It consists of a series of speeches to the people from Moses. This great leader realized that he was approaching the time of his death, so he repeated many of the laws that God had revealed to His people at Mount Sinai more than forty years before. Moses wanted to make sure that the people remained loyal to the Lord and His commands as they prepared to enter the land of promise.

Moses especially warned the Israelites of the perils of idolatry. He knew they would be settling a land where the Canaanites worshiped many false gods, especially the fertility god Baal. He called upon the people to remain faithful to the one true God, who demanded their exclusive loyalty and total commitment: "Thou shalt love the LORD thy God with all thine heart, and with all thy soul, and with all thy might" (6:5; see Matt. 22:37).

The final chapter of Deuteronomy departs from its speech format to report on the death of Moses. He died on Mount Nebo after God allowed him to look across the Jordan River to view the Promised Land. His greatness as a leader of God's people is acknowledged in these words: "There arose not a prophet since in Israel like unto Moses, whom the Lord knew face to face" (34:10).

Deuteronomy's significance was recognized by the New Testament writers, who quoted from this book more than eighty times. At the beginning of His public ministry, Jesus cited several passages from Deuteronomy to turn aside the temptations of Satan (Matt. 4:4, quoting Deut. 8:3; Matt. 4:7, quoting Deut. 6:16; Matt. 4:10, quoting Deut. 6:13).

Summary of Deuteronomy

1:1–18. Moses recalls the experiences of the Israelites after they first came out of Egypt, including his appointment of officials to help him lead the people (Exod. 18:1–27).

1:19–46. Moses reminds the people of their rebellion and refusal to enter Canaan after spies were sent to investigate the land (Num. 13:17–33).

2:1–23. Moses recounts the marching orders given the Israelites by the Lord after their

---

[2:1–23] CAMPING GROUNDS. *The Avims which dwelt in Hazerim* (Deut. 2:23).

This verse is part of an extended review by Moses of the different tribes and ethnic groups encountered by the Israelites during their years of wandering in the wilderness.

The Hebrew word *Hazerim* is not the name of a specific place. In this context it should be translated as "camping grounds." The Avims were probably a nomadic people who moved from place to place with their grazing livestock.

forty years of wandering in the wilderness came to an end.

2:24–37. Moses recalls the victory of the Israelites over King Sihon of Heshbon (Num. 21:21–32).

3:1–22. Moses reminisces about the victory of the Israelites over King Og of Bashan and the settlement of the tribes of Reuben, Gad, and one-half of the tribe of Manasseh in Og's territory (Num. 21:33–35; 32:1–42).

3:23–29. Moses reminds the people of God's decision that he—Moses—would not be allowed to enter the Promised Land (Num. 20:1–13).

4:1–49. Moses challenges the Israelites to remain faithful to the covenant that God established with His people and to follow the teachings of the law that God handed down through Moses at Mount Sinai.

5:1–22. Moses restates the Ten Commandments, which God delivered to him at Mount Sinai (Exod. 20:1–17).

5:23–33. Moses reminds the people that the awesome, unapproachable God of the universe has chosen to reveal Himself to the nation of Israel.

6:1–25. Moses reminds the people of their responsibility to teach the laws and commandments of God to their children.

7:1–26. God promises to give the Israelites victory over the pagan peoples who inhabit Canaan and bring prosperity to His people when they are settled in the land.

[6:1–25] WRITING ON THE DOOR. *Thou [Israelites] shalt write them upon the posts [doorframes, NIV] of thy house, and on thy gates* (Deut. 6:9).

The Israelites were commanded by the Lord to write passages from His law on the doorframes of their houses after they settled permanently in the land of Canaan. Every time they entered or left their dwellings, they would be reminded of God's Word and their promise to obey His commands.

[11:1–32] IRRIGATION OF EGYPTIAN CROPS. *The land, whither thou [Israelites] goest in to possess it, is not as the land of Egypt, from whence ye came out, where thou sowedst thy seed, and wateredst it with thy foot* (Deut. 11:10).

This verse contrasts the land of Egypt, where the Israelites had been enslaved, with the land of Canaan, which God had promised to His people. Egyptian crops grew in the fertile flood plain along the Nile River. But Canaan was a land of hills and valleys. Here the crops of the Israelites would flourish from the "waters of the rain of heaven" (Deut. 11:11).

Watering crops "with thy foot" in Egypt probably refers to the small waterwheels that were turned by foot to pump water from the Nile River into irrigation canals. This artificial watering system was essential for crop production in Egypt's hot, dry climate.

8:1–20. The Lord warns the people of the perils of prosperity. They must not forget Him after they have become comfortable and affluent in the land He is giving them.

9:1–29. Moses warns the people not to become overconfident after they settle in Canaan. They are capable of ignoring and rejecting God and turning to false gods, just as they did at Mount Sinai and during their years of wandering in the wilderness.

10:1–5. Moses recalls how God wrote the Ten Commandments a second time on two tablets of stone, which Moses placed in the ark of the covenant (Exod. 34:1).

10:6–22. Moses reminds the Israelites of the awesome God whom they serve and the signs and wonders He has performed on behalf of His people.

11:1–32. God places two choices before the Israelites. If they remain faithful to Him, He will bless them. But if they turn to false gods, He will curse them (Josh. 24:1–15).

12:1–32. After the Israelites settle in the land,

[19:14–21] BOUNDARY STONES. *Thou [Israelites] shalt not remove thy neighbour's landmark [boundary stone, NIV], which they of old time have set in thine inheritance* (Deut. 19:14).

After the Israelites settled in Canaan and received their land allotments, they marked their property by placing small stones around the edges of their plots.

Unlike permanent fences, these stones could be moved easily. A dishonest person on an adjoining plot could move these markers and encroach on his neighbor's property. The Lord specifically prohibited this practice because it was a form of stealing (Exod. 20:15).

Moving boundary stones is also forbidden in Proverbs 22:28; 23:10.

God promises to give the nation a central place of worship, where they will present various offerings and sacrifices.

13:1–18. A false prophet or any other Israelite who causes people to worship pagan gods is to be put to death.

14:1–21. The Lord reminds the Israelites of the animals that may be eaten and those that are prohibited as food (Lev. 11).

14:22–29. A tithe, or one-tenth of one's crops or livestock, is to be presented as an offering to the Lord (Num. 18:20–32).

15:1–18. God establishes guidelines for fair and just treatment of the poor.

15:19–23. Firstborn animals from herds of livestock are to be presented as offerings to God.

16:1–17. God reminds the people of the regulations for observing three major festivals or religious holidays: Passover and Feast of Unleavened Bread (vv. 1–8), Feast of Weeks (vv. 9–12), and Feast of Tabernacles (vv. 13–15) (Lev. 23).

16:18–20. Judges are expected to be fair and just in their decisions.

16:21–22. The making of idols or images of false gods is prohibited (Exod. 20:3–4).

17:1–7. A person found guilty of idolatry—on the testimony of at least two witnesses—is to be put to death.

17:8–13. A sentence handed down by judges and priests through due process is considered a binding judgment. Refusal to abide by the verdict will result in the death penalty.

17:14–20. If a king is ever appointed to rule over Israel, he must not trust in military might or marry many wives. He is expected to rule with justice and to fear God and obey His commandments.

18:1–8. Since the Levites will not receive an inheritance of land in Canaan, they are to be supported by tithes and offerings from the people (Num. 18:20–32).

18:9–14. All forms of "black magic"—witchcraft, fortune-telling, and communing with the dead—are prohibited for God's people.

18:15–22. God promises to send prophets—particularly a special prophet after the pattern of Moses—to declare His will to His people. True prophets are those whose predictions come true.

19:1–13. God repeats His instructions that

[16:21–22] NO TREES AROUND ALTARS. *Thou [Israelites] shalt not plant thee a grove of any trees near unto the altar of the LORD thy God* (Deut. 16:21).

Shrines devoted to worship of false gods were surrounded by thick groves of trees, perhaps to hide the immoral acts that occurred around these altars. The Lord prohibited the planting of trees around His altars to avoid any hint of idol worship among His people.

cities of refuge are to be established throughout the land after the Israelites have settled in Canaan. These cities are to serve as safe harbors for innocent people who are accused of murder (Num. 35).

19:14–21. Bearing false witness is a serious matter. Any person who wrongly accuses another of a crime is to bear the penalty the innocent person would have received if convicted (Exod. 20:16).

20:1–8. Any man who has just built a house, planted a new vineyard, or married a wife may be excused from military duty (Luke 14:16–20).

20:9–20. Israelite armies are expected to observe specific "rules of war" when engaging their enemies in battle.

21:1–9. The elders of a city are given a handwashing ritual by which they can proclaim their innocence when the body of a person is found near their city.

21:10–14. An Israelite man may marry a woman who is captured from their enemies in times of war, but specific guidelines are prescribed by the Lord for such a marriage.

21:15–17. If a man is married to more than one wife, he cannot play favorites by transferring inheritance rights from his firstborn son to a son born later to a favorite wife. The father's true firstborn son should receive a double portion when his property is divided at his death.

21:18–21. A son who is stubborn and rebellious toward his parents may be stoned to death if they bring charges against him before the elders of the city.

21:22–23. To avoid defiling the land, a person executed by hanging must be taken down and buried before nightfall.

22:1–25:4. The Lord issues regulations for the conduct of Israelites in various situations: the provision of a protective railing on the

---

[22:1–25:4] GUARDRAILS ON THE ROOF. *When thou [Israelites] buildest a new house, then thou shalt make a battlement [parapet, NIV] for thy roof, that thou bring not blood upon thine house, if any man fall from thence* (Deut. 22:8).

This verse is something of an ancient "building code." A house was to be built with a guardrail around the edge of the roof to protect people from accidental falls.

In Bible times the roofs of houses were flat. A stairway on the outside of the house allowed the residents to use the roof much like a patio or deck is used today. Particularly at night, the roof was a good place to relax and catch a cooling breeze. Sometimes a family would even sleep on the roof to escape the oppressive heat (2 Sam. 11:2).

Perhaps the most famous "rooftop incident" in the Bible was King David's chance encounter with Bathsheba. The king was tempted to commit adultery with her when he looked down from the roof of his palace and saw her taking a bath (2 Sam. 11:2).

---

roof of a house, the treatment of borrowed property, physical disabilities that prevent a person from entering the sanctuary, the restoration of an unclean person to cleanliness, the lending of money, and fair and just treatment of the poor (Exod. 21–23).

25:5–10. If an Israelite man should die without children, his brother is encouraged to marry his widow to produce children so the dead man's family name will continue. A brother who dodges this responsibility will be ridiculed and humiliated by the elders of the city.

25:11–19. Israelites are charged to be honest in all their business dealings, not using one pair of scales for buying and another for selling (Lev. 19:35–36).

26:1–19. The people are to present the firstfruits of their harvest as a special offering to God (Exod. 23:19).

27:1–10. Moses instructs the people to build

an altar of stones after they cross the Jordan River to enter the Promised Land (Josh. 4:1–9). On this altar, sacrifices of thanksgiving are to be offered to God.

27:11–26. The Levites are instructed to issue a series of warnings to the Israelites after they enter the Promised Land. These warnings will remind the people to obey God's commands.

32:48–52. The view toward Israel from Mount Nebo. From this elevated site, Moses got only a glimpse of the promised land.

28:1–30:20. If God's people obey Him, they will live long and prosper in their new land. But if they turn away from Him and worship other gods, they will be afflicted with pain and disaster.

31:1–13. Moses calls upon the Israelites to be brave and courageous, since the time for them to do battle with the Canaanites is drawing near. He charges them to be diligent in obedience to God's laws.

31:14–30. Moses recalls how the Lord directed him to write a song for the Israelites to remind them to remain loyal to the powerful God who brought them out of slavery and sustained them in the wilderness.

32:1–47. Moses reminisces about how he delivered a song he wrote to the people of Israel. He praised the Lord for His faithfulness and graciousness to His chosen people, in spite of their rebellion and worship of false gods (Exod. 15:1–22).

32:48–52. God commands Moses to climb to the top of Mount Nebo, the highest peak in the Abarim Mountains, and look across the Jordan River to view the land He has promised to Israel.

33:1–29. Moses blesses the people of Israel tribe by tribe, just as Jacob had spoken hundreds of years before to each of his sons (Gen. 49). The descendants of Jacob's sons have grown into the twelve tribes of Israel.

34:1–12. Moses dies in Moab after viewing the Promised Land and is succeeded by Joshua.

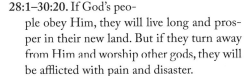

[33:1–29] CRUSHING OLIVES. *Of Asher he [Moses] said…let him be acceptable to his brethren, and let him dip his foot in oil* (Deut. 33:24).

Before his death, Moses predicted the future for each of the tribes of Israel after they settled in the land of Canaan (Deut. 32:1–25). The tribe of Asher would be known for its olive oil production. "Dip his foot in oil" refers to the ancient practice of crushing olives by foot to expel the oil.

Olive oil was used as fuel in oil-burning lamps (Exod. 27:20) and as an anointing agent (Lev. 2:1).

CHAPTER 2
BOOKS OF HISTORY

The second major section of the Old Testament contains twelve books classified as historical writings: Joshua, Judges, Ruth, 1 and 2 Samuel, 1 and 2 Kings, 1 and 2 Chronicles, Ezra, Nehemiah, and Esther.

These books trace the history of the nation of Israel across a period of more than 800 years—from the conquest of Canaan under Joshua about 1400 B.C. to their return from capivity by the Babylonians and Persians about 530 B.C. In between these two pivotal events were such happenings as rule by charismatic judges after the death of Joshua, the establishment of a central kingship form of government, the glory days of the Israelites under King David and his son Solomon, the division of the nation into northern and southern factions, the destruction of the Northern Kingdom by Assyria, and the fall of the Southern Kingdom to Babylonia.

OVERVIEW: Moses' successor, Joshua, leads the people to capture and settle the Promised Land.

Introduction to Joshua

The book of Joshua takes its name from its major personality, Joshua, who became the new leader of the Israelites upon the death of Moses (Deut. 34:9).

God charged Moses with the responsibility of leading the Israelites out of slavery and bringing them to the border of Canaan, the land that He had promised to Abraham and his descendants many centuries before (Gen. 12:1–5). Joshua would pick up where Moses left off, leading the people to conquer the territory and getting them settled in their new land.

Joshua was ideally suited for the task that he inherited. He had been trained and groomed for leadership by Moses himself (Num. 13:8; 14:6–9; 27:18–23). A stalwart follower of the Lord, Joshua realized that Israel could not overcome the Canaanites without God's help. He kept the people focused on following the Lord's leadership.

Joshua was also a good organizer and military commander. In a period of about twenty-five years, he led the people to victory over the Canaanites. Then he supervised the process of dividing the land among the twelve tribes and getting them settled in their new territory.

One of Joshua's legacies is his recognition that the worship of God is not to be mixed with the worship of false gods. The Lord will not tolerate such practices. He demands exclusive loyalty from His people. Joshua set the example for all Israel near the end of his life when he gathered the people and declared: "Choose you this day whom ye will serve; whether the gods which your fathers served that were on the other side of the flood, or the gods of the Amorites, in whose land ye dwell: but as for me and my house, we will serve the Lord" (24:15).

Joshua himself probably wrote most of the book that bears his name (see a description of his writing efforts in 24:26). The one exception to this is the final section that reports his death (24:29–33). These verses were probably added, under God's inspiration, by an unknown editor after Joshua died. They serve as a tribute to Joshua and his contribution to the nation of Israel.

Summary of Joshua

1:1–10. God orders Joshua, Moses' successor, to lead the people across the Jordan River and into the land of Canaan.

1:11–18. Joshua spreads the word for the people to get ready to move out. He reminds the tribes of Reuben and Gad and one-half of the tribe of Manasseh of their promise to help the other tribes when the time comes for them to conquer the Canaanites (Num. 32).

2:1–24. Joshua sends two spies to investigate

[2:1–24] **A HOUSE ON A WALL.** *She [Rahab] let them [Israelite spies] down by a cord through the window: for her house was upon the town wall, and she dwelt upon the wall* (Josh. 2:15).

Some walled cities of Bible times had an inner wall and an outer wall for maximum protection. To strengthen these walls, the space between them was filled with dirt and rubble at selected points. Houses were sometimes built right into the city wall by placing them on top of these piles of rubble.

Since Rahab "dwelt upon the wall" of Jericho, she must have lived in one of these "wall houses." She helped the Israelite spies escape over the city wall by lowering them with ropes from her window.

Another similar escape was made in New Testament times by the apostle Paul. Believers in the city of Damascus delivered him from his enemies, who were watching the city gates "day and night to kill him" (Acts 9:24). They placed Paul in a basket and lowered him over the city wall.

the Canaanite city of Jericho. Rahab the prostitute hides them in her house and helps them escape over the city wall. They report to Joshua that conditions are right for conquest of the land.

3:1–17. Led by the priests carrying the ark of the covenant, the people cross the flooded Jordan River on dry land as God miraculously stops the flow of water (Exod. 14).

4:1–24. Twelve stones are taken from the Jordan River and set up as a memorial in Gilgal to remind the Israelites of God's presence and protection (Deut. 27:1–10).

5:1. The Canaanites are frightened when they learn about the miraculous crossing of the Jordan River by the Israelites.

5:2–12. Joshua performs the rite of circumcision on all male Israelites who have not been circumcised (Gen. 17:9–14).

5:13–15. At Jericho, the mysterious captain of the host of the Lord meets and encourages Joshua.

6:1–27. God miraculously delivers the city of Jericho to Joshua and his warriors by causing the walls to collapse. Rahab the prostitute and her family are spared because she helped the two Israelite spies when they investigated the city (Josh. 2).

7:1–26. The Israelites fail to conquer the city of Ai because one of their own warriors, Achan, disobeyed the Lord by keeping some of the spoils of war for himself. The people stone Achan to death when they discover his sin.

8:1–29. After dealing with Achan, Joshua and his warriors capture the city of Ai by pretending to retreat, then ambushing Ai's pursuing army.

8:30–35. Joshua builds an altar on which sacrifices are offered. He reads to all the Israelites the book of the law that God delivered to Moses.

9:1–27. The Gibeonites trick Joshua into making a peace treaty with them. Joshua makes good on his promise not to harm them, but they become menial servants of the Israelites (2 Sam. 21:1–9).

10:1–11:23. Joshua and his army defeat the united forces of several Canaanite kings and occupy their territories.

[7:1–26] **MONUMENT TO A CRIME.** *They [Joshua and the Israelites] raised over him [Achan] a great heap of stones* (Josh. 7:26).

Achan was executed because he kept some of the spoils of war taken in battles against the Canaanites for himself (Josh. 7:20–21). This was a violation of the Lord's command (Josh. 6:19).

To commemorate Achan's crime, Joshua and other Israelite leaders piled stones on his grave. This makeshift monument served as a constant reminder to others of the seriousness of disobeying God.

Throughout Israel's history, stones were also heaped up to serve as memorials of positive events in the life of the nation (Exod. 24:4; Josh. 4:3–9; 24:26; 1 Sam. 7:12).

1–27. Walls tumble at the border town of Jericho as the Israelites begin their conquest of e promised land.

12:1–6. The territories east of the Jordan River—those captured by the Israelites under Moses' leadership—are listed. This area had already been settled by the tribes of Reuben and Gad and one-half of the tribe of Manasseh (Num. 32).

12:7–24. The kings and their territories west of the Jordan River in Canaan—those captured under Joshua's leadership—are listed.

13:1–7. The Lord reminds Joshua in his old age that the Canaanites still occupy parts of the land that He has promised to the Israelites.

13:8–14. God gives a general description of the territories east of the Jordan River that have already been settled by the tribes of Reuben and Gad and one-half of the tribe of Manasseh.

13:15–23. The territory east of the Jordan River assigned to the tribe of Reuben is listed.

13:24–28. The territory east of the Jordan River assigned to the tribe of Gad is listed.

13:29–31. The territory east of the Jordan River assigned to one-half of the tribe of Manasseh is listed (1 Chron. 5:23).

13:32–33. A summary statement about the territories east of the Jordan River assigned to the Israelites and a reminder that the Levites received no land inheritance.

14:1–5. A general statement about the division of the land of Canaan among the Israelite tribes.

14:6–15. Caleb receives a special inheritance of land, which includes the city of Hebron. Moses had made this promise of land to Caleb forty years before. Caleb was one of the twelve spies who investigated the land. Only he and Joshua had trusted God and recommended that the Israelites move forward immediately to conquer the land (Num. 14:5–10).

15:1–63. The territory, including cities, assigned to the tribe of Judah is listed.

16:1–4. A general statement about the territories assigned to the two tribes that sprang from Joseph's two sons, Ephraim and Manasseh.

16:5–10. The territory assigned to the tribe of Ephraim is listed.

17:1–13. The territory, including cities, assigned to the tribe of Manasseh is listed.

17:14–18. The tribes of Ephraim and Manasseh ask for additional land, and Joshua grants their request.

18:1–10. Joshua sends representatives from each tribe to survey the remaining land so it can be divided among the tribes that have not yet received an inheritance.

18:11–28. The territory, including cities, assigned to the tribe of Benjamin is listed.

19:1–9. The territory, including cities, assigned to the tribe of Simeon is listed.

19:10–16. The territory, including cities, assigned to the tribe of Zebulun is listed.

19:17–23. The territory, including cities, assigned to the tribe of Issachar is listed.

19:24–31. The territory, including cities, assigned to the tribe of Asher is listed.

19:32–39. The territory, including cities, assigned to the tribe of Naphtali is listed.

19:40–48. The territory, including cities, assigned to the tribe of Dan is listed.

19:49–51. The tribes of Israel grant Joshua a city as a reward for his faithful leadership.

20:1–9. Six cities throughout the territory of the tribes are designated as cities of refuge (Num. 35; Deut. 19:1–13). Three of these are to be on the western side and three on the eastern side of the Jordan River.

21:1–45. The Levites receive no land inheritance, so they are given forty-eight cities throughout the territory of the tribes. These cities are assigned to the three branches of the Levites: Kohathites (vv. 10–26), Gershonites (vv. 27–33), and Merarites (vv. 34–40) (see Num. 35).

22:1–9. Now that the war with the Canaanites is over, Joshua allows the warriors from the tribes of Reuben and Gad and one-half of the tribe of Manasseh to return to their homes on the eastern side of the Jordan River. They have made good on their promise to help the other tribes conquer the land (Num. 32).

22:10–34. The tribes of Reuben and Gad and one-half of the tribe of Manasseh build a huge altar on their side of the Jordan River. The tribes on the other side of the river fear this is an altar for pagan worship. But they are assured it has been built as a gesture of praise and thanksgiving to God.

23:1–16. In his old age, Joshua gathers the people and reminds them that God has fulfilled His promise to give them a land of their own. He challenges them to love the Lord and to keep His commandments.

24:1–28. In his farewell speech to Israel, Joshua gives the people a history lesson to show how gracious God has been to His people. He challenges them to remain faithful to God and to put away the worship of false gods; then he leads them to renew the covenant with the Lord.

24:29–33. Joshua dies and his accomplishments are summarized.

OVERVIEW: A series of judges, or military leaders, deliver the Israelites from their enemies.

Introduction to Judges

The book of Judges, written by an unknown author, covers a dark period of about 300 years in the history of the Israelites. This was the time between the conquest and settlement of Canaan by the tribes of Israel and the establishment of a centralized government under a human king about 1000 B.C.

These were chaotic years for Israel because the people turned away from the Lord and worshiped false gods. The writer of Judges tells us that it was a time when "every man did that which was right in his own eyes" (17:6; 21:25) rather than following the Lord.

God would punish His people by sending oppressors against them. These included tribal groups such as the Canaanites, Midianites, Moabites, and Philistines. The Israelites would repent and cry out to God for deliverance. Then the Lord would send a judge, or a military leader, to raise an army among the Israelite tribes to throw off the yoke of oppression.

After God's intervention on their behalf, the people would follow the Lord for a while, only to fall back again into the same old pattern of idolatry. Then the cycle of oppression-repentance-deliverance would begin all over again (see summary of 2:6–23 below). The onset of the cycle is introduced by the phrase "The children of Israel did evil in the sight of the LORD," which occurs seven times throughout the book (2:11; 3:7,12; 4:1; 6:1; 10:6; 13:1).

One of the subtle messages of the book of Judges is that God is no respecter of persons when He is looking for people to carry out His will. One of the judges whom He raised up to deliver His people was a woman named Deborah (4:1–24). This must have been surprising to the people, since ancient Israel was a male-dominated society.

6:11–16. Gideon is surprised when the angel of the Lord calls him to defeat Israel's enemy, the Midianites. The appointed judge twice requests confirmation by laying out a fleece, once to collect dew when the surrounding ground is dry, once to remain dry when the nearby ground is damp.

Deborah did enlist a male warrior named Barak to help her raise an army to defeat the Canaanites, but she was clearly the leader of the campaign (4:8).

Summary of Judges

1:1–36. When Joshua dies, pockets of Canaanites still live in the territory settled by the tribes of Israel. Battles with the Canaanites and other enemies continue.

2:1–5. An angel of the Lord reveals that God is not pleased because the Israelites have not driven all the Canaanites out of the land. They have allowed the pagan worship practices of the Canaanites to continue.

2:6–23. After Joshua's death, a new generation of Israelites that does not obey the Lord comes on the scene. They are corrupted by worshiping the false gods of their enemies. As punishment, God raises up a group to oppress them. The people then repent of their idolatry and cry out to God for deliverance. Then God empowers a judge, or military leader, to lead the Israelites to defeat the enemy.

3:1–6. Some of the nations or tribal groups that oppressed the Israelites during the period of the judges are listed.

3:7–11. The Lord empowers the judge Othniel, Caleb's brother (Josh. 14:6–15), to deliver the Israelites from oppression by King Chushan-rishathaim of Mesopotamia.

[1:1–36] MUTILATION OF CAPTIVES. *They [tribe of Judah] pursued after him [King Adoni-bezek], and caught him, and cut off his thumbs and his great [big, NIV] toes* (Judg. 1:6).

Adoni-bezek, a Canaanite king, was defeated by warriors from the tribe of Judah. In ancient warfare captive soldiers were sometimes mutilated like Adoni-bezek was to take away their fighting abilities. With both thumbs and both big toes missing, the king would not be able to move quickly or handle a bow or spear.

The ancient Assyrians were known to mutilate captives just for sport, cutting off body parts that had nothing to do with waging war. One monument left by an Assyrian king testifies to their military cruelty: "Their men, young and old, I took prisoners. Of some I cut off the feet and hands; of others I cut off the noses, ears, and lips; of the young men's ears I made a heap."

3:12–15. The Lord empowers the judge Ehud to deliver the Israelites from oppression by the Moabites (2 Sam. 8:2).

3:16–26. Ehud, pretending to bring a gift, assassinates King Eglon of Moab in his own house.

3:27–30. Ehud leads the Israelite army to victory over the Moabites.

3:31. The judge Shamgar leads Israel to defeat the Philistines (2 Sam. 5:17–25).

4:1–5. The Lord empowers the judge Deborah, a prophetess, to deliver the Israelites from oppression by the Canaanites.

[3:31] AN OX GOAD AS A WEAPON. *After him [Ehud] was Shamgar the son of Anath, which slew of the Philistines six hundred men with an ox goad* (Judg. 3:31).

As one of the judges, or military deliverers, of Israel, Shamgar used an ox goad as an efficient weapon against the Philistines. An ox goad was a pole about eight feet long and two inches in diameter. It was sharpened to a point on one end. A farmer used this end when plowing an ox to prod him into a faster gait. The other end had a metal blade that he used to clean roots or clay from the tip of the plow.

Jesus referred to an ox goad when He appeared to the apostle Paul on the road to Damascus: "Saul, Saul, why persecutest thou me? It is hard for thee to kick against the pricks [goads, NIV]" (Acts 26:14).

4:6–9. Deborah enlists Barak (Heb. 11:32) to lead the army of Israel against the Canaanites.

4:10–17. Barak gathers an army from the tribes of Zebulun and Naphtali. They defeat the Canaanites, whose commander, Sisera, escapes on foot.

4:18–24. Victory over the Canaanites is sealed by the assassination of Sisera. A woman named Jael drives a tent stake through his skull while he is in a deep sleep from exhaustion.

5:1–31. Deborah and Barak celebrate the defeat of the Canaanites with a song of praise to the Lord, "The Song of Deborah."

6:1–6. The combined forces of the Midianites and the Amalekites oppress Israel, destroying their crops and stealing their livestock.

6:7–10. A prophet arrives in Israel to remind the people that they are suffering because they have disobeyed the Lord.

6:11–16. The judge Gideon (Heb. 11:32) learns from an angel of the Lord that he has been selected to deliver Israel from oppression by the Midianites.

7:1–8. The Gideon Cave in Maayan Harod National Park in northern Israel. God thinned out Gideon's large army by sending home all but those who drank by scooping up water in their hands.

[7:16–25] GIDEON'S SECRET WEAPONS. *He [Gideon] divided the three hundred men into three companies, and he put a trumpet in every man's hand, with empty pitchers, and lamps within the pitchers* (Judg. 7:16).

Gideon relied on the Lord, as well as shock and surprise, to defeat the huge Midianite army with a force of only three hundred warriors. He and his men advanced on the enemy camp at night while most of the Midianites were still asleep. Then, at Gideon's signal, they blew their trumpets and broke their pitchers with torches inside, suddenly bathing the camp in light.

All the noise and light convinced the Midianites that they were being attacked by a huge army. In the shock and confusion, they "set every man's sword against his fellow" (Judg. 7:22) and fled into the night. Their disorganization made them easy prey for the pursuing Israelites.

6:17–24. The angel disappears after proving to Gideon through a miracle that he is God's messenger. Gideon builds an altar to the Lord to show he accepts God's call.

6:25–32. Obeying God's orders, Gideon tears down an altar devoted to the pagan god Baal. He builds in its place an altar dedicated to the Lord.

6:33–35. The combined forces of the Midianites and the Amalekites gather at the valley of Jezreel. Gideon raises an army from the tribes of Manasseh, Asher, Zebulun, and Naphtali.

6:36–40. Gideon asks God for two miraculous signs involving a fleece, or a piece of wool, to prove that He will use Gideon to deliver Israel.

7:1–8. The Lord trims Gideon's army—from 32,000 to 22,000 to 10,000 and finally to just 300—to show that the battle will not be won through military might but by dependence on the Lord to deliver on His promise.

7:9–15. Gideon hears two enemy soldiers discussing a dream about a battle in which the Midianites are defeated. This is another sign from the Lord that victory over the Midianites is assured.

7:16–25. Using torches, pitchers, and trumpets, Gideon and his 300 warriors launch a surprise attack on the Midianite army at night. The resulting chaos causes the warriors to attack and kill one another. Gideon seals the victory by capturing and executing two Midianite princes.

8:1–3. Warriors from the tribe of Ephraim complain because they were not summoned to join the battle against the Midianites. Gideon uses diplomacy to soothe their wounded pride.

8:4–21. Gideon captures and executes two kings of Midian, Zebah and Zalmunna, to break the power of the Midianite kingdom.

8:22–23. The Israelites ask Gideon to become their king, but he refuses.

8:24–27. Gideon makes a golden ephod, or apron, which apparently becomes an object of worship in the city where he lives.

8:28–35. After Gideon dies, the Israelites again turn away from God and begin to worship the pagan Canaanite god Baal.

9:1–6. Abimelech, a son of Gideon, is appointed king by the people of the city of Shechem. He kills the other sons of Gideon to eliminate any challengers for the throne. Only Gideon's youngest son, Jotham, escapes the slaughter.

9:7–21. Jotham ridicules Abimelech by telling a parable about the bramble, or thornbush, and the trees. Abimelech, just like the

[13:1–25] SAMSON THE NAZARITE. *Thou [Manoah's wife] shalt conceive, and bear a son; and no razor shall come on his head: for the child shall be a Nazarite unto God from the womb* (Judg. 13:5).

A Nazarite was a person who took an oath known as the Nazarite vow. He promised to avoid worldly things and to devote himself totally to the Lord. As evidence of this commitment, a Nazarite was not to drink wine or any intoxicating beverages and he was not to cut his hair (Num. 6:5).

The Nazarite vow was voluntary, and it was generally taken for a limited time, perhaps thirty or sixty days. But Samson was designated as a Nazarite for life; this choice was made for him by the Lord and his parents even before he was born.

Samson failed to live up to the vow that others had made for him. He indulged in worldly pleasures and sinned against the Lord. When Delilah succeeded in cutting his hair, the spirit of the Lord left him and his great strength was taken away (Judg. 16:19).

thornbush, isn't worthy of the kingship.

9:22–57. The people of Shechem turn against Abimelech. He is eventually killed by a woman who drops a piece of millstone on his head while he is leading a siege against a walled city.

10:1–5. Tola and Jair serve as judges to deliver Israel from their enemies.

10:6–18. The people of Israel turn to idol worship; God punishes them by raising up the Philistines and the Ammonites as their oppressors.

11:1–33. The judge Jephthah leads Israel to victory over the Ammonites (Deut. 23:3).

11:34–40. Jephthah is obligated to offer his own daughter as a sacrifice because of his rash vow to give God the first thing that came out to meet him when he returned from battle (see v. 31).

12:1–6. Jephthah leads his forces in a civil war against the tribe of Ephraim.

12:7. Jephthah dies and is buried in Gilead.

12:8–15. Three different men—Ibzan, Elon, and Abdon—serve for a brief time as judges over Israel.

13:1–25. The judge Samson (Heb. 11:32) is born to godly parents in the tribe of Dan. Consecrated as a Nazarite (Num. 6:1–21), his mission is to deliver Israel from oppression by the Philistines.

14:1–20. Samson selects a Philistine woman as his wife. He taunts his friends by giving them a riddle to solve.

15:1–20. Samson burns the crops of the Philistines and slaughters 1,000 men with the jawbone of a donkey.

16:1–3. Samson escapes from a Philistine trap by tearing a city gate out of the wall and carrying it off to Hebron.

14:1–20. Samson was a man of superhuman strength—and seemingly superhuman appetites.

16:4–21. Samson reveals to Delilah, a Philistine woman, that the source of his superhuman strength is his long hair that has never been cut. Delilah shaves his head while he is asleep. Samson is captured, blinded, and sentenced to a life of hard labor as a prisoner of the Philistines.

16:22–31. Samson dies, along with thousands of the Philistines, when he pushes down the support columns of a building where he was being taunted by his captors.

17:1–13. Micah fashions several objects of idol worship and hires a Levite as his household priest.

18:1–6. The tribe of Dan sends out scouts to find a territory or city they can claim as their own. Micah's household priest assures them that God will bless their efforts.

18:7–31. The Danite scouts recommend that Laish, a city of the Zidonians, be taken. Danite warriors stop at Micah's house on their way to Laish, stealing Micah's objects of idol worship and taking away his

[16:22–31] **DAGON OF THE PHILISTINES.** *The lords of the Philistines gathered them [the Philistines] together for to offer a great sacrifice unto Dagon their god, and to rejoice: for they said, Our god hath delivered Samson our enemy into our hand* (Judg. 16:23).

This pagan god to whom the Philistines attributed such power was their primary, national god. They must have gathered often in ceremonies such as this—probably in a temple devoted to Dagon—to worship and pay tribute to him.

Stone carvings of Dagon portray him with the head, hands, and upper body of a man and the lower part of his body as a fish. The Hebrew word for Dagon actually means "little fish." This pagan god represented the reproductive powers of nature. The fish was an appropriate image because of its ability to reproduce rapidly and in great numbers.

The Philistines boasted that Dagon had delivered their enemy Samson into their hands. But when he pushed down the pillars that held up Dagon's temple (Judg. 16:29–30), he proved that Israel's God was superior to this pagan idol.

household priest. These become part of the worship system of the Danites after they occupy Laish.

19:1–30. A Levite's concubine is violated and killed by perverted residents of the city of Gibeah in the territory of the tribe of Benjamin. The Levite informs the other Israelite tribes of this outrage and urges them to take action against the city of Gibeah and the Benjaminites.

20:1–48. The tribes of Israel raise an army and attack the Benjaminites at Gibeah. They wipe out most of the tribe, including the women.

21:1–25. Because of its great losses, the tribe of Benjamin is in danger of going extinct, especially since the other tribes made a vow not to give their daughters in marriage to the few remaining Benjaminite men. But the tribes find a way to produce wives for Benjamin so this tribe will not be "cut off from Israel" (v. 6).

OVERVIEW: Ruth's commitment to her mother-in-law exemplifies God's love and care.

Introduction to Ruth

The book of Ruth is only four chapters long, but it is one of the most inspiring books of the Bible. It takes its name from a Moabite (Gentile) woman who married into an Israelite family. When all the men of the family died, Ruth remained steadfastly loyal to her mother-in-law, Naomi. The name Ruth means "friendship," and she modeled love and friendship at their best.

Modern Christian wedding ceremonies often include the words of devotion spoken by Ruth to Naomi: "Intreat me not to leave thee... for whither thou goest, I will go; and where thou lodgest, I will lodge: thy people shall be my people, and thy God my God" (1:16).

The author of Ruth is unknown. What we do know is that the events of the book happened during "the days when the judges ruled" (1:1). This was a dark period in Israel's history (see the introduction to Judges on p. 49). Ruth shows us that even in the worst of times, God is at work in His world.

Summary of Ruth

1:1–5. Elimelech and his wife and two sons move to Moab from Judah to escape a famine in their homeland. Then Elimelech and his two sons die, leaving three widows in distress: his wife, Naomi, and the two Moabite women whom his sons had married.

1:6–22. Naomi decides to return to her homeland. One of her widowed daughters-in-law, Ruth, insists on going with her.

2:1–23. Ruth goes into the barley fields to gather left-behind stalks of grain to make bread for herself and Naomi. By chance, this field belongs to Boaz, a distant relative of Naomi's late husband, Elimelech. Ruth meets Boaz, who arranges with his harvesters to leave many stalks in the field for her to glean. Naomi is pleased when she learns that Ruth has met Boaz.

[2:1–23] GLEANING IN THE FIELDS OF BOAZ. *She [Ruth] went, and came, and gleaned in the field after the reapers* (Ruth 2:3).

Ruth's gathering of grain in the fields of Boaz is the best example in the Bible of the practice of gleaning. After crops had been harvested, poor people were allowed in the fields and orchards to pick up any grain or fruit that had been left behind.

Old Testament law specified that the corners of fields were not to be harvested by landowners. Grain in these spots was to be left for the poor (Lev. 23:22). Likewise, a sheaf of grain left accidentally in the field was to remain there as provision for the poor (Deut. 24:19).

Some generous landowners went beyond the letter of the law and deliberately left part of the harvest in the fields for the poor. For example, when Boaz learned about Ruth gleaning on his property, he instructed his workers, "Pull out some stalks for her from the bundles [of grain] and leave them for her to pick up" (Ruth 2:16 NIV).

[4:1–12] SIGN OF THE SHOE. *Now this was the manner in former time in Israel concerning redeeming and concerning changing, for to confirm all things; a man plucked off his shoe, and gave it to his neighbour: and this was a testimony in Israel* (Ruth 4:7).

Naomi's deceased husband, Elimelech, had some land in Bethlehem that she had been forced to sell because of her poverty conditions (Ruth 4:3). Elimelech had a relative who, as his next of kin, had the right to buy back or redeem this property to keep it in the family.

But this unnamed relative gave up that right by removing his sandal. Only the owner of a plot of land had the right to walk on it. Removal of his sandal symbolized that he was giving up his ownership rights and transferring them to Boaz, who could then proceed to buy back the property from the current owner.

3:1–18. Naomi sends Ruth to lie at the feet of Boaz at night, a custom that indicates she is willing to marry Boaz. The law of levirate marriage encouraged relatives of deceased males who had no children to marry their widows in order to produce children to carry on the family name (Deut. 25:5–10). Boaz, as a distant relative of Naomi's late husband, Elimelech, is willing to marry Ruth but indicates there is a relative closer to Elimelech who has first choice in the matter.

4:1–12. With the elders of the city looking on as witnesses, Boaz sits down with this relative at the city gate. The man gives up the right to marry Ruth, leaving Boaz free to take her as his wife.

4:13–22. Boaz marries Ruth, who gives birth to a son named Obed. Obed becomes the father of Jesse and the grandfather of the great King David of Judah (Matt. 1:5).

2:1–23. After the harvest, the widowed Ruth collects leftover grain—as Jewish law allowed the poor to do. Ruth later marrie the Bethlehem farm owner, Boaz, and they became great-grandparents of King David.

OVERVIEW: The Israelite tribes unite under a kingship form of government. Saul fails as the first king.

1. Hannah presents young Samuel to Eli the priest, fulfilling promise to "give him unto the LORD all the days of his life" Samuel 1:11).

Introduction to 1 Samuel

The book of 1 Samuel is a pivotal book in the history of Israel. Up to this point, about 1050 to 1000 B.C., the nation had no centralized form of government. It existed as a loose tribal society, with each of the twelve tribes living to itself and minding its own affairs. This changed when Saul was anointed the first king of Israel by the prophet Samuel (10:1). For the rest of their history during Old Testament times, God's people would be ruled by an earthly king.

First Samuel is named for the prophet Samuel, the author and one of the central personalities of the book. As the last of the judges and the first of the prophets, he served as the moral conscience of the nation during this critical period in its history.

As the first king of Israel, Saul got off to a good start. He showed humility, patience, and courageous leadership and was able to win some decisive victories over Israel's number one enemy, the Philistines. But over time he degenerated into a sullen, impatient, and rebellious leader who refused to follow the clear commands of the Lord. Samuel was finally commanded by the Lord to anoint the young shepherd boy David as Saul's successor (16:1–13).

David knew he was destined to become king someday. But in the meantime he showed loyalty to Saul by serving as his aide and becoming a heroic warrior in his army. Saul eventually became consumed by a jealous rage, and David was forced to flee for his life into Philistine territory.

The book of 1 Samuel ends tragically— with the death of Saul and his three sons at the hands of the Philistines (chap. 31). This paved the way for David to succeed to the kingship.

Summary of 1 Samuel

1:1–8. Hannah expresses her sorrow over her childlessness by weeping and refusing to eat.

1:9–18. Hannah prays for a son and promises to devote him to the Lord.

[1:9–18] ELI'S SEAT OF JUDGMENT. *Eli the priest sat upon a seat by a post of the temple of the Lord* (1 Sam. 1:9).

Since Eli was the high priest of Israel, the seat on which he sat was probably a "seat of judgment" from which he advised the people. As the final judge in religious matters, he helped people solve their problems by subjecting themselves to the Lord's will. Hannah, a godly woman who had been unable to have children, brought this problem before Eli for his advice and counsel.

Eli told Hannah, "Go in peace: and the God of Israel grant thee thy petition" (1 Sam. 1:17). She eventually did give birth to a son—the prophet Samuel.

1:19–28. Samuel is born as an answer to Hannah's prayer. She follows through on her promise to devote him to the Lord by presenting him to the priest Eli at Shiloh.

2:1–10. Hannah prays and sings a song of thanksgiving to God for the birth of Samuel and His continuing faithfulness to Israel.

2:11. The boy Samuel lives with the priest Eli at Shiloh and helps him with his ceremonial religious duties.

2:12–17. The dishonest sons of Eli cheat people when they offer sacrifices to the Lord at Shiloh.

2:18–21. The boy Samuel continues his work with Eli at Shiloh. Samuel's mother and father are blessed with other children.

2:22–36. A prophet warns Eli that he and his household will be judged by the Lord because of the wicked behavior of his two sons, Hophni and Phinehas.

3:1–9. The Lord speaks to the boy Samuel three times; he assumes he is being called by the priest Eli.

3:10–21. God speaks to Samuel for the fourth time, revealing that He will punish Eli and his descendants because he has failed to deal with his wicked sons. Samuel is recognized throughout the land as a true prophet of the Lord.

4:1–11. Eli's sons, Hophni and Phinehas, are killed in a battle with the Philistines. The Philistines carry away the Israelites' sacred chest known as the ark of the covenant (Exod. 37:1–9).

4:12–18. The aged priest Eli dies at the news that his sons have been killed and the ark of the covenant has been captured by the Philistines.

4:19–22. Eli's daughter-in-law names her newborn child Ichabod, symbolizing that God's glory has left Israel.

5:1–12. God punishes the Philistines for capturing the ark. He works miracles and sends plagues upon them in three different cities where it is being kept.

6:1–21. After keeping the ark for seven months, the Philistines return it to Israel, along with gifts of gold as a trespass offering.

7:1–2. The ark is kept at the Israelite city of Kirjath-jearim for twenty years.

7:3–6. Samuel calls on the Israelites to turn from their idolatry back to God and offers sacrifices to the Lord at Mizpeh.

7:7–14. Israel wins a victory over the Philistines after Samuel prays and makes a special offering to the Lord.

7:15–17. Samuel serves as a priest and judge for all Israel from his home at Ramah.

[6:1–21] PAGAN CHARMS. *Ye [Philistines] shall make images [models, NIV] of your emerods [tumors, NIV], and images of your mice that mar the land* (1 Sam. 6:5).

The Philistines captured the ark of the covenant from the Israelites and carried it to the city of Ashdod (1 Sam. 5:1). God punished the Philistines by sending swarms of mice throughout their land. These mice apparently carried a disease that caused the Philistines to break out in sores, or tumors.

Pagan priests among the Philistines recommended that they send the ark back to the Israelites, along with images of the mice and tumors that were causing their suffering. They thought these images would serve as magic charms to cure their sores and ward off evil spirits.

8:1–3. In his old age, Samuel appoints his two sons as judges over Israel, but they become dishonest and corrupt.

8:4–9. The elders of Israel ask Samuel to appoint a king to rule over all the tribes (Hosea 13:10).

8:10–22. At God's command, Samuel informs the people about the suffering they will experience under a human king. But his warnings fall on deaf ears. God tells Samuel to proceed to select a king to rule over Israel.

9:1–27. Saul, a handsome young man from the tribe of Benjamin, encounters Samuel while searching for his father's lost donkeys. The Lord informs Samuel that Saul is the person who should be anointed as Israel's king.

10:1. Samuel pours oil on Saul's head to anoint him as king over the Israelites.

10:2–16. Samuel tells Saul to look for several miraculous signs to show that he is the Lord's anointed to rule over Israel.

10:17–27. Samuel calls the tribes of Israel together for a public presentation of Saul as their new king. The reluctant Saul is summoned from his hiding place to begin his duties.

11:1–15. Saul gathers an army from among all the tribes and defeats the Ammonites at Jabesh-gilead. This quiets minority opposition to his kingship, and he is acclaimed king by all Israel at Gilgal.

12:1–25. Samuel reminds the people of how God has blessed them in past years; he challenges them to remain faithful to Him during this new era of their history under a human king (Josh. 24:1–28).

13:1–14. Preparing for battle with the Philistines, Saul offers a sacrifice to God on his own rather than waiting for Samuel the priest to present the offering with the prescribed ritual. Samuel informs him that this act of impatience and obedience will cost him the kingship.

13:15–23. Saul's warriors have only a few iron weapons to fight with. Their Philistine enemies have developed a monopoly on making and sharpening iron weapons throughout the entire territory of Israel (2 Kings 24:14).

14:1–19. Saul's son Jonathan, accompanied by his armorbearer, leads a secret mission against a company of Philistines, causing panic throughout the enemy camp.

14:20–23. Saul and his army join the battle and chase the Philistine garrison from the area.

14:24–42. Saul warns all Israelite warriors against partaking of food during the day when a great battle rages against the Philistines. His own son Jonathan violates the command.

14:43–46. Saul prepares to execute Jonathan for his disobedience, but other Israelite warriors intervene to save Jonathan's life.

14:47–52. Saul's victories over Israel's enemies are listed, along with the members of his family (1 Chron. 8:33).

15:1–9. The prophet Samuel directs Saul to destroy the Amalekites and all their livestock (Exod. 17:8–16). But Saul spares the life of

[17:40–51] DAVID'S SLING. *His [David's] sling was in his hand* (1 Sam. 17:40).

The sling that David carried was a simple but effective weapon used by shepherds, farmers, and even soldiers in Bible times. It was similar to the slingshot in its design and how it was used.

Like a slingshot, the sling had a pocket in which a small stone was placed. Attached to this pocket were two leather straps. The slinger grasped the ends of the straps, twirled the stone around several times in a circular motion, then released one of the straps at just the right time to hurl the stone toward its target.

In skilled hands, the sling was a formidable weapon. The force of the stone was strong enough to kill wild animals and—in Goliath's case—even a giant of a man (1 Sam. 17:49).

During the time of the judges, the tribe of Benjamin had a unit of seven hundred soldiers who specialized in use of the sling. All the slingers in this elite corps were left-handed, and they "could sling a stone at a hair and not miss" (Judg. 20:16 NIV).

King Agag and keeps some of the choice spoils of war.

15:10–35. Samuel reprimands Saul for his disobedience. He declares that the kingship has been taken away from him by the Lord and will be given to another.

16:1–13. At the Lord's command, Samuel anoints the shepherd boy David—the youngest son of Jesse—as Saul's replacement as king of Israel.

16:14–23. Saul selects David to serve as his armorbearer and to play the harp to soothe his troubled mind.

17:1–22. Saul's army is stationed for battle against the Philistines, but they are bullied into inaction by the taunts of a Philistine giant named Goliath.

17:23–39. The shepherd boy David arrives on the scene and prepares to fight Goliath, since no Israelite warrior will accept his challenge. David refuses to wear the armor of Saul for the battle.

17:40–51. David fells Goliath with a single stone from his sling, then executes the giant with his own sword.

17:52–58. At the death of their champion, the Philistine army flees in panic and suffers a

17:40–51. A man holds a sling of the sort young David used to fell Goliath. The sling would whirl the rock to build up centrifugal force before releasing it at his target.

humiliating defeat by the army of Israel.

18:1–4. David and Saul's son Jonathan make a pact of everlasting friendship.

18:5–16. David becomes a commander in Saul's army and is praised by the Israelites for his bravery. In a fit of jealousy, Saul tries to kill David.

18:17–30. David takes Saul's daughter Michal as his wife after leading a successful campaign against the Philistines.

19:1–7. Jonathan intercedes with his father, Saul, on behalf of David, receiving Saul's assurance that he will not harm David.

19:8–18. Saul breaks his promise and attempts to kill David again. David seeks sanctuary with the prophet Samuel.

19:19–24. Saul sends soldiers to capture David, but they are moved by God's Spirit to prophesy instead. The same thing happens to Saul when he comes looking for David in Samuel's household.

20:1–42. Jonathan warns David that Saul intends to kill him and that he should flee for his life. Then David and Jonathan bid each other a sorrowful farewell.

21:1–9. David visits the priest Ahimelech at Nob. Ahimelech gives him food and the sword of the Philistine giant Goliath to use as his own weapon.

21:10–15. David pretends to be insane in order to find sanctuary with Achish, king of Gath, in Philistine territory.

22:1–5. David gathers an army of 400 warriors while hiding from Saul.

22:6–23. Saul slaughters Ahimelech and scores of other priests at Nob for providing assistance to David.

23:1–5. David and his fighting men defeat a Philistine force to save the city of Keilah.

23:6–29. David eludes Saul and his army by hiding in various places in the wilderness.

24:1–15. David gets close enough to Saul in a dark cave to cut off a piece of his robe, but he refuses to kill him. From a distance, David condemns Saul for wasting his time by chasing him and trying to kill him.

24:16–22. Saul admits that David is a righteous man and that he is destined to become the new king of Israel. He secures David's promise that he will not murder all of Saul's descendants after he is anointed king.

25:1. Samuel dies and is buried at Ramah.

25:2–13. David asks a wealthy livestock owner named Nabal for food supplies for his hungry army, but Nabal insults David and refuses his request. David prepares to take the needed supplies by force.

25:14–35. Nabal's wife, Abigail, gathers food supplies and presents them to David to appease his anger.

25:36–44. Nabal dies, and David takes Abigail as one of his wives.

26:1–16. David and one of his warriors slip into Saul's camp at night. David gets close enough to Saul to kill him, but he refuses— once again (1 Sam. 24:1–15)—to do so.

[19:19–24] NOT QUITE NAKED. *He [Saul] stripped off his clothes also, and prophesied before Samuel in like manner, and lay down naked all that day and all that night* (1 Sam. 19:24).

The basic dress for both men and women of Bible times was a full-length outer garment, or robe, as well as a full-length undergarment of lighter material. Thus, the term *naked* as rendered by the KJV in this verse does not mean totally nude. A person who took off his outer robe was considered "naked," although he might still be wearing his undergarment.

This is the sense in which the prophet Isaiah went around "naked" (Isa. 20:2) at the Lord's command to symbolize the fate of the people of Judah unless they turned from their idolatry. The NIV says that Isaiah went around "stripped"— without his outer robe.

[25:1] SAMUEL'S TOMB. *Samuel died; and all the Israelites were gathered together, and lamented him, and buried him in his house at Ramah* (1 Sam. 25:1).

Some interpreters believe this verse means that Samuel was buried in a tomb in the house he lived in at Ramah. But it is likely that the term *house* was just a poetic way of referring to a tomb. Job spoke of the grave as a "house appointed for all living" (Job 30:23).

26:17–20. From a distance, David again condemns Saul for trying to kill him (1 Sam. 24:9–15).

26:21–25. Saul again admits his wrongdoing (1 Sam. 24:16–22) and predicts that David will be victorious and successful as king of Israel.

27:1–4. David and his army of 600 warriors again seek sanctuary with Achish, king of Gath, in Philistine territory (1 Sam. 21:10–15).

27:5–12. David lives among the Philistines for sixteen months. From his headquarters at the city of Ziklag, he conducts raids against several tribal enemies of the Israelites, including the Geshurites, Gezrites, and Amalekites.

28:1–4. A coalition of several Philistine armies assembles against Saul's forces at Gilboa.

28:5–25. Saul asks for the Lord's direction but gets no response. He hires a medium to conjure up the spirit of Samuel, who predicts that Saul's army will be defeated by the Philistines.

29:1–11. The commanders of the allied Philistine forces do not trust David. They insist that he and his fighting men not be allowed to go into battle against Saul, lest they turn against the Philistines. David is dismissed by his Philistine friend Achish, king of Gath.

30:1–21. David and his army defeat the Amalekites, who had raided his headquarters city of Ziklag and carried away captives and spoils of war.

30:22–31. David shows his kindness and fairness by sharing the spoils of war with 200 of his warriors who were too weak to pursue the battle with the Amalekites to the end. He shows his political astuteness by sharing the spoils with his fellow Israelites in several selected cities.

31:1–13. The Philistines defeat Saul's forces at Mount Gilboa (1 Chron. 10:1–4). Among the dead are Saul and his three sons, whose corpses are displayed on the wall of a Philistine city. Some brave Israelite warriors take the bodies down under the cover of darkness and give them a decent burial.

28:5–25. Dead Samuel's spirit, conjured up by a medium, appears to King Saul. Samuel warns that Saul and his three so will join him the following day, after a doomed battle with the Philistines.

OVERVIEW: David succeeds Saul as king and leads Israel to victory over its enemies.

Introduction to 2 Samuel

The book of 2 Samuel picks up where 1 Samuel leaves off—with the death of King Saul and the succession of David to the kingship. At first David was recognized by the people as king over only a part of Israel. But David eventually won out over other challengers and reigned over the entire territory of Israel. Second Samuel traces the events of David's administration across a period of about forty years.

This book is named for the prophet Samuel, the author of 1 Samuel (see the introduction to 1 Samuel on p. 57). But 2 Samuel could not have been written by him, since it reports on events that happened after Samuel's death (1 Sam. 25:1). Many scholars believe 2 Samuel was written by Abiathar, the high priest of the nation during David's administration (2 Sam. 15:24–35).

Unlike Saul, Israel's first king, who rejected God's counsel (see the introduction to 1 Samuel on p. 57), David followed the Lord and set a good example for his people. God rewarded him by giving him victory over all of Israel's enemies and expanding the borders of his kingdom. God even promised David that one of his descendants would always occupy the throne of Israel (7:1–17).

But even David had feet of clay. He committed adultery with Bathsheba and tried to cover up his crime by having her husband killed. When confronted by God's prophet, David repented of his sin and received God's forgiveness. But he would have to face the consequences of his sin through tragedies that would strike his own family (11:1–12:12).

Toward the end of David's reign, his son Absalom raised an army and tried to take the kingship from his father by force. David's army prevailed, but Absalom was killed in battle. The king mourned his son with some of the saddest words in the Bible: "O my son Absalom, my son, my son Absalom! would God I had died for thee, O Absalom, my son, my son!" (18:33).

Some of the events from David's reign that appear in 2 Samuel are also reported in the book of 1 Chronicles. These events are cross-referenced to 1 Chronicles in the summary of 2 Samuel below.

Summary of 2 Samuel

1:1–16. David is informed of the death of Saul and Saul's son Jonathan at the hands of the Philistines.

1:17–27. David laments the death of Saul and Jonathan.

2:1–7. David is recognized as king by the tribe of Judah in southern Israel. He makes Hebron his headquarters city.

2:8–11. Abner, commander of Saul's army, makes Saul's son Ish-bosheth king over the other tribes of Israel. For seven and one-half years, two opposing kingships exist in Israel.

> **[1:1–16] KING SAUL'S BRACELET.** *I [soldier from Saul's camp] took the crown that was upon his [Saul's] head, and the bracelet [band, NIV] that was on his arm* (2 Sam. 1:10).
>
> After King Saul died, a warrior removed his crown and bracelet and brought a report to David about the death of the king. The bracelet worn by Saul probably signified his royal status, just like his crown. Common among kings of the ancient world, these royal arm bands were often decorated with jewels and precious stones.

One faction recognizes David, and the other recognizes Ish-bosheth.

2:12–32. In an initial battle between the two factions, Ish-bosheth's forces under Abner are defeated by David's army under the leadership of Joab.

3:1–5. David's fortunes increase, while Ish-bosheth loses ground. Six sons from several different wives are born to David while he rules over the tribe of Judah at Hebron.

3:6–21. Abner offers to desert to David and to swing the support of the tribes that follow Ish-bosheth to David.

3:22–39. Joab assassinates Abner. David makes it clear that he had nothing to do with his death.

4:1–8. Ish-bosheth is assassinated by his two brothers; they cut off his head and present it to David.

4:9–12. David executes Ish-bosheth's assassins.

5:1–5. David is recognized by all the tribes as king over all Israel (1 Chron. 11:1–3).

5:6–10. David captures the city of Jerusalem from the Jebusites and turns it into his new headquarters city (Josh. 15:63; 1 Chron. 11:4–9).

5:11–16. Hiram, king of Tyre, pays honor to David as king of Israel (1 Chron. 14:1–2). Eleven sons from several different wives are born to David at Jerusalem (1 Chron. 14:3–7).

5:17–25. David defeats the Philistines in a major battle in the valley of Rephaim (1 Chron. 14:8–17).

6:1–11. David moves the ark of the covenant from the house of Abinadab to the house of Obed-edom. Uzzah is killed when he touches the ark while it is being moved (1 Chron. 13:1–14).

6:12–19. David dances before the ark of the covenant when it is moved from the house of Obed-edom to Jerusalem (1 Chron. 15:1–29).

6:20–23. David's wife Michal criticizes him for dancing before the ark of the covenant. David defends his behavior as an act of devotion and worship before the Lord.

7:1–17. God promises David that his kingship will be established forever—that a descendant of David will always occupy the throne of Israel (1 Chron. 17:1–15; Ps. 132:11).

7:18–29. David pours out his heart to God in a prayer of praise and thanksgiving (1 Chron. 16:7–36).

8:1–14. David extends his kingdom and

> **[3:22–39] MURDER IN THE GATE.** *When Abner was returned to Hebron, Joab took him aside in the gate [gateway, NIV] to speak with him quietly, and smote him there…that he died* (2 Sam. 3:27).
>
> Abner was the commander of King Saul's army. After Saul's death, David became king. Joab, a military leader who was loyal to David, killed Abner because Abner had tried to install one of Saul's sons as the new king.
>
> Joab took Abner "aside in the gate" of the city of Hebron, supposedly for a private talk. The vaulted openings through the massive walls of some ancient cities were ten to twelve feet thick. This dark passageway was an ideal place for Joab to commit this crime.

his influence by defeating the Philistines, Moabites, Syrians, Amalekites, and Edomites (1 Chron. 18:1–14).

8:15–18. The aides and chief officials in David's administration are listed (1 Chron. 18:15–17).

9:1–13. David provides for Mephibosheth, the lame son of his late friend Jonathan. David invites Mephibosheth to live in Jerusalem and to eat at his table like one of his own sons.

10:1–19. David's army, led by his commander Joab, defeats the allied forces of the Ammonites and the Syrians (1 Chron. 19:6–19).

11:1–5. David commits adultery with Bathsheba, the wife of Uriah the Hittite, while Uriah is away on duty with David's army. She informs David that she is pregnant with David's child.

11:6–13. David tries to cover his sin by granting Uriah a furlough to spend time with Bathsheba. But Uriah foils the king's scheme by refusing to spend the night with his wife.

11:14–25. David directs his commander, Joab, to move Uriah to the front of the battle so Uriah will be killed.

11:26–27. With Uriah disposed of, David takes Bathsheba as his own wife. She gives birth to a son by David.

12:1–9. Nathan the prophet condemns David for his sin and his crime against Uriah. Nathan convicts David of his sin by telling him a parable about a wealthy man (representing David) who stole a lamb from a poor man (representing Uriah).

12:10–12. Nathan announces God's judgment against David because of his sin with Bathsheba: David's own family will be afflicted with trouble and violence.

12:13–23. David repents of his sin and is assured by Nathan that he will not die. But the sickly child born to Bathsheba dies within a few days.

12:24–25. David comforts Bathsheba in the loss of their first child. She later gives birth to another son by David whom they name Solomon.

[12:13–23] **DAVID'S BEREAVEMENT PATTERN.** *Then said his servants unto him [David], What thing is this that thou hast done? thou didst fast and weep for the child, while it was alive; but when the child was dead, thou didst rise and eat bread* (2 Sam. 12:21).

The newborn child whom King David's servants referred to had been conceived during his adulterous affair with Bathsheba (see sidebar, "Temptation on the Roof," on p. 65).

David's servants were amazed because he reversed the normal pattern of grieving in Israelite culture. Following the death of a loved one, the survivors would stop all their normal activities and mourn and fast for a period of several days. Then they would be persuaded by other family members to return to their daily routine.

But David mourned for his newborn child for seven days before he died. He knew this child would die because the prophet Nathan had told him so (2 Sam. 12:13–17). He returned to his routine activities as soon as the child died.

12:26–31. David's commander, Joab, defeats the Ammonites at Rabbah, and they are made slaves in David's kingdom (1 Chron. 20:1–3).

13:1–19. Amnon, one of David's sons, rapes his half sister Tamar.

13:20–33. David's son Absalom, full brother of Tamar and half brother of Amnon, murders Amnon to avenge his crime against Tamar.

13:34–39. Absalom goes into hiding in Geshur and is greatly missed by his father, David.

14:1–24. David's commander, Joab, pleads with the king to let Absalom return to Jerusalem from Geshur. David agrees but refuses to have any contact with Absalom.

14:25–28. Absalom is portrayed as a handsome, vain, and arrogant man who takes great pride in his long, beautiful hair.

14:29–33. Absalom sets Joab's barley fields on fire to force him to arrange a meeting between him and the king. David and his son Absalom are finally reconciled after years of estrangement.

15:1–12. Absalom works behind the scenes to undercut his father's influence and to cultivate loyalty to himself throughout Israel. Absalom gathers a force at Hebron in opposition to David's kingship.

15:13–23. David and his family, his household servants, and the officials in his administration flee Jerusalem. They hide in the wilderness because of the threat from Absalom's rebellion.

15:24–29. David sends the priests Zadok and Abiathar back to Jerusalem with the ark of the covenant, since this city is considered its appropriate resting place.

15:30–37. David sends his friend and supporter Hushai the Archite into Jerusalem so he can spy on the rebellious Absalom.

16:1–4. Ziba, the servant of Mephibosheth, comes to the aid of the fleeing David and his officials by providing food and supplies.

16:5–14. Shimei, a distant relative of Saul, issues curses against David as he flees from Jerusalem.

[15:30–37] **DUST ON THE HEAD.** *Hushai the Archite came to meet him [David] with his coat rent [torn, NIV], and earth [dust, NIV] upon his head* (2 Sam. 15:32).

Hushai was a friend and supporter of King David. During Absalom's rebellion, Hushai expressed his sorrow at David's exile by tearing his clothes and throwing dust on his head.

Adam, the first man, was created by the Lord from "the dust of the ground" (Gen. 2:7), one of the most common substances on earth. Putting dust on one's head may have been a way of showing humility and helplessness in the face of sorrow.

The custom of putting dust on the head is also referred to in several other passages in the Bible (Josh. 7:6; 1 Sam. 4:12; 2 Sam. 1:2; 13:19; Neh. 9:1; Job 2:12; Lam. 2:10; Ezek. 27:30; Rev. 18:19).

16:15–19. Absalom enters Jerusalem with his supporters. The spy Hushai convinces Absalom he has switched loyalties from David to Absalom.

16:20–23. Ahithophel, a former aide of David, now supports Absalom's rebellion. Ahithophel advises Absalom to claim David's concubines as his own, an act that symbolizes Absalom is assuming the kingship.

17:1–14. Ahithophel advises Absalom to attack David and his forces while they are on the run. But the spy Hushai convinces him to wait until he has gathered a large army before pressing the attack.

17:15–22. Hushai sends messengers to warn David to flee into the wilderness, in case Absalom should decide to mount a surprise attack against him.

[17:15–22] HIDDEN IN A CISTERN. *They [Jonathan and Ahimaaz]…came to a man's house…which had a well in his court; whither they went down. And the woman took and spread a covering over the well's mouth, and spread ground corn [grain, NIV] thereon; and the thing was not known* (2 Sam. 17:18–19).

Jonathan and Ahimaaz were spies who reported on Absalom's activities to King David while David was in exile during Absalom's rebellion.

The "well" in which Jonathan and Ahimaaz were hidden was probably a cistern that was used to collect rainwater. It must have been dry at this time. With containers of grain or flour placed on top of its cover, this cistern was an ideal hiding place.

17:23. Ahithophel commits suicide because Absalom did not follow his advice to attack David immediately.

17:24–29. David and his forces hide out near the city of Mahanaim; here they are supplied with food and other necessities by local residents.

18:1–8. David's army, under three military leaders—Joab, Abishai, and Ittai—attack Absalom's forces in the forest of Ephraim. David instructs them not to harm his son Absalom.

18:9–18. Disregarding the king's orders, Joab kills Absalom after his long hair is entangled in the branches of a tree.

[18:19–33] DAVID'S SAD LAMENT. *The king [David] …wept…O my son Absalom, my son, my son Absalom! would God I had died for thee* (2 Sam. 18:33).

David's outpouring of grief over his son Absalom is one of the saddest passages in the entire Bible. Apparently such expressions of sorrow over deceased loved ones were common in Bible times. When Jacob died, his family "mourned with a great and very sore lamentation" (Gen. 50:10).

18:19–33. David weeps bitterly for his son after a messenger informs him that Absalom is dead.

19:1–8. David's extreme and extended grief over his son Absalom comes across to his supporters as lack of appreciation for their loyalty. Joab confronts David about this problem, and David agrees to meet with his soldiers and constituents at the city gate.

19:9–14. David builds political support throughout Israel to prepare for his return to Jerusalem as king. He names his nephew Amasa, who had commanded Absalom's army (2 Sam. 17:25), an officer in his army in order to reach out to those who had supported Absalom.

19:15–43. David is acclaimed king by several different segments of Israelite society as he crosses the Jordan River and enters the city of Jerusalem. He forgives Shimei for insulting him as he was fleeing the city (2 Sam. 16:5–14).

[19:15–43] **CROSSING THE JORDAN RIVER.** *There went over a ferry boat to carry over the king's household* (2 Sam. 19:18).

This verse describes David's return from exile to take up his duties as king over Israel after Absalom's rebellion had been put down. David and the rest of the royal household crossed over the Jordan River back into Israelite territory.

Many interpreters question the KJV's use of the term *ferry boat* to describe this crossing. The Jordan River is not very deep in most places. It is generally crossed at shallow places known as fords by just wading across.

The NIV's rendering of this verse—"they crossed at the ford to take the king's household over"—is probably a better translation.

20:1–7. A man named Sheba of the tribe of Benjamin incites a rebellion against David among the northern tribes of Israel. David dispatches his army under Joab and Amasa to put down the rebellion.

20:8–13. Joab murders Amasa, apparently because he had doubts about Amasa's loyalty to the king.

20:14–22. Sheba's rebellion ends when he is assassinated by citizens of the city where he sought refuge from David's army.

20:23–26. The chief officials in David's administration are listed.

21:1–9. About 400 years before David's time, Joshua had made a treaty with the Gibeonites that guaranteed their safety (Josh. 9:3–27). But Saul had broken this treaty by killing some of the Gibeonites. David makes amends with the Gibeonites by allowing them to execute seven of the surviving descendants of Saul.

21:10–14. David retrieves the bones of Saul and his son Jonathan from the city of Jabesh-gilead and has them buried in Saul's family plot in the territory of Benjamin.

21:15–22. David's army kills several Philistine giants, some of whom were descendants of the giant Goliath whom David had killed several years before (1 Sam. 17:32–52).

22:1–51. David utters a prayer of thanksgiving to God for giving him victory over all his enemies. This psalm also appears in the Bible as Psalm 18.

[20:8–13] **GRASPING THE BEARD.** *Joab said to Amasa, Art thou in health, my brother? And Joab took Amasa by the beard with the right hand to kiss him* (2 Sam. 20:9).

Grasping a person's beard and kissing his cheek was a customary greeting among men of Bible times. But Joab used it as a cover to assassinate Amasa (2 Sam. 20:10) because Amasa had supported Absalom's rebellion.

23:1–7. Apparently near the end of his life, David issues these words of praise to God for His faithfulness and His promise that David would enjoy an eternal reign on the throne of Israel (2 Sam. 7:1–17).

23:8–39. The names and brave deeds of David's

[22:1–51] **A PSALM REPEATED.** *David spake unto the LORD the words of this song in the day that the LORD had delivered him out of the hand of all his enemies* (2 Sam. 22:1).

The remaining verses in 2 Samuel 22 contain the words of this psalm that David wrote. This psalm also appears in the Bible as Psalm 18. Although there are a few minor variations between these two recordings of the same psalm, it is essentially the same in both locations.

This verse shows that David wrote many of the psalms in response to specific events in his life. He wrote this psalm to praise the Lord for giving him victory over the enemies of Israel and for establishing him as king throughout the land.

24:16–25. Egyptian farmers knock grain kernels loose on a threshing floor. The biblical David bought a stone threshing floor in Jerusalem and built a sacrificial altar there, where his son Solomon later built the temple.

"mighty men" are listed. These men may have been an elite group of warriors, perhaps David's personal bodyguards (1 Chron. 11:10–47).

24:1–9. David directs his commander, Joab, to take a census of all the fighting men throughout the tribes of Israel (1 Chron. 21:1–6).

24:10–15. The Lord sends a plague upon the people because of David's sin in ordering the census. Perhaps his sin was human pride over the kingdom he had built (1 Chron. 21:7–17).

24:16–25. David buys a threshing floor from Ornan/Araunah the Jebusite as the site for an altar on which sacrifices will be offered to God. These sacrifices bring an end to the plague (1 Chron. 21:18–30).

1 KINGS

OVERVIEW: The united kingdom splits into two factions: Judah (Southern Kingdom) and Israel (Northern Kingdom). The prophet Elijah challenges Israel's evil king Ahab.

Introduction to 1 Kings

The book of 1 Kings is so named because it traces the history of God's people through a succession of kings following the death of David about 970 B.C. and the succession of his son Solomon to the throne. But the pivotal event in the book is the split of the united kingdom into two rival factions—Judah (Southern Kingdom) and Israel (Northern Kingdom)—after the death of Solomon.

Solomon was noted for his wisdom and the expansion of his kingdom through international trade and diplomacy. But he was also very foolish about some things. He built his kingdom through burdensome taxation and even forced his subjects to work without pay on some of his lavish building projects.

The tribes in the northern section of Solomon's kingdom pulled away and formed their own nation (Israel) under their own king (Jeroboam). This happened when Solomon's son and successor, Rehoboam, vowed to continue—and even intensify—Solomon's oppressive policies (12:16–24).

First Kings does not name its author, and he remains unknown to this day. But we do know that he based his book at least partially on the official historical records of these two rival nations. The unknown author of 1 Kings mentions "the book of the chronicles of the kings of Israel" (14:19) and "the book of the chronicles of the kings of Judah" (14:29).

Several kings of both Judah and Israel are mentioned in the book of 1 Kings. But the author gives major attention to Ahab of Israel and his evil wife, Jezebel. They were responsible for promoting worship of the pagan Canaanite god Baal throughout Israel. God raised up a fiery prophet named Elijah to condemn their idolatry and predict that God would punish their evil deeds. This prophecy is fulfilled in the final chapter of the book when Ahab is killed in his royal chariot during a battle with the Syrians (22:29–40).

Elijah's sudden appearance on the scene (17:1) to challenge the powerful king of Israel shows that God is never without a witness, even in the darkest of times. Over and over again in 1 Kings we are told that "the word of the LORD came to Elijah" (18:1). And this faithful prophet always "went and did according unto the word of the LORD" (17:5).

Accounts of many of the events in 1 Kings are duplicated in the book of 2 Chronicles. These events are cross-referenced to 2 Chronicles in the summary of 1 Kings below.

Summary of 1 Kings

1:1–4. David's health declines with age, and he is unable to carry out his duties as king.

1:5–10. Adonijah, a son of David and brother

of Absalom, plots to seize the throne as David's successor.

1:11–31. David's wife Bathsheba and Nathan the prophet persuade David to designate Bathsheba's son Solomon as the royal successor.

1:32–40. Solomon is officially anointed at Gihon as David's successor (1 Chron. 23:1).

1:41–53. Adonijah seeks sanctuary from Solomon at the altar. Solomon promises Adonijah that he will not kill him if he causes no trouble for the new king.

[1:41–53] SAFETY AT THE ALTAR. *Adonijah feared because of Solomon, and arose, and went, and caught hold on the horns of the altar* (1 Kings 1:50).

Adonijah, a son of David, had hoped to succeed his father as king of Israel (1 Kings 1:11). But this honor went to Adonijah's brother Solomon.

Adonijah sought protection from Solomon's wrath by grasping the four corners, or horns, of the altar in the tabernacle. This provided temporary asylum or protection for a person who had committed a crime until the charges against him were thoroughly investigated.

This same protection could be sought in one of the cities of refuge throughout the land (Deut. 4:41–42).

2:1–9. David charges Solomon to remain faithful to the Lord as the new king of Israel. David gives Solomon permission to take revenge against two of his political enemies—Joab and Shimei.

2:10–12. David dies after forty years as king—seven years as king of the southern tribe of Judah and thirty-three years as king over all the tribes of Israel (1 Chron. 29:26–27).

2:13–25. Solomon has Adonijah killed because he requested that a former wife of David be given to Adonijah as his own wife.

2:26–27. Solomon deposes Abiathar from the priesthood because he supported Adonijah's quest for the kingship.

2:28–35. Solomon assassinates Joab, former commander of David's army, because he supported Adonijah's attempt to seize the throne. Joab had also killed two innocent men: Abner and Amasa.

2:36–46. Solomon has Shimei assassinated when he disobeys the king's orders and leaves the city of Jerusalem.

3:1–2. Solomon marries the daughter of the pharaoh of Egypt to seal a political alliance with that nation.

3:3–15. Solomon has a dream while offering sacrifices to the Lord at Gibeon. In the dream, Solomon asks for great wisdom so he might be a wise and just king. God promises to honor his request and to give Solomon great riches and honor, as well (2 Chron. 1:1–13).

3:16–28. Solomon's wisdom is revealed as he settles a dispute between two women who claim to be the mother of the same child.

4:1–20. The aides and officials in Solomon's administration are listed.

[4:1–20] SUPPLIES FOR SOLOMON. *Solomon had twelve officers [district governors, NIV] over all Israel, which provided victuals [supplies] for the king and his household: each man his month in a year made provision* (1 Kings 4:7).

Taxes are nothing new. They existed as early as King Solomon's time (about 950 B.C.). He needed revenue to support his lavish building projects and the huge army and staff that he assembled.

For taxation purposes, Solomon divided the nation into twelve administrative districts. Each of these districts supplied the king with what he needed to run the central government for one month out of the year.

Each district had a governor or administrator appointed by the king. This official was responsible for gathering needed supplies from the people in his district.

4:21–28. Solomon becomes wealthy and extravagant as the ruler of a kingdom that stretches from Egypt in the south to the Euphrates River in the north (Ps. 72:8–11).

4:29–34. Solomon is also acclaimed for his great wisdom. He writes thousands of songs and proverbs.

5:1–18. Solomon makes a trade agreement with King Hiram of Tyre, a friend and supporter of his father, David. Solomon trades food for cedar trees as well as cut stone, which are available in Hiram's territory. These building materials are to be used in the construction of a magnificent temple for worship of the Lord in Jerusalem (2 Chron. 2).

6:1–38. Solomon's temple in Jerusalem is completed in seven years (2 Chron. 3).

7:1–12. Solomon spends thirteen years constructing his own royal palace and other administrative buildings in the capital city.

7:13–22. Solomon hires a metalworker from Tyre to construct two magnificent pillars of brass, or copper, in the temple.

7:23–51. This metalworker also fashions other furnishings for the temple, including a huge water basin ("molten sea," v. 23) for sacrificial washing of the priests; candlesticks that stand before the altar; and pots, shovels, and other utensils to be used by the priests in handling sacrificial offerings (2 Chron. 4).

8:1–11. The ark of the covenant is placed in the Most Holy Place in the inner court of the temple. The Lord shows His pleasure and His presence by filling the Most Holy Place with a cloud.

8:12–66. In an elaborate ceremony of dedication for the temple, Solomon prays a prayer of gratitude to the Lord and leads the people to make sacrificial offerings to show their

7:23–51. An artist's conception of Solomon's temple, showing the "molten sea" at left and altar at right.

[8:12–66] HANDS LIFTED IN PRAYER. *Solomon stood before the altar of the LORD in the presence of all the congregation of Israel, and spread forth his hands toward heaven* (1 Kings 8:22).

When King Solomon dedicated the newly constructed temple with a prayer to the Lord, he stood with his hands open and the palms lifted toward heaven. This stance was often taken when praying, especially in Old Testament times (Exod. 9:33; Ezra 9:5; Ps. 28:2; Isa. 1:15).

dedication and obedience (2 Chron. 5–6).

9:1–9. God makes Solomon the same conditional promise He had made to his father, David. If Solomon follows the Lord, his kingship over Israel will be established forever. But if Solomon turns away from God and leads His people astray, the Lord will reject Solomon and bring punishment upon the land (2 Chron. 7:12–22).

9:10–28. Solomon builds supply cities and chariot cities for military purposes and establishes a port for conducting trade with other nations (2 Chron. 8).

10:1–13. The Queen of Sheba visits Solomon and is impressed with his wisdom and great riches (2 Chron. 9:1–12).

10:14–29. Solomon's riches multiply as he develops trade relationships with other nations. Other rulers honor him for his wisdom and power (2 Chron. 9:13–28).

11:1–8. Solomon's dozens of foreign wives, many of whom he married to seal political alliances, cause him to turn from the Lord and worship pagan gods.

11:9–13. God declares that He will divide Solomon's kingdom because of his sin of idolatry. But He will allow one tribe to remain under the kingship of Solomon's son and successor because of His promise of an eternal kingship to Solomon's father, David (2 Sam. 7:1–17).

11:14–25. Several Israelite leaders oppose Solomon's kingship. These include Hadad and Rezon.

11:26–40. The most serious threat to Solomon arises from within his own administration. Jeroboam, one of Solomon's officials, rebels against the king. The prophet Ahijah promises Jeroboam that Solomon's kingdom will be split into two factions. The northern tribes will unite under Jeroboam against Solomon. The southern tribe of Judah will remain loyal to the dynasty of David and will be ruled by Solomon's son.

11:41–43. Solomon dies and is succeeded by his son Rehoboam (2 Chron. 9:29–31).

12:1–15. Rehoboam disregards the complaints of the northern tribes under Jeroboam and vows to intensify the harsh practices of his father, Solomon (2 Chron. 10:1–15).

12:16–24. The northern tribes revolt against Rehoboam and acclaim Jeroboam as their king. For the next several centuries of Israel's history, two opposing nations of the Jewish people exist—the northern tribes known as the nation of Israel (or the Northern Kingdom) and the southern tribes known as the nation of Judah (or the Southern Kingdom). God's promise of an eternal kingship through David and his descendants continues through the Southern Kingdom (2 Chron. 10:16–19).

12:25–33. King Jeroboam of Israel (Northern Kingdom) sets up sanctuaries for worship at the cities of Bethel and Dan in his territory. He wants to remove the temptation for the people of his kingdom to return to the temple at Jerusalem in Judah (Southern Kingdom) to worship God and offer sacrifices (2 Chron. 11:14–17).

13:1–10. God sends a prophet from Judah to King Jeroboam of Israel. This prophet delivers the prediction that Josiah, a descendant

[14:1–18] **FOOD FOR A JOURNEY.** *Take with thee [King Jeroboam's wife] ten loaves, and cracknels [cakes, NIV], and a cruse of honey, and go to him [the prophet Ahijah]* (1 Kings 14:3).

When King Jeroboam's son became sick, he sent his wife to ask the prophet Ahijah whether his son would get well. The journey to Ahijah's house must have been long, since the king's wife carried enough food for several days.

Cracknels were bread that had been baked into thin, hard biscuits. They probably held up better under traveling conditions than soft-baked bread.

of King David, will burn the bones of Jeroboam's priests upon the altar at Bethel at a distant future time.

13:11–32. The prophet who delivers this message to King Jeroboam is killed by a lion after he disobeys God's commands to return immediately to Judah.

13:33–34. King Jeroboam continues his practice of using unauthorized and unqualified persons as priests in the sanctuaries he has established in the Northern Kingdom.

14:1–18. A prophet at Bethel predicts that King Jeroboam's ill son will die and that Jeroboam will be punished for his sin and idolatry.

14:19–20. Jeroboam dies after reigning over Israel for twenty-two years and is succeeded by his son Nadab.

14:21–31. Rehoboam dies after serving as king of Judah for seventeen years and is succeeded by his son Abijam/Abijah (2 Chron. 12:13–16).

15:1–8. Abijam/Abijah dies after reigning over Judah for three years and is succeeded by his son Asa (2 Chron. 13:21–14:2).

15:9–24. King Asa pleases the Lord while ruling Judah. He removes the idols and pagan shrines that had been established in the land. After reigning for forty-one years, Asa dies and is succeeded by his son Jehoshaphat (2 Chron. 15; 16:13–17:1).

15:25–31. King Nadab of Israel is assassinated and succeeded by Baasha after a reign of only two years.

15:32–16:7. The prophet Jehu predicts that the dynasty of King Baasha of Israel will end. Baasha dies and is succeeded by his son Elah.

16:8–14. Elah is assassinated and succeeded as king of Israel by Zimri, one of his chariot commanders. Zimri also murders all the relatives of Baasha and Elah to end the royal dynasty of Baasha, as the prophet Jehu had predicted (1 Kings 16:1–7).

16:15–20. Zimri commits suicide after he

[18:20–40] **A GOD WHO HEARS AND ACTS.** *Elijah mocked them [the prophets of Baal], and said, Cry aloud: for he [Baal] is a god; either he is talking, or he is pursuing, or he is in a journey, or peradventure he sleepeth, and must be awaked* (1 Kings 18:27).

The prophet Elijah challenged the prophets of the pagan god Baal to a contest on Mount Carmel. They laid a sacrificial animal on a pile of wood. The prophets of Baal would call on their god, and Elijah would call on his. The god who answered by sending fire to consume the sacrifice would be declared the superior god (1 Kings 18:22–25).

Elijah ridiculed Baal because he did not answer the cry of his priests, even though they called to him for several hours. Perhaps he was silent, Elijah suggested, because he was preoccupied with other matters, was away on a journey, or was taking a nap.

When Elijah called on the Lord, fire fell immediately from heaven and consumed the sacrificial animal on the altar (1 Kings 18:38). This proved that God heard the prayers of His people and was superior to Baal.

18:20–40. Part of an Israeli national park, Mount Carmel is today a tourist attraction. Thousands of years ago, God's prophet Elijah defeated several hundred prophets of Baal on Mount Carmel.

realizes his forces face defeat at the hands of Omri. He is succeeded as king of Israel by Omri.

16:21–30. Omri builds Samaria and makes it the capital city of Israel. After an evil reign of twelve years, he dies and is succeeded by his son Ahab.

16:31–34. Ahab marries Jezebel, a worshiper of the pagan god Baal, and sets up a shrine to Baal in the capital city of Samaria.

17:1. The prophet Elijah predicts that a drought will strike Israel as punishment for Ahab's sins.

17:2–7. Elijah is kept alive by ravens as he hides from Ahab beside the brook Cherith.

17:8–16. During the drought, Elijah and a widow and her son are kept alive miraculously by the Lord through a small amount of meal and oil that never runs out.

17:17–24. The son of the widow dies, and Elijah restores him miraculously to life.

18:1–14. God commands Elijah to meet King Ahab. The Lord assures Elijah that He will end the drought by sending rain. Elijah sends word through one of Ahab's servants that he wants to meet with the king.

18:15–19. Elijah talks with King Ahab and asks him to send the prophets of Baal to meet him on Mount Carmel.

18:20–40. Elijah prevails over the prophets of Baal in a dramatic encounter on Mount Carmel. The Lord sends a miraculous sign to show His superiority over all pagan gods. Elijah kills the prophets of Baal at the brook Kishon.

18:41–46. God ends the drought by sending rain in response to the prayer of Elijah (1 Kings 17:1).

19:1–18. Elijah flees to Mount Horeb to escape Jezebel's threat against his life. God directs him to return to Israel to anoint new kings for Syria and Israel and to select the prophet Elisha as his successor. The Lord assures Elijah in a still, small voice that many people in Israel remain faithful to Him.

19:19–21. Elisha follows Elijah after he is selected as the prophet's successor.

20:1–12. King Ben-hadad of Syria prepares to attack the forces of King Ahab of Israel at the capital city of Samaria.

20:13–21. Although outnumbered, Ahab's army defeats Ben-hadad because of the Lord's miraculous intervention.

20:22–34. Ahab defeats Ben-hadad a second time and spares his life.

20:35–43. A prophet of the Lord condemns King Ahab for not killing Ben-hadad when he had the opportunity.

21:1–4. Naboth refuses to sell his land with a vineyard to King Ahab.

21:5–16. Jezebel and Ahab have Naboth executed on a false charge so they can take over his property.

21:17–29. The prophet Elijah announces to King Ahab that he and Jezebel will be killed and that dogs will lick up his blood and ravage Jezebel's corpse. This will be the Lord's punishment for their crime against Naboth and their encouragement of idol worship throughout Israel.

22:1–4. The kings of Israel (Ahab) and Judah (Jehoshaphat) propose a joint campaign against the Syrians to capture the city of Ramoth-gilead (2 Chron. 18:1–3).

22:5–12. Several false prophets assure King Ahab of a great victory if he and Jehoshaphat attack the Syrian forces (2 Chron. 18:4–11).

22:13–28. Micaiah, a true prophet of the Lord, announces that Ahab will be defeated if he goes against the Syrians (2 Chron. 18:12–27).

22:29–40. King Ahab is killed in the battle at Ramoth-gilead. Dogs lick up his blood when it is washed from his chariot, in fulfillment of the prediction of the prophet Elijah (1 Kings 21:19; 2 Chron. 18:28–34).

22:41–50. After twenty-five years as king of Judah, Jehoshaphat dies and is succeeded by his son Jehoram/Joram (2 Chron. 20:31–21:1).

22:51–53. Ahaziah succeeds his father, Ahab, as king of Israel and continues his evil and sinful policies.

[21:1–4] NO SALE. *Naboth said to Ahab, The LORD forbid it me, that I should give the inheritance of my fathers unto thee* (1 Kings 21:3).

Naboth's refusal to sell his land in which his vineyard grew shows the dedication of the Israelites to the land they had inherited from their ancestors. By law, Israelites were not to sell their land inheritance, except in cases of extreme poverty or financial hardship (Lev. 25:23, 25; Num. 36:7).

King Ahab eventually brought false charges against Naboth, had him killed, and took his land (1 Kings 21:7–13). The Lord sent the prophet Elijah to condemn these brazen acts and to tell the king that he would pay for these crimes with his life (1 Kings 21:17–22).

OVERVIEW: Elisha succeeds the prophet Elijah. Israel falls to Assyria, and Judah falls to the Babylonians.

Introduction to 2 Kings

The book of 2 Kings picks up where 1 Kings leaves off, continuing the account of the reigns of various kings of Judah and Israel. The same unknown author who wrote 1 Kings also wrote this book (see the introduction to 1 Kings on p. 70). Second Kings covers a period of about 260 years in the histories of these two nations.

Israel, the breakaway nation of the northern territory, began its history with questionable worship practices instituted by King Jeroboam. This pattern continued under most of the successive kings, with some encouraging and even lending state support to worship of pagan gods. God's punishment fell upon Israel in 722 B.C., when the Assyrians overran the nation and carried away many of its citizens as captives and slaves (17:5–23).

One bright spot in the nation of Israel was the prophet Elisha, who succeeded Elijah as God's spokesman to the kings of the North. He worked many miracles among the people and was an influential force for righteousness. But not even this stalwart prophet could turn Israel from its rush toward destruction.

The kings of Judah, since they were descendants of the great King David, were generally a better lot than the kings of Israel. Several kings of Judah, including Hezekiah (chaps. 18–20) and Josiah (22:1–23:30), led reform movements to purge idolatry from the land and turn the people back to worship of the one true God.

But Judah also had its share of evil kings. Two of the worst were Ahaz, who practiced child sacrifice (2 Chron. 28:1–4), and Manasseh, who built altars for pagan worship and participated in black magic and witchcraft (21:1–9). About 135 years after Israel fell to a foreign power, God sent the same punishment upon Judah. The leading citizens of the nation were carried into exile when Jerusalem fell to the Babylonians in 587 B.C.

The book of 2 Kings ends with Jerusalem in shambles and the beautiful temple destroyed and looted by a pagan army (25:8–21)—a far cry from the glory days of David and Solomon. Perhaps the writer of Proverbs had this situation in mind when he declared, "Righteousness exalteth a nation: but sin is a reproach to any people" (Prov. 14:34).

Many of the events described in 2 Kings are also recorded in the book of 2 Chronicles. These events are cross-referenced to 2 Chronicles in the summary of 2 Kings below.

Summary of 2 Kings

1:1–18. Ahaziah, son and sucessor of Ahab as king of Israel, dies after suffering injuries in an accident. Since he has no son, he is succeeded by his brother Jehoram, another son of Ahab.

2:1–11. Elisha asks that a double portion of Elijah's spirit be given to him as Elijah's successor. Elijah is taken into heaven by a whirlwind.

[2:1–11] SONS OF THE PROPHETS. *And the sons of the prophets that were at Bethel came forth to Elisha* (2 Kings 2:3).

These "sons of the prophets" knew that Elisha had been chosen as Elijah's successor, so they came out to see the two prophets together when Elijah and Elisha approached the city of Bethel.

Several different groups of "sons of the prophets" are mentioned in the book of 2 Kings (2:5, 7; 4:38, 43; 6:1–2). They were apparently disciples or followers of prophets such as Elijah and Elisha who assisted the prophets in their work and learned from their example and instruction.

A "company of prophets" is also mentioned in connection witht the ministry of the prophet Samuel (1 Sam. 19:19–20). Samuel may have been the founder of this prophetic guild.

2:12–18. Elisha is recognized by the sons of the prophets as Elijah's legitimate successor, with the Spirit of the Lord that filled Elijah.

2:19–22. Elisha miraculously purifies the bad waters of a spring at Jericho.

2:23–25. Elisha curses several children who were mocking and taunting him as God's prophet; they are attacked by two bears.

3:1–3. Ahab's son Jehoram becomes king of Is-rael and continues his father's evil practices.

3:4–20. Elisha predicts that the combined forces of Israel, Judah, and Edom will be victorious over the Moabites.

3:21–27. As Elisha predicts, the Moabites are defeated.

4:1–7. Elisha works a miracle for a poor widow whose sons are about to be sold into slavery. A jar of oil is multiplied until she has enough to pay her debts.

4:8–37. Elisha brings back to life the only son of a woman at Shunem who had provided food and lodging for the prophet.

4:38–44. Elisha miraculously purifies and multiplies a meager supply of food to feed a large group of the sons of the prophets.

5:1–14. Naaman, commander of the Syrian army, is miraculously cured of his leprosy by the prophet Elisha (Luke 4:27).

5:15–27. Elisha refuses to accept the gifts of thanks offered by Naaman. But his servant Gehazi follows Naaman and claims the gifts. As punishment, Elisha declares that the leprosy that afflicted Naaman will fall on Gehazi.

6:1–7. Elisha miraculously causes an ax head to float so it can be retrieved from the Jordan River.

6:8–23. Elisha is miraculously delivered from a company of Syrian soldiers when the Lord strikes them blind.

6:24–7:20. The Syrians besiege Israel's capital

[8:7–15] SHOWING OFF WITH GIFTS. *So Hazael went to meet him [Elisha], and took a present with him, even of every good thing of Damascus, forty camels' burden, and came and stood before him* (2 Kings 8:9).

Hazael was a servant of Ben-hadad, king of Syria. When the prophet Elisha visited Damascus, Ben-hadad sent Hazael to meet him with royal gifts. Since the king was sick, he may have been trying to get Elisha to exercise his healing powers on his behalf.

In Old Testament times, even small gifts were often accompanied by great pomp and ceremony. The forty camels that greeted Elisha were probably not loaded down with all they could carry. Each camel may have carried only a small part of the total gift. The king wanted to impress Elisha with an extravagant outward display.

city of Samaria, and the people begin to run out of food. But Elisha predicts that the city will be saved through a miracle. The Lord sends panic and confusion among the Syrian army; the city is delivered, just as Elisha predicted.

8:1–6. The king of Israel restores the property of the woman of Shunem who had befriended Elisha (2 Kings 4:8–37) because of the prophet's reputation and influence.

8:7–15. Hazael assassinates and succeeds Ben-hadad as king of Syria. Elisha predicts that Hazael will commit many cruel acts against the nation of Israel.

9:30–37. Jezebel is thrown from a window to her death. God had ordered her death for her scheme against a vineyard owner named Naboth.

8:16–24. Jehoram/Joram succeeds his father, Jehoshaphat, as king of Judah. After a reign of eight years, Jehoram/Joram dies and is succeeded by his son Ahaziah.

8:25–29. The allied forces of Israel and Judah go to war against King Hazael of Syria. King Jehoram/Joram of Judah is wounded in a battle at Ramoth-gilead.

9:1–13. Elisha sends a prophet to Ramoth-gilead to anoint Jehu, a commander in Israel's army, as the new king of Israel. Jehu is directed to execute all claimants to the throne from the line of Ahab.

9:14–29. Jehu assassinates King Jehoram/Joram of Israel, the son of Ahab. Jehu also kills Jehoram's ally and friend, King Ahaziah of Judah (2 Chron. 22:2–9).

9:30–37. Jehu kills Jezebel, the wife of Ahab. Her body is eaten by dogs, in fulfillment of the prophecy of Elijah (1 Kings 21:17–29).

10:1–17. Jehu assassinates all the descendants of Ahab to end the royal dynasty of this wicked and idolatrous king. Jehu also murders several relatives of King Ahaziah of Judah because of their connection with Ahab.

10:18–28. Jehu kills the worshipers of Baal throughout Israel and destroys the images of this pagan god.

10:29–31. Jehu fails to abolish the golden calves that King Jeroboam of Israel had established at Bethel and Dan. God promises to extend Jehu's royal dynasty to the fourth generation because of his obedience of God's command to end the dynasty of Ahab.

10:32–36. King Hazael of Syria wins many victories in Israel. Jehu dies and is succeeded as king of Israel by his son Jehoahaz.

11:1–3. After King Ahaziah of Judah is killed by King Jehu of Israel (2 Kings 9:27–29), Ahaziah's mother, Athaliah, seizes the throne. She does so by murdering her own grandsons, who were legitimate claimants to the throne. Joash/Jehoash, one of Ahaziah's sons, is saved from Athaliah's massacre and hidden away in the temple for six years (2 Chron. 22:10–12).

11:4–21. When Joash/Jehoash is seven years old, he is brought out of hiding by Jehoiada the priest and acclaimed as the new king of Judah. Athaliah is deposed as queen and assassinated (2 Chron. 23).

[11:4–21] A ROYAL CORONATION. *He [Jehoiada] brought forth the king's son [Joash], and put the crown upon him, and gave him the testimony [presented him with a copy of the covenant, NIV]; and they [the people] made him king, and anointed him; and they clapped their hands, and said, God save the king* (2 Kings 11:12).

This verse gives us insight into a royal coronation ceremony in Old Testament times. After the royal crown was placed on Joash's head, the king was presented with a copy of God's law. This was to serve as his guide in governing the people. He was then formally anointed for his task by having oil poured on his head (1 Sam. 16:13).

A royal coronation must have been a public affair. The people showed their approval of Joash's coronation by clapping and shouting, "God save the king [Long live the king, NIV]."

12:1–16. Joash/Jehoash follows the Lord under the counsel of the priest Jehoiada. Joash/Jehoash authorizes a special offering to be taken among the people designated for making needed repairs to the temple (2 Chron. 24:1–14).

12:17–18. Joash/Jehoash pays tribute to King Hazael of Syria to keep him from invading Judah's capital city of Jerusalem.

12:19–21. Assassinated by his own servants, Joash/Jehoash is succeeded as king of Judah by his son Amaziah (2 Chron. 24:25–27).

13:1–9. In the Northern Kingdom (Israel), Jehoahaz succeeds his father, Jehu, as king. Israel is ravaged by the Syrians during Jehoahaz's administration. After a reign of seventeen years, Jehoahaz is succeeded by his son Joash.

13:10–13. The evil reign of Joash ends after sixteen years, and he is succeeded as king of Israel by his son Jeroboam II.

13:14–19. The prophet Elisha predicts from his deathbed that the Northern Kingdom will win several key battles against the Syrians.

13:20–21. After Elisha's death and burial, a dead man is revived when his body touches the prophet's bones.

13:22–24. After oppressing Israel for several years, King Hazael of Syria dies and is succeeded by his son Ben-hadad.

13:25. King Joash of Israel takes back from the Syrians the cities they had captured when his father, Jehoahaz, reigned in Israel. This fulfills Elisha's prophecy (2 Kings 13:14–19).

14:1–7. Amaziah defeats the Edomites during his reign as king of Judah.

14:8–14. The kingdoms of Judah and Israel go to war against each other. Israel's king, Joash, seizes gold and silver items from Judah's capital city, Jerusalem, and carries them to Israel's capital, Samaria (2 Chron. 25:17–24).

14:15–22. King Joash of Israel dies; King Amaziah of Judah dies.

14:23–29. Jeroboam II succeeds his father, Joash, as king of Israel (2 Kings 13:10–13). His evil reign displeases the Lord.

15:1–7. Azariah/Uzziah succeeds his father, Amaziah, as king of Judah. Azariah/Uzziah dies and is succeeded by his son Jotham (2 Chron. 26:16–23).

15:8–12. Zachariah succeeds his father, Jeroboam II, as king of Israel. Zachariah is assassinated and succeeded by Shallum after a brief reign. This fulfills God's promise to Jehu that his royal dynasty would extend to the fourth generation (2 Kings 10:29–31).

15:13–16. After a reign of only one month, Shallum is assassinated and succeeded by Menahem as king of Israel.

15:17–22. During his reign as king of Israel, Menahem is forced to pay tribute to King Pul (Tiglath-pileser) of Assyria. Menahem dies and is succeeded by his son Pekahiah.

15:23–26. After a reign of two years, Pekahiah is assassinated and succeeded as king of Israel by Pekah, a commander in Pekahiah's army.

15:27–31. During Pekahiah's reign over Israel, King Tiglath-pileser of Assyria invades his territory and enslaves some of his subjects. Pekah is assassinated and succeeded by Hoshea as king of Israel.

15:32–38. Azariah's/Uzziah's son Jotham becomes king of Judah (2 Kings 15:1–7). Jotham dies and is succeeded by his son Ahaz.

16:1–4. King Ahaz encourages worship of false gods thoughout Judah, even committing the abominable practice of child sacrifice to pagan gods (2 Chron. 28:1–4).

16:5–9. Ahaz pays tribute to the Assyrian king, Tiglath-pileser, who rescues Ahaz from his enemies.

16:10–18. Ahaz offers sacrifices on the altar of a pagan god and dismantles the altar in the temple devoted to worship of the one true God.

16:19–20. Ahaz dies and is succeeded as king of Judah by his son Hezekiah (2 Chron. 28:26–27).

17:1–4. Ahaz's son Hoshea reigns over Israel as a puppet king under the thumb of King Shalmaneser of Assyria. Hoshea is imprisoned by Shalmaneser after he quits paying tribute to Assyria and tries to form an alliance with Egypt to resist the Assyrian threat.

17:5–6. Assyria defeats Israel and carries away many of its citizens as captives to several Assyrian cities.

17:7–23. The end of Israel as a separate kingdom is attributed to the people's sin and rebellion against God and their worship of false gods.

17:24–41. Assyria settles people from pagan lands in the territory previously occupied by the citizens of Israel. The Israelites left in the land eventually adopt the pagan worship practices of these foreigners.

18:1–12. Hezekiah becomes king of Judah. Unlike his father, Ahaz (2 Kings 16:10–18), Hezekiah follows the Lord, tears down pagan altars, and leads the people to worship the Lord. At first, Hezekiah is able to resist the threat to his kingdom from Assyria.

18:13–37. Sennacherib, king of Assyria, captures several fortified cities of Judah. He stations his army outside Jerusalem and threatens to attack the city with a prolonged siege unless Hezekiah surrenders (2 Chron. 32:1–19).

19:1–7. King Hezekiah sends word about Judah's plight to the prophet Isaiah, who assures the king that God will deal with this threat from Assyria.

19:8–19. King Hezekiah receives a written threat from the Assyrian forces; he prays earnestly to the Lord for Judah's deliverance.

19:20–37. The prophet Isaiah assures King Hezekiah again of the Lord's protection. A mysterious plague strikes the Assyrian army, wiping out 185,000 warriors. Sennacherib returns to Assyria without attacking Jerusalem (2 Chron. 32:20–23; Isa. 37).

19:20–37. The angel of the Lord wipes out 185,000 Assyrian soldiers in a single night, protecting Jerusalem from King Sennacherib's threats.

20:1–11. King Hezekiah falls seriously ill and prays fervently to the Lord. The prophet Isaiah assures him that he will recover and live to reign as king of Judah for fifteen more years (Isa. 38). To confirm His promise of miraculous healing to the king, the Lord moves a sundial backwards by ten degrees (2 Chron. 32:24–26).

20:12–19. The prophet Isaiah reprimands King Hezekiah for showing his vast treasures of gold and silver to envoys from Babylonia. Isaiah predicts that these treasures will be captured and carried away someday by the Babylonians (2 Chron. 32:27–31).

20:20–21. King Hezekiah dies and is succeeded as king of Judah by his son Manasseh (2 Chron. 32:32–33).

21:1–9. As king of Judah for fifty-five years, Manasseh constructs altars for idol worship, performs child sacrifice to pagan gods, and participates in black magic and witchcraft. His long reign and acts of evil make him perhaps the worst king in the history of Judah (2 Chron. 33:1–10).

21:10–16. Because of Manasseh's wickedness and encouragement of pagan worship, God vows that He will punish the nation of Judah.

21:17–18. Manasseh dies and is succeeded as king of Judah by his son Amon (2 Chron. 33:20).

21:19–26. Amon continues the evil practices of his father, Manasseh. Amon is assassinated by his own servants after a reign of only two years and is succeeded by his son Josiah (2 Chron. 33:21–25).

22:1–7. As a faithful follower of the Lord, King Josiah authorizes repairs to the temple in Jerusalem (2 Chron. 34:8–13).

22:8–14. During the temple repairs, a copy of the book of the law (Genesis, Exodus, Leviticus, Numbers, and Deuteronomy) is discovered. Josiah realizes when this book is read that the people of Judah have wandered away from God's commands. He sends several priests to confer with a prophet to find out how God will deal with the sins of His people (2 Chron. 34:14–21).

22:15–20. Huldah the prophetess declares that the Lord will deal kindly with Josiah because of his determination to follow His will. But God will punish the nation of Judah for its waywardness and rebellion (2 Chron. 34:22–28).

23:1–3. King Josiah calls the leaders of Judah together to renew the covenant with the Lord (2 Chron. 34:29–33).

23:4–27. King Josiah launches a religious reform movement throughout Judah. He tears down pagan altars, destroys images of idols, puts to death pagan priests who were leading people astray, and reinstates observation of the Passover—a festival celebrating their deliverance from slavery in Egypt.

23:28–30. Killed in a battle with the Egyptians, Josiah is succeeded as king of Judah by his son Jehoahaz (2 Chron. 35:20–36:1).

23:31–37. After a reign of only three months, King Jehoahaz is captured and imprisoned by the Egyptians. The Egyptians put Eliakim, another son of Josiah, on the throne as a puppet king and demand that he pay tribute to the Egyptian government. The Egyptians also give Eliakim another name, Jehoiakim (2 Chron. 36:2–4).

24:1–7. During the reign of Eliakim/Jehoiakim, the Babylonians invade Judah. He dies and is succeeded by his son Jehoiachin.

24:8–19. King Nebuchadnezzar of Babylonia invades and subdues the nation of Judah. He takes King Jehoiachin and his royal household as well as all the key leaders of Judah to Babylon as captives. Nebuchadnezzar also places Mattaniah on the throne of Judah as a puppet king and renames him Zedekiah (2 Chron. 36:9–10).

24:20–25:7. Mattaniah/Zedekiah rebels against Babylonia. Nebuchadnezzar invades Jerusalem and takes the king to Babylon as a prisoner after forcing him to watch the murder of his sons.

[24:20–25:7] BLINDING OF PRISONERS. *They [the Babylonian army] slew the sons of Zedekiah before his eyes, and put out the eyes of Zedekiah, and bound him with fetters of brass [bronze shackles, NIV], and carried him to Babylon* (2 Kings 25:7).

Zedekiah was serving as king of Judah when the nation fell to the Babylonians in 587 B.C. The last thing he saw before being blinded by his captors was the death of his sons.

The blinding of prisoners was a cruel punishment often meted out by the Babylonians, Assyrians, and Persians. This was done by searing the pupils with a hot copper plate or by thrusting a sword or dagger into the eyes.

Samson was also blinded when he was captured by the Philistines (Judg. 16:21).

25:8–21. Nebuchadnezzar ransacks the city of Jerusalem, breaking down the city wall, burning the temple and other buildings, and carrying away gold and silver from the temple furnishings. Key leaders of Judah are murdered or enslaved and taken to Babylon, while peasants and farmers of Judah are left behind to cultivate the land.

25:22–26. A remnant of the citizens of Judah flees to Egypt after murdering Gedaliah, an official whom Nebuchadnezzar had appointed governor of Judah.

25:27–30. In Babylonia, Nebuchadnezzar is succeeded as king by his son Evil-merodach. The new king releases King Jehoiachin of Judah from prison and gives him a place of honor and privilege in the Babylonian court.

1 CHRONICLES

OVERVIEW: A chronicle of the reign of David as king of Israel. This book covers many of the same events as 2 Samuel.

Introduction to 1 Chronicles

The book of 1 Chronicles focuses on the reign of David as king of Israel. Many of the events in David's life covered in 2 Samuel are also included in 1 Chronicles. Why do two books of the Old Testament cover essentially the same territory?

Perhaps the best answer is that the author of 1 Chronicles wrote with a distinct purpose in mind. Many scholars believe it was written by Ezra the priest after the Jewish people returned to Jerusalem following their period of exile among the Babylonians and Persians. This was a time of great discouragement and disillusionment among God's people. Ezra wanted to give them hope by showing that God was with them. His promise that a descendant of David would always rule over His people (2 Sam. 7:1–17) had not been forgotten.

The books of 1 and 2 Chronicles were written originally as one unbroken book. Thus, Ezra began Chronicles with nine chapters of genealogical material that traced God's people all the way back to Adam. He ended Chronicles with the Jewish people returning from the Exile (2 Chron. 36:21–23). This "review of history" technique was a reminder that God had blessed His people in the past. He would continue to do so as they began to rebuild their lives back in their homeland.

First Chronicles does give us insights into David's character not found in 1 Samuel. For example, we learn that David organized the priests and Levites into several different groups and assigned them specific duties in the tabernacle (23:2–26:32). He gathered the materials for his son and successor, Solomon, to use in building the temple (28:9–29:19). David was more than a military king; he was also interested in honoring God through appropriate forms of worship.

Events from David's life in 1 Chronicles that also appear in 2 Samuel are cross-referenced to 2 Samuel in the summary below.

Summary of 1 Chronicles

1:1–4. Descendants of Adam up through Noah and his sons are listed.

1:5–7. Descendants of Noah's son Japheth are listed.

1:8–16. Descendants of Noah's son Ham are listed.

1:17–27. Descendants of Noah's son Shem up through Abraham are listed.

1:28–33. Descendants of Abraham's son Ishmael and other sons born to Abraham's concubine Keturah are listed.

1:34–54. Descendants of Abraham's son Isaac through Isaac's son Esau are listed.

2:1–2. The twelve sons of Isaac's son Jacob, or Israel, are listed.

2:3–15. Descendants of Jacob's son Judah up through King David are listed.

2:16–55. Other descendants of Judah are listed.

3:1–4. Sons of David born while he reigned at Hebron are listed.

3:5–9. Sons of David born while he reigned at Jerusalem are listed.

3:10–24. Descendants of David's son Solomon are listed.

4:1–23. Descendants of Jacob's son Judah are listed.

4:24–43. Descendants of Jacob's son Simeon are listed.

5:1–10. Descendants of Jacob's son Reuben are listed.

5:11–17. Descendants of Jacob's son Gad are listed.

5:18–26. A brief history is given of the tribes of Israel that settled on the eastern side of the Jordan River—Reuben, Gad, and one-half of the tribe of Manasseh (Josh. 22:1–9).

6:1–30. Descendants of Jacob's son Levi are listed. The Levites assisted the priests with sacrificial duties at the tabernacle and the temple.

6:31–48. Levites who assisted with the song service after David moved the ark of the covenant to Jerusalem are listed.

6:49–53. The son and successors of Aaron as priests of Israel are listed.

6:54–81. The cities assigned to the Levites throughout the territory of Israel are listed (Josh. 21:1–45).

7:1–5. Descendants of Jacob's son Issachar are listed.

7:6–12. Descendants of Jacob's son Benjamin are listed.

7:13. Descendants of Jacob's son Naphtali are listed.

7:14–19. Descendants of Jacob's grandson Manasseh are listed.

7:20–29. Descendants of Jacob's grandson Ephraim are listed.

7:30–40. Descendants of Jacob's son Asher are listed.

8:1–40. Descendants of Jacob's son Benjamin are listed. (This is a more detailed list than that given in 1 Chron. 7:6–12.)

9:1–9. Various Jewish leaders who lived in Jerusalem are listed.

9:10–34. Various priests and Levites who ministered in Jerusalem are listed.

9:35–44. Ancestors and descendants of Saul, the first king of Israel, are listed.

10:1–14. King Saul and his sons are killed in a battle against the Philistines on Mount Gilboa (1 Sam. 31:1–13).

[10:1–14] GOD KNOWS THE NEWS. *They [Philistines] took his [Saul's] head, and his armour, and sent into the land of the Philistines round about, to carry tidings unto their idols* (1 Chron. 10:9).

When the Philistines defeated King Saul and his army, they notified their fellow citizens to carry news about their victory to their pagan gods. This shows the weakness of idols and the superiority of the one true God, who sees all and knows all: "The eyes of the LORD are in every place, beholding the evil and the good" (Prov. 15:3).

11:1–3. David is acclaimed king over all Israel by all the tribes (2 Sam. 5:1–5).

11:4–9. David captures the fortified city of Jebus from the Jebusites. Later it becomes his capital city and is known as Jerusalem (2 Sam. 5:6–10).

11:10–47. The brave commanders and warriors among David's "mighty men" are listed (2 Sam. 23:8–39).

12:1–40. Warriors who joined David's forces while he was hiding from King Saul at Ziklag are listed.

13:1–14. David moves the ark of the covenant from the home of Abinadab to a temporary resting place at the house of Obed-edom. Uzza/Uzzah is killed when he reaches out to steady the ark and accidentally touches it (2 Sam. 6:1–11).

14:1–2. King Hiram of Tyre provides materials and workmen to build a house for David (2 Sam. 5:11–12).

14:3–7. Thirteen children are born to David at Jerusalem (2 Sam. 5:13–16; 1 Chron. 3:5–9).

14:8–17. David defeats the Philistines in a major battle in the valley of Rephaim (2 Sam. 5:17–25).

15:1–29. David makes plans for a great celebration with music and dancing as the ark of the covenant is moved to Jerusalem from the house of Obed-edom. This time the ark is moved as God directed—by Levites carrying it on their shoulders on poles inserted into rings on the ark (2 Sam. 6:12–19).

16:1–6. David presents burnt offerings and peace offerings to the Lord before the ark in the tent he has prepared for its dwelling place.

16:7–36. David offers a prayer of praise and thanksgiving to God for His wonderful works on behalf of His people (2 Sam. 7:18–29).

16:37–43. David appoints a group of Levites to minister continuously before the ark, offering burnt offerings and other sacrifices to the Lord.

17:1–15. David makes plans to build a house, or temple, devoted to worship of God. Instead, the Lord promises that He will build David a house, or memorial. He promises that David's kingdom will be established forever—that his descendants will reign from generation to generation on the throne of Israel (2 Sam. 7:1–17).

17:16–27. In a prayer of humility and gratitude, David praises God for His love and goodness.

18:1–14. David expands his nation's territory and power by defeating the Philistines, Moabites, Syrians, Amalekites, and Edomites (2 Sam. 8:1–13).

[18:1–14] CRIPPLING WAR HORSES. *David also houghed [hamstrung, NIV] all the chariot horses* (1 Chron. 18:4).

David extended his kingdom as far north as Syria by defeating Hadarezer, king of Zobah. He weakened Hadarezer's ability to wage war by capturing his chariots and crippling his chariot horses, probably by cutting a muscle or tendon in their legs.

Since David did not take the horses as booty, he probably had little use for chariots and horses in his own army. Chariots would have been impractical in the rocky and hilly terrain of Palestine.

18:15–17. Selected officials in David's administration are listed (2 Sam. 8:14–18).

19:1–5. David sends messengers to the Ammonites on a peaceful mission, but they are rejected and humiliated.

19:6–19. David's army, under the command of Joab, defeats the combined forces of the Ammonites and the Syrians (2 Sam. 10).

20:1–3. David seals his victory over the Ammonites by capturing their capital city, Rabbah (2 Sam. 12:26–31).

20:4–8. David's warriors are victorious over several Philistine giants, relatives of the giant Goliath whom David killed (1 Sam. 17:46–51).

21:1–6. David orders Joab, commander of his army, to take a census of all the fighting men throughout the tribes of Israel (2 Sam. 24:1–9).

25:1–31. David is remembered as a musician and composer, but he also organized Israel's religious leaders into praise and worship bands featuring trumpets, cymbals, and harps.

21:7–17. God sends a plague on the nation because of David's sinful pride that led him to order the census (2 Sam. 24:10–15).

21:18–30. David buys a threshing floor from Ornan/Araunah the Jebusite as the site for an altar on which sacrifices will be offered to the Lord. The plague ends when sacrifices are offered (2 Sam. 24:16–25).

22:1–19. God refuses to allow David to build the temple in Jerusalem because he has been

[25:1–31] MUSIC FOR WORSHIP. *All these were the sons of Heman the king's seer in the words of God, to lift up the horn* (1 Chron. 25:5).

David organized the priests and Levites into several different groups to serve at the tabernacle on a rotating basis. The Levites descended from Heman were to provide music for worship—specifically to play the horn, or trumpet.

Other Levite musicians were assigned to play different instruments, including cymbals, psalteries [lyres, NIV], and harps (1 Chron. 25:6).

a warrior king. But David gathers material for the project and challenges Solomon, his son and successor, to complete the task.

23:1. Solomon will succeed his father, David, as king of Israel (1 Kings 1:32–40).

23:2–32. David organizes the Levites into several different groups and assigns them specific duties as officers and judges, musicians, doorkeepers, and assistants to the priests.

24:1–19. David organizes the priests into twenty-four different groups that will officiate at the altar on a rotating basis.

24:20–31. Several different leaders of the divisions of the Levites are listed.

25:1–31. The Levites responsible for worship music are organized into twenty-four different groups to serve on a rotating basis.

26:1–19. Levites who serve as porters (doorkeepers and gatekeepers) for the tabernacle and temple are listed.

26:20–32. The Levites listed in these verses are responsible for storing and caring for offerings and sacrifices devoted to support and upkeep of the tabernacle and the temple.

27:1–15. David's military force is divided into twelve units of 24,000 warriors each. These units apparently served for one-month assignments on a rotating basis during the year. The captains of the twelve units are listed by name.

27:16–24. Leaders of the tribes of Israel during David's administration are listed.

27:25–34. Counselors, advisers, chief officials, and keepers of the royal herds in David's administration are listed (2 Sam. 8:14–18; 1 Chron. 18:15–17).

28:1–8. David gathers the leaders of Israel and informs them that his son Solomon will be his successor. He challenges them to remain faithful to the Lord as leaders of Israel.

28:9–21. David encourages his son Solomon to build the temple in Jerusalem, using the materials and funds that David has collected.

29:1–9. Encouraged by David, the leaders of Israel contribute additional gold and silver to pay for the temple's construction.

29:10–19. David offers a prayer of thanksgiving to God. He pledges all the money and supplies to construction of a temple that will bring glory and honor to the Lord.

29:20–25. The leaders of Israel offer sacrifices to God and acclaim Solomon as the new king of Israel.

29:26–30. David dies after forty years as king—seven years as king of the southern tribe of Judah and thirty-three years as king over all the tribes of Israel (1 Kings 2:10–12).

OVERVIEW: A chronicle of the reign of Solomon as king of Israel and division of the united kingdom into two nations. This book covers many of the same events as 1 and 2 Kings.

Introduction to 2 Chronicles

The book of 2 Chronicles picks up where 1 Chronicles ends—with Solomon's succession to the kingship following the death of his father, David, about 970 B.C. This book covers essentially the same period as the books of 1 and 2 Kings and repeats many of the events from these two books (see introductions to 1 and 2 Kings on pp. 70 and 77).

Ezra the priest was the author of both 1 and 2 Chronicles. His purpose for writing the books was to give hope to the Jewish people who were given permission to return to their homeland following the Exile (36:21–23; see the introduction to 1 Chronicles on p. 84).

One of the major differences between 2 Chronicles and the books of 1 and 2 Kings is that little attention is given to the kings of Israel (Northern Kingdom) in 2 Chronicles. This probably indicates that Ezra was concerned only with tracing the line of David and showing that Judah (Southern Kingdom) was the nation that remained loyal to the Lord.

Once the former residents of Judah were resettled in their homeland, Ezra may have been hinting that they needed to rebuild the temple. It was important to reestablish the traditions that proved they were the true worshipers of God.

Another striking difference between 2 Chronicles and 1 and 2 Kings is the role of the prophets Elijah and Elisha. They are prominent spokesmen for the Lord in 1 and 2 Kings, but Elijah is mentioned in only one verse in all of 2 Chronicles (21:12), and Elisha is not mentioned at all. This is explained by the fact that Ezra focused on Judah in 2 Chronicles, and Elijah and Elisha directed their prophecies against the kings of Israel.

Events from 2 Chronicles that also appear in 1 and 2 Kings are cross-referenced to these two books in the summary of 2 Chronicles below.

Summary of 2 Chronicles

1:1–13. As the new king of Israel, Solomon offers sacrifices to the Lord on an altar at Gibeon. He asks God for great wisdom in order to be a good leader. The Lord promises to honor this request and to give him riches and honor as well (1 Kings 3:3–15).

1:14–17. The symbols of Solomon's wealth include his chariots, chariot cities, gold and silver, and horses.

2:1–18. Solomon prepares to build the temple by securing cedar timber from King Hiram/Huram of Tyre (1 Kings 5). Hiram/Huram also provides skilled craftsmen for the project. Solomon presses into service thousands of non-Israelites who are living in his territory to serve as construction workers.

3:1–17. The huge, ornate temple compound built by Solomon is described (1 Kings 6).

[8:1–18] **WALLED CITIES.** *Also he [King Solomon] built Beth-horon the upper [Upper Beth Horon, NIV], and Beth-horon the nether [Lower Beth Horon, NIV], fenced cities, with walls, gates, and bars (2 Chron. 8:5).*

Cities of Bible times—like the twin cities of Upper and Lower Beth Horon—were surrounded by massive stone walls. Some of these structures were more than thirty feet high and ten to twelve feet thick. Residents of the city would retreat behind these walls when under attack by an enemy.

The attacking army would either scale the wall by using ladders or try to break down the city gate. The gate was made of heavy timbers, reinforced with iron. When closed, the gate would be secured by sliding heavy timbers or iron bars across its surface from the inside.

When in full lock-down mode, a heavily fortified or "fenced" city was an effective defense against an army of superior numbers. Often the besieging force would camp around the city for months and starve its citizens into submission.

4:1–22. The furnishings of the temple include the central altar, a huge water basin ("molten sea," v. 2), smaller basins, tables, candlesticks, and utensils used by the priests to handle sacrifices (1 Kings 7:23–51).

5:1–6:42. In an elaborate dedication ceremony, the ark of the covenant is placed in the completed temple. God's glory fills the temple in the form of a cloud. Solomon blesses the people gathered for the ceremony and praises God for His provision for His people. He prays that Israel will always remain faithful to the one true God (1 Kings 8:12–66).

7:1–3. Fire from heaven consumes a sacrifice that had been placed on the altar of the temple.

7:4–11. Additional sacrifices to the Lord are placed on the altar of the temple. This ceremony of thanksgiving continues for eight days.

7:12–22. The Lord renews with Solomon the covenant He had made with his father, David. Solomon's kingship over Israel will be eternal if he follows the Lord. But if Solomon does not obey God's commands, God will reject him and bring catastrophe upon the land (1 Kings 9:1–9).

8:1–18. Solomon builds storage cities and fortifies and equips other cities as defense outposts. He also establishes a port from which international trade is conducted (1 Kings 9:10–28).

9:1–12. Solomon receives a royal visitor, the Queen of Sheba, and impresses her with his wealth and wisdom (1 Kings 10:1–13).

9:13–28. Solomon multiplies his riches through international trade. He is honored by other nations for his power and wisdom (1 Kings 10:14–29).

9:29–31. Solomon dies after reigning for forty years and is succeeded as king by his son Rehoboam (1 Kings 11:41–43).

10:1–15. Rehoboam ignores the complaints of Jeroboam and the northern tribes about the harsh and oppressive practices of King Solomon. Rehoboam tells them he plans to multiply their misery (1 Kings 12:1–15).

10:16–19. The northern tribes revolt against Rehoboam and acclaim Jeroboam as their king. For the next several centuries of Israel's history, two opposing nations of the Jewish people exist—the northern tribes, known as the nation of Israel (or the North-ern Kingdom), and the southern tribes, known as the nation of Judah (or the Southern Kingdom). God's promise of an eternal kingship through David and his descendants continues through the

Southern Kingdom (1 Kings 12:16–24).

11:1–4. God speaks through a prophet to prevent Rehoboam from going to war against the Northern Kingdom.

11:5–13. King Rehoboam fortifies cities as defense outposts in the Southern Kingdom.

11:14–17. Many priests and Levites in the Northern Kingdom move to the Southern Kingdom to be near the central place of worship at the temple in Jerusalem. King Jeroboam sets up rival sanctuaries for worship and appoints his own priests (1 Kings 12:25–33).

11:18–23. The wives and children of King Rehoboam of Judah are listed.

12:1–12. To punish King Rehoboam for his unfaithfulness, God allows Shishak of Egypt to invade Judah and carry away the royal treasures.

12:13–16. After reigning for seventeen years, King Rehoboam of Judah dies and is succeeded by his son Abijah/Abijam (1 Kings 14:21–31).

[16:13–17:1] WAS KING ASA CREMATED? *They [Israelites]...laid him [King Asa] in the bed [bier, NIV] which was filled with sweet odours and divers kinds of spices prepared by the apothecaries' art: and they made a very great burning for him [made a huge fire in his honor, NIV]* (2 Chron. 16:14).

Was the body of King Asa of Judah cremated by being burned on a platform, or bier, sprinkled with spices? Some interpreters say yes; others say no.

Some believe the spices were first burned as an offering, then the king's body was laid in a coffin on top of the ashes from these spices. Others believe the king's body was actually burned along with the spices. This verse lends itself to either interpretation.

What is certain is that cremation was practiced on occasion among the Jews in Old Testament times. The bodies of King Saul and his sons were burned (1 Sam. 31:12). The prophets Jeremiah (Jer. 34:5) and Amos (Amos 6:10) also mentioned the practice of cremation.

–18. Walls of Jerusalem as built by the Ottomans in the 1500s, on the foundation of much …lier biblical walls. King Solomon had used his wealth to fortify cities throughout Israel, …ding walls and military facilities.

13:1–20. King Abijah/Abijam of Judah defeats the forces of King Jeroboam of Israel and captures several towns in the Northern Kingdom.

13:21–14:1. Abijah/Abijam dies and is succeeded as king of Judah by his son Asa (1 Kings 15:1–8).

14:2–8. Asa is a good king who follows the Lord and removes pagan altars and idols from the territory of Judah.

14:9–15. God gives Asa a decisive victory over King Zerah of Ethiopia.

15:1–19. A prophet encourages Asa to follow the Lord. Asa responds by implementing a religious reform movement throughout Judah, tearing down pagan altars, smashing idols, and leading the people to renew the covenant with God (1 Kings 15:9–24).

16:1–6. King Asa forms an alliance with the Syrian king Ben-hadad, who delivers Judah from oppression by the forces of King Baasha of Israel.

16:7–12. The prophet Hanani rebukes Asa because he relied on the military might of Syria for deliverance rather than the power of God.

16:13–17:1. Asa dies after reigning for forty-one years and is succeeded as king of Judah by his son Jehoshaphat (1 Kings 15:9–24).

17:2–5. King Jehoshaphat continues to follow the Lord as his father, Asa, had done. God rewards him for his faithfulness.

17:6–19. Jehoshaphat sends Levites throughout the land to teach God's law to the people. His kingdom thrives, and other nations pay tribute to him and honor his accomplishments.

18:1–3. King Jehoshaphat agrees to join an alliance with King Ahab of Israel against the Syrians (1 Kings 22:1–4).

18:4–11. False prophets who served as "yes men" for the king of Israel assure Ahab and Jehoshaphat that an attack against the Syrians will be successful (1 Kings 22:5–12).

18:12–27. Micaiah, a true prophet of the Lord, warns Ahab and Jehoshaphat that their campaign against Syria will fail (1 Kings 22:13–28).

23:1–21. Self-appointed queen Athaliah is executed at the "horse gate by the king's house" (2 Chronicles 23:15), not in the temple.

18:28–34. King Ahab of Israel is killed in the battle with the Syrians at Ramoth-gilead (1 Kings 22:29–40).

19:1–11. King Jehoshaphat implements additional religious reforms throughout the kingdom of Judah.

20:1–30. After Jehoshaphat and the people pray fervently to God, He gives them a great victory over the combined forces of the Moabites and the Ammonites.

20:31–21:1. Jehoshaphat dies after a twenty-five year reign as king of Judah and is succeeded by his son Jehoram/Joram (1 Kings 22:41–50).

21:2–7. On becoming king of Judah, Jehoram/Joram kills all his brothers to remove any challenge to his kingship. He fails to honor the Lord with his leadership.

21:8–10. The Edomites revolt against Judah and try to reestablish themselves as an independent kingdom.

21:11–22:1. As the prophet Elijah predicts, King Jehoram/Joram dies of a mysterious disease. His reign over Judah lasts for eight years. He is succeeded by his son Ahaziah.

22:2–9. Ahaziah's reign fails to please the Lord because of his connections with Ahab, the wicked king of Israel. When Jehu assassinates Ahab and becomes the new king of Israel, he also has Ahaziah executed (2 Kings 9:14–29).

22:10–12. Athaliah seizes the throne of Judah when her son Ahaziah is assassinated. She attempts to execute all claimants to the throne. But one of Ahaziah's sons, Joash/Jehoash, is hidden in the temple for six years (2 Kings 11:1–3).

23:1–21. Jehoiada the priest brings Joash/Jehoash out of hiding, and the people acclaim him as the new king of Judah. Athaliah is executed (2 Kings 11:4–21).

24:1–14. Joash/Jehoash follows the Lord as long as the priest Jehoiada is alive. Joash/Jehoash authorizes a special offering to be taken among the people and designates it for making needed repairs to the temple (2 Kings 12:1–16).

24:15–22. After the death of the priest Jehoiada, King Joash/Jehoash turns away from the Lord and encourages idol worship in the land. He even has Jehoiada's son killed because he condemned the king's waywardness and idolatry.

24:23–24. To punish Joash/Jehoash, the Lord allows the Syrians to defeat Judah and carry away the king's treasures.

24:25–27. Assassinated by his own servants, King Joash/Jehoash of Judah is succeeded by his son Amaziah (2 Kings 12:19–21).

25:1–16. At the beginning of his reign, Amaziah pleases the Lord. But he sins by setting up shrines for worship of pagan gods after defeating the Edomites (2 Kings 14:1–7).

25:17–24. King Jehoash of Israel invades the kingdom of Judah and carries away gold and silver from the temple in Jerusalem (2 Kings 14:8–14).

25:25–26:1. King Amaziah of Judah dies and is succeeded by his son Uzziah/Azariah (2 Kings 15:1–7).

26:2–5. Uzziah/Azariah is a good king who follows the Lord and reigns for fifty-two years in Judah.

26:6–15. Uzziah/Azariah strengthens the nation of Judah during his long reign by improving Jerusalem's defenses, developing a strong army, and subduing the Philistines and the Ammonites.

26:16–23. Uzziah/Azariah is struck with leprosy when he attempts to burn incense at the altar—a task reserved for priests only. After his death, he is succeeded by his son Jotham (2 Kings 15:1–7).

27:1–9. After reigning over Judah for sixteen

[26:6–15] **UZZIAH'S WAR MACHINES.** *He [King Uzziah] made in Jerusalem engines [machines, NIV], invented by cunning [skillful, NIV] men, to be on the towers and upon the bulwarks [corner defenses, NIV], to shoot arrows and great stones* (2 Chron. 26:15).

King Uzziah of Judah made Jerusalem's city wall defenses even more effective by increasing the firepower of the warriors on the wall. In the defense towers on top of the wall, he placed mechanical war machines that were capable of hurling huge stones and shooting arrows in bulk on the enemy below.

These "engines" were probably similar to the catapults used so effectively by the Roman army in later centuries.

years, Jotham dies and is succeeded by his son Ahaz.

28:1–4. Ahaz is an evil king who encourages idolatry throughout Judah. He even sacrifices his own children to a pagan god (2 Kings 16:1–4).

28:5–25. The Lord punishes Judah because of King Ahaz's abominable acts. The nation is pillaged by the Syrians, the Edomites, and the Philistines, as well as the nation of Israel (Northern Kingdom).

28:26–27. Ahaz dies and is succeeded as king of Judah by his son Hezekiah (2 Kings 16:19–20).

29:1–36. Hezekiah orders the priests to restore and purify the temple, since it had been desecrated during the reign of his father, Ahaz. Hezekiah leads the people to rededicate the temple and to resume the practice of bringing sacrifices and offerings to the altar.

30:1–27. Hezekiah leads the priests and the people to reinstate celebration of the Passover—a major religious festival that had not been observed in the land for many years.

31:1. The people destroy pagan altars and idols that had been set up throughout the land.

31:2–21. Hezekiah orders the people to bring firstfruits and other offerings to provide a livelihood for the priests and Levites. He directs that the surplus goods be stored for future use.

32:1–19. King Sennacherib of Assyria surrounds the city of Jerusalem. He taunts the God of Judah and orders Hezekiah to surrender (2 Kings 18:13–37).

32:20–23. Hezekiah and the prophet Isaiah pray earnestly to the Lord. Judah is delivered miraculously from the Assyrian forces (2 Kings 19:20–37).

32:24–26. King Hezekiah is struck by a serious illness, but he recovers when he prays to God in a spirit of humility (2 Kings 20:1–11).

32:27–31. God blesses Hezekiah, and his wealth increases. But the king commits a serious error when he displays his treasures to envoys from Babylonia (2 Kings 20:12–19).

32:32–33. King Hezekiah dies and is succeeded as king of Judah by his son Manasseh (2 Kings 20:20–21).

33:1–10. Manasseh reverses the religious reforms of his father, Hezekiah, and reinstates pagan worship throughout the land. He even participates in black magic and witchcraft and sacrifices some of his own children to pagan gods (2 Kings 21:1–9).

33:11–19. As punishment, God allows the Babylonians to capture Manasseh. He eventually continues his kingship under their jurisdiction. Manasseh tries to stem the tide of idol worship in Judah that he had started, but the people continue in their misguided ways.

33:20. Manasseh dies and is succeeded as king of Judah by his son Amon (2 Kings 21:17–18).

33:21–25. King Amon continues the evil practices of his father, Manasseh. Assassinated by his own servants after a brief reign, he

33:11–19. Evil king Manasseh disregarded God until he was captured and shackled by the Babylonians. Then he "besought the LORD his God, and humbled himself greatly before the God of his fathers" (2 Chronicles 33:12).

is succeeded by his son Josiah (2 Kings 21:19–26).

34:1–7. A good and godly king like his great-grandfather Hezekiah, Josiah tears down the pagan altars and images that had been placed throughout the land.

34:8–13. King Josiah orders that needed repairs be made to the temple in Jerusalem (2 Kings 22:1–7).

34:14–21. During the temple repairs, a copy of the book of the law (Genesis, Exodus, Leviticus, Numbers, and Deuteronomy) is discovered. Josiah realizes when this book is read that the people of Judah have wandered away from God's commands. He sends several priests to confer with a prophet to find out how God will deal with the sins of His rebellious people (2 Kings 22:8–14).

34:22–28. Huldah the prophetess declares that the Lord will deal kindly with Josiah because he has vowed to follow His will. But God will punish the nation of Judah for its sin and rebellion (2 Kings 22:15–20).

34:29–33. Josiah calls the elders of Judah and Jerusalem to meet at the temple to renew the covenant with the Lord (2 Kings 23:1–3).

35:1–19. King Josiah orders a nationwide observance of the Passover—a religious festival celebrating the deliverance of the Israelites from slavery in Egypt.

35:20–36:1. Josiah is killed in a battle with the Egyptians. Josiah's son Jehoahaz succeeds him as king of Judah (2 Kings 23:28–30).

[36:2–4] **FROM ELIAKIM TO JEHOIAKIM.** *The king of Egypt made Eliakim his [Jehoahaz's] brother king over Judah and Jerusalem, and turned [changed, NIV] his name to Jehoiakim* (2 Chron. 36:4).

Egypt siezed control of Judah, deposed King Jehoahaz, and installed Jehoahaz's brother Eliakim as king in his place. Then the Egyptian authorities changed the new king's name to Jehoiakim.

This renaming of the king sent a message to all the people that a new era in the life of their nation had begun—their subjection to Egypt. The power to change their king's name symbolized Egypt's supreme authority.

The nation of Judah was eventually overrun by the Babylonians. They carried away the leading citizens as captives, installed Mattaniah as a puppet king over what was left of the nation, and changed his name to Zedekiah (2 Kings 24:16–17).

36:2–4. Jehoahaz reigns only three months before he is captured by the Egyptians. They put Eliakim, another son of Josiah, on the throne as a puppet king and rename him Jehoiakim (2 Kings 23:31–37).

36:5–8. Judah is invaded by the Babylonian army under King Nebuchadnezzar during the reign of Eliakim/Jehoiakim. He is succeeded as king by his son Jehoiachin.

36:9–10. Jehoiachin reigns only three months and ten days before he is captured and deported to Babylonia. The Babylonians place Jehoiachin's brother Zedekiah/Mattaniah on the throne of Judah as a puppet king (2 Kings 24:8–19).

36:11–20. Zedekiah/Mattaniah rebels against the Babylonians, who ransack the city of Jerusalem and carry away all the temple treasures (2 Kings 24:20–25:21).

36:21–23. After seventy years as captives in a foreign land, the Jewish people are permitted to return to their homeland. This return is authorized by King Cyrus of Persia. This nation succeeds Babylonia as the dominant world power.

OVERVIEW: Ezra the priest leads the Jewish people to renew the covenant after their return from exile.

Introduction to Ezra

The book of Ezra belongs to the postexilic period of Israel's history—the time when God's people were allowed to return to their homeland following their years of exile in Babylonia and Persia.

Judah's leading citizens had been carried into exile by the Babylonians (2 Kings 25:8–21). But the Persians eventually defeated Babylonia. Persian policy was to allow subject peoples to live in their own territory and to worship their own god under a Persian-appointed military governor.

King Cyrus of Persia allowed the first group of Jewish exiles to return to Judah about 530 B.C. under the leadership of their duly-appointed governor, Zerubbabel (Ezra 2:1–2). The account of this group of exiles and their accomplishments is found in chapters 1–6 of Ezra.

About seventy years later, Ezra the priest returned to Jerusalem with another group of exiles. His accomplishments are related in chapters 7–10 of the book. Just as the first group of Jews rebuilt the temple, Ezra led the people to rebuild their commitment to God and His requirements in the law.

Ezra wrote the book that bears his name as well as the books of 1 and 2 Chronicles and Nehemiah (see the introductions to these books on pp. 84, 89, and 100. His book teaches an enduring message about the providence of God, who sometimes works through surprising circumstances—even the edict of a pagan Persian king—to accomplish His will in the lives of His people.

Summary of Ezra

1:1–4. King Cyrus of Persia conquers Babylonia, the nation that had overrun Judah and carried away captives to Babylon about seventy years before. In the first year of his reign, Cyrus allows the Jews who want to do so to return to their homeland and rebuild the city of Jerusalem and the temple (2 Chron. 36:22–23).

1:5–11. A group of Jewish leaders, along with priests and Levites, agree to return to Jerusalem to conduct the rebuilding project. Cyrus sends with them gold and silver and items from the temple that had been taken away by the Babylonians when they pillaged Jerusalem (2 Kings 24:13).

2:1–67. The leaders of the first group of Jewish exiles—more than 42,000—who return to their homeland under Zerubbabel (Hag. 2:20–23) are listed.

2:68–70. The returning exiles settle in various cities of their native land and contribute to a special rebuilding fund (1 Chron. 26:20).

3:1–6. People gather at Jerusalem from throughout their homeland to begin rebuilding.

They offer sacrifices of thanksgiving to God on the altar of the temple when it is restored.

3:7–13. Skilled workmen are enlisted, and materials are gathered to lay the foundation of the temple. Some of the Israelites are saddened that this new temple is not as ornate and beautiful as the first temple built by Solomon.

4:1–3. Zerubbabel, governor of Judah under appointment by the Persian king, refuses to allow non-Israelites to join in the rebuilding project.

4:4–16. These non-Jews take revenge for this rejection by trying to stop the construction project. They send a false report to King Artaxerxes of Persia, Cyrus's successor, that the Jews are plotting a rebellion against the Persian government.

4:17–24. Artaxerxes orders the work on the reconstruction of Jerusalem to stop until this charge against the Jews is investigated. The work does not resume until the accession of Darius to the Persian throne.

5:1. The prophets Haggai and Zechariah urge the people to resume work on the temple.

5:2–17. The leaders of Israel petition King Darius of Persia to allow the work on the temple to resume.

6:1–12. Darius permits the Jews to begin building again. He orders the enemies of the Jews to quit interfering with their building efforts. He sends gold and silver and building materials to assist in the construction work so they can resume their worship in the temple.

6:13–22. The temple is completed, the priests and Levites are organized for service at the altar, and celebration of the Passover festival is reinstated.

7:1–10. Ezra, a priest and scribe, prepares to leave Persia and join his countrymen who have already returned to their homeland. As an expert in the law of the Lord, he plans to teach the law to his fellow Israelites, probably because it had been neglected during their years in exile (Neh. 2:8, 18).

7:11–26. Ezra carries with him a letter from King Artaxerxes of Persia, giving him permission to return to Israel and to lead his countrymen in renewing their commitment to the law of the Lord. Artaxerxes also gives Ezra gold and silver and other valuable commodities to assist him in this restoration effort.

7:27–28. Ezra gives thanks to God for selecting him for this important task.

8:1–14. The exiles who returned to Jerusalem with Ezra are listed.

8:15–23. Ezra sends word for Levites to join his group of travelers. Several answer the call, and Ezra proclaims a fast of dedication to God before they begin the trip.

8:24–36. Ezra delivers the gold and silver and vessels from the temple to a group of priests for safekeeping. These were sent to Jerusalem as a gift from the Persian king Artaxerxes.

9:1–2. The leaders of Israel inform Ezra that many Jewish men have defiled themselves during the exile by marrying women from pagan backgrounds (Exod. 34:16).

9:3–15. In an eloquent prayer of confession and repentance, Ezra asks the Lord to forgive His people for their transgression.

10:1–17. All the Israelite men who have married women from pagan backgrounds gather at Jerusalem and agree to give up these wives.

10:18–44. The names of Israelite men who gave up their pagan wives are listed.

7:1–10. A priest and a scholar, Ezra taught the laws of Moses to Jews who returned from exile in what is now Iraq.

NEHEMIAH

OVERVIEW: Nehemiah leads the people to rebuild the walls of Jerusalem after their return from exile.

Introduction to Nehemiah

The book of Nehemiah emerged from the same background and circumstances that are reflected in the book of Ezra (see the introduction to Ezra on p. 97).

Nehemiah was a servant of King Artaxerxes of Persia. When he heard about the hardships of his fellow Jews who had returned to their homeland, he gained the king's permission to go there to assist in the rebuilding effort. His great accomplishment was leading his people to rebuild the defensive wall around Jerusalem. He also assisted Ezra the priest in his moral and legal reform movements among the people.

Nehemiah is a good case study in effective leadership. Under his supervision, the people rebuilt Jerusalem's wall in fifty-two days (6:15–19). He accomplished this challenging job by first seeking God's guidance and praying for the people of Judah. He took the time to do a careful analysis of the work to be done and to organize his workforce for maximum effectiveness.

Throughout the building project, Nehemiah also motivated and encouraged his workers and solved problems as soon as they arose with an aggressive leadership style. He persevered in the task and led the people to stay the course, even when their enemies threatened to attack them while they worked on the wall.

The world needs more courageous, visionary leaders like Nehemiah!

Summary of Nehemiah

1:1–3. In Persia, Nehemiah learns of the plight of the people who were left behind in Jerusalem when the Babylonians ransacked the nation of Judah many years before (2 Kings 25:1–4).

1:4–11. Nehemiah prays for his homeland and pleads with the Lord to forgive the sin and rebellion of His people.

> **[1:4–11] A ROYAL CUPBEARER.** *For I [Nehemiah] was the king's cupbearer* (Neh. 1:11).
>
> A cupbearer was one of the most important servants in the household of a king. His task was to taste the king's wine before he drank it to make sure it had not been poisoned by his enemies.
>
> Although Nehemiah was a Jew, he had risen to a position of prominence in the Persian court. Artaxerxes, the king, trusted him and allowed him to return to Jerusalem to rebuild the walls of the city (Neh. 2:3–7).

2:1–10. Nehemiah is the cupbearer for King Artaxerxes of Persia (Neh. 1:11). The king gives Nehemiah permission to go to Jerusalem to help rebuild the devastated city.

2:11–16. After arriving in Jerusalem,

Nehemiah surveys the broken defensive wall of the city under the cover of darkness to determine the repairs needed.

2:17–18. Nehemiah challenges the rulers of Jerusalem to rebuild the wall around the city.

2:19–20. Several enemies of the Jews scoff at Nehemiah's plan to rebuild the wall. But he insists that the project will be completed with the help of the Lord.

3:1–32. The names of several people who worked with Nehemiah on this building project are listed.

4:1–3. Sanballat and Tobiah, enemies of the Jews, ridicule Nehemiah's attempt to rebuild the wall of Jerusalem.

4:4–6. Nehemiah answers their taunts with a prayer for God's guidance and protection in the building project.

4:7–12. Sanballat and Tobiah and other enemies of the Jews vow to stop the building project with military force.

4:13–23. Nehemiah organizes a defensive force and arms his workers so they can protect themselves against an enemy attack. Many workers labor on the wall with their construction tools in one hand and their weapons in the other.

5:1–5. Some of the people complain to Nehemiah about their economic hardship. Their own fellow Jews are charging them excessive interest on money they have borrowed and are even holding their children in slavery as collateral against their debts (Ezra 4:13).

5:6–13. Nehemiah confronts the wealthy Jews who are exploiting their poor neighbors. They agree to restore the land and children that are being held as collateral.

5:14–19. Nehemiah is serving as governor of Judah under appointment by the Persian king. But he refuses to use his position and power to line his own pockets.

6:1–14. The enemies of the Jews continue their

2:1–10. A model of ancient Jerusalem indicates how the city may have looked in Bible times. Nehemiah led the work of repairing Jerusalem's walls after Babylonian invaders tore them down.

[5:6–13] **AN EMPTY POCKET.** *I [Nehemiah] shook my lap [shook out the folds of my robe, NIV], and said, So God shake out every man from his house, and from his labour, that performeth not this promise, even thus be he shaken out, and emptied* (Neh. 5:13).

The "lap" in this passage was a pocket in the loose outer robe where people carried items such as money or important papers. It served the same purpose as a man's wallet in modern times.

Nehemiah had just received a promise from the wealthy Jews of Jerusalem that they would no longer mistreat and defraud their poorer fellow Jews. When he shook out the pocket in his robe, he was saying to the wealthy, "God will make you just as empty as this pocket if you fail to keep the promise you have made."

plots to stop the building project. They even hire a false prophet to lure Nehemiah into an error in order to undermine his leadership. But Nehemiah is not fooled by their tricks.

6:15–19. The defensive wall around Jerusalem is rebuilt in fifty-two days—to the disappointment of Tobiah and other enemies who had tried to stop the project.

7:1–4. Nehemiah selects priests and Levites to preside over sacrifices in the temple. He also appoints civil leaders to provide security for the city of Jerusalem.

7:5–69. The Jewish tribes who have returned to Judah under the leadership of Zerubbabel (Hag. 2:20–23) are listed by clans and family groups.

7:70–73. Contributors to a special fund to assist in the rebuilding effort in Jerusalem are listed.

8:1–12. The people gather in the streets of Jerusalem and listen reverently as Ezra reads the book of the law (Genesis, Exodus, Leviticus, Numbers, and Deuteronomy). The priests and Levites are stationed among the crowd to explain these commands from God.

8:13–18. Ezra reads God's directions from the book of the law on how the Feast of Booths, or Tabernacles, is to be observed (Lev. 23:39–43). The people cut branches from trees and build themselves huts, or booths,

to remember their living conditions during the years of wandering in the wilderness.

9:1–38. All the people, including civil leaders, priests, and Levites, repent and confess their sins to God. They vow to keep the covenant between the Lord and Israel.

10:1–27. The names of the leaders who sealed the covenant between the Lord and the Israelites are listed.

10:28–39. The people agree to follow God's commands from the book of the law. They agree to resume the practice of bringing tithes, offerings, and sacrifices to the priests and Levites in the temple.

11:1–2. The leaders of Israel cast lots (Matt. 27:35) to determine the settlement of the returned exiles in the land. Ten percent are to settle in Jerusalem, and the remaining 90 percent will live in other cities throughout Judah.

11:3–24. The people selected to live in Jerusalem are listed.

11:25–36. Other cities of Judah where the exiles will settle are listed.

12:1–26. The names of priests and Levites who returned from the exile under Zerubbabel are listed (Ezra 2:1–67).

12:27–43. The names of priests and Levites whom Nehemiah appointed for a special function are listed. They lead the celebration at the dedication of the restored defensive wall of Jerusalem.

12:44–47. Nehemiah appoints priests and Levites to store the goods offered by the people for the support of the priesthood. He also organizes the priests and Levites to serve at the altar in the temple on a rotating basis. This restores the procedure established by David and Solomon (1 Chron. 25:1–26:32).

13:1–31. Nehemiah institutes religious reforms throughout the land of Judah. He restores the sanctity of the Sabbath, casts foreigners out of the temple, and forbids the Jewish people from marrying people from pagan backgrounds.

[10:28–39] **WOOD FOR THE ALTAR.** *We cast the lots among the priests, the Levites, and the people, for the wood offering, to bring it into the house of our God, after the houses of our fathers, at times appointed year by year, to burn upon the altar of the LORD our God* (Neh. 10:34).

Supplying wood for priests to use in offering burnt sacrifices on the altar was a task assigned to the Nethinims, or temple servants (see sidebar, "Temple Servants," on p. 98). But not enough of these servants returned from the Exile in Babylonia and Persia to handle this task.

Nehemiah solved the problem by assigning other people from among the Levites and the general population to do this work. He cast lots to set up a rotating system under which wood would be supplied for this purpose throughout the year.

ESTHER

OVERVIEW: Esther delivers her people, the Jews, from their enemies while they are living among the Persians.

Introduction to Esther

Following their years of exile among the Babylonians and Persians, the Jewish people were allowed by the Persians to return to their homeland (see the introduction to Ezra on p. 97). But the book of Esther shows clearly that not all the Jews took advantage of this opportunity. Many chose to remain in Persia, probably because this had become home to them during their long separation from Judah, their native land.

Esther, the young Jewish woman for whom

1:10–12. Persia's queen, Vashti, refuses a summons to appear before King Ahasuerus' drinking party for men. She is banished, opening the door for Esther to become queen.

the book is named, rose to the position of queen under the Persian king, Ahasuerus. Her cousin Mordecai was also an important official who served at the king's palace.

King Ahasuerus reigned from about 485 to 465 B.C., so the book of Esther can be dated to this time period. This was about forty years after the Persians allowed the first group of exiles to return to Judah. The author of the book is unknown.

The main characters in the book of Esther are King Ahasuerus; his wife, Queen Esther; his top official, an evil man named Haman; and Mordecai, Esther's cousin, who was also a palace official and a leader among the Jewish people who were living throughout Persia.

Haman developed a hatred for the Jews because he felt they did not pay him the respect he deserved as a high official of the Persian government. He tricked the king into issuing an order for their wholesale execution. But Queen Esther, at Mordecai's encouragement, used her influence with the king to expose Haman's plot. Haman was hanged on the gallows that he had built for Mordecai's execution, and Mordecai was promoted by the king to a higher position.

The Jewish people were allowed to resist their enemies, and they were granted victory by the Lord. The book ends with their celebration of this miraculous deliverance through a special holiday known as the Feast of Purim.

Summary of Esther

1:1–9. King Ahasuerus of Persia invites the leaders throughout his kingdom to a lavish banquet at his royal palace in Shushan.

1:10–12. The king asks his queen, Vashti, to appear before his guests to showcase her beauty, but she refuses.

1:13–22. On the advice of his aides, King Ahasuerus decrees that Vashti will be deposed as queen and replaced by another woman.

2:1–4. Ahasuerus begins a search throughout his kingdom for a woman to replace Vashti as queen.

2:5–18. Esther, also known as Hadassah, is a beautiful young Jewish woman who was adopted by her cousin Mordecai after the death of her parents. She wins the king's favor and replaces Vashti as the queen.

2:19–23. Mordecai, who serves in the palace of King Ahasuerus (Esther 2:5), saves the king's life when he stops an assassination plot.

3:1–6. Haman, a high official in King Ahasuerus' administration, is enraged when Mordecai refuses to bow before him and show him honor and respect.

3:7–15. In order to kill Mordecai, Haman devises a plan to destroy all the Jews. He convinces King Ahasuerus that the Jewish people are reckless and dangerous revolutionaries who refuse to abide by the king's laws. Ahasuerus issues an order that all the Jews throughout his kingdom are to be wiped out on a

---

[1:10–12] HAREM CARETAKERS. *The seven chamberlains [eunuchs, NIV] that served in the presence of Ahasuerus the king* (Esther 1:10).

A chamberlain was a male servant in a king's court who was responsible for the king's harem. To minimize the danger to these women, a chamberlain was emasculated. King Ahasuerus of Persia must have had a large harem, since he had seven of these servants.

Sometimes these male servants rose to positions of prominence as advisers in the king's administration. This must have been the case with two chamberlains of King Ahasuerus, since they participated in a plot to assassinate the king (Esther 2:21–23).

Other references to chamberlain or eunuchs include 2 Kings 9:32; Jer. 29:2; and Dan. 1:10.

specific day in the future.

4:1–9. Mordecai mourns for the Jewish people in front of the royal palace. He sends word to Esther that she must use her influence with the king to save the Jews from destruction.

4:10–17. Esther reminds Mordecai of the law that any person who approaches the Persian king without authorization runs the risk of being executed. But she promises Mordecai that she will take this risk on behalf of her own people, the Jews.

5:1–2. Esther makes an unauthorized appearance before the king. He agrees to receive her by extending his royal scepter for her to touch.

5:3–8. Esther asks the king to invite Haman to a banquet that she has prepared. At this banquet, she asks the king, along with Haman, to attend another banquet that she is preparing for the next day. During this second banquet she will make known her request to King Ahasuerus.

5:9–14. Filled with pride, Haman boasts to his wife and friends about his achievements and his special invitation to attend a banquet with the king and Queen Esther the next day. But Haman admits that all these achievements mean little as long as Mordecai refuses to bow down and show him honor. At his wife's suggestion, he builds a gallows on which he plans to have Mordecai hanged.

[4:10–17] DON'T BOTHER THE KING. *Whosoever... shall come unto the king...who is not called, there is one law...to put him to death, except such to whom the king shall hold out the golden sceptre* (Esther 4:11).

Mordecai asked Esther to seek an audience with King Ahasuerus of Persia to plead for the Jewish people. In this verse, Esther reminded Mordecai that anyone who approached the king without a personal invitation ran the risk of immediate execution.

The purpose of this harsh law may have been to keep the king from being pestered by grumblers and favor-seekers. He had the option of granting an audience to uninvited visitors by touching them with his royal scepter.

Esther did decide to approach the king—uninvited—on behalf of her people, the Jews. The king touched her with his scepter and agreed to hear her request (Esther 5:1–2).

6:1–14. While reading the royal archives, Ahasuerus discovers the account of Mordecai's intervention on the king's behalf (Esther 2:19–23). The king orders Haman to prepare and lead a tribute to Mordecai for his brave action. Haman's humiliation at being forced to honor the Jew grows deeper when his wife predicts that he will fall before Mordecai.

7:1–10. During the banquet with Haman and the king, Queen Esther exposes Haman's plot to have the Jews destroyed. King Ahasuerus orders that Hamon be put to death. He is hanged on the gallows he

[9:20–32] A CELEBRATION OF DELIVERANCE. *Wherefore they [the Jews] called these days Purim after the name of Pur* (Esther 9:26).

The Jewish people celebrated their deliverance from the death edict issued by Haman (Esther 3:5–15) with a special holiday known as the Feast of Purim.

The Hebrew word *purim* means "lots." The feast was named for the lots that Haman cast to determine the time when the Jews would be annihilated (Esther 3:7). Thanks to the brave actions of Esther and Mordecai, Haman was annihilated and the Jewish people prospered throughout the land.

9:1–19. Throughout the kingdom of Persia, the Jews destroy many of their enemies, including ten sons of Haman. Mordecai, on the other hand, grows in popularity and power.

9:20–32. Mordecai and Esther proclaim the fourteenth and fifteenth days of the month of Adar as an official religious holiday among the Jews. Known as Purim, it memorializes God's deliverance of His people from their enemies.

10:1–3. The Jewish Mordecai becomes an important and highly respected official under King Ahasuerus. He is also respected and honored by his own countrymen throughout the kingdom of Persia.

9:20–32. Jewish children dress up for the ongoing celebration of Purim. When the book of Esther is read aloud, noisemakers drown out the name of Haman, the story's villain.

had prepared for Mordecai's death (Esther 5:14).

8:1–2. Mordecai is promoted to a high position in King Ahasuerus's administration.

8:3–8. Queen Esther pleads with the king to spare her countrymen, the Jewish people.

8:9–17. King Ahasuerus issues a decree that authorizes the Jews to resist when their lives are threatened under the earlier order issued by Haman (Esther 3:13).

CHAPTER 3
BOOKS OF POETRY AND WISDOM

One of the most beloved books in the entire Bible—the book of Psalms—is included among the books of poetry and wisdom of the Old Testament. Other books in this category are Job, Proverbs, Ecclesiastes, and Song of Solomon.

Old Testament poetry does not include such elements as rhyme and alliteration, which we normally associate with poetic writings. Rather, the main feature of Old Testament poetic literature is parallelism. In this form of literary construction, the content of one line is advanced, contrasted, or repeated by the content of the next line. (See the introduction to the book of Psalms on p. 113–114 for a more detailed explanation of the technique of parallelism.)

Writings in this section of the Old Testament that deal with issues such as the meaning of life, the nature of human suffering, and how to have a happy and successful life are known as wisdom literature. The books of Job, Proverbs, and Ecclesiastes fall into this category. Several of the individual psalms are also classified as wisdom psalms: 1, 19, 37, 49, 104, 107, 112, 119, 127, 128, 133, 147, and 148.

JOB

OVERVIEW: In debates with his three friends, Job examines the problems of evil and human suffering.

Introduction to Job

The book of Job, written in the form of a dramatic poem by an unknown author, deals with a question as old as humankind: Why do the righteous suffer? Although Job was a righteous man who worshiped God and shunned evil (1:1), God allowed Satan to take away everything he owned, as well as his children.

As Job cried out to God in his misery, three friends arrived to offer comfort. But they actually drove Job into deeper despair because of their outspoken conviction that Job was being punished by the Lord because of his sins. Job protested that he was a righteous man and that God was treating him unjustly.

After Job and his friends had debated this question for a long time, God Himself finally spoke from a whirlwind. Revealing Himself as the powerful, all-knowing God, He declared that He could be trusted to do what was right, although His ways might seem strange and puzzling.

Humbled by this outpouring of God's power, Job finally learned to trust God, in spite of his imperfect understanding. He stopped questioning God and His ways and declared, "I abhor myself, and repent in dust and ashes" (42:6). God was pleased with this profession of faith and trust. He restored Job's fortunes and gave him additional children to replace those he had lost.

The book of Job teaches us that it is futile to try to understand the reason behind our suffering. It is enough to know that God is in control and that He is our refuge and strength in times of trouble. Like Job, we also need to learn that God is not bound by our understanding or by our lack of it. He is free and subject to no will but His own. He does not owe us an explanation for His actions.

Summary of Job

1:1–5. Job is a righteous and upright man who has been abundantly blessed by the Lord. He owns large herds of livestock and has many sons and daughters.

[1:1–5] A MAN OF MEANS. *His [Job's] substance also was seven thousand sheep, and three thousand camels, and five hundred yoke of oxen, and five hundred she asses [female donkeys, NKJV]* (Job 1:3).

In Old Testament times, a man's wealth was measured by the size of his flocks and herds. Job was a rich man by these standards. Female donkeys are mentioned in this passage because they were more valuable than male donkeys. The milk produced by females was a valuable food substance.

1:6–12. In a dialogue with God, Satan charges that Job serves Him for selfish reasons—what is in it for him. God gives Satan permission to test Job to determine if his charge is true.

1:13–22. In one disastrous day, Job loses everything: his large herds of livestock, his servants, and his own sons and daughters. But Job remains faithful to God.

2:1–10. Satan tells God that Job will certainly deny Him if he is afflicted with physical suffering. With God's permission, Job is struck with boils and sores. But still he refuses to cry out against God.

2:11–13. Three of Job's friends—Eliphaz, Bildad, and Zophar—hear about Job's misfortune. They come to mourn with Job and to comfort him in his anguish and pain.

3:1–26. Before his friends say a word, Job issues a plaintive cry of self-pity. He curses the day of his birth and wishes he had never been born. This chapter begins the first cycle of debate between Job and his friends. This cycle continues through chapter 14, with Eliphaz responding to Job (chaps. 4–5); Job replying to Eliphaz (chaps. 6–7); Bildad's first speech to Job (chap. 8); Job's response to Bildad (chaps. 9–10); Zophar's first speech to Job (chap. 11); and Job's reply to Zophar (chaps. 12–14).

4:1–5:27. In his response to Job's outburst, Eliphaz reminds his friend that the innocent do not suffer like Job is suffering. He calls on Job to turn to God and repent; then his troubles will go away.

6:1–7:21. Job protests that he is innocent. How can God be punishing him when he has done nothing wrong?

8:1–22. Bildad steps up the tempo when he enters the debate. God always acts with justice and fairness, he declares. Is Job suggesting otherwise by claiming that God is punishing an innocent man?

9:1–10:22. Job expresses his confusion and frustration. He agrees in theory with Bildad that God is just. But in Job's case He seems to be punishing a person who is righteous. Job laments his condition and again wishes he had never been born.

11:1–20. Zophar now jumps into the debate and turns it up a notch. He attacks Job personally and accuses him of being filled with pride and of uttering meaningless words. He charges that there must be some hidden sin in Job's life. God knows about it and is giving Job what he deserves.

12:1–14:22. Job grows angry and sarcastic with his know-it-all friends. He declares that he knows as much about God and how He works as they do. He appeals his case directly to God and calls on Him to declare him innocent. He also laments the brevity of life and the lot of all human beings on earth: "Man that is born of a woman is of few days, and full of trouble" (Job 14:1).

15:1–35. Eliphaz replies to Job's outburst, calling him a vain man whose stomach is filled with the east wind (in other words, a windbag!). His speech kicks off the second cycle of debate in the book of Job. This cycle continues through chapter 21, with Job's response to Eliphaz (chaps. 16–17); Bildad's second speech to Job (chap. 18); Job's

[9:1–10:22] MESSAGES ON FOOT. *My [Job's] days are swifter than a post [runner,* NIV*]: they flee away, they see no good* (Job 9:25).

Job complained about the brevity of human life by declaring that his days went by faster than a swift runner. He was probably referring to the fleet-footed messengers used by Old Testament kings to carry important messages to distant places.

King Hezekiah of Judah restored several important religious practices, including observance of the Passover, which had been neglected by the people. He sent "posts [couriers, NIV]…with…letters…throughout all Israel and Judah" (2 Chron. 30:6), summoning all citizens to gather at Jerusalem for this solemn occasion.

reply to Bildad (chap. 19); Zophar's second speech to Job (chap. 20); and Job's response to Zophar (chap. 21).

16:1–17:16. Job continues his complaining. He calls his friends "miserable comforters" (16:2) because of their lack of sensitivity and compassion.

18:1–21. Bildad insists that Job is being punished for his sin. He describes the destiny of the wicked in graphic terms, apparently to frighten Job into repentance.

19:1–29. Broken and depressed, Job begs his friends to have pity on him. They have become accusers and tormentors instead of comforters, accusing him unfairly and providing no answers to his probing questions.

19:1–29. Job recoils from the accusations of his friends Bildad, Eliphaz, and Zophar. They assumed Job's ordeal was due to sin in his life.

[19:1–29] CAUGHT IN GOD'S NET. *God hath overthrown me [Job], and hath compassed [surrounded, NKJV] me with his net* (Job 19:6).

Birds and other animals were often trapped with nets. These were also effective weapons in combat. A warrior would restrain an enemy by throwing a thick net around him. Then he would finish him off with a sword or spear.

In his suffering and struggles with God, Job compared himself to an animal or a man trapped in a net. He believed God was wielding the net. As an innocent sufferer, he thought he was being punished by God for no reason.

20:1–29. Zophar picks up the subject that Bildad had discussed in chapter 18: the terrible fate of the wicked. The implication of his remarks is that Job is being punished by God for his wickedness.

21:1–34. Job agrees with Zophar and the others that the wicked are ultimately punished, but he insists that they often prosper and flourish during this life.

22:1–30. Eliphaz intensifies his assault on Job.

He accuses him of serious sins, including oppression of the poor. His speech launches the third and final cycle of debate between Job and his friends. This cycle continues through chapter 26, with Job's response to Eliphaz (chaps. 23–24); Bildad's third speech to Job (chap. 25); and Job's reply to Bildad (chap. 26).

23:1–24:25. Job wishes he could stand in God's presence and present his case directly to Him. He protests that life is not fair—that God sometimes seems to punish the righteous and reward the wicked.

25:1–6. Bildad feels compelled to defend God against Job's accusations. He declares that man has no right to question God's actions.

26:1–14. Job ends the three cycles of debate with a strong affirmation about God: He is all-powerful, and His ways are beyond human understanding: "The thunder of his power who can understand?" (v. 14).

27:1–31:40. In these five chapters, Job issues his final defense against his accusers. He looks back on his days of plenty and compares them with his present state of poverty. But through it all he has kept his integrity before God. He claims, as he has throughout the debate, that he is an innocent sufferer.

32:1–37:24. These six chapters contain the angry outburst of a young man named Elihu. Apparently he had listened to the debate between Job and his three friends and was not pleased with what they were saying. Job was wrong because he had justified himself rather than God. And his three friends had failed to convince Job of the error of his ways. Elihu feels he needs to defend God's honor and set the record straight. In his long speech, he upholds God's works,

[38:1–41:34] SEALING WITH CLAY. *It [the earth] is turned as clay to the seal* (Job 38:14).

This verse is part of God's response to Job's charge against Him that He was unjust and unfair for causing Job to suffer.

In Bible times clay tablets or clay bricks were often stamped or sealed with a symbol that identified their owner or creator. God declared to Job that He was the all-powerful, omnipotent Lord who had created the earth and stamped it with His own seal. He did not owe Job an explanation for His actions.

wisdom, and justice. He declares that Job is getting what he deserves because of his sin.

38:1–41:34. Elihu's diatribe is not dignified by a response from either Job or God. Instead, God finally replies to Job after Job's whining throughout the book. God does not give Job an explanation for his suffering. But He reminds Job that He is the sovereign, all-powerful, omnipotent Creator of the universe whose ways are beyond human understanding. He does not have to justify and defend His actions to mere mortals (Hab. 2:2–20).

42:1–6. Job's prideful desire for understanding and justification gives way to trust and submission. With faith and humility he declares, "I have heard of thee by the hearing of the ear: but now mine eye seeth thee. Wherefore I abhor myself, and repent in dust and ashes" (vv. 5–6).

42:7–17. The Lord reprimands the three friends of Job because He is not pleased with their treatment of Job. Then He restores Job's fortunes by giving him twice as much as he had before (Isa. 40:2).

OVERVIEW: Prayers of praise, joy, and agony of soul addressed to God.

Introduction to Psalms

Several things about the book of Psalms make it unique among the books of the Bible: (1) It is the longest book of the Bible, (2) it was written by many different authors across a period of several centuries, and (3) parts of the book were used as a hymnal in the worship services of God's people, the Israelites.

The name of David appears in the titles of 73 of the 150 individual psalms in this book. But several other people are named in the titles of other psalms, and at least 50 psalms have no authors identified in the titles.

From the content of the individual psalms, it is clear that they were written by many different people across a long period of time. They were eventually compiled as a book of 150 psalms by an unknown editor. Musical terms in some of the psalms (for example, "To the chief

Psalm 23. Some of the Bible's most beloved imagery—such as the Lord as shepherd of His people—is found in the Psalms.

Psalm 8. The full moon rises over modern-day Jerusalem. Many ancient Jewish songs praise the wonder of God's creation.

Musician," Ps. 46 title) show that many of the psalms were chanted or sung during worship services in the tabernacle or temple.

All the psalms were written in poetic form. Many of these poems demonstrate the nature of Hebrew poetry. The psalm writers used a technique known as parallelism rather than rhyme or rhythm. In parallelism, one phrase is followed by a second phrase that repeats, adds to, or contrasts with the first phrase. Here are two examples of parallelism from the Psalms:

> For I will declare mine iniquity;
> I will be sorry for my sin.
> (repetition; Ps. 38:18)

> For the LORD knoweth the way of the righteous:
> but the way of the ungodly shall perish.
> (contrast; Ps. 1:6)

Several of the psalms look forward to the coming of the Messiah. Psalm 22 predicts the suffering of the Savior on the cross (Ps. 22:1; fulfilled in Matt. 27:46). Other psalms indicate that He would pray for His enemies (Ps. 109:4; fulfilled in Luke 23:34) and that His reign would last forever (Ps. 45:6; fulfilled in Heb. 1:8).

The book of Psalms is one of the most beloved books of the Bible, perhaps because it expresses the thoughts about God that believers sometimes feel in their hearts but can't seem to put into words. For example, these words from Psalm 95 are an appropriate prayer of praise for every circumstance of life: "O come, let us sing unto the LORD: let us make a joyful noise to the rock of our salvation. Let us come before his presence with thanksgiving, and make a joyful noise unto him with psalms. For the LORD is a great God, and a great King above all gods" (Ps. 95:1–3).

Summary of Psalms

Psalm 1. Blessed is the person who walks in accordance with the word of God (Prov. 4:14).

Psalm 2. A messianic psalm that declares that God's ultimate rule over the world will be established by His Son.

Psalm 3. God is a shield who protects the believer in troublesome times. This psalm was written by David when he fled from the rebellion of his son Absalom (2 Sam. 15–16).

Psalm 4. God hears the prayers of believers and grants peace and rest in the dark experiences of life.

Psalm 5. The Lord will reward the righteous and punish the wicked.

Psalm 6. A prayer for God to show mercy to the psalmist and to punish his enemies.

Psalm 7. This psalm focuses on righteousness. David wants God to know that he has lived a righteous life. He asks God to deliver him from wicked enemies.

Psalm 8. As he meditates on the wonders of God's physical creation, the psalmist realizes that man is weak and insignificant. But God has placed him in a position of honor and glory.

Psalm 9. A psalm of praise for the mercy and grace shown by the Lord to the nation of Israel. The psalmist also declares that God will punish the pagan nations.

Psalm 10. The wicked are persecuting and cheating the poor. The psalmist calls on the Lord to rise to their defense.

Psalm 11. God is in control, and the psalmist affirms his confidence in His wisdom and guidance.

Psalm 12. Surrounded by those who speak false, flattering words, the psalmist declares that "the words of the LORD are pure words" (v. 6). He can be trusted to be honest and fair.

Psalm 13. Although he is feeling lonely and abandoned, the psalmist vows to "sing unto the LORD, because he hath dealt bountifully with me" (v. 6).

Psalm 14. Wicked, depraved people who live as if God does not exist are fools (v. 1). The apostle Paul quoted the first two verses of this psalm to show that no person is sinless in God's eyes (Rom. 3:10–12).

Psalm 15. The psalmist gives a brief description of the godly person who walks in the ways of the Lord.

Psalm 16. This is a messianic psalm because of its reference to the resurrection of Christ (vv. 9–11; see Acts 13:35–37).

Psalm 17. Overwhelmed by his enemies, the psalmist looks to God for guidance and deliverance.

Psalm 18. This psalm of thanksgiving from David celebrates his deliverance by the Lord from threats against his life by King Saul. It closely parallels David's song of deliverance in 2 Samuel 22.

Psalm 19. A majestic celebration of God's revelation of Himself through nature and the law, God's written Word.

Psalm 20. This is a public prayer for the king of Israel, encouraging him and the people to trust in the Lord rather than military might.

Psalm 21. A prayer for victory over Israel's enemies under the leadership of the nation's earthly, political king.

Psalm 22. A well-known messianic psalm. Christ quoted from it while He was on the cross: "My God, my God, why hast thou forsaken me?" (v. 1; see Matt. 27:46).

Psalm 23. Because it portrays God as a tender, caring shepherd, this beloved psalm is known as the "Shepherd Psalm."

Psalm 24. As worshipers traveled to the temple in Jerusalem, they may have chanted this psalm as a recessional hymn. The Lord is portrayed as "the King of glory" (v. 10).

Psalm 25. Deeply aware of his unworthiness because of his sin, the psalmist prays passionately for God's mercy and forgiveness.

Psalm 26. A prayer of a person of integrity who has always sought to walk before the Lord in trust and obedience.

Psalm 27. An affirmation of faith from a person who has found solace in worship: "That I may dwell in the house of the LORD all the days of my life" (v. 4).

Psalm 28. The psalmist appeals to God as a rock and a shield. The Lord offers protection and deliverance to those who trust in Him.

Psalm 29. God's power and majesty are displayed in the forces of nature, even in a thunderstorm (v. 3).

Psalm 30. A psalm of thanksgiving to God for deliverance from sickness and death.

Psalm 31. The psalmist cries out to God in his anguish and distress. Christ quoted from this psalm on the cross just before He died: "Into thine hand I commit my spirit" (v. 5; see Luke 23:46).

Psalm 32. Sin in the believer's life brings remorse and misery, but repentance and confession result in God's forgiveness and the restoration of joy.

Psalm 33. The psalmist issues a public call for people to praise the Lord because of the wonders of His creation and the blessings that He showers on believers.

Psalm 34. David apparently wrote this psalm out of his experience of pretending to be insane before Achish, the Philistine king of Gath (1 Sam. 21:10–15). The psalm affirms that God provides for His people.

Psalm 35. The psalmist calls on God to pay back his enemies for their treachery and to restore his reputation and good name.

Psalm 36. This psalm paints a striking contrast between the goodness of God and the evil of human beings.

Psalm 37. Righteous people are encouraged to remain faithful to God, even though evil seems to be winning. The ultimate victory belongs the LORD and those who are his.

Psalm 38. The psalmist is crushed and humiliated by divine discipline because of his sin. He issues an eloquent plea for God's forgiveness and deliverance.

Psalm 39. Life is fleeting and filled with suffering and disappointment. The psalmist has learned to put his ultimate hope in the Lord.

Psalm 40. A psalm of praise and thanksgiving to God for answering the psalmist's prayer and coming to his aid.

Psalm 41. God is faithful, even though the psalmist has been betrayed by a close friend (v. 9). Jesus may have had this psalm in mind when He predicted that one of his own disciples would betray Him (John 13:18).

[41] BETRAYAL BY A FRIEND. *Yea, mine own familiar [close, NIV] friend, in whom I trusted, which did eat of my bread, hath lifted up his heel against me* (Ps. 41:9).

The ultimate insult of Bible times was betrayal by a close friend. In this psalm David may have been referring to Ahithophel, a friend and royal adviser, who joined Absalom's rebellion against the king (2 Sam. 15:12, 31).

Jesus cited this psalm when He predicted that Judas, one of His disciples, would betray Him: "He that eateth bread with me hath lifted up his heel against me" (John 13:18).

Psalm 42. The psalmist expresses despair because God seems far away, but he hopes for a restoration of their previous close relationship.

Psalm 43. The psalmist asks the Lord to plead his cause before the ungodly and to guide his life with divine light and truth.

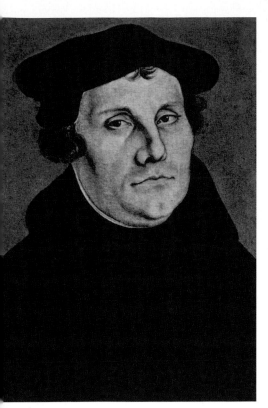

Psalm 46. Martin Luther, father of the Protestant movement, found encouragement in the Psalms. Psalm 46 inspired him to write one of his most famous hymns: "A Mighty Fortress Is Our God."

Psalm 44. Israel had apparently suffered defeat at the hands of an enemy. The psalmist calls on God to come to their aid as He has in the past.

Psalm 45. This is a royal wedding song celebrating the marriage of an unnamed king of Israel. Considered a messianic psalm, it emphasizes God's universal rule.

Psalm 46. God and His kingdom are like a place of refuge, a stronghold, a mighty fortress that cannot be overcome by the forces of evil. This psalm was the inspiration for Martin Luther's stirring Reformation hymn, "A Mighty Fortress Is Our God."

Psalm 47. A praise psalm that exalts God as the "great King over all the earth" (v. 2).

Psalm 48. The city of Jerusalem, referred to as Zion in this Psalm (v. 2) is portrayed as a place especially blessed and honored by the Lord.

Psalm 49. This psalm focuses on the folly of amassing great wealth in the belief that it will provide security. True security consists of following God and obeying His commands.

Psalm 50. Honoring God with an obedient, godly life is more important than offering sacrifices at the altar.

Psalm 51. David wrote this plea for forgiveness after he committed adultery with Bathsheba: "Create in me a clean heart, O God; and renew a right spirit within me" (v. 10; see 2 Sam. 11).

Psalm 52. This psalm grew out of Doeg's betrayal of David (1 Sam. 22). David proclaims that wicked people like Doeg will be rejected by the Lord, but the righteous will always enjoy God's blessings.

Psalm 53. This psalm, similar to Psalm 14, proclaims the universal sinfulness of humankind.

Psalm 54. In this psalm David affirms that God protected him during the time when the Ziphites told King Saul where David was hiding (1 Sam. 23:19–23).

Psalm 55. This psalm portrays a person in agony of soul after being betrayed by a close friend. But the psalmist looks to God as a never-failing friend and refuge.

Psalm 56. A psalm that affirms reliance on God during a time of fear and uncertainty.

Psalm 57. David expresses his confidence in God's protection, even as he seeks refuge in a cave from the wrath of King Saul (1 Sam. 24).

[56] GOD KNOWS OUR TEARS. *Thou [God] tellest my wanderings: put thou my tears into thy bottle: are they not in thy book?* (Ps. 56:8).

David may have been referring in this psalm to an ancient custom observed by mourners at funerals. They would collect the tears they shed for departed loved ones in small flasks and place them in their tombs as memorials of their love.

This was David's way of saying that God knows all about us. He even keeps a record of the tears we shed in our moments of sorrow and sadness. Jesus expressed the same truth when He declared, "The very hairs of your head are all numbered" (Matt. 10:30).

Psalm 58. This psalm calls for God's judgment on leaders who use their authority to defraud and cheat the innocent.

Psalm 59. David recalls the time when King Saul posted soldiers around his house to ambush and kill him (1 Sam. 19:11–18). He denounces his enemies and affirms his trust in God.

Psalm 60. Although Israel suffers from temporary setbacks, the psalmist is convinced that God will give them the ultimate victory over their enemies.

Psalm 61. A prayer for the earthly king of Israel. He and the psalmist will find security and safety in "the rock that is higher than I" (v. 2).

Psalm 62. The psalmist urges all people to put their trust in God, not riches or prestige. He is a never-failing source of strength and power.

Psalm 63. In "a dry and thirsty land" (v. 1), David longs for God's presence rather than water. This psalm may reflect the time when David was hiding in the wilderness from King Saul (1 Sam. 24).

Psalm 64. The psalmist expresses his conviction that God will protect him from his enemies and give them what they deserve.

Psalm 65. A hymn of thanksgiving for God's physical creation (Gen. 1:1–25) and the abundant crops He provides throughout the land.

Psalm 66. An eloquent expression of praise and thanksgiving for the Lord's mighty acts on behalf of His people.

Psalm 67. A call to worship that invites everyone, even the nations beyond Israel, to join in joyous praise of the Lord.

Psalm 68. This psalm is a battle march or victory hymn celebrating Israel's defeat of its enemies under the leadership of God.

Psalm 69. This messianic psalm, with its graphic description of human suffering, portrays the agony of Christ (compare Ps. 69:9 with John 2:17 and Ps. 69:21 with Matt. 27:34, 48).

Psalm 70. An urgent prayer for God's speedy deliverance. This psalm closely parallels Psalm 40:13–17.

Psalm 71. The psalmist thanks God for walking with him since his youth. He expresses confidence in the Lord's continuing presence in his senior years.

Psalm 72. A messianic psalm that looks toward the time when God will rule with righteousness throughout the world.

Psalm 73. Although the ungodly seem to be winning at the present time, they will eventually be judged and punished by the Lord. The righteous will be rewarded for their faithfulness.

Psalm 74. A plea for God to punish the enemies of Israel who destroyed the temple in Jerusalem (2 Kings 25:1–12). This psalm was probably written during Israel's period of exile in Babylon.

Psalm 75. A hymn of warning to the wicked. God is portrayed as the righteous judge.

Psalm 76. A hymn of victory celebrating God's deliverance of Israel from its enemies.

Psalm 77. A historical psalm that reviews

Psalm 82. This psalm is directed to rulers or leaders. God will judge those who use their authority to oppress and cheat others (Isa. 28).

Psalm 83. The psalmist calls on God to exercise His sovereignty and defend His people against their enemies.

Psalm 84. A hymn sung by worshipers as they approached God's temple: "My soul longeth, yea, even fainteth for the courts of the LORD" (v. 2).

Psalm 85. An optimistic psalm that looks to the future under God's leadership.

Psalm 86. Out of a deep sense of spiritual need ("O LORD, hear me: for I am poor and needy," v. 1), the psalmist pleads for God's mercy and forgiveness.

the Lord's wondrous acts on behalf of His people.

Psalm 78. Looking back on Israel's history, this psalm warns future generations to remain loyal to God and His commands.

Psalm 79. This psalm describes a time of national disaster, perhaps the destruction of Jerusalem and the temple by the Babylonians (2 Kings 25:1–12). The psalmist calls on God to deliver Israel from its shame and humiliation.

Psalm 80. Israel was once like a healthy vine (vv. 8–11; see Isa. 5:1–7), but now it has been cut down and defeated. The psalmist asks the Lord to restore the nation to its former glory.

Psalm 81. The psalmist paints a graphic contrast between God's faithfulness and the waywardness of Israel.

Psalm 82. Assyrian soldiers. Psalm 82 vows judgment on those who oppress others. Assyria, known for its vicious treatment of conquered people, was overrun by Babylonian invaders in 612 B.C.

Psalm 87. A short psalm on the glories of Jerusalem, referred to as Zion (v. 2).

Psalm 88. This is perhaps the most desperate of all the psalms, prayed by a person who was seriously ill. But the Lord did not seem to hear his plea. The tone of this psalm is similar to that of the book of Job.

Psalm 89. This psalm refers to the everlasting covenant that God made with David (2 Sam. 7:1–17). But tragic events since that time make the psalmist wonder if God has given up on Israel.

Psalm 90. This is the only psalm in the book of Psalms attributed to Moses. He contrasts the eternity of God with the brief human life span.

Psalm 91. This is one of the most beloved of the psalms. God is a refuge and fortress for the believer: "He that dwelleth in the secret place of the most High shall abide under the shadow of the Almighty" (v. 1).

Psalm 92. A majestic hymn of praise and thanksgiving for God's goodness to His people.

Psalm 93. A short psalm that celebrates God's reign over the world in glory and majesty.

Psalm 94. The Lord is a God of justice. He will ultimately judge the wicked and reward those who follow His law.

Psalm 95. A call to worship: "O come, let us sing unto the LORD: let us make a joyful noise to the rock of our salvation" (v. 1).

Psalm 96. The psalmist calls on all the earth to sing praises to God. This psalm is one of the greatest affirmations in the Bible of the believer's missionary witness.

Psalm 97. The Lord is to be praised because He is superior to all other gods.

Psalm 98. The Lord is to be praised with music and song because of His salvation and righteousness.

Psalm 99. The Lord is to be praised because He is a holy God who has remained faithful to His people.

Psalm 100. A short psalm of praise to God because "the LORD is good; his mercy is everlasting; and his truth endureth to all generations" (v. 5).

Psalm 101. The psalmist pledges to remain faithful to God and not to associate with evil and ungodly people.

Psalm 102. In anguish and affliction, the psalmist pours out his heart to God. He prays that the Lord will have mercy on Jerusalem, or Zion. This psalm may have been written during Israel's period of exile under the Babylonians.

Psalm 103. This is a psalm of overflowing gratitude to God for His goodness, mercy, and love: "Bless the LORD, O my soul: and all that is within me, bless his holy name" (v. 1).

Psalm 104. The psalmist marvels at the display of God's glory in the universe that He has created (Ps. 8).

Psalm 105. This psalm reviews God's mighty acts on behalf of His people Israel, especially His dealings with Abraham and His miracles during the Exodus.

Psalm 106. This psalm also reviews the history of Israel's relationship with God, but it emphasizes the sin and disobedience of the people.

Psalm 107. People in many different situations experience anguish and suffering, but God is the great comforter of all who walk in His ways.

Psalm 108. A psalm of praise to the Lord, who has formed Israel into His own people. This psalm is made up of verses from Psalm 57:7–11 and Psalm 60:5–12.

Psalm 109. The psalmist describes his distress because of persecution by his enemies. He asks God to take up his case against them.

Psalm 110. This messianic psalm looks toward

[110] GOD GIVES THE VICTORY. *Sit thou at my [God's] right hand, until I make thine enemies thy footstool* (Ps. 110:1).

A footstool was a piece of furniture, similar to a modern ottoman, on which a person rested his or her feet while in a reclining or resting position. To treat one's enemies as a footstool was to defeat them and bring them into total subjection. Thus, God assured the psalmist that he would be victorious over his enemies if he trusted in the Lord.

This passage has been interpreted as a reference to the Messiah. Following His victory over death and the grave, Jesus is now seated at God's right hand as our Savior and Mediator (Acts 2:32–35; 1 Cor. 15:27).

the reign of the coming Messiah, who will be exalted as "a priest for ever after the order of Melchizedek" (v. 4; see Heb. 5:6).

Psalm 111. The psalmist praises the Lord for His goodness and His gracious deeds. He reminds the people that "the fear of the LORD is the beginning of wisdom" (v. 10).

Psalm 112. The person who respects and follows the Lord will be safe and secure, having nothing to fear from the forces of evil.

Psalm 113. A psalm of praise to God because He lifts up the poor and showers them with mercy.

Psalm 114. The psalmist praises the Lord because of His deliverance of Israel from slavery in Egypt during the Exodus (Exod. 12:31–42).

Psalm 115. This psalm describes the futility of trusting in false gods and the wisdom of trusting in the Lord.

Psalm 116. Delivered from the snares of death, the psalmist vows to serve God and to present sacrifices and offerings before Him in the temple.

Psalm 117. A two-verse psalm of praise—the shortest of all the psalms.

Psalm 118. A messianic psalm. Jesus quoted this psalm to show that He had been

Psalm 125. "As the mountains are round about Jerusalem, so the LORD is round about his people from henceforth even for ever" (v. 2).

rejected by His own people: "The stone which the builders refused is become the head stone of the corner" (v. 22; see Matt. 21:42).

Psalm 119. This psalm on the written Word or law of God is the longest of the psalms and the longest chapter in the entire Bible. It is divided into twenty-two sections of eight verses each, with each section identified by a different letter of the Hebrew alphabet. The eight verses in each section begin with their respective Hebrew letter.

Psalm 120. The psalmist prays for deliverance from lies and slanderous words that are being uttered against him by his enemies.

Psalm 121. Pilgrims traveling to the temple at Jerusalem for worship may have sung this prayer for safety along the way.

Psalm 122. A prayer for the peace and prosperity of the city of Jerusalem.

Psalm 123. A short psalm imploring the Lord's mercy.

Psalm 124. The psalmist admits that Israel would not have been victorious over its enemies without the Lord's help.

Psalm 125. Just as the hills and mountains surround Jerusalem, God places His love and mercy around His people.

Psalm 126. This psalm is associated with the return of Jewish exiles to their homeland following the exile in Babylon (2 Chron. 36:22–23). The people are overwhelmed with joy.

Psalm 127. A psalm that celebrates family life, particularly the joys of children.

Psalm 128. This psalm may have been recited as a blessing on the groom at a wedding: "Thy wife shall be as a fruitful vine by the sides of thine house: thy children like olive plants round about thy table" (v. 3).

Psalm 129. This psalm celebrates the victories of the Israelites over their enemies.

Psalm 130. The psalmist waits patiently and expectantly before the Lord as he pleads for mercy and forgiveness.

Psalm 131. A brief prayer of quiet and humble trust in the Lord's goodness.

Psalm 132. This messianic psalm rejoices in God's promise to David of an eternal kingship (2 Sam. 7:1–17).

Psalm 133. A brief psalm celebrating unity and brotherly love.

Psalm 134. The psalmist encourages the priests and Levites who are on watch duty in the temple at night.

Psalm 135. God's mighty acts in history display His greatness and show that He is superior to all pagan gods.

Psalm 136. This psalm was probably a responsive hymn sung in the temple. As the choir or priests recited the main part of the hymn, the people responded, "His mercy endureth for ever."

Psalm 137. This psalm from the exile in Babylon shows how the Israelites missed their homeland: "By the rivers of Babylon...we wept, when we remembered Zion" (v. 1).

Psalm 138. A prayer of thanksgiving for God's kindness, truth, and mercy.

Psalm 139. The psalmist celebrates God's unlimited knowledge and universal presence. There is nothing God doesn't know—even the psalmist's unexpressed thoughts (v. 2).

Psalm 140. Dangerous people are threatening the life of the psalmist, and he prays for God's protection.

Psalm 141. The psalmist prays that he will not use the same tactics against his enemies that they are using against him—and thus fall into sin.

Psalm 142. A prayer of David for protection when he was hiding in a cave from King Saul (1 Sam. 22:1–5).

Psalm 143. A plaintive cry for God's guidance and direction: "Teach me to do thy will" (v. 10).

[150] **PRAISE WITH CYMBALS.** *Praise him [God] upon the loud cymbals; praise him upon the high sounding cymbals* (Ps. 150:5).

The cymbals of Bible times were similar to our modern cymbals. Two circular plates of brass were struck against each other to produce a clanging or ringing sound.

Two different types of cymbals are apparently mentioned in this verse. "Loud" cymbals were probably similar to the large metal plates used in modern marching bands. The "high sounding" cymbals may have been similar to our modern castanets. Worn on the fingers of both hands, these were struck together rapidly to produce a distinctive rattling or rhythmic sound.

Psalm 144. A battle song asking for victory under the leadership of the Lord. The army of Israel may have sung or chanted psalms like this as it went into battle.

Psalm 145. A psalm of pure praise to God for His wondrous works: "Great is the LORD, and greatly to be praised; and his greatness is unsearchable" (v. 3).

Psalm 146. The psalmist celebrates God's universal reign and calls on people to place their trust in Him.

Psalm 147. A hymn of praise focusing on God as protector of His people Israel and as Creator of the universe.

Psalm 148. A hymn of universal praise. Let everything praise God: angels, sun and moon, heavens, waters, mountains, animals, kings, men, women, and children.

Psalm 149. The psalmist exhorts all the people of Israel to praise the Lord, their faithful and mighty King.

Psalm 150. The book of Psalms ends with a ringing affirmation of praise to God: "Let every thing that hath breath praise the LORD" (v. 6).

PROVERBS

OVERVIEW: Wise sayings and observations on life designed to motivate believers to walk in the way of wisdom.

Introduction to Proverbs

The book of Proverbs is one of three books in the Old Testament classified as wisdom literature. The other two are Job and Ecclesiastes. They are known as books of wisdom because they deal with philosophical issues such as the meaning of life and behavior that leads to happiness and contentment in daily living.

Proverbs is the most practical of these three books. It contains wise sayings on how to live in harmony with God as well as other people. The underlying theme of Proverbs is that true wisdom consists of showing respect for God and living in harmony with His commands.

The very first verse of Proverbs identifies its author as "Solomon the son of David, king of Israel" (1:1). Even among other nations beyond Israel, Solomon was noted for his great wisdom (1 Kings 4:29–34). So he certainly had good qualifications for writing this book.

But some chapters within the book are attributed to other writers, including Agur (30:1) and King Lemuel (31:1). Solomon probably wrote the basic core of Proverbs but added some writings from other sources and gave proper credit to their writers.

The book of Proverbs is the most practical, down-to-earth book in the Old Testament. It reads like a manual of instructions for daily living, even using occasional humor to make an important point: "Even a fool, when he holdeth his peace, is counted wise: and he that shutteth his lips is esteemed a man of understanding" (17:28).

In this realistic book you will find advice on the importance of home and family, dealing with pride, getting along with others, the perils of adultery, getting ahead through hard work, the dangers of strong drink, treating the poor with kindness and compassion, and dealing honestly and forthrightly with others in business relationships.

Summary of Proverbs

1:1–7. This brief introduction to the book of Proverbs states its purpose: to give instruction in wisdom.

1:8–33. The phrase "my son" (v. 8) is repeated often throughout Proverbs. The authors of Proverbs are imparting good advice and practical rules for living, as a father might do with his son. Those who heed the counsel of wisdom will not fall into evil.

2:1–22. The Lord is the true source of wisdom. Those who seek Him will avoid the pitfalls of sin and will not be enticed into adulterous relationships.

3:1–12. It is best to trust God for insight and direction and not to depend on human understanding: "In all thy ways acknowledge him, and he shall direct thy paths" (v. 6).

3:13–26. Happy is the person who finds

1:1–7. King Solomon, depicted here with the queen of Sheba, was famous for his wisdom. He probably wrote most of Proverbs. Scripture says Solomon composed 3,000 proverbs and 1,005 songs (1 Kings 4:32).

wisdom and understanding. He will have nothing to fear, since his confidence is in the Lord.

3:27–35. Treat your neighbors with kindness. Do not envy or copy the ways of the wicked.

4:1–27. Avoid evil and the company of those who commit evil deeds. Follow the straight and narrow path of righteousness. Do not criticize others or speak idle words.

5:1–23. Marriage is sacred in the eyes of the Lord. Stay away from extramarital affairs, and cultivate your relationship with your spouse.

6:1–5. Do not enter into contracts carelessly or make foolish promises to others.

6:6–15. Idleness and laziness lead to poverty. Follow the example of the ant; it works diligently without having to be hounded by a supervisor!

[6:6–15] FROM NAUGHTY TO WORTHLESS. *A naughty person [scoundrel, NIV], a wicked man, walketh with a froward [corrupt, NIV] mouth* (Prov. 6:12).

The word translated as "naughty person" or "scoundrel" in this verse literally means "son of Belial." In the Hebrew language, *Belial* means "worthless" or "useless." Thus, one mark of a worthless person is the evil or corrupt speech that comes from his or her mouth.

People in the Bible who were called "worthless" or "son of Belial" include the evil sons of Eli the priest (1 Sam. 2:12), those who supported Jeroboam's rebellion against the southern tribes of Israel (2 Chron. 13:7), and those who gave false testimony against Naboth at the urging of Jezebel (1 Kings 21:11–13).

6:16–19. A list of seven things that the Lord hates: pride, lying, murder, wickedness, the spreading of gossip, the bearing of false witness, and the stirring up of trouble among people.

6:20–35. A second exhortation to avoid adulterous relationships (Prov. 5).

7:1–27. A third exhortation to avoid adulterous relationships (Prov. 5; 6:20–35).

8:1–36. In this hymn of praise, wisdom is exalted as something that is more valuable than gold and silver or precious stones. Wisdom was present with God when He created the world. This is another way of saying that God is the author of all wisdom.

9:1–18. Both foolishness and wisdom are personified as women. They illustrate the two different approaches to life.

10:1–32. These proverbs draw a contrast between the wise/righteous/godly and the foolish/unrighteous/wicked: "The mouth of a righteous man is a well of life: but violence covereth the mouth of the wicked" (v. 11).

11:1–31. The contrast between the wise and the foolish continues: "He that trusteth in his riches shall fall: but the righteous shall flourish as a branch" (v. 28).

12:1–28. The contrast between the wise and the foolish continues: "Lying lips are abomination to the LORD: but they that deal truly are his delight" (v. 22; see Rev. 22:15).

13:1–25. The contrast between the wise and foolish continues: "Every prudent man dealeth with knowledge: but a fool layeth open his folly" (v. 16).

14:1–35. The contrast between the wise and the foolish continues. But some of these proverbs have a touch of humor: "The poor is hated even of his own neighbour: but the rich hath many friends" (v. 20).

15:1–33. The contrast between the wise and the foolish continues: "The thoughts of the wicked are an abomination to the LORD: but the words of the pure are pleasant words" (v. 26; see Ps. 37:30).

16:1–33. These proverbs give moral and ethical advice on various subjects: "Pride goeth

[17:1–28] **KEEP THE GATE LOW.** *He that exalteth his gate [builds a high gate, NIV] seeketh destruction* (Prov. 17:19).

The typical house of Bible times consisted of four to six rooms built around a central courtyard. This courtyard was similar to a modern hallway. First you entered the courtyard through the front door, or gateway. Then you used the courtyard to gain access to all the rooms in the house.

The gateway into a house was normally only about four feet high. These low entrances may have been designed to keep thieves from riding horses into the courtyard. Thus, the writer of Proverbs states that anyone who built his gate high was asking for trouble. This was a symbolic way of saying that pride or self-exaltation also leads to destruction.

23:1–35. More proverbs with moral and ethical advice: "Let not thine heart envy sinners: but be thou in the fear of the Lord all the day long" (v. 17; see Ps. 37:1).

24:1–34. More proverbs with moral and ethical advice: "Be not a witness against thy neighbour without cause; and deceive not with thy lips" (v. 28; see Eph. 4:25).

25:1–28. More proverbs with moral and ethical advice: "Confidence in an unfaithful man in time of trouble is like a broken tooth, and a foot out of joint" (v. 19; see Job 6:15).

26:1–28. More proverbs with moral and ethical advice: "Answer not a fool according to his folly, lest thou also be like unto him" (v. 4).

before destruction, and an haughty spirit before a fall" (v. 18; see Jer. 49:16).

17:1–28. More proverbs with moral and ethical advice: "A reproof entereth more into a wise man than an hundred stripes into a fool" (v. 10).

18:1–24. More proverbs with moral and ethical advice: "Death and life are in the power of the tongue: and they that love it shall eat the fruit thereof" (v. 21; see Matt. 12:37).

19:1–29. More proverbs with moral and ethical advice: "House and riches are the inheritance of fathers: and a prudent wife is from the Lord" (v. 14).

20:1–30. More proverbs with moral and ethical advice: "Bread of deceit is sweet to a man; but afterwards his mouth shall be filled with gravel" (v. 17).

21:1–31. More proverbs with moral and ethical advice: "The horse is prepared against the day of battle: but safety is of the Lord" (v. 31).

22:1–29. More proverbs with moral and ethical advice: "Train up a child in the way he should go: and when he is old, he will not depart from it" (v. 6; see Eph. 6:4).

[25:1–28] **BEAUTIFUL WORDS.** *A word fitly [aptly, NIV] spoken is like apples of gold in pictures [settings, NIV] of silver* (Prov. 25:11).

This verse refers to the beautiful metal engravings that were displayed in the homes of kings and the wealthy in Bible times. "Apples of gold" were probably carvings of apples that were made from gold or painted to look like gold. These were placed in a highly polished silver frame to give the entire work of art an ornate appearance.

The point of this proverb is that an appropriate word spoken at just the right time is a thing of beauty. Or to put it another way, "A wholesome tongue is a tree of life" (Prov. 15:4).

27:1–27. More proverbs with moral and ethical advice: "Let another man praise thee, and not thine own mouth; a stranger, and not thine own lips" (v. 2).

28:1–28. More proverbs with moral and ethical advice: "He that covereth his sins shall not prosper: but whoso confesseth and forsaketh them shall have mercy" (v. 13; see Job 31:33).

31:10–31. A woman in Iran spins yarn by hand, like the Proverbs 31 woman: "she layeth her hands to the spindle, and her hands hold the distaff" (v. 19).

31:1–9. People in positions of authority should avoid strong drink, lest it impair their judgment. They also have the responsibility to treat the poor and helpless with fairness and compassion.

31:10–31. The book of Proverbs ends with words of praise for a wife of noble character. She works hard to take care of her household, and she performs acts of kindness in her community. A wife like this is a priceless asset to her family: "Her price is far above rubies" (v. 10).

29:1–27. More proverbs with moral and ethical advice: "The fear of man bringeth a snare: but whoso putteth his trust in the Lord shall be safe" (v. 25).

30:1–9. God has infinite wisdom. Consider His wonderful works. By comparison, humans are weak and foolish.

30:10–33. The natural order reveals the wisdom and power of God. Humans are awestruck by many things in nature that they cannot understand (Ps. 104).

[30:10–33] CHURNING UP ANGER. *The churning of milk bringeth forth butter…so the forcing of wrath [stirring up anger, niv] bringeth forth strife (Prov. 30:33).*

In Bible times butter was produced by placing milk in a bag made from an animal skin and shaking it vigorously back and forth until the butter fat separated from the milk.

This proverb has a "just as" construction. Just as surely as shaking milk produces butter, giving vent to one's anger will cause strife and trouble. The phrase "stirring up anger" suggests that a person can feed his or her anger until it becomes uncontrollable.

OVERVIEW: A philosophical essay on the futility and emptiness of life apart from God.

Introduction to Ecclesiastes

The book of Ecclesiastes takes its title from the Greek word *ekklesiastes*, meaning "assembly" or "congregation." The author of the book identifies himself as "the Preacher" (1:1), or one who assembles a congregation.

This author reveals the theme of Ecclesiastes in the second verse of his book: "Vanity of vanities; all is vanity" (1:2). He wants us to understand what he has learned through his own experience—that all human achievements are empty and unfulfilling when pursued as ends in themselves.

He repeats this phrase throughout the book, showing how wisdom, hard work, wealth, learning, fame, and pleasure—in and of themselves—do not bring happiness. Life's highest good, he delares at the conclusion of the book, is to "fear God, and keep his commandments" (12:13).

This preacher of the-things-in-life-that-really-matter further identifies himself as "the son of David, king in Jerusalem" (1:1). This must have been Solomon, the king who was noted for his superior wisdom and great riches (1 Kings 4:29–34; 10:14–23). He probably wrote Ecclesiastes near the end of his life as he looked back and measured the meaning of all his achievements.

This book shows that earthly possessions, popularity, and great accomplishments do not bring lasting happiness. True joy is a result of serving God and following His will for our lives.

Summary of Ecclesiastes

1:1–11. The author of the book identifies himself as the Preacher (probably Solomon). He observes that life is vain and meaningless, and it seems to go around and around in an endless circle.

1:12–18. Even the accumulation of much learning and wisdom does not give meaning and purpose to life.

2:1–3. The pursuit of fun and pleasure fails to satisfy (Prov. 14:13).

2:4–11. Great wealth and accomplishments in themselves are empty and meaningless.

2:12–23. Both the wise man and the foolish man are destined to die—and neither of them knows what will happen after they are gone. Man's brief life on earth is filled with pain and sorrow (Job 14:1–2; James 4:13–14).

2:24–26. Perhaps the most sensible thing a person can do while on earth is to enjoy life's simple pleasures and take pride in his work.

3:1–8. There is an appropriate time for everything in life: "a time to keep silence, and a time to speak" (v. 7).

3:9–15. God's gift to man is his ability to take pleasure in the daily routine and to enjoy his work.

3:16–22. God judges the righteous and the

9:1–10. For much of Ecclesiastes, Solomon seems to take the attitude "Life is hard, and then you die." So he urges the living to "eat thy bread with joy, and drink thy wine with a merry heart" (v. 7).

wicked. Eventually all life turns to dust, the substance from which man was originally created (Gen. 2:7).

4:1–16. The vanity of life is multiplied by man's idleness, envy, and greed.

5:1–7. Do not make a vow to God unless you intend to keep your promise and follow through on your commitment (Gen. 28:20–22).

5:8–20. A rich person doesn't sleep as soundly as a working man. The man of means is always worrying about what might happen to his possessions.

6:1–12. Another problem with wealth is that rich people are never satisfied with what they have. The more possessions they acquire, they more they want. Thus, they are ruled by their desires (Luke 18:18–30).

7:1–22. These verses consist of miscellaneous proverbs on many different subjects. They are similar to the sayings in the book of Proverbs.

7:23–29. While wisdom does not bring meaning to life, acting wisely is preferable to acting foolishly.

8:1–5. Wise people respect the king and bow to his authority (Dan. 4:35).

8:6–17. Solomon complains that life is not fair. Sometimes the righteous suffer while the wicked flourish and prosper.

9:1–10. Solomon laments the plight of those who have died. They are soon forgotten by the living. He exhorts the living to enjoy their brief days on earth.

9:11–18. Wisdom is better than brute strength and the weapons of war.

10:1–20. Miscellaneous proverbs on various subjects, particularly careless speech: "The

> **[9:1–10] DRESSED IN WHITE.** *Let thy garments be always white* (Eccles. 9:8).
>
> In the hot climate of Palestine, white was a sensible color for clothes. So it was only natural for Solomon, the author of Ecclesiastes, to express this wish for others.
>
> The wearing of white clothes was also a symbol of purity and holiness—a characteristic of God and those who follow His commands. When Daniel saw God in a vision, He was dressed in white clothes (Dan. 7:9). In the end time, the redeemed are also to be "arrayed in white robes" (Rev. 7:13).

words of a wise man's mouth are gracious; but the lips of a fool will swallow up himself" (v. 12).

11:1–6. Solomon's advice in these verses is twofold: Don't put all your eggs in one basket ("Give a portion to seven, and also to eight," v. 2), and have a backup strategy in case your original plan does not work out ("Thou knowest not whether [it] shall prosper," v. 6).

11:7–12:7. Old age, with the inevitable loss of physical strength, arrives sooner than one expects. In their youthful years, people should enjoy life and honor their Creator.

12:8–14. Solomon concludes his search for meaning in life with this ringing affirmation: "Fear God, and keep his commandments: for this is the whole duty of man" (v. 13).

SONG OF SOLOMON

OVERVIEW: A love song celebrating human love relationships and God's love for His people.

Introduction to the Song of Solomon

This book is also called the "Song of Songs" because the author, Solomon, claimed it was his favorite or the most important among all the songs he wrote (1:1). This is significant, because Solomon is reported to have written 1,005 songs (1 Kings 4:32).

Perhaps this was Solomon's favorite song because it describes his love for a young woman who is referred to as a "Shulamite" (6:13). This wealthy king had hundreds of wives and concubines in his harem (1 Kings 11:3). But many of his marriages were political arrangements to seal treaties with other nations.

Is it possible that Solomon's marriage to the Shulamite—a peasant vineyard keeper whose skin had been darkened by long exposure to the sun—was the only meaningful and intimate marriage relationship he ever experienced?

Many people are shocked by the frank language of physical attraction between a husband and wife that appears in the Song of Solomon (7:1–9). But the physical side of marriage is a beautiful part of God's plan. God created man and woman for each other and declared, "Therefore shall a man leave his father and his mother, and shall cleave unto his wife: and they shall be one flesh" (Gen. 2:24).

Like the book of Genesis, the Song of Solomon says a bold yes to the sanctity of marriage and the physical side of the husband-wife relationship.

Summary of the Song of Solomon

1:1. Introduction to Solomon's Song.

1:2–7. The bride expresses her love for her groom. She is dissatisfied with her appearance, since she is a girl from the country whose skin has been darkened by the sun (vv. 5–6).

> **[1:2–7] A MIDDAY REST.** *Tell me, O thou whom my soul loveth, where thou feedest, where thou makest thy flock to rest at noon* (Song 1:7).
>
> These are the words of King Solomon's bride as she searched for her beloved, the king. She referred to a common practice in Bible times of shepherds protecting their sheep by having them rest at midday in order to avoid the oppressive heat.
>
> David may have referred to this practice when he compared God to a watchful shepherd: "The LORD is my shepherd; I shall not want. He maketh me to lie down in green pastures" (Ps. 23:1–2).

1:8–11. The groom reassures his bride that he is pleased with how she looks: "Thy cheeks are comely with rows of jewels" (v. 10).

1:12–17. Both bride and groom continue to express their affection for each other.

2:1–17. The setting for these verses is springtime in the country (vv. 11–13). The couple

3–11. A newly married Jewish couple kisses. Solomon's "song of songs" celebrates the devotion between a married man and woman. Some scholars musicians may have performed the song at the king's wedding.

as pillars of marble, set upon sockets of fine gold" (v. 15).

6:1–3. In answer to the question "Whither is thy beloved gone?" (v. 1), the bride says he is with her, referring to herself as "his garden" (v. 2).

6:4–13. The groom describes the beauty of his one true love. All the queens and concubines in a king's harem do not compare to her.

7:1–13. The bride and groom express their mutual love and devotion to each other. They take great delight in the time they spend together.

8:1–14. The Song of Solomon ends with the bride and groom united in their mutual love for each other. The writer declares that true love is eternal: "Many waters cannot quench love, neither can the floods drown it" (v. 7).

express their joy that they are committed in love to each other: "My beloved is mine, and I am his" (v. 16).

3:1–6. The bride dreams about her groom and expresses sorrow over their separation.

3:7–11. The groom, symbolized by King Solomon in a royal procession, arrives for the wedding ceremony.

4:1–16. The groom expresses great delight in the beauty of his bride.

5:1–8. The bride has another dream that she is separated from her groom. She asks other people to join her frantic search for him.

5:9–16. The bride takes great pleasure in the appearance of her groom: "His legs are

[3:7–11] SOLOMON'S PORTABLE CHAIR. *King Solomon made himself a chariot of the wood of Lebanon. He made the pillars [posts, NIV] thereof of silver, the bottom thereof of gold, the covering of it of purple* (Song 3:9–10).

The Hebrew word translated as "chariot" in this passage actually refers to a palanquin—a portable couch or chair in which kings were carried from place to place by royal servants. Poles were fastened to each side of the palanquin. Four servants would then hoist the king in his chair and place the poles on their shoulders.

Solomon's gold and silver palanquin had a purple awning or cover to protect him from the sun. Purple was the color that signified royalty.

CHAPTER 4
BOOKS OF THE MAJOR PROPHETS

The last seventeen books of the Old Testament are classified as books of prophecy. Five of these books—Isaiah, Jeremiah, Lamentations, Ezekiel, and Daniel—are known as major prophets, while the remaining twelve are called minor prophets.

These terms do not mean that some of these books are more important than others. Rather, as the Old Testament was compiled, the longer—or major—books were placed first in the prophetic section, while the shorter—or minor—books were placed second. The exception is Lamentations, a short book of only five chapters. This book was placed after Jeremiah because the prophet Jeremiah wrote Lamentations.

The word *prophet* comes from two Greek words that mean "to speak for." The prophets of the Old Testament received God's message by direct revelation and passed it on to others in written or spoken form. They literally spoke for God and prevailed upon His people to remain obedient and loyal to Him.

ISAIAH

OVERVIEW: God will punish His people for their rebellion, but He also promises to send the Messiah, who will save them from their sins.

Introduction to Isaiah

The book of Isaiah is the best-known prophetic book of the Old Testament, probably because of its emphasis on the theme of salvation and its prophecies about the coming Messiah. Because of its anticipation of the coming of Jesus Christ and His message of redemption, Isaiah is sometimes called the fifth Gospel.

Isaiah was called to the prophetic ministry "in the year that king Uzziah died" (6:1; about 740 B.C.) in a dramatic vision of the Lord in the temple. He preached God's message of judgment and hope to the people of the Southern Kingdom (Judah) for the next forty years.

In the early part of Isaiah's ministry, Judah's sister nation, the Northern Kingdom (Israel) fell to the Assyrians because of its sin and rebellion against God (2 Kings 17:5–23). Isaiah

The famed Dead Sea caves where sacred Jewish writings were found in the late 1940s. Isaiah's prophecy was among the preserved scrolls, dating much earlier than previous copies.

declared to Judah that the same thing would happen to it unless the people quit worshiping false gods and followed the one true God.

But the prophet's message of God's coming judgment was intermingled with prophecies of hope for the future. These positive prophecies are those for which Isaiah is best known.

About 700 years before Jesus was born, Isaiah foretold His coming. As a spiritual ruler who would bring redemption for His people, He would establish a spiritual kingdom that would be a counterpart to the physical kingdom established by King David. These are the titles by which He would be known: "Wonderful, Counseller, The mighty God, The everlasting Father, The Prince of Peace" (9:6).

The book of Isaiah is also known for its Servant Songs (42:1–25; 49:1–55:13). The nations of Judah and Israel failed to follow God's commission to act as His servant. So this commission would be passed on to the coming Messiah.

When Jesus launched His public ministry, He quoted from these Servant Songs to show that this prophecy was being fulfilled in His life and ministry. His mission was "to preach the gospel to the poor...to set at liberty them that are bruised, to preach the acceptable year of the Lord" (Luke 4:18–19, quoting Isa. 61:1–2).

Summary of Isaiah

1:1–31. Isaiah compares the sins of idolatry in the nation of Judah to the evils committed by the cities of Sodom and Gomorrah. Judah must repent and turn back to God or suffer the Lord's punishment.

2:1–4:6. In the future, Jerusalem will become the city of God and a safe haven for all people of the earth (2:1–5). But before that happens, God will judge His people severely because of their pride, rebellion, and evil deeds (2:6–4:6).

[1:1–31] BAD NEWS FOR JERUSALEM. *The daughter of Zion is left as a cottage [shelter, NIV] in a vineyard, as a lodge [hut, NIV] in a garden of cucumbers [melons, NIV] (Isa. 1:8).*

Farmers of Bible times had to keep a close watch on their crops to protect them from animals and thieves. They would build crude huts from tree branches in the fields to provide shelter for those who watched the crops. After the harvest these huts would soon fall and rot.

Isaiah compared Jerusalem, referred to in this passage as "the daughter of Zion," to one of these abandoned and useless shelters. He declared that the city would fall to an enemy and become utterly desolate unless the people turned from their worship of false gods and renewed their commitment to the Lord.

5:1–7. These verses are known as Isaiah's "song of the vineyard." He compares the nation of Judah to a vineyard that God has preserved and cultivated. But the people have produced nothing but bitter, useless grapes. Jesus also used this imagery of the vineyard for the Jewish people (Matt. 21:33–41).

5:8–30. Because of Judah's sins of idolatry, injustice, and rebellion, God will raise up an enemy nation to carry His people into captivity: "They shall roar, and lay hold of the prey, and shall carry it away safe, and none shall deliver it" (v. 29).

6:1–13. Isaiah is called to the prophetic ministry in a dramatic encounter with the awe-inspiring Lord in the temple.

7:1–25. Through the prophet Isaiah, God warns King Ahaz of Judah not to form an alliance with the Assyrians against other enemy nations. Assyria will eventually become an instrument of judgment in God's hands against His people.

8:1–22. Isaiah names his newborn son Maher-shalal-hash-baz, meaning "fast plunder."

This signifies that the nations that oppose Assyria will fall quickly, leaving other nations an easy target for the mighty Assyrian army.

9:1–7. Although dark days are just ahead for God's people, He will eventually restore them by sending the Messiah, the Prince of Peace. As the leader of a spiritual kingdom, He will become the heir to the "throne of David" (v. 7; see 2 Sam. 7:1–17).

9:8–10:34. Israel (Northern Kingdom), with Samaria as its capital, will be overrun by the Assyrians. The people will be carried away as captives, but the Lord will preserve a remnant of His people who remain faithful to Him.

11:1–12:6. The coming messianic King will rule with righteousness and perfect justice. Although He will spring from the lineage of David as "a root of Jesse" (11:10), He will be sought by the Gentiles and all nations of the earth.

13:1–14:23. Just as God's people will be judged for their sins, His judgment will also fall on the Babylonians. They will be defeated by the Medes and the Persians (13:17).

14:24–27. The nation of Assyria is also destined to feel God's wrath.

14:28–32. The remnants of the Philistines who still live among the Jewish people will be judged by the Lord.

15:1–16:14. Isaiah delivers God's message of judgment against the Moabites, ancient enemies of His people.

[15:1–16:14] NO SINGING AT WORK. *Gladness is taken away, and joy out of the plentiful field; and in the vineyards there shall be no singing* (Isa. 16:10).

The people of Bible times sang while working in the fields to escape from the monotony of farmwork. Isaiah declared that the singing and gladness of the Moabites would be taken away when God judged them for their idolatry.

17:1–14. The nation of Syria, with its capital at Damascus, will be punished by the Lord for its idolatry and pride.

18:1–7. God's punishment will also fall upon the Ethiopians.

19:1–25. The proud Egyptians will tremble in fear before the terrible punishment of the Lord.

20:1–6. At God's command Isaiah walks around without his outer robe to show that Assyria will strip the Egyptians and the Ethiopians of their possessions and take them away as captives.

21:1–17. No nation will escape the marauding Assyrian army—not Babylonia (vv. 1–10), Edom ("Dumah," vv. 11–12), or the tribes of Arabia (vv. 13–17).

22:1–25. In the midst of these prophecies of judgment against foreign nations, Isaiah declares that the city of Jerusalem, Judah's capital, is also destined for destruction. This prophecy was fulfilled about 135 years after Isaiah's time when the Babylonians overran the nation of Judah (2 Kings 25:1–12).

23:1–18. Isaiah pronounces God's judgment against Tyre, a flourishing seaport and trade center north of Judah.

24:1–23. This chapter summarizes the impact of God's judgment against Israel (Northern Kingdom) and Judah (Southern Kingdom) as well as the foreign nations. The entire earth will be shaken by His judgment against sin.

25:1–27:13. These three chapters are affirmations of hope. Although God will judge and discipline his people, He will not reject them. After they have been exiled among a foreign nation for a time, they will be restored to their homeland (2 Chron. 36:22–23). This brings a song of praise to the lips of God's people: "Trust ye in the Lord for ever: for in the LORD JEHOVAH is everlasting strength" (26:4).

[28:1–29] **METHODS OF THRESHING GRAIN.** *The fitches [caraway, NIV] are not threshed with a threshing instrument, neither is a cart wheel turned about upon the cummin; but the fitches are beaten out with a staff, and the cummin with a rod* (Isa. 28:27).

In this verse Isaiah contrasts two different methods of separating grain from the stalk in Bible times.

Small grains such as caraway and cummin were threshed by beating them with a stick. This method was also used when theshing a small amount of grain (Ruth 2:17). Dragging a stone threshing sledge ("threshing instrument") over the grain was the preferred method for threshing wheat or barley in large quantities.

Isaiah's point is that God knows us, and He knows our needs. He will use whatever method is appropriate as His discipline to keep us focused on Him.

28:1–29. Isaiah condemns both Judah (Southern Kingdom) and Israel (Northern Kingdom) because they have turned away from the Lord to worship false gods. He has harsh words especially for the leaders of these nations who have led the people astray (Jer. 8).

29:1–24. A woe is pronounced against Ariel, or Jerusalem, "the city where David dwelt" (v. 1). God is not impressed with those who flatter Him with words but refuse to obey His commands.

30:1–31:9. Through Isaiah the prophet, the Lord condemns the leaders of Judah who have formed an alliance with Egypt against the Assyrian threat. They should be turning to the Lord instead for protection against their enemies.

32:1–20. Isaiah calls on the people to look for the Messiah, the coming King, who will "reign in righteousness" (v. 1). But before this King arrives, the people must turn from their sinful and complacent ways.

33:1–24. The Lord alone is the hope and salvation of His people: "The LORD is our judge, the LORD is our lawgiver, the LORD is our king; he will save us" (v. 22; see Ps. 77:1–2).

34:1–17. Isaiah returns to the theme of God's judgment against the foreign nations (chaps. 13–23).

35:1–10. This chapter portrays a future time when God will redeem and restore His people. They will return to Jerusalem ("Zion," v. 10) with songs of joy and gladness.

36:1–22. King Sennacherib of Assyria invades Judah and captures several walled cities. He sends word to King Hezekiah of Judah that Assyria will attack with a superior force unless Judah surrenders.

37:1–38. King Hezekiah and the prophet Isaiah pray to the Lord, asking Him to save Judah from the Assyrian threat. God miraculously delivers the nation by destroying 185,000 warriors in Sennacherib's army (2 Kings 18:13–19:37).

[40:1–31] **GET READY FOR THE KING.** *Prepare ye the way of the LORD, make straight in the desert a highway for our God.... The crooked shall be made straight, and the rough places plain* (Isa. 40:3–4).

Roads of Bible times were little more than paths, rough and crude by modern standards. When a king traveled, his servants would go ahead of him, removing stones, filling in low places, and straightening curves so the king's journey would be more pleasant.

Isaiah found in this practice a spiritual principle. The people needed to prepare the way for the coming of the Lord in a new and fresh way—a reference to the future Messiah. In the New Testament, this passage was applied to John the Baptist, who prepared the way for the ministry of Jesus Christ (Luke 3:4–5).

49:1–55:13. Jesus endures beating and whipping before His crucifixion, an ordeal that New Testament writers said fulfilled Isaiah's prophecy of a Suffering Servant: "He was wounded for our transgressions. . .and with his stripes we are healed" (53:5).

38:1–22. King Hezekiah of Judah is seriously ill, and Isaiah tells him he will die. But Hezekiah prays humbly to the Lord, who graciously extends the king's life for fifteen more years (2 Kings 20:1–11).

39:1–8. Hezekiah foolishly shows off his royal riches to a messenger from the king of Babylon. Isaiah predicts that the Babylonians will defeat the nation of Judah and carry off these treasures at some future time (2 Kings 20:12–19).

40:1–31. The prophet Isaiah follows his prediction of disaster for Judah with words of encouragement. The Lord is the great comforter who never stops loving His people. He gives power and strength to those who depend on Him.

41:1–29. In contrast to lifeless idols that are fashioned by human hands, God is the living, awesome Lord who brought all of creation into being (Gen. 1:1–24). He alone is worthy of worship.

42:1–9. This is one of several "Servant" passages or "Servant Songs" in Isaiah (chaps. 49–55). The nations of Judah and Israel have failed to carry out the mission of world redemption that God intended. Therefore, He will accomplish this through one person—His coming Servant, the Messiah, His Son, Jesus Christ.

42:10–16. This redemptive mission of God's Servant is reason for rejoicing: "Give glory unto the Lord, and declare his praise in the islands" (v. 12).

42:17–25. In contrast to the faithfulness of God's Servant, the nations of Judah and

Israel have rejected the Lord and followed their own desires.

43:1–44:5. In spite of the unfaithfulness of His people, God forgives. He will walk with them in their humiliation and suffering.

44:6–20. These are some of the most striking verses in the Bible on the worship of false gods. How foolish it is for a person to worship something he has conceived in his mind and fashioned with his hands (Jer. 10:1–25).

44:21–28. In contrast to lifeless and powerless idols, the one true God is the living and powerful redeemer of His people.

45:1–13. The Lord promises to restore His people to their homeland after a period of exile in Babylonia and Persia. This will be accomplished by the Lord, who will use King Cyrus of Persia as an instrument in His plan (v. 1; see 2 Chron. 36:22–23).

45:14–25. The entire world will eventually turn to God because He alone offers salvation: "Look unto me, and be ye saved, all the ends of the earth: for I am God, and there is none else" (v. 22).

46:1–13. Isaiah reminds the people that the worship of idols is futile, since they are weak and helpless and offer no hope.

47:1–15. The nation of Babylonia will be devastated by the Lord because of its wickedness and pride.

48:1–22. Throughout their history the nations of Judah and Israel have rejected God. But He continues to love them and call them back from their wayward ways.

49:1–55:13. These seven chapters of Isaiah contain more of the prophet's famous "Servant Songs" (Isa. 42:1–9). At times the prophet seems to speak of the nations of Judah and Israel as God's servant. But in other places in these passages, it is clear that he is referring to the Servant who is to come—the

[47:1–15] NO HELP FROM STARGAZERS. *Let now the astrologers, the stargazers, the monthly prognosticators, stand up, and save thee from these things that shall come upon thee* (Isa. 47:13).

The words *astrologers, stargazers,* and *monthly prognosticators* refer to people who studied the stars and the movement of the moon in order to foretell the future. This was especially popular among the ancient Babylonians.

In Babylonia the astrologers were members of a specific caste. Persons born into this caste continued to practice the star-gazing and sign-reading skills inherited from their ancestors. Astrologers were among the people with magical powers summoned by King Nebuchadnezzar of Babylonia to interpret his strange dream (Dan. 2:2).

Isaiah declared that God would judge the people of Judah for their sins, and nothing could thwart His purpose. He—the Creator of the moon and stars—was more powerful than those who read the moon and stars.

Messiah. Chapter 53 is clearly messianic in nature. It portrays the "Suffering Servant"— Jesus Christ—who gave His life to secure redemption for others: "He was wounded for our transgressions, he was bruised for our iniquities: the chastisement of our peace was upon him; and with his stripes we are healed" (v. 5).

56:1–12. God is bringing a new age of salvation for His people. But He expects them to live as people who belong to Him, keeping His laws and practicing justice.

57:1–21. The Lord's people cannot worship the one true God and participate in idol worship at the same time. He demands their exclusive loyalty (Josh. 24:15).

58:1–14. True religion does not consist of observing rituals such as fasting and offering sacrifices. The Lord honors such things as obeying His commands and treating others with justice and fairness (Amos 5:18–27).

59:1–21. The prophet catalogs the wicked and sinful actions that have separated the people of Judah from the Lord: lying, vanity and pride, murder of innocent people, and rebellion against God.

60:1–62:12. In these three chapters, Isaiah gives us a glimpse of the future glory of Jerusalem. God will take delight in His people. They will shine like a beacon of righteousness, drawing all nations of the earth to bow before the Lord. Jesus quoted from Isaiah 61:1–2 when He identified Himself as the Messiah who had been sent by God "to preach good tidings unto the meek...to bind up the brokenhearted, to proclaim liberty to the captives" (v. 1; see Luke 4:18–19).

63:1–64:12. But before these blessings fall upon God's people, He must punish them for their sin and rebellion. This leads Isaiah to offer a

60:1–62:12. Jesus fulfilled another prophecy of Isaiah by preaching "good tidings unto the meek" (61:1).

beautiful prayer that God will uphold and sustain them during their days of trouble and suffering (2 Kings 25:1–12).

65:1–66:24. Isaiah ends his book by drawing a contrast between two different destinies. Total destruction awaits those who continue in their sin and refuse to turn to God. But a life of joy and peace is the destiny of those who follow the Lord.

[60:1–62:12] AN OPEN GATE POLICY. *Therefore thy gates shall be open continually; they shall not be shut day nor night* (Isa. 60:11).

The gates of walled cities (see the note "Walled Cities" on p. 90) were closed and bolted at night as a security measure. Residents of the city who didn't make it back inside before darkness fell were forced to spend the night outside.

Isaiah portrayed a future time under the reign of the Messiah when city gates would never be closed. God would be all the protection the people would need.

JEREMIAH

OVERVIEW: The Lord will use the pagan Babylonians as His instrument of judgment against Judah (Southern Kingdom).

Introduction to Jeremiah

For about forty years, the prophet Isaiah had tried to turn the Southern Kingdom (Judah) from its sinful ways (see the introduction to Isaiah on p. 135). About seventy-five years after Isaiah died, God raised up another spokesman, the prophet Jeremiah, to continue delivering His message to His people. Like Isaiah, Jeremiah also ministered in Judah for a period of forty years—from about 625 to 585 B.C.

4:1–31. Jeremiah is often called "the weeping prophet." God told him to tell the people of Jerusalem that their nation would fall. It was a prophecy Jeremiah lived to see.

But these two prophets were very different in the type of message they were called on to deliver. Isaiah was a prophet of hope, but Jeremiah was a prophet of despair. By Jeremiah's time the nation of Judah had degenerated into such a godless state that its destruction was assured. It was Jeremiah's task to deliver this bad-news message from the Lord: As punishment for its sin and idolatry, Judah would be defeated by the pagan Babylonians.

When God called Jeremiah to the prophetic ministry, He made it clear that his job would not be easy. But He promised to strengthen and protect him: "I have made thee this day a defenced city, and an iron pillar...against the kings of Judah....And they shall fight against thee; but they shall not prevail...for I am with thee...to deliver thee" (1:18–19).

Jeremiah needed this assurance and protection because he was mocked, criticized, and abused by his own people throughout his entire ministry.

As the power of the Babylonians grew, Jeremiah was accused of treason because he called on the leaders of Judah to surrender, since their fate was already sealed by the Lord. Citizens of his own hometown threatened his life. He was imprisoned several times for delivering the Lord's unpopular message.

This faithful prophet's message from the Lord was verified with the fall of Jerusalem to the Babylonian army in 587 B.C. Jeremiah will always be remembered as a prophet who spoke God's truth without compromise, in spite of strong opposition.

Summary of Jeremiah

1:1–3. This brief introduction to the book tells us that Jeremiah prophesied during the reigns of three different kings of Judah—Josiah, Jehoiakim, and Zedekiah—or a period of about forty years.

1:4–19. God calls Jeremiah to his prophetic ministry. His task is to proclaim God's forthcoming judgment against the nation of Judah because the people are worshiping false gods. The prophet's vision of a budding almond tree shows that God's judgment is coming soon. The vision of a boiling pot facing toward the north indicates the direction from which this judgment will come.

2:1–37. God led His people out of slavery in Egypt and brought them into the Promised Land (Exod. 12:32–42). But they have rejected Him to serve the pagan gods of the surrounding nations. God's charge against them through the prophet Jeremiah is that "they have forsaken me the fountain of living waters, and hewed them out cisterns, broken cisterns, that can hold no water" (v. 13).

[2:1–37] DRINKING FROM A CISTERN. *They have forsaken me [God] the fountain [spring, NIV] of living waters, and hewed them out cisterns, broken cisterns, that can hold no water* (Jer. 2:13).

Cisterns of Bible times were little more than deep pits dug in the ground or shallow reservoirs carved out of limestone rock. Rainwater was directed into these holding tanks and stored for use during the dry season.

Compared to a spring from which fresh groundwater flowed, a cistern left a lot to be desired. The water could get contaminated, or the cistern could lose its water supply because of a leak.

Jeremiah criticized the foolish people of Judah for drinking water from a cistern when fresh springwater was available. They had forsaken the living Lord and were worshiping lifeless pagan gods.

3:1–25. The Lord compares the idolatry of Judah with the sin of adultery (Hosea 2:1–13). God's people promised to remain faithful to Him alone. But they have gone back on their promise and are committing spiritual adultery through their worship of idols.

4:1–31. God's declaration that He will devastate the land of Judah leads Jeremiah to inspect the destruction and to lament the fate of his fellow citizens: "I beheld, and, lo, the fruitful place was a wilderness, and all the cities thereof were broken down at the presence of the LORD, and by his fierce anger" (v. 26).

5:1–6:30. God reveals that He will use a foreign power as His instrument of judgment against His people. This mighty and ancient nation will invade Judah, destroy crops and livestock, and overrun all its walled cities.

7:1–34. The Lord commands Jeremiah to stand in the entrance to the temple in Jerusalem. Here he denounces their sin and calls on them to turn back to the Lord before it is too late. The people have substituted religious rituals, such as offering sacrifices at the temple, for obedience of God's commands. But God is not fooled by such practices. He demands total loyalty and commitment from His people.

8:1–22. The leaders of Judah have led the people astray. For this, they will be judged severely by the Lord: "They shall not be gathered, nor be buried; they shall be for dung upon the face of the earth" (v. 2; see Isa. 28; Zech. 10–11).

9:1–26. This chapter is a graphic portrait of the depths to which people can sink when they turn their backs on God. The sins of Judah enumerated by Jeremiah include lying, slandering, and bearing false witness against others.

10:1–25. People who worship idols are vain and foolish. They bow down before a wooden statue decorated with gold that they have made with their own hands. Such gods are

[9:1–26] NOT A RUNAWAY. *Oh that I [Jeremiah] had in the wilderness a lodging place of wayfaring men [travelers, NIV]; that I might leave my people, and go from them!* (Jer. 9:2).

Jeremiah is known as the "weeping prophet" because it broke his heart to see his countrymen rejecting the Lord and following false gods. In this verse he expressed his desire to leave his familiar surroundings, escape to the desert, and live among strangers. Then he would not be exposed every day to the sin and rebellion of the nation of Judah.

But Jeremiah never acted on his desire. For about forty years he stayed at the prophetic task to which God had called him. He is one of the Bible's best examples of faithfulness and obedience to the Lord.

weak and powerless. But the Lord is the one true God, awesome in majesty and power, who is able to deliver and protect His people (Isa. 44:6–20).

11:1–17. The Lord charges His people with breaking the covenant they had formed with Him in their early history. They have turned from Him and worshiped other gods. They will be punished for their waywardness.

11:18–23. Jeremiah learns that certain "men of Anathoth" (v. 21), his hometown, have plotted to kill him because of his prophecies against Judah. But God promises to protect the prophet and to punish these people for their actions.

12:1–17. Jeremiah complains to God because the wicked people in the land seem to be prospering, while the righteous followers of the Lord are suffering. God assures the prophet that this situation will be remedied when He exercises His judgment throughout the land.

13:1–11. The Lord commands Jeremiah to place a linen girdle (belt or sash) among the rocks on the bank of the Euphrates River. The prophet retrieves it some time later after it has rotted. Just as the girdle was ruined, God declares, He will eventually "mar the pride of Judah, and the great pride of Jerusalem" (v. 9).

13:12–27. At God's command, Jeremiah tells the people of Judah that "every bottle shall be filled with wine" (v. 12). But this is not a symbol of prosperity. It actually means that the inhabitants of Jerusalem will be as if they were drunk, helpless to defend themselves against the coming invasion from a foreign nation.

14:1–22. Jeremiah complains that false prophets are denying his message that God will punish Judah through a great disaster. They are predicting peace and prosperity for the land (1 Kings 22:1–28). God assures Jeremiah that he is the true prophet who is delivering the message He intends for His people.

15:1–21. Jeremiah reminds the Lord that he has been mocked and persecuted by his own people for proclaiming God's message of forthcoming judgment. He wonders how much longer he can stand up under the pressure. And what will happen to him when Jerusalem falls? God assures His faithful prophet of His strength and protection: "I will make thee unto this people a fenced brasen wall: and they shall fight against thee, but they shall not prevail against thee: for I am with thee to save thee and to deliver thee" (v. 20).

16:1–21. The Lord tells Jeremiah that he will not be permitted to marry and have children. To do so would be futile, since children have no future in a land marked for destruction.

17:1–8. Jeremiah declares that the sin of the people of Judah is no surface problem. It has infected and corrupted their total being. They can be delivered from their evil only if they repent and turn to God.

17:9–27. Judah is so corrupt that the people have stopped observing the Sabbath (Exod. 20:8–11). Such ungodly behavior will be punished severely by the Lord.

18:1–17. A potter shapes clay. After Jeremiah watched a potter reshaping a marred vessel, God said He would do the same with the Jewish nation.

18:1–17. Jeremiah watches a potter reshape a piece of clay until he makes exactly the vase or bowl he had in mind. Just like this human craftsman, God has the right to shape the nation of Judah into the people He wants them to be. If they refuse His shaping influence, He will discipline them by scattering them before their enemies.

[18:1–17] A LESSON FROM THE POTTER. *Then I [Jeremiah] went down to the potter's house, and, behold, he wrought a work on the wheels* (Jer. 18:3).

The Lord instructed Jeremiah to watch a potter at work and He would give the prophet a special message for the people. Ancient potters made pots by shaping wet clay with their hands as it turned on a foot-powered pedestal.

As Jeremiah watched the potter, the vessel he was making collapsed. The potter massaged the clay into a lump and began to form it into another pot. The message for the people was that Judah was like clay in the hands of God. They should allow Him to shape them into a vessel of His own choosing (Jer. 18:6).

18:18–23. The enemies of Jeremiah threaten his life again (11:18–23). He prays a bitter prayer of vengeance against them. This prayer is similar to outcries against the enemies of the psalmist in the Psalms (Ps. 59).

19:1–15. At God's command the prophet breaks a bottle, or jug, before the people of Judah. This object lesson is a warning that God will shatter the nation unless the people forsake their worship of pagan gods and turn back to God.

20:1–6. Pashur, son of Immer the priest, beats Jeremiah and puts him in shackles because he is proclaiming God's message of judgment against Judah. The prophet predicts that Pashur and his household as well as other citizens of Judah will be carried away as captives by the Babylonians.

20:7–18. Jeremiah cries out to God because of the burden he bears as a spokesman for the Lord against his country. This is such a difficult job for the prophet that he laments the day he was born (Job 3:1–4).

21:1–14. The setting for this chapter is apparently the final siege of Jerusalem by the Babylonians while Zedekiah was king of Judah (2 Kings 25:1–12). Resistance against the Babylonians is futile, the prophet tells the king. Their only hope for survival is to surrender.

22:1–30. This chapter contains Jeremiah's prophecies of disaster against three different kings of Judah: Shallum (vv. 11–17), Jehoiakim (vv. 18–23), and Coniah, or Jehoiachin (vv. 24–30). Chronologically, these prophecies were delivered before the events described in Jeremiah 21.

23:1–8. Jeremiah predicts that a faithful remnant of God's people will return to their homeland after their period of captivity by a foreign nation is over. He also speaks of the future Messiah, "THE LORD OUR RIGHTEOUSNESS" (v. 6). This prophecy was fulfilled with the birth of Jesus about 600 years after Jeremiah's time (Luke 2:1–7).

23:9–40. Jeremiah denounces the false prophets of Judah who are telling the leaders of the nation what they want to hear rather than declaring the word of the Lord (Jer. 14).

24:1–10. God shows Jeremiah a basket of good figs and a basket of spoiled figs. The good figs represent the faithful remnant of God's people whom He will return to their homeland after the Babylonian captivity is over (2 Chron. 36:22–23). But the spoiled figs represent King Zedekiah of Judah and his sons, who will be wiped out when the nation is defeated (2 Kings 25:1–12).

25:1–38. Because of their idolatry, the people of Judah will be carried away as captives to

Babylon for a period of seventy years. The nations that surround Judah will also fall to the Babylonian invasion.

26:1–19. After Jehoiakim becomes king of Judah, God sends Jeremiah to proclaim His message to the people: Jerusalem will fall because of the sin of the people. The leaders of Judah push for Jeremiah's execution, but he is spared when a group defends his prophetic ministry.

26:20–24. King Jehoiakim has Urijah the prophet executed because he is proclaiming God's forthcoming judgment just like Jeremiah. The prophet Jeremiah must have wondered if he would be next in line for the executioner.

27:1–22. The setting for this chapter is the continuing Babylonian threat against Judah. The Babylonian army had already defeated King Jeconiah/Jehoiachin, ransacked Jerusalem, carried some citizens into exile, and robbed the temple treasures (vv. 18–20). Jehoiakim was ruling over Judah (v. 1). God directed Jeremiah to put on a yoke—a symbol of submission—and to wear it in the city of Jerusalem to show that the nation's only hope for survival was unconditional surrender to Babylonia.

28:1–17. Hananiah, a false prophet, denies Jeremiah's prophecy that the Babylonians will defeat the nation of Judah. Instead, Hananiah predicts peace and prosperity for the land. As Jeremiah predicts, Hananiah dies within a short time because he delivered a false prophecy in the Lord's name and led the people astray (Jer. 14; 23:9–40).

29:1–9. Jeremiah writes a letter to the Jewish captives who had already been taken to Babylon (see summary of 27:1–22). He advises them to settle down and make the best of life in Babylon, since they will be there for many years (25:11).

29:10–19. God promises that a faithful remnant of His people will eventually return from captivity to their homeland.

29:20–32. The Lord pronounces judgment against several false prophets who have been leading the people to trust in a lie.

30:1–31:40. Even in the midst of the punishment of His people, God will show mercy. A remnant will be saved and restored to their homeland. At the same time, God will establish a new covenant with those who belong to Him. This new spiritual covenant, written on their hearts, will replace the covenant of law, which they were unable to keep. Ultimately, this promise of a new covenant was fulfilled with the coming of Jesus Christ and His sacrificial death and offer of eternal life for all who accept Him as Lord and Savior (Heb. 9:11–15).

32:1–44. While the Babylonians are attacking Jerusalem, Jeremiah buys a plot of land in Anathoth, his hometown. This shows his confidence in the promise of the Lord that the land throughout Judah will eventually be valuable again. This will happen when the remnant of God's people return from captivity to their homeland.

33:1–26. This chapter is messianic in nature. The Lord reminds His people of the promise He had made to David several centuries before—that one of David's descendants would always occupy the throne of Judah (2 Sam. 7:12–16). Jesus as the "son of David" (Matt. 1:1) is the ultimate fulfillment of this prophecy.

34:1–7. The Lord sends Jeremiah to King Zedekiah of Judah with a message while Jerusalem is under siege. The message is that the city will fall to Babylonia and Zedekiah will be captured by the enemy.

34:8–22. God expresses His displeasure that the citizens of Judah have broken His law about enslavement of their own countrymen. They are keeping Jewish slaves in perpetual slavery rather than freeing them after seven years, as the law commands (Deut. 15:12–15).

35:1–19. A group of people known as the Rechabites seeks refuge in Jerusalem because of the Babylonian threat. Their refusal to drink wine—a commitment they had made many years before—emphasizes the failure of the people of Judah to keep their covenant with the Lord.

36:1–10. Jeremiah enlists a scribe named Baruch to write down his prophecies of God's judgment against the nation of Judah. Baruch then reads the prophet's words to the people in the temple.

36:11–26. King Jehoiakim of Judah sends for the scroll after he hears about Jeremiah's written message. To show his contempt for the prophet, he burns the scroll bit by bit as it is read by one of his aides.

36:27–32. Jeremiah reproduces the destroyed scroll by dictating God's message again to

[36:11–26] BARUCH'S INK AND PAPER. *Then Baruch answered them, He [Jeremiah] pronounced all these words unto me with his mouth, and I wrote them with ink in the book [scroll, NIV]* (Jer. 36:18).

Baruch was the faithful scribe of Jeremiah who wrote down the messages of the prophet in order to preserve them for future generations.

The ink used by Baruch and other ancient scribes was made by mixing soot, lampblack, or ground charcoal with water and gum. The scroll on which he wrote Jeremiah's prophecies was probably made from the papyrus plant or from animal skins.

While this writing was primitive by modern standards, it held up well. The manuscripts in the collection known as the Dead Sea Scrolls, discovered in 1947, were still legible, even though they had been written about 2,000 years before.

Baruch. He also expands the original message of judgment. The Lord declares that King Jehoiakim will be judged severely for destroying the scroll.

37:1–21. Jeremiah is imprisoned on the false charge that he is deserting his own people to seek refuge among the Babylonian army. King Zedekiah asks him if he has any word from the Lord for Judah, since the nation is under attack by the enemy. Jeremiah's reply is not what the king wants to hear: "Thou shalt be delivered into the hand of the king of Babylon" (v. 17).

38:1–13. Jeremiah's enemies throw him into a dungeon or pit—perhaps a cistern with mud in the bottom—and leave him to die. With King Zedekiah's permission, Ebed-melech, a servant of the king, pulls the prophet out of the pit.

38:14–28. King Zedekiah summons Jeremiah in secret and asks him what he should do. Jerusalem is running out of food and water because of the prolonged Babylonian siege. The prophet tells him the only way to save himself and the city is to surrender to the Babylonian army.

39:1–10. Just as Jeremiah had predicted for many years, the Babylonians conquer Judah. After a long siege, they break down the walls of Jerusalem and burn the city. King Zedekiah and his sons are captured when they try to escape. The proud king of Judah is forced to watch as his sons are executed. Then the Babylonians put out his eyes and carry him away in chains to their capital city. Also forced into exile are the elite members of Jewish society. The peasants are left behind to cultivate the land (2 Kings 25:1–12).

39:11–14. King Nebuchadrezzar of Babylon releases Jeremiah from prison, treats him with kindness, and allows him to remain in Judah.

39:1–10. Babylonian soldiers ransacking Jerusalem may have looked something like this.

39:15–18. Jeremiah assures Ebed-melech, who had pulled him out of a cistern (38:1–13), that his life will be spared because of his trust in the Lord.

40:1–6. The Babylonians treat Jeremiah with kindness and allow him to decide whether he wants to go to Babylon or stay in Jerusalem. He decides to stay with the poor of the land who have been left behind.

40:7–41:18. The Babylonians place Gedaliah in charge of affairs in Judah. Ishmael, a Jewish zealot, incites a mob and assassinates Gedaliah, along with several Babylonian citizens who were helping to keep order in the land (2 Kings 25:22–25).

42:1–22. Representatives of the Jewish remnant left in Judah ask Jeremiah what they should do. They are apparently afraid of retaliation from the Babylonians for Gedaliah's assassination; they wonder if they should seek safety in Egypt. Jeremiah predicts they will be destroyed if they flee to Egypt. He advises them to stay in Judah.

43:1–7. Disregarding Jeremiah's advice, the Jewish remnant seeks refuge in Egypt, carrying Jeremiah and Baruch with them.

43:8–44:30. Jeremiah warns the Jewish remnant in Egypt that it is futile to try to hide from God's judgment in a foreign land. The Babylonians will eventually conquer Egypt, and they will be carried into exile to join their Jewish countrymen who have already been settled in Babylon.

45:1–5. Jeremiah assures his faithful scribe, Baruch, that Baruch's life will be spared in the devastating events that lie ahead.

[46:1–51:64] JUDGMENT AGAINST MOAB. *Moab... hath not been emptied from vessel to vessel...therefore his taste remained in him, and his scent is not changed* (Jer. 48:11).

This verse refers to a step in the process of making wine when it was poured from one jar to another to improve its taste. Jeremiah declared that Israel's enemy, Moab, had not yet experienced devastation by an enemy nation—or being "emptied from vessel to vessel."

But this would change in the future when Moab would be judged by the Lord for its sin. God would "empty his [Moab's] vessels, and break their bottles" (Jer. 48:12).

46:1–51:64. These five chapters contain Jeremiah's prophecies against the nations. God's judgment will be poured out against the nations that surround Judah as well as Judah itself. Marked for destruction because of their idolatry are Egypt (chap. 46), the Philistines (chap. 47), Moab (chap. 48), the Ammonites (49:1–6), Edom (49:7–22), Damascus (49:23–27), Kedar and Hazor (49:28–33), Elam (49:34–39), and Babylonia (chaps. 50–51).

52:1–34. The book of Jeremiah ends with a review of one of the greatest tragedies in the history of God's people: the fall of Jerusalem to the Babylonian army. This chapter covers the same events as those described in chapter 39 (see also 2 Kings 24–25). Perhaps Jeremiah revisited this national tragedy to remind his readers of the perils of refusing to follow the Lord.

OVERVIEW: Jeremiah laments the fall of Jerusalem to the Babylonian army.

Introduction to Lamentations

A lament is a cry of despair. Thus, Lamentations is appropriately named because it expresses great despair over the destruction of Jerusalem by the Babylonian army in 587 B.C.

This book was probably written by the prophet Jeremiah. He had warned Judah for many years that they would be defeated by a foreign power unless the people repented of their idol worship and turned back to the one true God (see the introduction to Jeremiah on p. 142).

Lamentations shows the sensitive side of Jeremiah's personality. He loved the city of Jerusalem and his native land, although he was compelled by the Lord to deliver a harsh message of judgment against his fellow citizens. When the inevitable finally happened, he was overcome with grief and despair: "For these things I weep; mine eye, mine eye runneth down with water, because the comforter that should relieve my soul is far from me: my children are desolate, because the enemy prevailed" (1:16).

Summary of Lamentations

1:1–22. Jerusalem, capital of the nation of Judah, was once a proud and prosperous city. But now it lies in ruins, devastated and looted by the Babylonian army. Its streets

[1:1–22] TRAMPLED BY GOD'S JUDGMENT. *The Lord hath trodden the virgin, the daughter of Judah, as in a winepress* (Lam. 1:15).

Jeremiah referred to the city of Jerusalem as "the virgin, the daughter of Judah." He lamented the destruction of the city by the Babylonian army in 587 B.C.

Jerusalem had been trodden down like grapes in a winepress. In Bible times the juice was extracted from grapes to make wine by crushing them underfoot in a vat, or winepress, carved out of solid rock.

God's judgment is also described as a winepress in Isaiah 63:3 and Revelation 14:19–20; 19:15.

were once filled with people, but now it is almost deserted. The Babylonians have carried the leading citizens of Judah into captivity, leaving behind only a few peasants and farmers (2 Kings 25:1–12). The city is like a destitute widow who mourns for her family.

2:1–22. Why did this happen? The prophet Jeremiah declares that Jerusalem has only itself to blame for its predicament. The Lord had warned Judah for many years that the nation would be defeated by a foreign enemy unless it forsook its worship of false gods and turned back to the one true God. Now God has "thrown down, and hath not pitied: and he hath caused thine enemy to rejoice over thee" (v. 17).

3:1–42. Out of his despair over Jerusalem's plight, Jeremiah sees a glimmer of hope.

After all, the Babylonians have spared the lives of most of the Jewish people (v. 22). Perhaps through God's mercy and grace they will survive their ordeal of captivity in Babylon and be restored to their homeland at some future time.

3:43–66. Once again, Jeremiah is overwhelmed by the suffering and humiliation of the people of Judah. Their enemies had laughed and cheered when Jerusalem fell. The prophet asks God to pay them back for their cruelty.

4:1–20. These verses contain more stark pictures of the devastation of Jerusalem. Jeremiah condemns the priests and prophets for failing to lead the people back to God. This would have kept divine judgment from falling on the city.

5:1–22. A jackal, likely the "fox" of the King James Version that prowled the devastated city of Jerusalem.

4:21–22. The nation of Edom, an enemy of the Israelites for many years, apparently participated in the capture and destruction of Jerusalem (see the book of Obadiah). Jeremiah predicts that Judah will eventually be restored, but Edom will be permanently wiped out by the Lord.

5:1–22. Jeremiah reviews the numerous sufferings of the people of Judah. Then he prays for God to grant them restoration and forgiveness: "Turn thou us unto thee, O LORD, and we shall be turned; renew our days as of old" (v. 21).

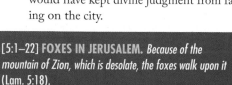

[5:1–22] FOXES IN JERUSALEM. *Because of the mountain of Zion, which is desolate, the foxes walk upon it* (Lam. 5:18).

Jeremiah used this word picture to show the desolation of Jerusalem (referred to as "Zion") after it was captured, plundered, and destroyed by the Babylonians.

The city was virtually empty, since the leading citizens of Judah had been carried away to Babylon as captives. Once-thriving Jerusalem was now the haunt of foxes and other wild animals.

The Hebrew word for "foxes" is often rendered as "jackals" (see the NIV). These animals, similar to wild dogs, were scavengers. Jackals prowling through Jerusalem gives an even more vivid portrait of the plight of the city.

OVERVIEW: Prophecies of judgment and hope to God's people while they are in exile in Babylon.

Introduction to Ezekiel

The prophet Ezekiel received his messages from God through a series of visions. He addressed his prophecies to the Jewish exiles in Babylon across a twenty-year period, from about 593 to 573 B.C.

Ezekiel himself was one of those exiles. He was carried away from Judah about 597 B.C. during the first Babylonian invasion of his nation. Ten years later the Babylonians returned to Judah and destroyed the city of Jerusalem. Thus, Ezekiel's messages to the Jewish exiles

1:1–28. Ezekiel's vision of four winged cherubim is captured in a stained glass window. The prophet is also reaching for a scroll, which God instructed him to eat.

referred to tragedies that had already happened as well as those that would happen in the future.

Their period of exile in Babylon was a time of great disillusionment for the Jewish people. Now that they were reaping the fruits of their sins, there was little need for harsh condemnation. Ezekiel's major task was to encourage the people and give them hope for the future.

In the first part of Ezekiel's book, the prophet reminded the people of their sins and the losses they had suffered and predicted other disasters. But beginning with chapter 36, he began to give them assurance that better days were ahead. God would lead them back to their homeland and establish His univeral rule among His people through a descendant of David. This prophecy was fulfilled when Jesus was born in Bethlehem more than five hundred years after Ezekiel's time (Luke 2:1–7).

One of the great contributions of the book of Ezekiel is the doctrine of personal accountability. The Jewish people had such a strong sense of group identity that they often glossed over their personal sins. Ezekiel told the exiles that each of them was responsible for his or her own sin. They must stand before God and take responsibility for their wrongdoing.

The book of Ezekiel has an important message for modern believers. We cannot depend on the beliefs of our parents, a church, or a denomination to give us favor in God's sight. He demands that we stand before Him and make our own personal, deliberate choice to follow His will and obey His commands.

Summary of Ezekiel

1:1–28. Ezekiel has a vision of four winged creatures known as cherubim. God's glory appears among these creatures.

2:1–10. The Lord informs Ezekiel that He has called him as His messenger to the Jewish exiles in Babylon.

3:1–27. Ezekiel eats a roll, or scroll, on which God's message to His rebellious people is written. This symbolizes the prophet's acceptance of God's message and mission to the Jewish exiles.

4:1–17. At God's command, Ezekiel uses a clay tile and an iron pan to enact the Babylonian siege against Jerusalem. He eats tiny amounts of food for several days to show the starvation conditions that existed in Jerusalem before the city fell.

> **[4:1–17] A RECORD IN CLAY.** *Son of man [Ezekiel], take thee a tile [clay tablet, NIV], and lay it before thee, and pourtray upon it the city, even Jerusalem (Ezek. 4:1).*
>
> God made a strange request of the prophet Ezekiel. He asked him to draw upon a clay tablet a picture of the city of Jerusalem under siege by the Babylonian army. This was to serve as a warning to the people about the forthcoming judgment of God against Jerusalem and the nation of Judah.
>
> In Bible times clay tiles or tablets about six by nine inches in size were often used as writing material, just like paper is used today. Characters were etched into these tablets with a metal pen while the clay was soft. When hardened in a kiln, the writing on these tiles was virtually indestructible.
>
> Archaeologists have discovered many of these clay tablets in the ruins of ancient cities. They shed light on the culture and customs of the ancient world.

5:1–17. Ezekiel shaves his beard and his head with a sword. Then he burns the hair to show that God has judged His people with the sword of the Babylonians because of their unfaithfulness.

6:1–14. God's destruction has fallen upon the mountains of Judah and those who worshiped false gods upon these high places.

7:1–27. The doom that God has promised against Judah because of the idolatry of the people is now unleashed in full force against the land: "According to their deserts will I judge them; and they shall know that I am the LORD" (v. 27).

8:1–18. Ezekiel is transported in a vision to the temple in Jerusalem. Here God shows him how the temple has been desecrated through the worship of false gods.

9:1–11. God commands that a special mark be placed on every person in Jerusalem who is grieved by the desecration of the temple. They will be saved when Jerusalem falls, but everyone without this mark will be destroyed (Rev. 9:4; 14:1).

10:1–22. Ezekiel has a vision of the same four winged creatures, or cherubim, that he had in chapter 1. God's glory leaves the temple and rests above these cherubim. This signifies that God's glory will eventually leave the temple because His people have polluted this holy place with their pagan worship practices.

11:1–25. Ezekiel speaks against certain leaders of Jerusalem who are predicting prosperity rather than disaster for the city. He declares that the future of God's people rests with the Jewish exiles in Babylon. God will eventually restore His remnant to their homeland (2 Chron. 36:22–23).

12:1–28. At God's command, Ezekiel acts out the fall of Jerusalem and the exile of the people to Babylon.

13:1–23. Ezekiel denounces false prophets who are telling the people what they want to hear rather than proclaiming God's message of judgment (Jer. 28). He also condemns false prophetesses who are leading the people astray through witchcraft and the reading of signs to foretell the future.

14:1–23. God will not tolerate the worship of false gods by His people. He demands their exclusive loyalty (Josh. 24:15). He will judge the nation of Judah for their false worship.

15:1–8. God's people were often compared to a vine (Isa. 5:1–7; Hosea 10:1), but their idolatry has turned them into a vine that bears no fruit. They will be cut down and burned by the fire of God's judgment (Luke 13:6–9).

16:1–63. This long chapter is a parable about

> **[15:1–8] USELESS AS A WILD VINE.** *Shall wood be taken thereof [from a vine] to do any work? or will men take a pin of it to hang any vessel thereon?* (Ezek. 15:3).
>
> Ezekiel compared the nation of Judah to a wild vine. Just as a vine of this type yields no lumber—not even as much as a pin or peg to hang a pot on—so Judah had become useless to the Lord because of the sin and rebellion of the people.
>
> Domestic vines such as the grape are useful because of the fruit they produce. Throughout their history the Israelites were often spoken of as a fruitful vine (Gen. 49:22). But even a grapevine is useless if it fails to produce grapes (Jer. 2:21). Ezekiel looked in vain for the fruits of righteousness and holiness among the people of his time.

God's relationship with His people Israel. The Lord adopted Israel when she was an orphan, lavishing her with His love and care. But she rejected Him and turned to the worship of pagan gods. While Israel will receive its deserved punishment, God will not give up on His people. He remains faithful to His covenant promises: "I will establish my covenant with thee; and thou shalt know that I am the LORD" (v. 62).

17:1–24. The two eagles in this chapter represent Babylonia and Egypt. The vine represents the nation of Judah, which broke its oath of allegiance to Babylonia and turned to Egypt for help. God will punish Judah for this act of disobedience, but He will eventually rebuild His people through a faithful remnant who follow His commands.

18:1–32. The people of Judah were sometimes

fatalistic in their attitudes, blaming their ancestors for their current problems. Ezekiel declares that each person is accountable for his or her own sins: "The soul that sinneth, it shall die. The son shall not bear the iniquity of the father, neither shall the father bear the iniquity of the son" (v. 20).

19:1–14. In this mournful poem, Ezekiel laments the kings who ruled Judah during the tragic period just before the nation fell to the Babylonians.

20:1–44. Several leaders of Judah ask Ezekiel if he has a message from the Lord. The prophet responds by giving them a history lesson, showing that the Israelites have tended to be sinful and rebellious from the very beginning of their existence as a nation.

20:45–21:32. Because of their rebellious history, God will send His wrath against His people. His agent of judgment will be the Babylonians, who will destroy Jerusalem as well as the capital of the Ammonites.

22:1–31. Jerusalem was supposed to be the "holy city." Instead, it has become the "bloody city" (v. 2) because of its sin, idolatry, and denial of justice to the poor. Jerusalem will be judged severely by the Lord for its corruption.

23:1–49. In this parable of two adulterous sisters, Ezekiel portrays the nation of Israel (Northern Kingdom) as Aholah and the nation of Judah (Southern Kingdom) as Aholibah. Their lust leads them to pursue their lovers with reckless abandon. Judah saw Israel punished with defeat and exile because of Israel's sins, but in spite of this warning, Judah continued her sinful ways.

24:1–14. Ezekiel portrays Jerusalem as a cooking pot. Its citizens will be stewed like meat in the fire of God's judgment when the Babylonians besiege the city (2 Kings 25:1–12).

24:15–27. God warns Ezekiel that his wife will soon die, but he is not to mourn her death. This is a sign to the Jewish exiles in Babylon that they will soon be cut off from their relatives in Jerusalem when the city is overrun by the Babylonians.

25:1–32:32. These chapters contain Ezekiel's prophecies of God's judgment against the nations: Ammon (25:1–7); Moab (25:8–11); Edom (25:12–14); the Philistines (25:15–17); Tyrus, or Tyre (26:1–28:19); Zidon, or Sidon (28:20–26); and Egypt (chaps. 29–32).

33:1–20. The Lord tells Ezekiel that the duty of a watchman is to sound a warning in times of danger. This is also the mission of a true prophet of God.

[20:45–21:32] BABYLONIAN SIGN-READING. *The king of Babylon stood...at the head of the two ways [at the junction of the two roads, NIV], to use divination [seek an omen, NIV]: he made his arrows bright, he consulted with images, he looked in the liver* (Ezek. 21:21).

Ezekiel told the people of Judah that the king of Babylonia was coming into their territory on a mission of conquest. He would stop at a fork in the road and decide whether to take the road toward Jerusalem or to go the other way and attack the capital city of the Ammonites (Ezek. 21:19–20).

To decide which road to take, the king would read the signs by using one of three possible methods. He might cast lots by drawing an arrow out of his quiver and throwing it down to see which way it pointed. He could consult his pagan gods. Or he could have one of his priests "read" the liver of a sacrificial animal and advise him on which city to attack.

Such superstitious sign-reading was practiced by the pagan nations of Bible times. But God declared black magic and divination off-limits to His people (Deut. 18:10–11).

37:1–14. Ezekiel's most famous vision takes place in a valley filled with human skeletons that suddenly grow flesh and come to life. God says He will do the same for Israel, resurrecting the dead nation.

33:21–33. News that the city of Jerusalem has fallen reaches Ezekiel. He passes this on to the other Jewish exiles in Babylon.

34:1–31. The leaders of Judah will be punished because they have exploited and misled the people rather than guiding them in the ways of the Lord. In contrast to such undependable human leaders, God is a true shepherd. He will eventually bring His people back to their homeland to feed on fertile pastures.

35:1–15. The nation of Edom, referred to as "mount Seir" (v. 2) by Ezekiel, joined in the humiliation of Judah when Jerusalem fell to the Babylonians. God will repay this callous act. The prophet Obadiah also condemned Edom for these acts of treachery (see the book of Obadiah).

36:1–38. This chapter represents a turning point in the book of Ezekiel. Up to now, the prophet has spoken mainly of God's judgment against the nation of Judah. But now that God's judgment has reached its climax with the fall of Jerusalem, Ezekiel will spend the rest of his book giving hope to the Jewish exiles in Babylon. In the future God will restore His people to their homeland. He will give them a new heart and fill them with a new spirit.

37:1–14. Ezekiel has a vision of a valley filled with dry, lifeless bones. God's Spirit enters the bones, and they spring to life. This symbolizes the forthcoming spiritual restoration of the nation of Israel.

37:15–28. At God's command, Ezekiel picks up two sticks. These represent the two separate nations of Israel (Northern Kingdom) and Judah (Southern Kingdom). The prophet

---

[37:15–28] MESSAGES ON WOOD. *The sticks whereon thou [Ezekiel] writest shall be in thine hand before their [Israel's and Judah's] eyes (Ezek. 37:20).*

God told Ezekiel to write messages on two separate sticks, representing the nations of Judah (Southern Kingdom) and Israel (Northern Kingdom). Then he was to place the two sticks together. This represented the time when the two nations would become one again and be ruled over by the messianic king.

Messages were often written on long, narrow strips of wood in Bible times. The practice is referred to as early as the time of Moses (Num. 17:2–3).

---

declares that God will unite His people into one kingdom under one king—"David my servant" (v. 24). This is a title for the promised Messiah. This prophecy was fulfilled with the coming of Jesus.

38:1–39:29. Ezekiel looks into the future and predicts a great battle between the forces of evil and the people of God. Several evil nations, under the leadership of Gog, attack God's people, but they are defeated when God intervenes. The apostle John, writing in the book of Revelation, uses Gog's evil forces to represent all who oppose God in the final battle in the end times under the leadership of Satan (Rev. 20:8).

40:1–48:35. The book of Ezekiel ends with the prophet's glorious vision of a new temple rebuilt on the site of Solomon's temple in Jerusalem. This must have brought hope to the Jewish exiles in Babylon, since Solomon's temple had been destroyed when Jerusalem fell to the Babylonian army.

OVERVIEW: Daniel and his three friends model faithfulness to God while living among pagan nations. Daniel also issues prophecies of the future and the end-time.

Introduction to Daniel

The prophet Daniel, author of the book that bears his name, was taken into exile about 600 B.C., along with other citizens of Judah, when the Babylonians invaded his country. He was probably in his late teens at the time.

The events recorded in the book of Daniel show that he remained in exile for at least fifty years. Daniel served as an aide in the administration of King Nebuchadnezzar of Babylonia soon after he was carried away (2:46–49). Eventually Babylonia was defeated by the Persians. Daniel also served under the Persian king Darius (6:1–13). This king brought the exile to an end when he allowed Jewish captives who wished to do so to return to their homeland (2 Chron. 36:22–23).

One of the problems that confronted the Jewish captives in Babylonia and Persia was how to remain faithful to God in the midst of pagan surroundings. Was this possible? Two episodes recorded by Daniel gave a bold yes to this question.

Three of Daniel's friends were thrown into a hot furnace because they refused to worship an image of the Babylonian king. When they emerged unharmed because of God's miraculous intervention, the Babylonians developed a reverent respect for this awesome God (3:8–27).

This respect for God grew even stronger when Daniel was miraculously delivered from a den of lions, where he was thrown when he continued to pray to his own God rather than the pagan Persian gods. The Lord had demonstrated that He was superior to all other gods.

The book of Daniel serves as an inspiration for modern believers. In a critical and unbelieving world, we can rest assured of God's presence and protection if we remain faithful to Him.

Summary of Daniel

1:1–7. Daniel and his three friends—Shadrach, Meshach, and Abednego—are carried to Babylon as captives after Judah

---

[1:1–7] LOOTING OF THE TEMPLE. *He [King Nebuchadnezzar] brought the vessels into the treasure house of his god* (Dan. 1:2).

When the Babylonian army captured and plundered the city of Jerusalem, King Nebuchadnezzar siezed the golden utensils, spices, jewels, and other valuable items that belonged to the Jewish temple. He carried these valuables to Babylon, where he deposited them in the treasure house of a temple devoted to the worship of a pagan Babylonian god.

This fulfilled a prophecy that Isaiah had issued to the people of Judah about 100 years before: "The days come, that all...which thy fathers have laid up in store...shall be carried to Babylon" (Isa. 39:6).

3:19–30. The "fiery furnace" that Shadrach, Meshach, and Abednego were thrown into may have been a type of ore smelter, similar to this modern steel plant.

is defeated by the Babylonians under King Nebuchadnezzar (2 Kings 25:1–12). These four young Jewish men are selected for training in Babylonian customs and culture before being placed in government service in Babylon.

1:8–21. Daniel and his three friends refuse to defile themselves with the rich foods and strong wine they are required to eat while in training for government service. Eating only vegetables ("pulse," v. 12) and water, they grow stronger than all the other young men in the training program.

2:1–11. King Nebuchadnezzar of Babylonia has a dream that he is not able to recall. None of his wise men or magicians can tell him what he dreamed.

2:12–45. Daniel is able to tell Nebuchadnezzar what he dreamed and what it meant. The prophet tells the king that he will continue for a while as a mighty ruler over a broad territory. But his successors will not be able to hold this kingdom together.

2:46–49. King Nebuchadnezzar appoints Daniel to a high position in his administration. Also promoted are Daniel's three friends: Shadrach, Meshach, and Abednego.

3:1–7. King Nebuchadnezzar fashions a statue of himself from gold and has it set up at a prominent site in Babylonia. He orders all the people in his kingdom to bow down and worship the image at his command.

3:8–18. Enemies of Daniel's three friends inform the king that these young Jewish men will not worship the golden image. When Nebuchadnezzar questions them about this, they reply: "O king...we will not serve thy gods, nor worship the golden image which thou hast set up" (v. 18).

3:19–30. Because of their disobedience of the king's order, Shadrach, Meshach, and Abednego are thrown into a hot furnace. But an angel protects them, and they emerge untouched and unharmed by the flames. King Nebuchadnezzar is so impressed by this miracle that he orders everyone in Babylonia to be respectful toward the God whom they worship. He also promotes Shadrach, Meshach, and Abednego to higher positions in his administration.

4:1–37. Daniel interprets another dream of King Nebuchadnezzar—and it happens just as Daniel predicts. Toward the end of his reign, the king is struck by a strange disease—perhaps mental illness. Convinced he is an animal, he forages in the pastures, eating grass with the livestock. But he apparently recovers from this illness long enough to recognize Daniel's God as the one true God (vv. 34–37).

5:1–12. Belshazzar, successor of Nebuchadnezzar as king of Babylonia, is partying with friends and officials of his administration. In the midst of the merrymaking, a hand appears and writes some words on the wall. None of his wise men or magicians can make sense of the message.

5:13–31. Called to interpret the handwriting, Daniel gives Belshazzar the bad news: The days of the Babylonian kingdom are numbered. God will deliver the nation into the hands of the Medes and Persians. That very night Belshazzar is killed, and the glory days of Babylonia come to an end.

6:1–13. Daniel wins the favor of the new Persian regime and the victorious king, Darius,

[6:1–13] UNCHANGEABLE PERSIAN LAWS. *O king, establish the decree...that it be not changed, according to the law of the Medes and Persians, which altereth not* (Dan. 6:8).

The enemies of Daniel in Persia asked King Darius to issue a law against worshiping any god other than the king himself. They knew this would trap Daniel, since he would refuse to bow down to any god other than the supreme Lord of the universe.

The ancient Medes and Persians considered their laws infallible and irreversible. Once a decree was ordered by the king, it could not be changed or wiped off the books. For example, the Persian law authorizing the extermination of the Jews in Esther's time was not canceled. But the king issued another decree warning the Jews about the death warrant and authorizing them to act in self-defense against their enemies (Esther 8:5–11).

who names him to a high position in his administration. But Daniel has some political enemies, and they conspire to have him killed. They persuade King Darius to issue a decree making it unlawful for anyone to pray to any god except the king. Daniel continues his practice of praying to God as he has always done.

6:14–28. Because of his disobedience, Daniel is thrown into a den of lions. The next day Darius finds him standing among the lions unharmed because God sent an angel to protect him. The king issues an order for all the people to "tremble and fear before the God of Daniel" (v. 26).

7:1–28. Daniel has a vision that foretells events of the future. He sees four beasts that represent four future earthly kings. The fourth beast will triumph over all the nations of the earth. A horn on the fourth beast represents a ruler who will oppose God and persecute those who follow the Lord. But eventually God's eternal kingdom will be established.

8:1–27. Daniel has a vision of a ram and a goat. The ram, representing the kingdoms of Media and Persia, is defeated by a goat. This foretells the rise of Alexander the Great and the Greek Empire that he would establish. At Alexander's death, his empire would be divided among his generals: "Four kingdoms shall stand up out of the nation" (v. 22).

9:1–19. Daniel realizes that the seventy-year captivity of the Jewish people by the Babylonians and Persians is almost over (Jer. 29:10). So he prays a beautiful prayer of intercession and deliverance for his people.

9:20–27. These verses contain the famous "seventy weeks" prophecy of Daniel, revealed to him by the angel Gabriel. Most interpreters believe these seventy weeks should be interpreted as seventy times seven years—or a period of 490 years. Thus, this prophecy refers to the coming of the Messiah, Jesus Christ, about 490 years from the time when the Jews were allowed to return to Jerusalem from the exile to resettle their homeland.

10:1–11:45. This vision is revealed to Daniel after a period of fasting and prayer while he stands by the Hiddekel (Tigris) River in Persia. Strengthened by an angel after his period of fasting, Daniel falls into a trance and receives a revelation of events of the future. He foresees a struggle between a "king of the south" and a "king of the north." Many interpreters believe this refers to the battle for supremacy between two generals of Alexander the Great after Alexander's death about 300 years after Daniel's time.

12:1–13. An angel reveals to Daniel that the Jewish people can expect a period of tribulation in the future. But those who persevere will experience joy and a new beginning in the Lord. Even Daniel is not given perfect understanding of events that will happen in the end-time (vv. 8–9). But he is assured of God's eternal presence as he waits for Him to act: "Go thou thy way till the end be: for thou shalt rest, and stand in thy lot at the end of the days" (v. 13).

CHAPTER 5
BOOKS OF THE MINOR PROPHETS

The last twelve books of the Old Testament are known as the minor prophets. This does not mean they are of minor importance. The title refers to the short length of the books and the fact that they were placed after the major prophets (Isaiah, Jeremiah, Lamentations, Ezekiel, and Daniel) in the compilation of the Old Testament.

If all the minor prophets were compiled into one book, their total length would be about equal to that of the book of Isaiah. Though brief, the books and the prophets who wrote them delivered God's powerful message to several different situations over a period of about 400 years.

Amos and Hosea preached to the Northern Kingdom before that nation fell to the Assyrians in 722 B.C. Six of the minor prophets—Obadiah, Joel, Micah, Nahum, Zephaniah, and Habakkuk—ministered in the Southern Kingdom. God sent the prophet Jonah to preach judgment and repentance to the pagan nation of Assyria. Three of these prophets—Haggai, Zechariah, and Malachi—encouraged and challenged the Israelites after they returned to their homeland following the exile among the Babylonians and Persians.

HOSEA

OVERVIEW: Hosea's own tragic marriage to an unfaithful wife shows that God's people have rejected Him to worship false gods.

Introduction to Hosea

The book of Hosea paints a beautiful picture of God's faithful love for His people. It was written by the prophet Hosea, who ministered in the nation of Israel (Northern Kingdom) during a period of forty years, from about 755 to 715 B.C.

Hosea declared to the people of his homeland that they were marked for destruction by the Lord because of their sinful ways, especially their worship of false gods. As the prophet predicted, Israel fell to the Assyrians in 722 B.C.

But the message for which Hosea is most remembered is his declaration that God had not given up on His people. Even though they were sinful and rebellious, He still loved them and worked patiently to restore them to their favored status as His special people.

This truth about God was demonstrated in Hosea's own life. At the Lord's direction, the prophet married a prostitute. Several children were born into this marriage. But just as it appeared that his wife had given up her sinful ways, she left Hosea and returned to her life of prostitution.

Hosea searched for his wayward spouse and found that she had been sold into slavery. He bought her from her master and restored her as his wife. This object lesson showed that God had not rejected Israel, although the people had turned their back on Him by worshiping false gods.

The message of Hosea is that God's punishment of His people is motivated by His love. He loves us too much to let us continue in our wayward ways. His goal is to restore us to full fellowship with Him.

Summary of Hosea

1:1–11. God calls Hosea to deliver His message to the wayward nation of Israel (Northern Kingdom). At God's command, Hosea marries a prostitute named Gomer. She bears three children, and they are given symbolic names that represent God's intention to punish Israel.

2:1–13. Just as Gomer had committed adultery before she married Hosea, so has Israel been guilty of spiritual adultery in God's sight (Isa. 3:1–25). The people have worshiped false gods and have been unfaithful to the one true God. He will judge them for these rebellious acts.

2:14–23. After God has punished and disciplined His people, He promises to restore them to His favor. His kindness and mercy will be showered upon them once again.

3:1–5. Hosea's wife, Gomer, apparently returns to her life as a prostitute and is sold as a slave. God directs Hosea to buy her back. This shows God's redemptive love. For a while, the people of Israel will also lose their

The prophet Hosea condemned the people of the Northern Kingdom for their worship of Baal, a pagan fertility god. He described them as indulgent worshippers who loved "flagons of wine."

The Hebrew word rendered as "flagons of wine" by the KJV is translated as "sacred raisin cakes" by the NIV. This is probably a more accurate translation, since cakes made of raisins, or dried grapes, were considered a delicacy in Bible times. They may have been eaten in connection with immoral worship ceremonies at the altars of Baal.

freedom to an enemy nation as punishment for their sin. But God will eventually redeem them and restore them as His people.

4:1–19. God gives a detailed list of the sins that Israel has committed. These include killing, stealing, lying, and committing adultery. But their greatest sin is worshiping false gods.

5:1–15. Even the priests have turned away from following God and are leading the people astray. Hosea also declares that the nation of Judah is just as guilty as Israel of forsaking the Lord and going its own way (v. 10).

6:1–7:16. Some of the people of Israel have been convicted of their sin and have turned back to God. But their repentance was a sham, and they have fallen right back into idolatry. Hosea declares that their goodness "is as a morning cloud, and as the early dew it goeth away" (6:4).

8:1–14. The nation of Israel will experience God's law of sowing and reaping. They will reap God's terrible punishment for the sins they have sown: "They have sown the wind, and they shall reap the whirlwind" (v. 7).

9:1–10:15. Hosea announces the specific punishment that God has in store for Israel.

Because of their idolatry, the people will be carried away as captives by the Assyrians (10:6; see 2 Kings 18:9–12).

11:1–12. This chapter shows God's everlasting love for His people. He compares the nation of Israel to a little child whom He guided and taught as He led them out of slavery in Egypt. Now Assyria will rule over them for a time, but the Lord will eventually restore His people through His grace.

[11:1–12] **RELIEF FROM THE YOKE.** *I [God] drew them [Israelites] with cords of a man, with bands of love: and I was to them as they that take off the yoke on their jaws* (Hosea 11:4).

In this verse Hosea portrays the love of God for His special people, the Israelites. Although they had rebelled against Him again and again, He kept pulling them back into His fellowship with "bands of love."

Hosea also compared the love of God to relief given to oxen when they were wearing heavy wooden yokes while working in the fields. These yokes had to be lifted up by their masters to enable the animals to lower their heads so they could eat or drink.

God is the great "yoke lifter" who shows mercy and love to His people.

12:1–13:16. These chapters return to the theme of God's judgment against Israel because of the people's worship of false gods. The prophet declares that Samaria (captial city of Israel) "shall become desolate; for she hath rebelled against her God" (13:16).

14:1–9. Hosea closes his book with a plea for Israel to repent and return to the Lord before it is too late. The path to forgiveness and restoration is open if the people will turn from their rebellious ways.

JOEL

OVERVIEW: A plague of locusts serves notice that God will judge His people for their sin and rebellion.

Introduction to Joel

This brief prophetic book paints a disturbing picture of the coming judgment of God against His people because of their sin. It was written by the prophet Joel about 590 B.C., during the dark days before the nation of Judah fell to the Babylonians.

Joel begins his book with a description of the devastation of Judah by a swarm of locusts. These destructive insects, similar to grasshoppers, destroyed all the crops and stripped the leaves from shrubs and trees. This was a foretaste of the judgment of God that would fall upon the land unless the people repented and turned from their wicked ways.

Along with this message of judgment, Joel also had words of hope. God promised to bless His people if they would turn to Him and obey

2:1–11. Locusts swarm the Indian Ocean island of Madagascar. The prophet Joel apparently used such an infestation to warn that even worse disaster was coming for Israel, as invaders would destroy the Jewish nation for its sins.

His commands. He would renew their zeal and commitment through a great outpouring of His Spirit (2:28–29). The entire world would be impressed as He gathered His people in Jerusalem to serve as their sovereign ruler (3:2).

The prophecy about the outpouring of God's Spirit was fulfilled several centuries later during the days of the early church. The Holy Spirit came in great power upon the followers of Jesus while they were in Jerusalem praying for God's guidance (Acts 2:16–21).

This same Spirit is alive and well today in the lives of those who belong to Christ.

Summary of Joel

1:1–20. The land of Judah is invaded by a huge swarm of locusts. The flying insects, similar to grasshoppers, destroy all the vegetation in their path, even stripping leaves and bark from the trees (Exod. 10:12–15). With their crops destroyed, the people face the prospect of starvation. Joel calls on the priests to proclaim a fast and to gather the people to God's house for prayer and repentance.

2:1–11. The prophet declares that this locust plague is only a shadow of what the approaching "day of the Lord" (v. 1) will be like. This time of God's judgment and punishment will be "a day of darkness and of gloominess, a day of clouds and of thick darkness" (v. 2; see Jer. 46:10).

2:12–17. But it is not too late for Judah to repent. Joel calls on the people to forsake their sinful ways and turn to the Lord.

2:18–27. In response to the repentance of His people, God will withhold His judgment and give them many blessings instead. He will send the rains and give them an abundant harvest, more than enough to replace the crops devastated by the locusts.

2:28–32. Even more abundant are the spiritual blessings that God will send upon His

[1:1–20] DESTRUCTION BY LOCUSTS. *That which the palmerworm hath left hath the locust eaten; and that which the locust hath left hath the cankerworm eaten; and that which the cankerworm hath left hath the caterpiller eaten* (Joel 1:4).

A locust plague, such as the one described by Joel in this verse, was one of the worst disasters that could happen in the agricultural society of Bible times. Millions of these insects, similar to grasshoppers, would descend on the land and devour the crops. Scarcity of food—and even widespread starvation—could follow.

The eighth plague that God sent against the Egyptians to convince Pharaoh to release the Hebrew slaves was a swarm of locusts (Exod. 10:12–15).

Joel's account of a swarm of locusts in his time details the four stages in the development of this destructive insect: (1) a hatchling emerges from the egg (palmerworm); (2) it develops wings and begins to fly (locust); (3) it becomes strong enough to begin eating vegetation (cankerworm); and (4) as a fully grown adult, it flies in a swarm with millions of others to do its most destructive work (caterpiller).

people if they remain faithful to Him. He promises to send His Spirit "upon all flesh" (v. 28)—not just on prophets and priests but on ordinary people. The apostle Peter quoted this passage on the day of Pentecost to show that God had fulfilled this promise by sending His Spirit to empower the early Christian believers (Acts 2:16–21).

3:1–21. Joel looks into the future to the day of messianic blessing for the people of God. But this will also be a day of judgment for the pagan nations as well as individuals who have refused to acknowledge Jesus as Savior and Lord: "Multitudes, multitudes in the valley of decision: for the day of the Lord is near in the valley of decision" (v. 14).

AMOS

Overview: Genuine religion consists of treating others with justice and mercy rather than observing rituals and offering sacrifices.

Introduction to Amos

Like Hosea, Amos was also a prophet to the Northern Kingdom (Israel). But Amos was a native of Judah (Southern Kingdom). He was sent by the Lord into Israel to denounce the sin and corruption of the people. Amos's prophecy is dated at about 760 b.c., a few years before Hosea began his public ministry (see the introduction to Hosea on p. 164).

Amos is known as the great prophet of righteousness and social justice of the Old Testament. He condemned the wealthy people of Israel who were cheating the poor. He criticized the wives of the rich leaders of the nation for their selfishness and greed. The prophet also declared that the religion of the people was shallow and meaningless. Worship had degenerated into empty rituals and ceremonies that had no relationship to daily life.

According to Amos, authentic religion results in holy and righteous behavior. True worship does not consist of offering burnt offerings, observing all the religious holidays, and worshiping at the temple. Worship that honors God will lead people to treat others with justice and to follow the Lord's commands.

Amos was a lowly shepherd from the tiny village of Tekoa in Judah (1:1) who left his flocks to serve as the Lord's spokesman among the affluent classes in another country. God often surprises us with the people whom He calls out as His special servants.

Summary of Amos

1:1–2. Amos is from the village of Tekoa in Judah (Southern Kingdom). But he is sent to proclaim God's judgment against Israel (Northern Kingdom).

1:3–2:5. God's judgment is first pronounced against the cities and nations surrounding Israel: Damascus (1:3–5), Gaza (1:6–8), Tyrus, or Tyre (1:9–10), Edom (1:11–12), Ammon (1:13–15), Moab (2:1–3), and Judah (2:4–5).

2:6–16. God lists the sins for which the nation of Israel will be punished. These include worshiping idols instead of the one true God, cheating the poor, and persecuting the prophets whom God sends as His spokesmen.

3:1–15. The Lord reminds the citizens of Israel that He brought them out of Egypt when they were a slave people and made them into a nation that belongs to Him (Exod. 12:33–42). But He will just as surely punish them unless they turn from their rebellious ways.

4:1–3. Amos refers to the wives of the wealthy Israelites as "kine [cows] of Bashan" (v. 1). They are just as guilty as their husbands because they encourage the men to oppress the poor to support their extravagant lifestyle.

[2:6–16] BAD NEWS FOR THE WEALTHY. *They [wealthy class of Israel] sold the righteous for silver, and the poor for a pair of shoes* (Amos 2:6).

Two of God's highest expectations for His people, the Israelites, were that they would practice righteousness and show compassion toward the poor. In this verse Amos charged the wealthy class of Israel—the Northern Kingdom—with violating both these commands.

They were so calloused toward righteousness that they thought they could buy and sell it like any other commodity. Rather than treating the poor with fairness and justice, they were selling them into slavery because they could not pay their debts. Sometimes these debts were no more than the minor sum required to buy a cheap pair of sandals!

Amos declared that God would judge the wealthy for such greed and lack of compassion.

4:4–13. God has punished Israel for its sin and extravagance in many different ways. But these reprimands have failed to turn the people back to Him.

5:1–17. Amos issues a lament against Israel, as if the nation has already fallen to a foreign oppressor and experienced God's judgment. But he also declares that the people can avoid this fate if they will turn to God: "Seek the LORD, and ye shall live" (v. 6).

5:18–27. Commitment to the Lord must go deeper than worship rituals such as bringing offerings to the altar and singing songs of praise. God requires genuine repentance and righteous living from His people: "Let judgment run down as waters, and righteousness as a mighty stream" (v. 24; see Isa. 58).

6:1–14. Amos makes it clear what will happen to Israel if the people do not turn from their sinful ways. They will be taken away as captives into a foreign land.

7:1–9. Amos sees three visions of judgment promised by the Lord against Israel: grasshoppers (vv. 1–3), fire (vv. 4–6), and a plumb line (vv. 7–9). The plumb line is a dramatic demonstration that Israel does not measure up to God's standards.

7:10–17. Amaziah the priest rejects Amos's message and tells him to go back to Judah. Amos pronounces God's judgment against Amaziah because he refuses to hear the word of the Lord.

[7:10–17] AMOS AND SYCAMORE FIGS. *I [Amos] was no prophet, neither was I a prophet's son; but I was an herdman, and a gatherer of sycomore fruit* (Amos 7:14).

Amos was a lowly shepherd from the tiny village of Tekoa (Amos 1:1) in Judah (Southern Kingdom). But he was called to declare God's judgment against the rich people of the neighboring nation, Israel (Northern Kingdom). This verse shows that he did not claim to be a learned and sophisticated messenger. His only credential was his call from the Lord.

The "sycomore fruit" that Amos mentioned was a type of wild fig that grew in his native Judah. These figs were inferior in quality to the domesticated figs that are mentioned several times in the Bible (Num. 13:23; 1 Sam. 25:18; Mark 11:12–21). Only the poorest people of the land grew and ate sycamore figs.

8:1–14. Amos sees a vision of a basket of ripe fruit. This shows that Israel is ready for God's judgment, just as ripe fruit is ready to eat.

9:1–15. God's judgment falls on Israel. Although the people try to hide, He hunts them down. But God's grace is also evident in the midst of His judgment. He promises to preserve a faithful remnant of people who will eventually return to their homeland.

OBADIAH

OVERVIEW: God will punish the Edomites for participating in the humiliation of Jerusalem.

Introduction to Obadiah

Obadiah is the shortest book in the Old Testament, containing only twenty-one verses. The author is identified in the first verse of the book, but this is all we know about him.

Obadiah's brief prophecy was against the Edomites, ancient enemies of the nation of Israel. They had participated in the destruction and looting of the city of Jerusalem when it fell to the Babylonian army in 587 B.C. Because of this despicable act, the Edomites would be destroyed by the Lord.

The message of Obadiah's book is that God keeps faith with His people. He had promised many centuries before Obadiah's time that He would guide and protect His people and deal harshly with anyone who tried to do them harm (Gen. 12:1–3). God is the rock to whom we can flee in times of trouble and distress.

Summary of Obadiah

Verse 1. The Lord gives Obadiah the prophet a message of judgment that he is to speak against the nation of Edom.

Verses 2–5. God condemns the pride and vanity of Edom. The Edomites considered themselves invincible in their fortress cities—particularly the capital of Sela. But the Lord makes it clear through Obadiah that He will bring them down (Ezek. 25:12–14).

Verses 6–9. References to Esau in these verses show the ancestry of the Edomites. They were descendants of Esau, the twin brother of Jacob (Gen. 25:9–28). The problems between the nations of Israel and Edom had begun with the conflict between these two brothers many centuries before Obadiah's time (Gen. 25:19–28; 27:1–41).

Verses 10–16. The Lord will use an enemy nation to defeat Edom. Such punishment is deserved because of Edom's treatment of Judah. The Edomites stood by when foreigners attacked Jerusalem. They even carried away spoils from the city and prevented Jewish fugitives from fleeing to safety.

Verses 17–21. In contrast to the humiliation and defeat of Edom, God will bless His people Israel. After the exile in Babylon, they will return and possess the land that God has promised to Abraham and his descendants.

OVERVIEW: God uses a prejudiced prophet to show that He loves all people, even the enemies of the Israelites.

Introduction to Jonah

The book of Jonah shows that God can use a negative example to teach a positive lesson.

The negative example is the prophet Jonah, whom God called to preach to the citizens of Nineveh. This great city was the capital of the Assyrian Empire. The Jews hated the Assyrians because they were their sworn enemies who worshiped pagan gods. So Jonah tried to run away from God's call.

Eventually Jonah did travel to Nineveh and preach to the Ninevites, as God commanded him to do. But when they repented and turned to God, he sulked and pouted because the Lord refused to destroy them.

The positive lesson taught through this negative prophet is that God loves everyone, not just the Jewish people. Their religious pride led them to the false belief that they had an exclusive claim on God's love. But no one is outside the scope of His grace.

One positive thing we can say about Jonah is that he did dare to tell the truth about himself and his prejudice by writing the book that bears his name. It was probably written about 760 B.C. during the glory days of the Assyrian Empire. Jonah ministered during the days of King Jeroboam II of Israel (Northern Kingdom), who reigned about 793–753 B.C. (2 Kings 14:25).

Summary of Jonah

1:1–3. God calls Jonah to pronounce judgment against Nineveh, capital city of the Assyrian Empire. But Jonah runs from God and catches a ship bound for Tarshish in the opposite direction from Nineveh.

1:4–16. A violent storm strikes the ship. The superstitious crew casts lots to determine who is responsible for the storm. The lot falls on Jonah, who admits he is running from God's call. He advises the sailors to toss him overboard to appease the Lord's anger.

[1:4–16] **SUPERSTITIOUS SAILORS.** *Come, and let us [sailors on Jonah's ship] cast lots, that we may know for whose cause this evil is upon us* (Jon. 1:7).

Sailors of ancient times tended to be very superstitious because of their constant exposure to the dangers of the sea. When a storm struck the ship in which Jonah was escaping from the call of the Lord, they assumed the pagan gods were punishing them because of their displeasure with one person on board.

To find out who this person was, they cast lots—a custom similar to rolling dice or drawing straws in modern times. These lots may have been round stones or flat sticks of various lengths. Exactly what they looked like is not known.

The casting of lots as a method of decision making is mentioned several times in the Bible (Lev. 16:8–10; Num. 33:54; Josh. 14:2; 1 Chron. 25:8–9; Acts 1:26).

2:1–10. The great fish spits Jonah onto the shore. After three days in the creature's belly, he would now do what God told him to: preach to wicked Nineveh.

1:17. God saves Jonah by sending a great fish to swallow him and keeping him alive for three days in the stomach of the fish (Matt. 12:40).

2:1–10. Jonah prays an eloquent prayer for deliverance. The Lord hears his prayer and has him ejected from the fish unharmed and placed on the shore.

3:1–4. The Lord calls on Jonah again to proclaim His message to the city of Nineveh. This time Jonah obeys and delivers God's message of judgment against the Ninevites (Luke 11:32).

3:5–10. The citizens of Nineveh repent of their wicked ways and turn to the Lord in repentance. God withholds the disaster He had threatened against the city.

4:1–3. Jonah gets angry because the Lord extends mercy and forgiveness to the Ninevites. In self-pity, he asks God to take his life.

4:4–8. Jonah builds a hut on the eastern side of Nineveh. Here he waits to see what will happen to the city. God causes a vine to grow up over his head to shelter him from the sun and to cool his anger. Then the Lord causes the vine to die, and Jonah is miserable in the sun and hot wind. He again wallows in self-pity and wishes he were dead.

4:9–11. God condemns Jonah because he is more concerned about a vine than he is about the people of the city of Nineveh. He reminds Jonah that He is a merciful and forgiving God who loves all people, even the pagan Assyrians.

OVERVIEW: God's judgment will fall, but better days are ahead for God's people. He will send the Messiah, who will be born in Bethlehem.

Introduction to Micah

The prophet Micah delivered God's message to the citizens of both Judah (Southern Kingdom) and Israel (Northern Kingdom). He mentioned the reigns of three kings of Judah—Jotham, Ahaz, and Hezekiah (1:1)—a period that stretched from about 750 to 687 B.C. He must have written his book toward the end of this period.

Like most of the prophets of the Old Testament, Micah's book included prophecies of both judgment and promise. God would send His punishment upon His people because of their sin. But He was just as determined to bless them to fulfill the promises He had made to Abraham many centuries before (Gen. 12:1–5).

Micah made it clear that the people of both Judah and Israel would be punished by the Lord for their sin and rebellion. But in the future, God would restore His people through a remnant of those who would remain faithful to Him.

The book of Micah is best known for its promise of the coming Messiah. Micah even foretold the place where He would be born: the village of Bethlehem (5:2). This is one of the most remarkable messianic prophecies in the entire Old Testament.

Summary of Micah

1:1–16. God announces through the prophet Micah that He will judge the cities of Samaria and Jerusalem (v. 1). Jerusalem was the capital city of Judah (Southern Kingdom), while Samaria was the capital of Israel (Northern Kingdom). God plans to punish both nations because they have turned away from Him to worship false gods.

2:1–11. Micah condemns the wealthy people of Judah and Israel because they are

5:1–15. Modern-day Bethlehem. Micah prophesied Bethlehem by name as the birthplace of the Messiah. Jesus was born there some seven hundred years later.

cheating the poor. He accuses them of lying awake at night, making plans to strip the poor of their houses and fields. But God is also making plans. He intends to send disaster against the rich and proud.

2:12–13. Judah and Israel will be defeated by a foreign nation. But God will preserve a small group of people—a faithful remnant—who will remain loyal to Him. He will use this minority to rebuild His people.

3:1–4. Many of the problems of Judah and Israel can be traced to their political leaders. They have lost the ability to distinguish between good and evil, so they lead the people astray (Ezek. 11:3).

3:5–7. Even the prophets fail to follow the Lord. They are called to be the moral conscience of the people. But instead they are prophesying that good times will continue and that Judah and Israel have nothing to fear (Jer. 14).

3:8–12. The Lord repeats His promise of judgment against the two nations because of their widespread sin and corruption.

4:1–13. This chapter mixes the themes of judgment and blessing in reverse order. Judah will be defeated and carried into exile by the pagan nation of Babylonia (vv. 9–13; see 2 Kings 25:1–12). But after the exile is over, the Jewish people will return to their homeland (2 Chron. 36:22–23). They will enjoy an era of peace and prosperity. From Jerusalem, God will extend His witness and influence to all the nations (vv. 1–8).

5:1–15. This chapter foretells the defeat of Israel (Northern Kingdom) by the Assyrians. But in the midst of this prophecy is another look into the future that has universal implications. A deliverer or "ruler in Israel" (v. 2) will be born in Bethlehem. This

> **[4:1–13] SITTING IN THE SHADE.** *They shall sit every man under his vine and under his fig tree; and none shall make them afraid* (Mic. 4:4).
>
> Micah used these word pictures to portray the future for God's people. After the coming of the Messiah, they would enjoy peace and prosperity, symbolized by resting in the shade.
>
> In the hot, dry climate of Palestine, people often escaped from the sun's oppressive heat by sitting under a grapevine or fig tree. Its thick branches and broad leaves made the fig tree an ideal shade.
>
> When Philip found Nathanael and brought him to Jesus, Nathanael was sitting under a fig tree. He was probably resting in its shade and meditating on God's Word (John 1:45–51).

messianic prophecy was fulfilled with the birth of Jesus about 700 years after Micah's time (Luke 2:1–7).

6:1–16. The Lord rehearses all the mighty deeds He has performed for His people. What does He expect in return? Not burnt offerings, fasting, and empty rituals—but obedience to His commands and commitment to His principles of love and justice: "What doth the Lord require of thee, but to do justly, and to love mercy, and to walk humbly with thy God?" (v. 8).

7:1–20. Micah mourns ("Woe is me!" v. 1) when he reviews the sins of Judah and Israel. He wonders if there is one righteous person left in the land. This drives him to place his trust in the holy and righteous God. He is also a God of justice and forgiveness. After His people receive their deserved punishment, He will shower them with mercy and love: "He will have compassion upon us; he will subdue our iniquities; and thou wilt cast all their sins into the depths of the sea" (v. 19).

OVERVIEW: Nineveh, capital city of the Assyrian Empire, will fall before God's judgment.

Introduction to Nahum

The book of Jonah shows that God loved the pagan Assyrians (see the introduction to Jonah on p. 171); this book shows that He held them accountable for their sins, just like everyone else.

Nahum consists of a prophecy written by the prophet Nahum about 615 B.C. that Nineveh—capital city of the Assyrian Empire—would fall as a result of God's judgment against its rebellion and cruelty. This happened in 612 B.C., just as the prophet predicted, when the Assyrians were defeated by the Babylonians.

Assyria had been the dominant world power for more than a century when Nahum

1:1. Nineveh's cruelty included the mistreatment of both humans and animals.

proclaimed his prophecy against it. God's judgment does not always come quickly, but it is thorough and efficient when it does arrive.

Summary of Nahum

1:1. The prophet Nahum receives a message of judgment from God. This message is to be proclaimed against Nineveh, capital of the Assyrian Empire.

1:2–8. Nahum paints a graphic picture of a powerful God who will judge the pagan city of Nineveh. But at the same time, those who serve Him have nothing to fear: "The Lord is good, a strong hold in the day of trouble" (v. 7).

1:9–15. God will destroy the idols and images of the pagan Assyrian religious system. But He will restore the nation of Judah and its system of worship of the one true God.

2:1–13. This chapter describes Nineveh under siege as God's judgment falls upon the city. Once known as "the dwelling of the lions" (v. 11), Nineveh is now weak and helpless as it cowers before its enemies. Just as Assyria had once robbed and looted other nations, now it will be stripped of its treasures.

3:1. Nahum declares, "Woe to the bloody city!" Assyria was known for its violence and cruelty in warfare. They disabled captive enemy soldiers by cutting off their hands. Rival political leaders were often impaled on stakes. Now these acts of cruelty will be carried out against the Assyrians.

3:2–19. Nahum continues his description of the defeat of Nineveh. Its streets will be littered with corpses, and it will be ransacked and burned. Not a single person will mourn the fall of Nineveh, because everyone has felt the effects of its evil and wickedness during its glory days.

[2:1–13] ASSYRIAN TERROR. *The shield of his mighty men is made red, the valiant men are in scarlet: the chariots shall be with flaming torches in the day of his preparation* (Nah. 2:3).

Nahum's description of Assyrian warriors and their battle gear shows why they struck terror in the hearts of those who faced them in battle.

The uniforms of Assyrian soldiers were scarlet in color, and they carried shields painted red, or perhaps overlaid with copper. They may have used these colors to make the blood from their wounds hard to see. In hand-to-hand combat, they wanted to give no sign that would infuse the enemy with hope and courage.

The "flaming torches" on their war chariots may have been whirling blades on the axles designed to damage and immobilize the wheels of enemy chariots. Or this could refer to the weapons in their chariots that flashed in the sunlight, giving the appearance of burning torches.

Assyria was noted for its cruelty in warfare. Their warriors would cut off the feet and hands of captives as a terror tactic to intimidate nations into surrendering to their rule (see the note "Mutilation of Captives" on p. 50).

OVERVIEW: Because God is sovereign, He can use any agency He desires—even a pagan enemy nation—to bring judgment upon His people.

Introduction to Habakkuk

Habakkuk was a prophet to the Southern Kingdom (Judah) who wrote his book about 600 B.C. Like Job, he had the audacity to question the ways of God (see the introduction to Job on p. 109).

First, the prophet thought God was being lenient for not punishing the people of Judah for their sin. The Lord assured him that punishment was coming in the form of the Babylonian army from the north.

Then Habakkuk questioned whether it was just and fair for the Lord to use a pagan nation as an instrument of His judgment. Weren't they more sinful than those whom God was sending them against?

The Lord told Habakkuk that He was the sovereign ruler of the universe who could do as He pleased. He did not owe the prophet an explanation for His actions. Habakkuk finally accepted this truth about the Lord and His ways in submissive faith.

One of the great truths from the book of Habakkuk is that God has no problem with honest questions from His followers. He does not reject us if we bring our doubts and questions to Him. He will listen and sympathize and help us in the struggle to learn more about Him and His sometimes mysterious ways.

Summary of Habakkuk

1:1–4. Habakkuk begins his book not with a declaration of the word of God to others but with a question directed to God Himself. The prophet wants to know why God allows His people, the nation of Judah, to continue committing sin without subjecting them to judgment.

1:5–11. The Lord assures Habakkuk that He does intend to hold His people accountable for their wrongdoing. Even now He is raising up an enemy nation, the Chaldeans (Babylonians), who will serve as His instrument of punishment against the people of Judah. When He does judge His people, it will be harsh and effective. The Babylonians are a "bitter and hasty nation" (v. 6) known to be "terrible and dreadful" (v. 7).

[1:12–2:1] BABYLONIAN WEAPONS WORSHIP. *They [Babylonian warriors] sacrifice unto their net, and burn incense unto their drag [dragnet, NIV]* (Hab. 1:16).

This verse apparently refers to the practice among the pagan Babylonians of worshiping and offering sacrifices to their weapons of war. The Babylonians were on a mission of world conquest in Habakkuk's time. Bowing down to these weapons was the Babylonians' way of strengthening and dedicating them for this purpose.

This pagan practice made it difficult for Habakkuk to accept the reality that God would use the Babylonians as an instrument of judgment against His own people, the nation of Judah.

1:12–2:1. The Lord's answer presents Habakkuk with another dilemma. The Babylonians are unrighteous people who worship pagan gods. Are they not more evil and wicked than those whom God will send them against? How can God use them to carry out His will? The prophet climbs upon a tower to wait for God's answer to this question.

2:2–20. God honors Habakkuk's question with a forthright answer. He is using the Babylonians not because of who they are or are not but because He can work His sovereign will as He desires. After He finishes with the Babylonians, He will also judge them for their evil ways. The Lord ends His answer to the prophet with a gentle rebuke that shows He does not have to justify His actions to anyone: "The LORD is in his holy temple: let all the earth keep silence before him" (v. 20; see Job 42:1–6).

3:1–19. In a beautiful prayer of submission, Habakkuk accepts the judgment of God against His people and the method He will use to bring it about. Praising God for His wonderful works, he declares, "I will rejoice in the LORD, I will joy in the God of my salvation" (v. 18).

1:1–4. In Rio de Janeiro, Brazil, slums and high-rise condominiums stand side by side. The prophet Habakkuk complained to God that wicked people prospered while the good suffered. God responded by promising to send invaders who would punish Israel for its sin.

Overview: Judah (Southern Kingdom) will fall to a foreign enemy because the people are bowing down to idols.

Introduction to Zephaniah

The prophet Zephaniah tells us more about himself and his background than any of the other minor prophets of the Old Testament. He traces his ancestry back to his great-great-grandfather King Hizkiah (Hezekiah) of Judah (1:1; see 2 Chron. 29:3–36).

Zephaniah also reveals that he ministered during the days of Josiah (1:1), a godly king who reigned in Judah from about 641 to 609 B.C. Zephaniah probably wrote his book about 627 B.C.

The prophet addressed his prophecies to the nation of Judah (Southern Kingdom), which was soon to be punished by the Lord for its sin and idolatry. His prophecies were fulfilled when the nation was overrun by the Babylonian army several years after he issued his warning.

Even as the Lord was punishing His people and sending them into exile, Zephaniah declared, He would preserve a remnant who would remain faithful to Him. These would eventually inherit the promise God made to Abraham hundreds of years before (Gen. 12:1–5). People of all nations would gather in Jerusalem to worship the Lord when the remnant of Judah returned to their homeland. The King of kings, the Messiah would rule among them (3:9–13).

Summary of Zephaniah

1:1. During the days of King Josiah of Judah, God calls the prophet Zephaniah to deliver His message of judgment.

1:2–18. Judah has turned away from the Lord and is worshiping false gods. Punishment for this serious sin will come upon Judah on the great day of the Lord. This will be "a day of trouble and distress, a day of wasteness and desolation...a day of clouds and thick darkness" (v. 15). No one in Judah will escape this time of judgment.

2:1–3. But even while preaching God's coming judgment, Zephaniah holds out hope. He urges the people of Judah to seek the Lord and follow His commands. Those who do so may possibly "be hid in the day of the LORD's anger" (v. 3).

2:4–15. God's wrath will extend beyond the land of Judah to the surrounding pagan nations. He will also punish the Philistines (vv. 4–7), the Moabites (vv. 8–11), the Ethiopians (v. 12), and the Assyrians (vv. 13–15).

3:1–7. As the capital city of Judah, Jerusalem will suffer the same fate as the rest of the nation. Because it has been polluted through worship of false gods, it will fall to foreign oppressors (2 Kings 25:1–12).

3:8–20. Although God is angered by Judah's idolatry, He has not given up on His people. He will preserve a faithful remnant who will remain loyal to Him. God will use them to resettle the land and bear witness of Him to others when they return from their time of captivity in a foreign land.

OVERVIEW: A message of hope for the Jewish exiles who have returned to Jerusalem and a call for them to complete the task of rebuilding the temple.

Introduction to Haggai

Haggai is one of three prophets in the Old Testament known as postexilic prophets. The other two are Zechariah and Malachi. They wrote their books during the turbulent period after the return of the Jewish exiles to Judah following their period of captivity by the Babylonians and Persians.

The years after the exile were discouraging times for God's people. They literally had to rebuild their lives following an absence from their homeland of more than fifty years. Neglected farmland had to be cleared before it could be cultivated. Destroyed homes had to be rebuilt. Customs and traditions had to be reestablished.

Haggai wrote his book to encourage the people to remain faithful to God, to rebuild the Jewish temple as a central place for worship, to practice holiness and righteousness in the midst of tough times, and to look forward to the coming of the Messiah and the establishment of His kingdom.

The book of Haggai emphasizes the truth that all of us need encouragement at times. One of the greatest ministries we can perform is to serve as encouragers to others.

Summary of Haggai

1:1–11. The Lord commands the prophet Haggai to address the people who have returned to Jerusalem after the exile in Babylon (2 Chron. 36:22–23). He is to challenge them to resume the task of rebuilding the temple. Haggai declares that they are suffering hard times because they have not rebuilt God's house as a place of worship.

1:12–15. The people respond to Haggai's challenge by beginning the work. The prophet delivers God's promise that He will be with them during the reconstruction project.

[2:10–19] THIRTY VESSELS SHORT. *When one came to the pressfat [wine vat, NIV] for to draw out fifty vessels out of the press, there were but twenty* (Hag. 2:16).

The Hebrew word rendered as "pressfat" by the KJV refers to a winepress or an olive press. These stone presses were used in Bible times to squeeze the oil out of olives for making fuels to burn in lamps or to press the juice out of grapes for making wine.

What Haggai is saying is that God will give the people less harvest than they expect unless they get their priorities straight and resume the task of rebuilding the temple. We can't shirk our responsibility to God and expect Him to shower us with blessings.

2:1–9. God realizes some of the people will be discouraged because the rebuilt temple will not be as large or as beautiful as the original temple. So Haggai encourages the people not to make such comparisons. What really matters is whether the temple brings glory and honor to God. The Lord promises to fill it with His presence so "the glory of this latter house shall be greater than of the former" (v. 9).

2:10–19. Haggai declares to the priests that a defiled object cannot be made clean through contact with a holy object. In the same way, the completed temple will have no magical qualities. The people should not think they will be made clean through contact with the temple. Holiness comes through devoting oneself to God and following His commands.

2:20–23. Haggai encourages Zerubbabel, a Jewish leader who has been appointed governor of Judah by the Persians (Hag. 1:1). God makes it clear that Zerubbabel has

[2:20–23] ZERUBBABEL AS A SIGNET RING. *In that day...will I [God] take thee, O Zerubbabel...and will make thee as a signet: for I have chosen thee, saith the LORD of hosts* (Hag. 2:23).

In ancient times a signet ring functioned much like a personal signature does today. A king or other high official would stamp an official document with the symbol on his ring to establish its legality and show that it was issued under his authority.

God compared Zerubbabel, the Jewish governor of Jerusalem, to a signet ring. He had invested Zerubbabel with the highest honor and would use him as His representative to bring about His purposes in the city of Jerusalem.

When the pharaoh of Egypt appointed Joseph to a high position in his administration, he gave Joseph his signet ring to show that he had the authority to act in his behalf (Gen. 41:42).

been placed in this important position for a good reason. He will use the governor to bring many blessings to His people.

ZECHARIAH

OVERVIEW: God will bless His people in the future by sending the Messiah. Meanwhile, the returned Jewish exiles need to rebuild Jerusalem and the temple.

Introduction to Zechariah

Zechariah addressed his prophecy to the same situation faced by Haggai (see the introduction to Haggai on p. 180). Like Haggai, he also encouraged the people to complete the task of rebuilding the temple in Jerusalem.

This building had been destroyed by the Babylonian army when it ransacked the city in 587 B.C. The temple was the center of religious life for the nation of Judah. So it was imperative that it be rebuilt as quickly as possible.

But the greatest contribution of Zechariah's book is his description of the coming Messiah. He described a coronation scene (6:9–15), in which a priest named Joshua, symbolizing the Messiah, is crowned as king as well as priest. He declared that the Messiah would reign in justice from the city of Jerusalem (8:3, 15–16).

Zechariah even described the manner in which the Messiah would enter the city: "He is just, and having salvation; lowly, and riding upon an ass, and upon a colt the foal of an ass" (9:9). This prophecy was fulfilled when Jesus rode into Jerusalem on a young donkey just a few days before His crucifixion (Matt. 21:5).

Summary of Zechariah

1:1–6. Zechariah calls upon the people to repent and turn from their sinful ways back to the Lord (James 4:8).

1:7–17. The prophet has a vision of four horsemen, or watchmen, who report that "all the earth...is at rest" (v. 11). This is a sign that it is time for the Jewish exiles to return from Persia to their homeland to rebuild the city of Jerusalem (2 Chron. 36:22–23).

> **[1:7–17] MONTH OF SEBAT.** *Upon the four and twentieth day of the eleventh month, which is the month Sebat [Shebat, NIV], in the second year of Darius* (Zech. 1:7).
>
> Zechariah had eight visions that he recorded in his book. In this verse he tells us the exact month and day on which his first vision occurred. The Jewish month of Sebat closely parallels our month of February.
>
> Many scholars believe this vision of the prophet—a man on a red horse among the myrtle trees (1:8)—can be precisely dated at February 24, 519 B.C., by using the phrase "the second year of Darius." We know from secular history that King Darius began his reign over Persia about 521 B.C.

1:18–21. The four horns in Zechariah's vision in these verses represent the nations that had defeated Judah. These foreign nations have been defeated, so the return of Jewish exiles to Jerusalem can now proceed with no interference.

2:1–13. In this vision, Zechariah sees a man with a measuring line who is preparing

9:9–17. With crowds cheering Him, Jesus rides into Jerusalem on a donkey—just as the prophet Zechariah predicted.

to measure the wall of Jerusalem. But this measurement is not necessary, since God will serve as the protector of the city: "I, saith the LORD, will be unto her a wall of fire" (v. 5).

3:1–10. The high priest Joshua is cleansed and restored to his office in this vision of Zechariah. This prepares the way for the coming of the Messiah, who is referred to as "the BRANCH" (v. 8; see also 6:9–15).

4:1–14. In this vision, Zechariah sees a golden candlestick, or lamp stand, with an olive tree on the left side and another olive tree on the right side. The message of the vision is that God will provide the resources to enable Zerubbabel, the governor of Jerusalem, to complete the rebuilding of the temple (Hag. 2:20–23).

5:1–4. Zechariah's vision of the flying scroll ("roll," v. 1) represents God's curse against any person who steals from others or swears falsely.

5:5–11. The basket ("ephah," v. 6) in this vision represents the cleansing of the land of

Judah. The sins of the people are in the basket, which is taken away to Babylonia.

6:1–8. Zechariah's vision of the four chariots is similar to his first vision (1:7–17). God is in control, and He exercises His sovereignty over the entire world.

6:9–15. A crown is placed on the head of Joshua the high priest. He symbolizes the promised Branch, or the Messiah (chap. 3).

7:1–8:23. These chapters address the question of fasting among God's people. Since the temple is being rebuilt, should the people continue to fast? God replies that He intends to bless His people and to turn their fasts into occasions of joy.

9:1–8. God declares that He will punish the pagan nations surrounding Judah because of their worship of false gods.

9:9–17. These verses describe the arrival of the long-promised messianic King, riding on a young donkey. This passage was fulfilled by Jesus when He made His triumphant entry into Jerusalem in this fashion (Matt. 21:5).

10:1–11:17. The earthly leaders of Judah have led the nation astray (Jer. 8). God promises that He will guide His people; they can count on Him to lead them with justice and mercy.

[13:1–14:21] HOLINESS AND HORSES. *In that day shall there be upon the bells of the horses, HOLINESS UNTO THE LORD* (Zech. 14:20).

In this verse Zechariah foresees a future time when all the nations will acknowledge and worship the one true God. The praise of the Lord will be so widespread that even horses will have "HOLINESS UNTO THE LORD" inscribed on the bells on their harnesses. These are the same words embroidered on the hat worn by the high priest of Israel (Exod. 28:36).

It was customary among the nations of Bible times to hang bells on the harnesses of their warhorses. This gave them a regal, military appearance. The noise produced by the bells also may have conditioned the horses for the noise of battle.

12:1–14. God empowers His people for a great battle against the nations, and victory is assured. The phrase "They shall look upon me whom they have pierced" (v. 10) has been interpreted as a reference to Christ and His suffering (John 19:37).

13:1–14:21. In the final days, the Lord will cleanse and bless Jerusalem and establish His eternal rule throughout the world.

OVERVIEW: A prophetic call for spiritual renewal among the Jewish exiles who have returned to Jerusalem.

Introduction to Malachi

Malachi was a postexilic prophet, so he faced the same situation as Haggai and Zechariah (see the introduction to Haggai on p. 180). The name Malachi means "messenger of the Lord," and he was bold and forthright as God's appointed spokesman.

The prophet Malachi delivered his messages to God's people about 450 b.c., or about 100 years after their return from captivity. This was a time of great moral laxity and indifference in the nation of Judah.

Many of the people stopped bringing their tithes and offerings to the temple. Others offered defective animals as sacrifices rather than the finest from their flocks, as the Lord demanded. Intermarriage with pagan people was commonplace. Even the priests grew careless and indifferent in presiding over ceremonies at the temple.

Malachi declared that these lax practices were unacceptable to the Lord. Unless the people and the leaders changed their ways, they would face His punishment.

To make God's message more forceful, Malachi wrote parts of his book in a debate format. God made a statement of truth that was denied by the people. The Lord then overturned their argument to emphasize the truth of His original statement (1:2–7; 2:10–17; 3:7–10).

It is futile to argue with God; He always has the last word!

Summary of Malachi

1:1–5. Malachi begins his message to the exiles who have returned to Jerusalem by assuring them of God's love. His love for Israel is evident because He allowed the Jewish exiles to return and resettle their land (2 Chron. 36:22–23). God continues to honor the covenant He made centuries ago with Abraham (Gen. 12:1–5). By contrast, the land of Edom has been destroyed and will not be reclaimed by the Edomites.

1:6–14. But God is displeased with the response of the people to His love. They have grown cold and casual in their devotion to Him. They are bringing sick and defective animals to offer as sacrifices rather than presenting the best from their flocks. This is a flagrant violation of His commands (Lev. 22:20).

2:1–9. Even the priests are neglecting their responsibilities. As spiritual leaders, they are supposed to be leading the people in the ways of the Lord. But they are actually leading people astray through their waywardness and neglect.

2:10–16. The spiritual condition of the people is reflected in their family problems. Many Israelite men have married women from the surrounding nations who worship pagan gods (Ezra 10:10–17). And some of the older men are divorcing the wives of their youth to marry younger pagan women. God is displeased with these practices.

2:17–3:5. The Lord declares that He is getting tired of the whining of the people about His apparent lack of judgment against the ungodly. He assures them that He is aware of the actions of the wicked and He will deal with them as they deserve when the time is right.

3:6–10. God declares that the people are guilty of withholding tithes and offerings that belong to Him. This is another example of their lack of commitment and spiritual zeal.

3:11–18. Apparently, some Israelites were complaining that their service to God had not been rewarded. God seemed to bless the unrighteous while bringing suffering upon the righteous. The Lord rebukes this pessimistic attitude. Those who truly belong to Him, He says, will "discern between the righteous and the wicked, between him that serveth God and him that serveth him not" (v. 18).

1:6–14. The prophet Malachi complained that worshippers we[re] bringing diseased and crippled animals as sacrifices to God, wh[en] Jewish law required only the best animals.

4:1–3. The coming day of the Lord, when God exercises His judgment, will have two different realities. To the wicked, it will be like a consuming hot oven. But those who belong to God will experience joy when they see "the Sun of righteousness arise with healing in his wings" (v. 2; see Joel 2:1–11).

4:4–6. These verses form a fitting conclusion not only to Malachi but to the entire Old Testament. They look back to God's law that was revealed to Moses many centuries before. But they also look forward to the fulfillment of this law with the coming of Christ. Four hundred years after the end of Malachi, God sent one final prophet known as John the Baptist to prepare the way for the promised Messiah. Jesus identified John as the Elijah who is promised in verse 5 (Matt. 17:10–13).

[3:11–18] GOD'S BOOK OF REMEMBRANCE. *A book of remembrance was written before him [God] for them that feared the LORD (Mal. 3:16).*

God promised through the prophet Malachi that He would write in a "book of remembrance" the names of all the people who honored and worshiped Him.

This metaphor probably comes from the ancient Persian custom of keeping an official record of those who rendered special service to the king. King Ahasuerus of Persia was looking through such a book when he discovered that Mordecai the Jew had saved him from an assassination plot (Esther 6:1–2).

PART 2

THE NEW TESTAMENT

The second grand division of the Bible is the New Testament. Unlike the Old Testament, which was written over a period of many centuries, the twenty-seven books of the New Testament were inspired by God and written down by human authors across a period of about sixty years.

The great event that brought the New Testament into being was the life and ministry of Jesus Christ. He fulfilled the promises that God made to His people in the Old Testament by establishing a new covenant (the word *testament* means "covenant") based on the spiritual principles of grace and forgiveness rather than the keeping of the law. This new covenant between God and His people was sealed with the atoning death of His own Son.

The four major divisions of the New Testament are (1) the four Gospels, accounts of the life and ministry of Jesus; (2) the Acts of the Apostles, a book of history that traces the growth of the early church after the death and resurrection of Jesus; (3) the thirteen epistles, or letters, of the apostle Paul; and (4) the eight letters classified as general epistles, written by early church leaders other than Paul to various churches and individuals. These divisions of the New Testament are discussed in the following chapters.

CHAPTER 6
THE GOSPELS

Jesus Christ is the cornerstone of the church and the Christian faith, so it is appropriate that the New Testament opens with not one account but four separate records of His life and ministry—the Gospels of Matthew, Mark, Luke, and John. These reports were written either by Jesus' apostles who witnessed His work firsthand (Matthew and John) or by persons who recorded the eyewitness testimony of those who had known Jesus in the flesh (Mark and Luke).

These Gospels are selective accounts rather than complete biographies of the life of Jesus. The Gospel writers focused on the final three years of Jesus' life when He conducted His teaching and healing ministry. Their purpose was to show how God revealed Himself supremely in the life of His Son. Even with their narrow three-year focus, they tell us only a few of the things He did. The apostle John declared in his Gospel: "There are also many other things which Jesus did, the which, if they should be written every one, I suppose that even the world itself could not contain the books that should be written" (John 21:25).

The Gospels of Matthew, Mark, and Luke are known as the Synoptic Gospels. This designation comes from the Greek word *synopsis*, which means "seeing together." There is a great deal of overlap and repetition among these three Gospels. They report many of the same events from the life of Jesus, using a similar chronology and even repeating the information almost word for word in many cases. Of course, each of these Gospels also contains material about Jesus not found in any other account.

In contrast to the Synoptic Gospels, the Gospel of John takes a unique approach to the life of Jesus. The apostle John does more than just tell us about the things that Jesus said and did. He goes beyond the obvious to give us the theological meaning behind His teachings and miracles.

We are fortunate to have four separate Gospel witnesses to the Jesus event. While they overlap and repeat one another at certain points, together they enrich and expand our understanding of who He was and what He did.

OVERVIEW: As the teacher who is greater than Moses, Jesus is the fulfillment of the Old Testament Scriptures.

Introduction to Matthew

The Gospel of Matthew is an ideal bridge between the Old Testament and the New Testament. It was written to show that Jesus is the fulfillment of Old Testament prophecy. For centuries the Jewish people had looked forward to the coming of the Messiah. Matthew affirmed that Jesus is this long-awaited Savior and King.

Matthew is never identified by name as the author of this Gospel. But since the early days of the church, he has been accepted as the writer. Matthew, also known as Levi (Mark 2:14), was called away from his duties as a tax collector to become one of the twelve disciples, or apostles, of Jesus (9:9–13).

Several clues in the Gospel of Matthew indicate that it was written to a Jewish audience to show that Jesus is the Messiah. Matthew quoted more than seventy times from the Old Testament—more than all the other three Gospels combined—using the refrain "that it might be fulfilled" (1:22) to show that Jesus fulfilled the prophecies of the Old Testament. Matthew also began his Gospel by tracing Jesus' ancestry back to Abraham, the father of the faith (1:1–2).

Another characteristic of this Gospel is its emphasis on the teaching ministry of Jesus.

The Sermon on the Mount (chaps. 5–7) summarizes the ethical standards that Jesus established for those who belong to the kingdom of God. In addition to these teachings, other important pronouncements of Jesus are grouped into major sections that end with a refrain such as "when Jesus had ended these sayings" or "when Jesus had finished these parables" (see 7:28; 11:1; 13:53; 19:1; 26:1).

Some accounts of Jesus' life and ministry in Matthew also parallel events reported in Mark, Luke, and John. These parallel passages are identified in the following summary of Matthew. The parallel passages in bold type with "see" references refer to pages in this book where expanded summaries of specific Gospel accounts may be found.

Summary of Matthew

1:1–17. Matthew begins his Gospel by tracing Jesus' genealogy through forty-two generations from Abraham up to Joseph and Mary. (For a different genealogy of Jesus, see Luke 3:23–38.)

1:18–25. Joseph is disturbed when Mary becomes pregnant while they are betrothed to each other. But an angel assures him that this pregnancy is of divine origin. Joseph marries Mary, and they name their firstborn son Jesus.

2:1–12. Wise men from the east arrive in Jerusalem to worship the newborn "King of the Jews" (v. 2). They are sent to Bethlehem,

[1:18–25] JOSEPH AND MARY'S BETROTHAL. *When as his mother Mary was espoused [pledged to be married, NIV] to Joseph, before they came together, she was found with child of the Holy Ghost* (Matt. 1:18).

In Bible times a marriage was arranged through a legal agreement between the parents of the groom and the bride. The groom's parents selected a woman for their son to marry, then paid the bride's parents a dowry, or bride price, to compensate them for the loss of her services as a daughter.

The period between the time of this legal agreement and the actual marriage of the couple was known as the betrothal. The future groom and bride were espoused or pledged to each other during this time in a formal agreement that was as legally binding as marriage itself. The betrothal could be broken only by a legal proceeding similar to a divorce.

It was during the time of her betrothal to Joseph that Mary discovered she was pregnant. This was certainly grounds for Joseph and his family to dissolve their marriage agreement with Mary and her parents.

But Joseph was informed by an angel that Mary's pregnancy was due to the miraculous action of the Holy Spirit. This child from her womb would be the Messiah, the Son of God, who would "save his people from their sins" (Matt. 1:21).

Joseph believed this message from the Lord, and he went forward with his plans to take Mary as his wife (Matt. 1:24).

where the Scriptures predicted this king would be born (Mic. 5:2). In Bethlehem, the wise men present gifts of gold, frankincense, and myrrh to the young Jesus.

2:13–18. The jealous and paranoid King Herod of Judah slaughters all the male children under two years of age around Bethlehem in an attempt to kill the young Jesus. But Joseph is warned in a dream to take the boy and His mother to a safe place in the land of Egypt.

2:19–23. After Herod dies, Jesus and His family return to Judah. They settle in the city of Nazareth, the ancestral home of Mary and Joseph (parallel passage: Luke 2:39–40).

3:1–12. In the wilderness of Judea, the forerunner of Jesus, John the Baptist, begins preaching his message of repentance and the coming kingdom (parallel passages: Mark 1:1–8; **Luke 3:1–20,** see p. 218).

3:13–17. Jesus is baptized by John the Baptist in the Jordan River. God shows His approval by declaring, "This is my beloved Son, in whom I am well pleased" (v. 17) (parallel passages: Mark 1:9–11; Luke 3:21–22).

4:1–11. At the beginning of His public ministry, Jesus faces a series of temptations from Satan (parallel passages: Mark 1:12–13; **Luke 4:1–13,** see p. 218).

4:12–17. Leaving His hometown of Nazareth, Jesus moves to Capernaum in Galilee and launches His public ministry. He continues the message that John the Baptist, His forerunner, had been preaching: "Repent: for the kingdom of heaven is at hand" (v. 17) (parallel passages: Mark 1:14–15; John 4:45).

4:18–22. Jesus calls two different pairs of brothers—Peter and Andrew, James and John—away from their fishing nets to become His followers and disciples (parallel passages: Mark 1:16–20; **Luke 5:1–11,** see p. 218).

[5:1–7:29] SALT OF THE EARTH. *Ye [followers of Jesus] are the salt of the earth: but if the salt have lost his savour [loses its saltiness, NIV], wherewith shall it be salted? it is thenceforth good for nothing* (Matt. 5:13).

Salt added flavor to food, and it was also used to preserve meat in a society in which refrigeration and cold storage did not exist.

Jesus used the imagery of salt to describe His followers. If they did not demonstrate their distinctive purity and holiness as His people, they would have no influence in the world. Christians have no higher calling than to serve as the "salt of the earth" in a sinful and decadent culture.

4:12–17. An eight-sided church built over the presumed site of Peter's house in Capernaum overlooks the ruins of an early synagogue. Jesus selected this fishing village, hometown of several of His disciples, as His ministry headquarters.

4:23–25. Jesus travels throughout the region of Galilee, preaching the gospel of the kingdom of God and healing the sick. As His fame spreads, crowds flock to Him from as far away as Judea and the city of Jerusalem in southern Palestine (parallel passages: Mark 1:35–39; Luke 4:42–44).

5:1–7:29. Jesus delivers His famous Sermon on the Mount to His followers. It describes the type of behavior expected of those who are true citizens of the kingdom of God. Jesus covers several distinctive themes in these teachings:

(1) The Beatitudes (5:3–12). The word *blessed*, meaning "happy," describes the rewards in store for those who live as citizens of God's kingdom.

(2) Salt and light (5:13–16). Christian living by citizens of God's kingdom bears a positive witness in the world.

(3) Authentic righteousness (5:17–48). We must go beyond rituals and external appearances and live by the deeper meaning of God's laws.

(4) The dangers of hypocrisy (6:1–18). Matters of worship such as giving, praying, and fasting must grow out of the right motives.

(5) Getting priorities in order (6:19–34). Anxiety over lesser matters will disappear when we put God's kingdom first.

(6) Not judging (7:1–6). The citizens of God's kingdom must not judge and condemn people with a harsh, critical attitude.

(7) The importance of prayer (7:7–12). We may claim the blessings of prayer that God has promised to those who follow Him.

(8) The two ways (7:13–14). Believers must choose the narrow way that leads to life, not the broad and popular way that leads to certain destruction.

(9) Fruit-bearing (7:15–20). A genuine follower of the Lord will perform deeds and render service that bring honor and glory to Him.

(10) Actions versus words (7:21–23). Obeying God is more important than a long speech about how committed we are to Him.

(11) The solid foundation (7:24–29). Jesus' parable about the man who built his house on a rock shows how important it is to plant our lives on the unshakable foundation of the Lord and His Word.

8:1–4. Jesus heals a man with leprosy (parallel passages: **Mark 1:40–45,** see p. 206; Luke 5:12–16).

8:5–13. Jesus expresses His surprise at the faith of a centurion, a Roman military officer. He heals the man's servant at a distance (parallel passage: Luke 7:1–10).

8:14–17. Many sick people from Capernaum seek Jesus for healing after He heals Peter's mother-in-law (parallel passages: Mark 1:29–34; Luke 4:38–41).

8:18–22. Jesus challenges His followers to be fully committed to Him (parallel passage: Luke 9:57–62).

8:23–27. Jesus calms a storm on the Sea of Galilee. The disciples are amazed at His power (parallel passages: Mark 4:35–41; Luke 8:22–25).

8:28–34. Jesus casts demons out of two wild men among the tombs (parallel passages: **Mark 5:1–20,** see p. 208; Luke 8:26–39).

9:1–8. Several scribes accuse Jesus of blasphemy after He heals a paralyzed man and forgives his sins (parallel passages: **Mark 2:1–12,** see p. 206; Luke 5:17–26).

9:9–13. Jesus calls Matthew, a tax collector, to leave his tollbooth and follow Him and become His disciple (parallel passages: Mark 2:13–17; **Luke 5:27–32,** see p. 218).

9:14–17. Jesus is asked why He and His disciples do not fast. He replies that fasting is an

[9:1–8] TOTAL PARALYSIS. *Then saith he [Jesus] to the sick of the palsy [the paralytic, NIV], Arise, take up thy bed* (Matt. 9:6).

The word *palsy* is used in the KJV to describe a person who is totally paralyzed. The Gospels use this word only of the man whose friends let him down through the roof of a house on a blanket so he could be healed by Jesus (Matt. 9:1–6; see also Mark 2:1–12; Luke 5:17–26).

Matthew's Gospel eliminates the details about this man being let down through the roof. But scholars believe this is the same healing miracle—with these details added—reported by Mark and Luke.

The apostle Peter also healed a man who was totally paralyzed (Acts 9:32–34).

external law or rite that is being displaced by spiritual principles. The kingdom of God that has arrived in Jesus cannot conform to the rituals of the Pharisees (parallel passages: Mark 2:18–22; Luke 5:33–39).

9:18–26. Jesus heals a woman with a hemorrhage and raises the daughter of a synagogue ruler from the dead (parallel passages: **Mark 5:21–43,** see p. 208; Luke 8:40–56).

9:27–31. Jesus heals two blind men and orders them not to tell anyone about this miracle.

9:32–35. Jesus heals a demon-possessed man who is unable to speak. The Pharisees charge Him with performing miracles through the power of Satan.

9:36–38. The spiritual needs of the people move Jesus to compassion. He prays for more workers to minister to these needs.

10:1–4. From among all His followers, Jesus selects twelve men to serve as His disciples (parallel passages: Mark 3:13–19; **Luke 6:12–16,** see pp. 218–220).

10:5–42. Jesus sends His twelve disciples out to preach the gospel of the kingdom of God and to heal the sick. He warns them that they will be rejected and persecuted in some places. But they can depend on God's promise of guidance and protection (parallel passages: Mark 6:7–13; Luke 9:1–6).

11:1–19. After being imprisoned by King Herod, John the Baptist wonders if Jesus really is the Messiah whom he has announced in his preaching. He sends two of his followers to Jesus to find out. Jesus assures John that He is indeed the spiritual deliverer whom God has sent. He also commends John for his faithfulness to the task of paving the way for His work (parallel passage: Luke 7:18–35).

11:20–24. Jesus condemns the cities of Chorazin, Bethsaida, and Capernaum in the region of Galilee for their spiritual stubbornness and lack of belief in Him and His teachings.

11:25–30. Jesus commends the common people ("babes," v. 25), who are open to His teachings, in contrast to the proud Pharisees ("the wise and prudent," v. 25), who are critical of His ministry. He invites all who are burdened down by a religion of legalistic rule-keeping to find relief and rest in Him.

12:1–8. The Pharisees criticize Jesus and His

[12:1–8] EATING GRAIN OFF THE STALK. *His [Jesus'] disciples were an hungered, and began to pluck the ears of corn [heads of grain, NIV], and to eat* (Matt. 12:1).

While passing by a field of wheat or barley on the Sabbath, Jesus' disciples stripped some grain from the stalks. They rubbed it in their hands to remove the outer husks, then popped the grain into their mouths.

Wheat or barley was usually ground into flour, then baked into bread. But when bread was not available, eating grain right off the stalk was a quick way to satisfy one's hunger.

The Old Testament law permitted hungry travelers to pick and eat handfuls of grain from fields along the road (Deut. 23:25).

disciples for picking grain on the Sabbath to satisfy their hunger. According to their interpretation, this breaks the law that prohibits working on the Sabbath (Exod. 31:14). Jesus replies that human needs must take precedence over ritual laws. Besides, as the Messiah, God's Son, He is "Lord even of the sabbath day" (v. 8) (parallel passages: Mark 2:23–28; Luke 6:1–5).

12:9–14. Jesus heals a man's withered hand in the synagogue on the Sabbath. The Pharisees again accuse Him of breaking the Sabbath law and begin to plot His destruction (parallel passages: Mark 3:1–6; Luke 6:6–11).

12:15–21. Jesus heals many sick and diseased people among the crowds that follow Him. Matthew the Gospel writer identifies Jesus with the Suffering Servant in the book of Isaiah (vv. 17–21; see Isa. 42:1–4) (parallel passage: Mark 3:7–12).

12:22–23. Jesus heals a demon-possessed blind man who cannot speak.

12:24–37. The Pharisees charge that Jesus heals people by the power of Satan. He responds by stating that Satan would not act against himself by casting demons (satanic beings) out of a person. He turns this charge back on the Pharisees by showing that they are committing blasphemy by attributing the work of God to Satan (parallel passage: Mark 3:20–30).

12:38–45. The scribes and Pharisees ask Jesus to show them some spectacular sign to prove that He is the Messiah. He refuses, knowing that no sign will be strong enough to overcome their unbelief. He does tell them that they will be given a continuing sign at some future time—His resurrection from the dead after three days in the grave.

12:46–50. According to Jesus, His true relatives, in a spiritual sense, are those who "do the will of my Father" (v. 50) (parallel passages: Mark 3:31–35, see p. 207; Luke 8:19–21).

13:1–9. Jesus delivers the parable of the sower to a crowd beside the Sea of Galilee. The sower threw seed on four different types of soil: wayside soil (v. 4), rocky soil (v. 5), soil where thorns grew (v. 7), and good soil (v. 8) (parallel passages: Mark 4:1–9; Luke 8:4–8).

13:10–17. Jesus explains to His disciples why He speaks in parables. These stories drawn from everyday life communicate spiritual truths to people with open minds. But they conceal truth from proud know-it-alls such as the Pharisees who are not open to new revelation from God (parallel passages: Mark 4:10–12; Luke 8:9–10).

13:18–23. Jesus tells His disciples that the four types of soil in the parable of the sower represent the different responses that people make to the claims of the kingdom of God (parallel passages: Mark 4:13–20; Luke 8:11–15).

13:24–30. The parable of the wheat and the tares (weeds) teaches that good and evil will exist in intermingled fashion until the final judgment. Then they will be separated. Good will be rewarded, and evil will be punished.

13:31–35. These two parables—mustard seed and leaven—teach the same truth: The kingdom of God may seem small and insignificant in the beginning, but it will grow to render an effective influence throughout the world (parallel passage: Luke 13:18–21).

13:36–43. Jesus explains the meaning of the parable of the wheat and the tares (weeds) to His disciples.

13:44–46. These two parables—the hidden treasure and the pearl of great price—teach that a person should be willing to pay any price to claim the blessings of God's kingdom.

9:27–31. Healing miracles, such as curing the blind, draw crowds of people to Jesus. His rising popularity made Jewish leaders jealous.

14:13–21. Jesus feeds a crowd of more than 5,000 with just five loaves of bread and two fish.

13:47–50. This parable of the net is similar to the parable of the wheat and the tares (weeds). The kingdom of God, symbolized by the net, will inevitably collect people who are both good and bad. But they will be separated at the final judgment.

13:51–52. This brief parable depicts a householder or landowner mixing both old and new to provide for his family. With His fresh teachings, Jesus brings many new insights to the traditions from the past. Both are essential for those who belong to the kingdom of God.

13:53–58. Jesus returns to His hometown of Nazareth, where He teaches in the local synagogue. But He is rejected because of the "hometown boy" syndrome. He declares that "a prophet is not without honour, save in his own country, and in his own house" (v. 57) (parallel passage: Mark 6:1–6).

14:1–12. John the Baptist is imprisoned by King Herod because he condemned Herod's adulterous marriage to his brother Philip's wife, Herodias. She succeeds in having John the Baptist executed (parallel passage: Mark 6:14–29).

14:13–21. Jesus multiplies a little bread and a few fish to feed more than 5,000 hungry people (parallel passages: **Mark 6:30–44**, see p. 208; Luke 9:10–17; John 6:1–14).

14:22–33. Jesus walks on the water to join His disciples in a boat on the Sea of Galilee. Peter tries his "water legs" but sinks because of a lack of faith. The disciples are amazed and declare that Jesus is "the Son of God" (v. 33) (parallel passages: Mark 6:45–52; John 6:15–21).

14:34–36. Jesus heals many sick and diseased people in the land of Gennesaret (parallel passage: Mark 6:53–56).

15:1–20. Several scribes and Pharisees criticize Jesus because He and His disciples do not perform a ritual washing of their hands before eating. He replies that externals such as food that go into the body do not defile a person. The impure thoughts and ideas that come from within a person are the real sources of defilement (parallel passage: Mark 7:1–23).

15:21–28. Jesus heals the daughter of a Gentile woman and expresses amazement at her great faith (parallel passage: Mark 7:24–30).

15:29–39. Jesus feeds a hungry crowd of more than 4,000 people by miraculously multiplying seven loaves of bread and a few fish (parallel passage: Mark 8:1–10). This miracle was performed for non-Jews in Gentile territory. Earlier He had fed more than 5,000 Jews in Jewish territory (see Matt. 14:13–21).

16:1–12. Jesus condemns the hypocrisy of the Pharisees and Sadducees and warns His disciples to avoid their teachings (parallel passage: Mark 8:11–21).

16:13–20. In the region of Caesarea-Philippi, Jesus commends the apostle Peter for his faith after he proclaims Jesus as the Messiah and the Son of God (parallel passages: Mark 8:27–30; Luke 9:18–20).

16:21–28. Jesus reveals to His disciples that He will be killed by the religious leaders and then resurrected. He condemns Peter for refusing to believe this prediction (parallel passage: Mark 8:31–9:1).

17:1–13. Jesus demonstrates His future glory by being transfigured before three of His disciples—Peter, James, and John. God speaks from a cloud, "This is my beloved Son, in whom I am well pleased; hear ye him" (v. 5) (parallel passages: Mark 9:2–13; Luke 9:28–36).

17:14–21. Jesus casts a stubborn demon out of a boy. He expresses disappointment in His disciples because their lack of faith prevented them from healing the boy (parallel passages: Mark 9:14–29; Luke 9:37–42).

17:22–23. Jesus again predicts His death and resurrection (parallel passages: Mark 9:30–32; Luke 9:43–45).

17:24–27. Jesus miraculously produces a coin to pay the yearly temple tax for Himself and Peter.

[17:24–27] A TAX FOR THE TEMPLE. *They [temple officials] that received tribute money came to Peter, and said, Doth not your master [Jesus] pay tribute?* (Matt. 17:24)

This verse refers to the annual tax designated for maintenance and support of the temple in Jerusalem. Every Jewish male was required to pay this tax. Perhaps the temple officials who collected this tax approached Peter about paying it because Jesus and His disciples were hard to pin down. Their teaching and healing ministry kept them moving from place to place.

The NIV translates the Greek word for "tribute money" in this verse as "two-drachma tax." The standard Greek coin of that time was the drachma. It took two of these coins to pay the tax.

The drachma was roughly equivalent to the Roman coin known as the denarius. A common laborer of Bible times would often be paid one denarius for a full day's work.

18:1–10. Jesus uses a child as an illustration to teach His disciples about the meaning of humility and service to others (parallel passages: Mark 9:33–50; Luke 9:46–50).

18:11–14. Through the parable of the lost sheep, Jesus shows His disciples that His mission is to seek and save lost and hurting people.

18:15–22. Jesus teaches His disciples just how far citizens of the kingdom of God should go to reclaim those who have wronged them. Love and forgiveness have no limit.

18:23–35. Through the parable of the unforgiving servant, Jesus teaches that all who have been forgiven should extend forgiveness to others.

19:1–12. In answer to a question from the Pharisees, Jesus discusses the meaning of marriage and the issue of divorce (parallel passage: Mark 10:1–12).

19:13–15. Jesus welcomes and blesses little children (parallel passages: **Mark 10:13–16,** see p. 210; Luke 18:15–17).

19:16–30. The rich young ruler turns away with regret because his wealth is more important to him than becoming a follower of Jesus (parallel passages: Mark 10:17–31; Luke 18:18–30).

20:1–16. This parable is known as the workers in the vineyard. The laborers worked for different lengths of time, but all were paid the same. The message is that God relates to citizens of His kingdom with mercy and grace and gives us more than we deserve.

20:17–19. On His way to Jerusalem, Jesus again tells His disciples that He will be executed in that city—but He will be resurrected on the third day after His death (parallel passages: Mark 10:32–34; Luke 18:31–34).

20:20–28. The mother of James and John, two of Jesus' disciples, asks Him to give her sons prominent places in His kingdom. He teaches the disciples that His kingdom is spiritual rather than physical in nature (parallel passage: Mark 10:35–45).

20:29–34. Jesus heals two blind men at Jericho (parallel passages: Mark 10:46–52; Luke 18:35–43).

21:1–11. Jesus is acclaimed by the crowds as the long-expected Messiah when He rides into Jerusalem on a donkey. Riding a lowly donkey fulfills the prophecy of Zechariah 9:9 and also shows that Jesus is a spiritual king, not the political deliverer whom the people were expecting (parallel passages: Mark 11:1–11; Luke 19:28–44; John 12:12–19).

21:33–46. Rich farmland lays a pattern of bounty on the fields of northern Israel, where Jesus once ministered. There Jesus told many parables about farming. These parables were a way of teaching the people about God and His kingdom. One story was about tenant farmers who killed the landowner's son—a metaphor of Jesus' coming crucifixion.

not), but their stubbornness and traditions kept them from entering God's kingdom. But the sinners were open and teachable (they refused to work in the vineyard at first but then did so) and thus able to become citizens of the kingdom.

21:33–46. The wicked husbandmen, or tenant farmers, in this parable represent the religious leaders of Israel. They are rejecting Jesus as God's Son, so God will turn to others—even Gentiles (Acts 13:46)—and offer them the opportunity to become citizens of God's kingdom (parallel passages: Mark 12:1–12; Luke 20:9–19).

22:1–14. This parable of the marriage feast teaches essentially the same truth as the parable of the wicked husbandmen (Matt. 21:33–46). The Jewish people who have rejected the Messiah will be turned away from the messianic feast, and Gentiles will be brought in to take their place at the table (Rom. 15:16).

22:15–22. The Pharisees and Herodians try to trap Jesus with a question about paying taxes to the Roman government. Jesus silences them by pointing out that people have a dual obligation—to the state or civil government as well as to God, the ultimate authority (parallel passages: Mark 12:13–17; Luke 20:20–26).

22:23–33. Jesus also deals skillfully with a question from the Sadducees that is designed to make Him look foolish. Whose wife would a woman be in the afterlife if she had been married to several different men? Jesus tells the Sadducees they are assuming the afterlife will be like life here on earth. But the spiritual realities of the life beyond will be different: "In the resurrection they neither marry, nor are given in marriage, but are as the angels of God in heaven" (v. 30) (parallel passages: Mark 12:18–27; Luke 20:27–40).

[21:12–22] COMMERCIALISM IN THE TEMPLE. *Jesus went into the temple…and cast out all them that sold and bought in the temple, and overthrew the tables of the moneychangers, and the seats of them that sold doves* (Matt. 21:12).

These commercial activities that upset Jesus were being conducted in an outer court of the Jewish temple during the observance of the Passover in Jerusalem.

All male Jews were expected to attend this festival, even if they lived a long distance from Jerusalem. The moneychangers were probably exchanging foreign coins of these pilgrims for the appropriate coins with which to pay the temple tax (see the note "A Tax for the Temple" on p. 197).

These pilgrims were also expected to provide animals for sacrifice on the altar of the temple during this celebration. Merchants were selling animals for this purpose as a convenience so pilgrims would not have to bring them along on their trip to the holy city.

Jesus was angry about the crass commercialism of the scene. Temple officials may have been profiting personally from the buying and selling. He quoted Isaiah 56:7 ("Mine house shall be called an house of prayer") and accused the merchants of defiling the temple: "But ye have made it a den of thieves" (Matt. 21:13).

21:12–22. Jesus drives out merchants who are buying and selling in the temple. He pronounces a curse on a fig tree that is bearing no fruit. The barren fig tree symbolizes the dead traditions of the Pharisees and other religious leaders of the nation (parallel passages: Mark 11:12–26; Luke 19:45–48).

21:23–27. Jesus answers the objections of the Pharisees and asserts His divine authority over the temple (parallel passages: Mark 11:27–33; Luke 20:1–8).

21:28–32. In this parable of the vineyard workers, a contrast is drawn between the Pharisees and the sinners. The Pharisees were supposed to be doing God's work (they promised to work in the vineyard but did

22:34–40. Jesus tells a teacher of the law that the command to love your neighbor as yourself (Lev. 19:18) is just as important as the command to love God (Deut. 6:4–9) (parallel passage: Mark 12:28–34).

22:41–46. In a discussion with the Pharisees, Jesus rejects the popular thinking of the day that the Messiah would be a human descendant of King David (2 Sam. 7:8–16). Jesus identifies Himself as the Messiah and the divine Son of God (parallel passages: Mark 12:35–37; Luke 20:41–44).

23:1–36. Jesus condemns the scribes and Pharisees because of their hypocrisy, dishonesty, pride, spiritual blindness, and preoccupation with external matters in religion (parallel passages: Mark 12:38–40; Luke 20:45–47).

23:37–39. Jesus expresses His sorrow over the city of Jerusalem because of its failure to accept Him as the Messiah (parallel passage: Luke 13:34–35).

24:1–51. This chapter is known as Jesus' great prophetic discourse. He predicts the destruction of the temple in Jerusalem and discusses events that will take place in the end-time before His second coming (parallel passages: Mark 13:1–37; Luke 21:5–38).

25:1–13. Through the parable of the ten virgins, Jesus teaches His followers to be in a state of watchful readiness at all times. His second coming may occur at any time—probably when it is least expected (1 Thess. 5:1–11).

25:14–30. In the parable of the talents, two servants multiplied the money entrusted to them by their master. But one was lazy and earned no interest on his talent. This parable teaches that we are to be good stewards of the gifts and abilities granted to us by the Lord.

25:31–46. Jesus compares the separation of people at the final judgment to the work of shepherds, who would separate the sheep from the goats in their flocks at the end of the day. Jesus identifies so closely with people in extreme need—the lonely, hungry, and imprisoned—that ministry to such people will be counted as service to Christ Himself.

26:1–5. Members of the Jewish Sanhedrin meet to plot how they can capture Jesus and have Him executed. They realize they must do this discreetly because of Jesus' popularity among the people (parallel passages: Mark 14:1–2; Luke 22:1–2).

26:6–13. A woman (according to the Gospel of John, it was Mary of Bethany) anoints the head of Jesus with an expensive perfume. Jesus interprets this as an anointing in preparation for His death and

---

[23:1–36] PHYLACTERIES AND TASSELS. *They [the Pharisees] make broad their phylacteries, and enlarge the borders [tassels, NIV] of their garments* (Matt. 23:5).

In this verse, as in all of Matthew 23, Jesus denounced the scribes and Pharisees for their hypocrisy and legalism.

The Pharisees were noted for their attempts to keep the Old Testament law in every minute detail. Over the centuries they had added their own interpretations of the law that they considered as binding as the original law itself.

Phylacteries were little boxes containing strips of parchment on which portions of the law were written. The Pharisees wore these boxes on their foreheads and hands as a literal obedience of the Lord's command, "Thou shalt bind them [God's laws] for a sign upon thine hand, and they shall be as frontlets between thine eyes" (Deut. 6:8). Tassels were decorative fringes that the Pharisees wore on their clothes to remind them of God's laws (Deut. 22:12).

The problem with these displays of piety among the Pharisees is that they were done just for show. Jesus declared that they worked hard to observe the externals of religion while omitting "the weightier matters of the law, judgment, mercy, and faith" (Matt. 23:23).

burial (parallel passages: Mark 14:3–9; John 12:1–8).

26:14–16. Judas, a disciple of Jesus, agrees to betray Jesus for thirty pieces of silver and lead the religious leaders to Him at an opportune time (parallel passages: Mark 14:10–11; Luke 22:3–6).

26:17–19. Jesus instructs His disciples to make preparations for a meal that they will eat together to observe the Jewish Passover (parallel passages: Mark 14:12–16; Luke 22:7–13).

26:20–25. During the Passover meal, Jesus identifies His disciple Judas as His betrayer (parallel passages: Mark 14:17–21; Luke 22:21–23; **John 13:21–30,** see p. 233).

26:26–30. Jesus observes the Last Supper with His disciples (parallel passages: Mark 14:22–26; **Luke 22:14–20,** see pp. 225–230).

26:31–35. Jesus predicts that all His disciples will abandon and deny Him during His arrest and trial (parallel passages: Mark 14:27–31; **Luke 22:31–38,** see p. 226; John 13:31–38).

26:36–46. Jesus agonizes in prayer in the Garden of Gethsemane about His forthcoming suffering and death. His disciples fall asleep and fail to support Him in His hour of need (parallel passages: Mark 14:32–42; Luke 22:39–46).

26:26–30. Judas Iscariot, at front left, prepares to leave the disciples' final meal with Jesus. He would soon sell out his teacher for thirty pieces of silver. This "Last Supper" would become a pattern for a Christian ritual known as the Lord's Supper, communion, or the Eucharist.

[26:47–56] **CHIEF PRIESTS.** *Judas, one of the twelve, came, and with him a great multitude. . .from the chief priests and elders of the people* (Matt. 26:47).

The phrase "chief priests" in this verse probably refers to the leaders or directors of the twenty-four groups of priests into which the priesthood was divided in David's time (1 Chron. 24:1–5). These twenty-four divisions of the priesthood probably presided at the altar in the tabernacle or temple on a rotating basis.

In New Testament times, these "chief priests" may have included the high priest as well as priestly members of his immediate family.

26:47–56. Judas leads a group of temple guards sent by the Sanhedrin to the place where Jesus is praying in the Garden of Gethsemane. He identifies Jesus by greeting Him with a kiss. Jesus is arrested and taken away (parallel passages: Mark 14:43–52; Luke 22:47–53; John 18:1–12).

26:57–68. Jesus appears before the high priest Caiaphas and the rest of the Jewish Sanhedrin. Peter follows and waits outside the house of the high priest to see what will happen. The Sanhedrin declares Jesus guilty of blasphemy when He admits He is the Son of God (parallel passages: Mark 14:53–65; Luke 22:63–71).

26:69–75. Outside the house of the high priest, Peter denies that He knows Jesus when he is questioned by three different people. The crowing of a rooster makes Peter realize that Jesus' prediction of his denial has come true (parallel passages: Mark 14:66–72; Luke 22:54–62; John 18:15–27).

27:1–2. The Sanhedrin finds Jesus guilty of blasphemy under the Jewish law. Determined to have Him executed, they take Him to Pontius Pilate, the Roman provincial governor of Judea. Only the Romans had the authority to pronounce and carry out the death sentence (parallel passages: Mark 15:1; Luke 23:1).

27:3–10. Judas has a change of heart when he realizes his actions have condemned an innocent man. He returns the betrayal money and then commits suicide (Acts 1:16–20).

27:11–26. Jesus appears before Pontius Pilate, the Roman governor. Pilate realizes Jesus is an innocent man. But he is also under pressure from the religious leaders, who are determined to have Him executed. He tries to get Jesus released by using the custom of setting one prisoner free at the whim of the people during a major Jewish holiday. But the people call for the release of another prisoner named Barabbas instead. Finally, Pilate condemns Jesus to death by crucifixion (parallel passages: Mark 15:2–15; Luke 23:13–25; John 18:28–19:16).

27:27–31. Jesus is mocked and abused by Roman soldiers before they lead Him away to the crucifixion site (parallel passage: Mark 15:16–20).

27:32. A bystander, Simon of Cyrene, is pressed into service to carry the cross of Jesus (parallel passages: Mark 15:21; **Luke 23:26–31,** see p. 226).

27:33–37. Jesus is crucified at a site known as Golgotha ("place of the skull") just outside the walls of Jerusalem (Heb. 13:12). The placard on His cross that specifies His crime reads, "THIS IS JESUS THE KING OF THE JEWS" (v. 37). This indicates that He was probably executed on the false charge that He was a political revolutionary who challenged the power and authority of the Roman government (parallel passages: Mark 15:22–26; Luke 23:32–38; John 19:17–24).

27:38–44. Jesus is mocked and ridiculed by people in the crowd as well as two thieves

28:16–20. The resurrected Jesus met several times with His disciples over the course of forty days. Shortly before returning to heaven, He gave the disciples the Great Commission, commanding them to take His message to people throughout the world.

who are being crucified at the same time (parallel passages: Mark 15:27–32; **Luke 23:39–43**, see p. 227).

27:45–54. Jesus' suffering and death are accompanied by several mysterious events, including an earthquake at the moment when He dies (parallel passages: **Mark 15:33–39**, see p. 213; Luke 23:44–48).

27:55–56. Several women from Galilee who are followers of Jesus are among the crowd at the crucifixion site (parallel passages: Mark 15:40–41; Luke 23:49; **John 19:25–27**, see p. 234).

27:57–60. Joseph of Arimathea buries the body of Jesus in his own tomb (parallel passages: Mark 15:42–46; Luke 23:50–54; **John 19:38–42**, see p. 235).

27:61. Mary Magdalene and "the other Mary" (probably the mother of Jesus' disciple James, the son of Alphaeus), followers of Jesus, mourn at the tomb where Jesus is buried (parallel passages: Mark 15:47; Luke 23:55–56).

27:62–66. After talking to Pilate, the religious leaders station guards at the tomb where Jesus is buried and seal the entrance with a large stone.

28:1–10. Mary Magdalene and "the other Mary" (see Matt. 27:61) visit the tomb of Jesus on Sunday morning after His death and burial two days before. They are greeted by an angel, who tells them He has been raised from the dead. The angel instructs them to tell His disciples this good news. Then Jesus Himself greets the women to assure them and calm their fears (parallel passages: Mark 16:1–8; Luke 24:1–8; John 20:1–2).

28:11–15. The Jewish Sanhedrin bribes the guards who were on duty at Jesus' tomb in an attempt to deny the claims of His resurrection. These guards spread the rumor that Jesus' disciples took His body out of the grave before daybreak on Sunday morning.

28:16–20. Jesus meets with His disciples in Galilee and charges them with His Great Commission (Acts 1:8). They are to continue His mission of bringing people into the kingdom of God (parallel passages: Mark 16:14–18; Luke 24:44–49).

OVERVIEW: Probably the first Gospel written, Mark focuses on the power of Jesus and presents Him as the Suffering Servant.

Introduction to Mark

Mark is the shortest and most concise of the four Gospels—only sixteen chapters in length. It's the Gospel of choice for those who want a quick, to-the-point overview of the life and ministry of Jesus.

Most scholars believe that Mark was the first Gospel written. It appeared about A.D. 60—about thirty years after the death and resurrection of Jesus. Matthew and Luke were written after Mark. These two Gospels apparently included material from Mark as well as additional accounts of Jesus' life from other sources. A careful study of these three Synoptic Gospels (see the introduction to the Gospels on p. 188) shows that all but a few verses from Mark appear in Matthew and Luke.

The author of Mark was John Mark, the young man who turned back to Jerusalem after accompanying Paul and Barnabas for a while on their first missionary journey (Acts 13:1–3). Mark later overcame this initial failure in Christian service and was associated with the apostle Peter in his ministry (1 Pet. 5:13). Before his death, Peter must have recounted events that he remembered from his experience as one of the twelve disciples of Jesus. John Mark wrote these eyewitness accounts down in the Gospel that bears his name.

While the Gospel of Matthew was written to a Jewish audience (see the introduction to Matthew on p. 189), Mark's Gospel has a Gentile orientation. Mark was careful to translate Jewish terms into Roman equivalents (for example, he indicated that the Aramaic word *Boanerges* meant "the sons of thunder," 3:17) and to explain Jewish customs to his non-Jewish audience. Mark also emphasized the miracles of Jesus rather than His teachings. Jesus comes across in this Gospel as a person of action who has power over sickness, the natural order, and the forces of evil.

Above all, Mark tells us about a Savior who was obedient to the will of His Father, even to the point of becoming the Suffering Servant on our behalf. Even the Roman centurion at the cross recognized this when he declared, "Truly this man was the Son of God" (15:39).

Some accounts of Jesus' life and ministry in Mark also parallel events reported in Matthew, Luke, and John. These parallel passages are identified in the following summary of Mark. The parallel passages in bold type with "see" references refer to pages in this book where expanded summaries of specific Gospel accounts may be found.

Summary of Mark

1:1–8. John the Baptist, forerunner of Jesus, begins preaching (parallel passages: Matt. 3:1–12; **Luke 3:1–20,** see p. 218).

1:9–11. Jesus is baptized by John (parallel

passages: **Matt. 3:13–17**, see p. 190; Luke 3:21–22).

1:12–13. Jesus is tempted by Satan (parallel passages: Matt. 4:1–11; **Luke 4:1–13**, see p. 218).

1:14–15. Jesus begins preaching in the region of Galilee (parallel passages: **Matt. 4:12–17**, see p. 190; John 4:45).

1:16–20. Jesus beckons Peter and Andrew and James and John to follow Him (parallel passages: Matt. 4:18–22; **Luke 5:1–11**, see p. 218).

1:21–28. Jesus casts demons out of a man in the synagogue at Capernaum on the Sabbath. The people are amazed at His power and authority (parallel passage: **Luke 4:31–37**, see p. 218).

1:29–34. Jesus heals Peter's mother-in-law; many sick people come to Him for healing (parallel passages: Matt. 8:14–17; Luke 4:38–41).

1:35–39. Jesus preaches and heals throughout Galilee (parallel passages: **Matt. 4:23–25**, see p. 192; Luke 4:42–44).

1:40–45. Jesus heals a man with leprosy. He ignores Jesus' instructions not to tell anyone about his miraculous healing, and people from a wide area flock to Jesus (parallel passages: Matt. 8:1–4; Luke 5:12–16).

2:1–12. Four men lower their paralyzed friend through the roof to Jesus for healing. Jesus also forgives his sins and is accused of blasphemy by a group of scribes (parallel passages: Matt. 9:1–8; Luke 5:17–26).

2:13–17. Jesus calls the tax collector Matthew, also known as Levi, to become His disciple (parallel passages: Matt. 9:9–13; **Luke 5:27–32**, see p. 218).

2:18–22. Jesus explains to the Pharisees why He and His disciples do not observe the ritual of fasting (parallel passages: **Matt. 9:14–17**, see pp. 192–193; Luke 5:33–39).

2:23–28. The Pharisees condemn Jesus for violating the law against working on the Sabbath (Exod. 20:8–11) by picking grain to eat (parallel passages: **Matt. 12:1–8**, see pp. 193–194; Luke 6:1–5).

3:1–6. Jesus angers the Pharisees by healing a man's withered hand on the Sabbath (parallel passages: **Matt. 12:9–14**, see p. 194; Luke 6:6–11).

3:7–12. People from many distant cities flock to Jesus because they have heard about His ability to heal (parallel passage: **Matt. 12:15–21**, see p. 194).

3:13–19. Jesus chooses twelve followers to serve as His disciples (parallel passages: Matt. 10:1–4; **Luke 6:12–16**, see pp. 218–220).

3:20–30. Jesus answers the charge of the Pharisees that He is healing people who are possessed by demons through the power of

---

[2:1–12] GOING THROUGH THE ROOF. *They [four friends of the paralyzed man] uncovered the roof where he [Jesus] was: and when they had broken it up, they let down the bed wherein the sick of the palsy [paralyzed man, NIV] lay* (Mark 2:4).

This verse shows the determination of the friends of a disabled man to get him to Jesus for healing. They brought their friend in a blanket or pallet to the house where Jesus was teaching. Unable to get into the building because of the crowd, they climbed an exterior stairway to the roof. After ripping a hole in the roof, they lowered him down to Jesus.

The roofs of most houses in Bible times were built in three steps. First, beams or logs were laid across the tops of the exterior walls. These beams were then overlaid with thatch, consisting of tree branches and straw. Finally, the thatch was topped with a layer of clay that was hardened in the sun. In a climate in which rainfall was minimal, these roofs would hold up well if the clay was rolled and hardened on a regular basis.

Tearing through a roof like this was a simple matter. It was also easy to repair.

4:30–32. A ridge of yellow mustard plants grows wild in Israel. Jesus said that God's kingdom is like the tiny mustard seed, which starts small but grows large.

Satan (parallel passage: **Matt. 12:24–37,** see p. 194).

3:31–35. Jesus' mother and brothers come to the place where He is teaching. They send word that they would like to see Him. Jesus affirms that His true relatives are those who do the will of God (parallel passages: Matt. 12:46–50; Luke 8:19–21).

4:1–9. Jesus delivers the parable of the sower from a fishing boat on the Sea of Galilee (parallel passages: **Matt. 13:1–9,** see p. 194; Luke 8:4–8).

4:10–12. In answer to a question from His disciples, Jesus explains why He teaches through parables (parallel passages: Matt. 13:10–17; Luke 8:9–10).

4:13–20. Jesus explains the meaning of the parable of the sower to His disciples (parallel passages: **Matt. 13:18–23,** see p. 194; Luke 8:11–15).

4:21–25. Citizens of the kingdom of God should let their influence penetrate the world, just as a candle or lamp is placed on a stand to light a room (parallel passage: Luke 8:16–18).

4:26–29. This parable of the seed growing quietly is found only in the Gospel of Mark. It teaches that the kingdom of God is God's work. He allows us as His followers to sow the seed, but God causes the seed to grow and produce a harvest.

4:30–32. Jesus in this parable compares the kingdom of God to a mustard seed. Although it is a tiny seed, it grows into a large plant. The kingdom of God is also destined to grow from obscurity into an influential force throughout the world.

4:33–34. Jesus continues to speak in parables and to explain their meaning to His disciples.

4:35–41. Jesus calms a storm and rebukes His disciples for their lack of faith (parallel passages: Matt. 8:23–27; Luke 8:22–25).

5:1–20. Jesus casts numerous demons out of a wild man who lived among the tombs in the country of the Gadarenes. The demons enter a herd of pigs, and they drown in the Sea of Galilee. Jesus sends the healed man into the cities of that region to tell others what Jesus has done for him (parallel passages: Matt. 8:28–34; Luke 8:26–39).

[5:1–20] LIVING AMONG THE DEAD. *There met him [Jesus] out of the tombs a man with an unclean spirit, who had his dwelling among the tombs* (Mark 5:2–3).

This man who met Jesus was possessed by demons. He may have been driven out of the villages of "the country of the Gadarenes" (Mark 5:1) and forced to live a life of isolation in a cemetery because of his violent, unpredictable behavior (Mark 5:5).

The "tombs" mentioned in this passage were probably natural caves or burial chambers that had been dug out of solid rock. Tombs like this were commonly used by the upper-class families of Bible times.

This poor, deranged man may have been living among the bones of the dead in one of these burial caves. The NIV states specifically that he was living "in the tombs," not "among the tombs."

5:21–43. Jesus heals a woman with a hemorrhage who slips through the crowd to touch the edge of His robe. He also raises from the dead the daughter of a synagogue ruler named Jairus (parallel passages: Matt. 9:18–26; Luke 8:40–56).

6:1–6. Jesus is rejected by the unbelieving citizens of His hometown of Nazareth (parallel passage: **Matt. 13:53–58,** see p. 196).

6:7–13. Jesus sends His disciples out to preach and heal (parallel passages: **Matt. 10:5–42,** see p. 193; Luke 9:1–6).

6:14–29. Herodias, the wife of King Herod, uses her daughter's influence with the king to have John the Baptist executed. Herodias wanted John killed because he had condemned her adulterous affair with the king (parallel passage: Matt. 14:1–12).

6:30–44. A huge crowd follows Jesus to an isolated area when He withdraws to rest and pray. As the day draws to a close, He has compassion on them because they have not eaten all day. He multiplies five loaves of bread and two fish to feed the crowd of more than 5,000 people. So thorough is this miracle that twelve baskets of food are left over (parallel passages: Matt. 14:13–21; Luke 9:10–17; John 6:1–14).

6:45–52. Jesus joins His disciples in a boat on the Sea of Galilee by walking on the water (parallel passages: **Matt. 14:22–33,** see p. 196; John 6:15–21).

6:53–56. Jesus and His disciples put ashore at the land of Gennesaret, where He heals many people (parallel passage: Matt. 14:34–36).

7:1–23. Jesus explains to the scribes and Pharisees why He and His disciples do not perform ritualistic hand-washings before eating (parallel passage: **Matt. 15:1–20,** see pp. 196–197).

7:24–30. Jesus heals a Gentile woman's daughter (parallel passage: **Matt. 15:21–28,** see p. 197).

7:31–37. Jesus heals a deaf man with a speech impediment, and he begins to speak clearly.

8:1–10. Jesus performs a second feeding miracle—this one for Gentiles (parallel passage: **Matt. 15:29–39,** see p. 197).

8:11–21. Jesus warns His disciples to stay away from the Pharisees and their teachings (parallel passage: Matt. 16:1–12).

8:22–26. Jesus heals a blind man outside the city of Bethsaida.

6:45–52. A fishing boat on the Sea of Galilee. Much of Jesus' ministry took place along the shores of this freshwater lake. And in one dramatic miracle, Jesus walked on its waters.

[7:1–23] JESUS AND THE SCRIBES. *Then came together unto him [Jesus] the Pharisees, and certain of the scribes [teachers of the law, NIV] (Mark 7:1).*

The scribes and Pharisees are often mentioned together as if they were united in their opposition to Jesus (see Matt. 15:1; Luke 5:21; John 8:3).

The office of scribe developed in Old Testament times when they were charged with the responsibility of copying the Scriptures. Laboriously copying a sacred document by hand was the only way to reproduce and pass on God's commands in written form.

By New Testament times scribes had assumed the task of interpreting and teaching God's law as well as copying it. This is why they are mentioned often with Pharisees as those who were opposed to Jesus. Both were committed to preserving the traditions that had grown up around the original written law. They considered these additions as binding as the law itself (see the note "Phylacteries and Tassels" on p. 200).

Jesus criticized these "sacred traditions," broke many of them Himself during His teaching and healing ministry, and insisted they were not as authoritative as God's law in its original form (Matt. 15:5–6; Mark 7:5–6; Luke 6:1–5).

8:27–30. Peter confesses Jesus as the Christ, God's Anointed One. Jesus cautions them to tell no one that He is the Messiah (parallel passages: **Matt. 16:13–20**, see p. 197; Luke 9:18–20).

8:31–9:1. Jesus informs His disciples about His future death and resurrection (parallel passage: **Matt. 16:21–28**, see p. 197).

9:2–13. Jesus is transfigured before three of His disciples, and He talks again about His forthcoming death (parallel passages: **Matt. 17:1–13**, see p. 197; Luke 9:28–36).

9:14–29. Jesus encourages the faith of the father of a demon-possessed boy. Then He casts out the stubborn demon and heals his son (parallel passages: Matt. 17:14–21; Luke 9:37–42).

9:30–32. Jesus again predicts He will be killed and then resurrected (parallel passages: Matt. 17:22–23; Luke 9:43–45).

9:33–50. Jesus teaches His disciples the meaning of true greatness for those who are citizens of God's kingdom (parallel passages: Matt. 18:1–10; Luke 9:46–50).

10:1–12. Jesus discusses with the Pharisees the meaning of marriage and the problem of divorce (parallel passage: Matt. 19:1–12).

10:13–16. The disciples try to keep children away from Jesus, but He welcomes and blesses them and declares that a citizen of the kingdom must become "as a little child" (v. 15) (parallel passages: Matt. 19:13–15; Luke 18:15–17).

10:17–31. The rich young ruler refuses to follow Jesus (parallel passages: **Matt. 19:16–30**, see p. 198; Luke 18:18–30).

10:32–34. Jesus again speaks with His disciples about His forthcoming death (parallel passages: **Matt. 20:17–19**, see p. 198; Luke 18:31–34).

10:35–45. Jesus' disciples James and John ask for places of prominence and honor in His kingdom (parallel passage: **Matt. 20:20–28**, see p. 198).

10:46–52. On His way to Jerusalem, Jesus heals a blind man named Bartimaeus at Jericho (parallel passages: Matt. 20:29–34; Luke 18:35–43).

[11:12–26] STRAIGHT-UP PRAYER. *When ye [Jesus' followers] stand praying, forgive, if ye have aught against any (Mark 11:25).*

This teaching of Jesus on prayer and forgiveness shows that standing was one common stance while praying in Bible times. The person would address his prayer to God by lifting his hands toward heaven with the palms up.

This is the way King Solomon prayed when he dedicated the newly constructed temple in Jerusalem to the Lord (1 Kings 8:22).

11:1–11. Jesus makes His triumphal entry into Jerusalem (parallel passages: **Matt. 21:1–11**, see p. 198; Luke 19:28–44; John 12:12–19).

11:12–26. Jesus places a curse on a barren fig tree and drives out merchants who are conducting business in the temple (parallel passages: **Matt. 21:12–22**, see p. 199; Luke 19:45–48).

11:27–33. Jesus assures the Pharisees of His divine authority over the temple (parallel passages: Matt. 21:23–27; Luke 20:1–8).

12:1–12. In this parable, Jesus compares the religious leaders of Israel to wicked husbandmen, or tenant farmers (parallel passages: **Matt. 21:33–46**, see p. 199; Luke 20:9–19).

12:13–17. The Pharisees and Herodians question Jesus about paying taxes to the Roman government (parallel passages: **Matt. 22:15–22**, see p. 199; Luke 20:20–26).

12:18–27. Jesus deals with a question from the Sadducees about the resurrection (parallel passages: **Matt. 22:23–33**, see p. 199; Luke 20:27–40).

12:28–34. Jesus answers a question from a teacher of the law on which is the greatest commandment (parallel passage: **Matt. 22:34–40**, see p. 200).

12:35–37. Jesus challenges the thinking of the Pharisees about the Messiah who would spring from the line of David (parallel passages: **Matt. 22:41–46**, see p. 200; Luke 20:41–44).

12:38–40. Jesus denounces the Pharisees for their pride and hypocrisy (parallel passages: **Matt. 23:1–36**, see p. 200; Luke 20:45–47).

12:41–44. Jesus praises a poor widow for her sacrificial offering (parallel passage: Luke 21:1–4).

13:1–37. Jesus predicts the destruction of the temple in Jerusalem and discusses end-time events (parallel passages: **Matt. 24:1–51**, see p. 200; Luke 21:5–38).

14:1–2. The Jewish Sanhedrin plots to arrest Jesus and have Him executed (parallel passages: **Matt. 26:1–5**, see p. 200; Luke 22:1–2).

14:3–9. A woman anoints Jesus with an expensive perfume (parallel passages: **Matt. 26:6–13**, see pp. 200–201; John 12:1–8).

14:10–11. Judas makes arrangements to betray Jesus (parallel passages: **Matt. 26:14–16**, see p. 201; Luke 22:3–6).

14:12–16. Two of Jesus' disciples select a location where they will partake of a Passover meal with Jesus (parallel passages: Matt. 26:17–19; Luke 22:7–13).

14:17–21. Jesus predicts that one of His disciples will betray Him (parallel passages: Matt. 26:20–25; Luke 22:21–23; **John 13:21–30**, see p. 233).

[14:17–21] BREAD OF BETRAYAL. *He [Jesus] answered... It is one of the twelve, that dippeth with me in the dish* (Mark 14:20).

People of Bible times did not use utensils such as forks and spoons to eat their meals. They picked up the food with their hands. But some dishes such as stew or gravy had to be scooped up with a piece of bread. This is the method of eating to which Jesus referred in this verse.

In John's Gospel this bread used to pick up liquid food is call a "sop." Jesus handed the bread to Judas, clearly identifying him as the betrayer (John 13:26).

14:22–26. Jesus institutes the memorial meal (1 Cor. 11:23–26), known today as the Lord's Supper (parallel passages: Matt. 26:26–30; **Luke 22:14–20**, see pp. 225–226).

14:27–31. Jesus predicts that all His disciples, including Peter, will deny Him (parallel passages: Matt. 26:31–35; **Luke 22:31–38**, see p. 226; John 13:31–38).

15:22–26. After a secret, all-night trial, Jesus is crucified on Friday morning.

14:32–42. Jesus prays with a heavy heart in the Garden of Gethsemane (parallel passages: **Matt. 26:36–46,** see p. 201; Luke 22:39–46).

14:43–52. Jesus is arrested in the Garden of Gethsemane (parallel passages: **Matt. 26:47–56,** see p. 202; Luke 22:47–53; John 18:1–2).

14:53–65. Jesus is declared guilty of blasphemy when He appears before the Jewish Sanhedrin (parallel passages: Matt. 26:57–68; Luke 22:63–71).

14:66–72. Peter denies that he knows Jesus (parallel passages: **Matt. 26:69–75,** see p. 202; Luke 22:54–62; John 18:15–27).

15:1. The Sanhedrin delivers Jesus to the Roman governor in an attempt to have Him sentenced to death (parallel passages: **Matt. 27:1–2,** see p. 202; Luke 23:1).

15:2–15. Pilate, the Roman governor, sentences Jesus to death by crucifixion (parallel passages: **Matt. 27:11–26,** see p. 202; Luke 23:13–25; John 18:28–19:16).

15:16–20. Jesus is mocked by Roman soldiers (parallel passage: **Matt. 27:27–31,** see p. 202).

15:21. Simon of Cyrene, a bystander, carries the cross of Jesus to the crucifixion site (parallel passages: Matt. 27:32; **Luke 23:26–31,** see p. 226).

15:22–26. Jesus is crucified at a site known as Golgotha (parallel passages: **Matt. 27:33–37,** see p. 202; Luke 23:32–38; John 19:17–24).

15:27–32. As He hangs on the cross between two thieves, Jesus is taunted by the crowd (parallel passages: Matt. 27:38–44; **Luke 23:39–43,** see p. 227).

15:33–39. For three hours before Jesus dies, darkness covers the earth. He quotes from Psalm 22:1 and cries out in despair, "My God, my God, why hast thou forsaken me," (v. 34). Upon His death, the huge curtain in the temple is ripped from top to bottom. Shaken by these mysterious happenings, a Roman centurion declares, "Truly this man was the Son of God" (v. 39) (parallel passages: Matt. 27:45–54; Luke 23:44–48).

15:40–41. Several women stand watch at the cross as Jesus is crucified (parallel passages: Matt. 27:55–56; Luke 23:49; **John 19:25–27,** see p. 234).

15:42–46. Jesus is buried in the tomb of Joseph of Arimathea (parallel passages: Matt. 27:57–60; Luke 23:50–54; **John 19:38–42,** see p. 235).

15:47. Women mourn at the tomb where Jesus is buried (parallel passages: Matt. 27:61; Luke 23:55–56).

16:1–8. Women discover that Jesus is gone when they visit the tomb to anoint His body on Sunday morning (parallel passages: Matt. 28:1–10; Luke 24:1–8; John 20:1–2).

16:9–11. The resurrected Jesus appears to Mary Magdalene (parallel passage: **John 20:11–18,** see p. 235).

16:12–13. Jesus appears to two of His followers on their way to Emmaus (parallel passage: **Luke 24:13–35,** see p. 228).

16:14–18. Jesus commissions His disciples (Acts 1:8) to continue His work (parallel passages: **Matt. 28:16–20,** see p. 204; Luke 24:44–49).

16:19–20. Jesus ascends to His Father (Acts 1:9), and His disciples continue His ministry, as they were commanded (parallel passage: Luke 24:50–53).

LUKE

OVERVIEW: The most complete account of the life and ministry of Jesus, Luke was written for Gentiles.

Introduction to Luke

Perhaps the most unique characteristic of the Gospel of Luke is that it has a sequel in the book of Acts. Both books are addressed to a person named Theophilus (1:3; Acts 1:1). This name means "lover of God," and Theophilus was probably a Roman of high rank. In this Gospel, Luke apparently wanted to show Theophilus and other Roman citizens like him the truth about Jesus and His ministry and those who had become His followers.

Luke did not identify himself as the author of this Gospel, but early church tradition ascribed this writing to him. Luke was a physician (Col. 4:14) and a missionary associate of the apostle Paul (2 Tim. 4:11; Philem. 24). Luke was not an eyewitness of the ministry of Jesus. But he tells us in the opening words of Luke that he had access to information from actual eyewitnesses that he included in the Gospel that bears his name (1:1–4).

The Gospel of Luke gives us the most complete picture we have of the life of Jesus. It is the only Gospel that tells us anything about the birth of Jesus (2:1–12). We also learn only in Luke that Jesus was aware of His unique mission as God's Son as a twelve-year-old boy (2:41–52).

With the exception of Matthew, which records the visit of the wise men to Jesus when He was a two-year-old child (Matt. 2:1–12), we find nothing in the other Gospels about Jesus' childhood years. Many of Jesus' most beloved parables appear only in the Gospel of Luke—for example, the lost coin and the lost son, also known as the prodigal son (chap. 15).

Luke is also the most inclusive of all the Gospels. He portrays Jesus associating with people of all classes—the poor, outcasts, sinners, women, and tax collectors. The hero of one of Jesus' parables is even a compassionate Samaritan—a member of a race of half-breeds whom the Jewish people despised (10:25–37).

More than the other Gospels, Luke also emphasizes the Holy Spirit in the life and ministry of Jesus (4:14; 10:21) and portrays Jesus as a person of prayer (3:21; 6:12; 9:29; 22:39–46).

Some accounts of Jesus' life and ministry in Luke also parallel events reported in Matthew, Mark, and John. These parallel passages are identified in the following summary of Luke. The parallel passages in bold type with "see" references refer to pages in this book where expanded summaries of specific Gospel accounts may be found.

Summary of Luke

1:1–4. Luke begins his Gospel by addressing his friend Theophilus. He wants Theophilus to hear from him the truth about Jesus and His work. Luke also wrote the book of

2:15–20. Bethlehem shepherds come to see the baby Jesus, who was born in a place where livestock were kept. Early church tradition said he was born in a cave that now rests like a basement beneath the oldest church in the world: Bethlehem's Church of the Nativity.

Acts. He also began this book with a word to Theophilus (Acts 1:1).

1:5–7. An elderly priest named Zacharias and his wife, Elisabeth, are godly, righteous people. But they have not been able to have children.

1:8–17. The angel Gabriel appears to Zacharias while he is burning incense in the temple. He informs the elderly priest that he and Elisabeth will be blessed with a son whom they are to name John. He will grow up to become a great prophet who will prepare the way for the coming of the long-expected Messiah.

1:18–25. Zacharias expresses doubt that this

will happen. The angel informs him that he will be punished for his disbelief by not being able to speak until the child is born.

1:26–33. The angel Gabriel also visits Mary, a young woman who lives in the city of Nazareth in the region of Galilee. Gabriel informs Mary that she will become pregnant and give birth to the long-expected Messiah. She is to give Him the name Jesus, which means "Savior."

1:34–38. Mary wonders how this birth can happen, since she is a virgin. The angel assures her that her pregnancy will occur supernaturally through the power of the Holy Spirit. The angel also informs Mary of the pregnancy of her cousin Elisabeth in the region of Judea.

1:39–56. Mary visits her cousin Elisabeth. They rejoice together about God's actions in their lives. Mary sings a beautiful song of thanksgiving known as the Magnificat (vv. 46–55). It expresses her joy that God will fulfill His promise of a Messiah for Israel through this child who will come from her womb.

1:57–66. The child of their old age is born to Zacharias and Elisabeth. Following the orders of the angel Gabriel, they name him John. The punishment for Zacharias's doubt is lifted, and he is able to speak again.

1:67–80. In this prophetic song known as the Benedictus, Zacharias expresses his thanks to God for the coming of the Messiah and the role his son, John, will play in preparing the way for His mission.

2:1–5. Mary and Joseph, the man to whom Mary is engaged, travel from Nazareth to the city of Bethlehem, Joseph's ancestral home, to register in a census. This registration for taxation purposes had been ordered for all residents throughout the Roman Empire by the emperor, Augustus Caesar.

2:6–7. While Mary and Joseph are in Bethlehem, Jesus is born in a stable. Their accommodations are crude because all the inns are filled with people in town for the census. Jesus' first crib is a feeding trough for livestock.

2:8–14. Angels announce the birth of Jesus to a group of shepherds who are watching over their sheep in the fields outside Bethlehem.

2:15–20. The shepherds hurry into Bethlehem, where they find Mary and Joseph and the baby Jesus. These humble shepherds become the first to announce the birth of "a Saviour, which is Christ the Lord" (Luke 2:11) to others.

2:21–24. When Jesus is eight days old, His parents take Him to the temple in Jerusalem for circumcision and dedication to the Lord, in accordance with Jewish custom (Gen. 17:12; Lev. 12:3).

2:25–35. When Jesus is brought into the temple, an aged man named Simeon recognizes Him as the long-expected Messiah. He prophesies that Jesus will be a light for Gentiles as well as the Jewish people (Eph.

[4:16–30] READING IN A SYNAGOGUE. *He [Jesus] went into the synagogue on the sabbath day, and stood up for to read* (Luke 4:16).

This synagogue in which Jesus read the Old Testament Scriptures was in Nazareth, his hometown in the province of Galilee. Synagogues were built in towns and cities throughout Palestine. Their purpose was not to replace the temple in Jerusalem that served as the central place of worship and sacrifice for all Israel. Synagogues existed to teach the law to local people.

A community synagogue was presided over by a leader who had been elected by its members. Priests had no official role in synagogues, although they often attended and were honored by being asked to read the Scriptures during the service.

Jesus was not a priest or a member of the religious establishment. His reading in the Nazareth synagogue shows that common, everyday "laypeople" who were known in the community were often asked to participate in the service. In addition, His ministry as a teacher and healer had begun to attract attention throughout Galilee (Luke 4:14–15).

Jesus read from the book of Isaiah and identified Himself as the Servant of the Lord whom the prophet had written about (Luke 4:17–21).

2:11–22). He also declares that His mother's heart will be broken by the suffering He is destined to endure.

2:36–38. An aged prophetess named Anna overhears Simeon's prophecy. She joins in with thanksgiving to God for sending redemption to Israel through this newborn Messiah.

2:39–40. Jesus grows up under the nurture of His earthly parents, Mary and Joseph, in the village of Nazareth in the region of Galilee (parallel passage: Matt. 2:19–23).

2:41–52. These verses in Luke give us the only information we have about Jesus' childhood years. When He is twelve years old, He accompanies His parents to Jerusalem to observe the Passover festival (Josh. 5:10–12). On their way back to Nazareth, Mary and Joseph discover that

4:1–13. After His baptism and before launching His ministry, Jesus retreated for a time of solitude and prayer into the wilderness badlands of what is now southern Israel.

Jesus is missing. Returning to Jerusalem, they find Him sitting among the learned interpreters of the Scriptures, both learning from them and contributing His own ideas. It is obvious to everyone that this is no ordinary twelve-year-old boy.

3:1–20. John the Baptist, forerunner of Jesus, launches his preaching ministry (parallel passages: Matt. 3:1–12; Mark 1:1–8). He challenges the people to repent of their sins and get ready for the coming of God's kingdom. Many of his hearers think John is the Messiah, but he makes it clear that he is preparing the way for "one mightier than I" (v. 16) who is the deliverer sent from God.

3:21–22. Jesus is baptized by John (parallel passages: **Matt. 3:13–17,** see p. 190; Mark 1:9–11).

3:23–38. Luke's genealogy of Jesus begins with Joseph and goes all the way back to Adam. (For a different genealogy of Jesus, see Matt. 1:1–17.)

4:1–13. Beginning in the wilderness, Satan presents a series of temptations to Jesus at the beginning of His public ministry. Jesus rises above these temptations through the power of prayer and the Scriptures (parallel passages: Matt. 4:1–11; Mark 1:12–13).

4:14–15. Jesus begins His preaching ministry in the region of Galilee.

4:16–30. Jesus preaches in the synagogue in His hometown of Nazareth. He identifies Himself as God's Suffering Servant depicted in the book of Isaiah (Isa. 61:1–2). The townspeople are enraged because they consider this blasphemous, so they try to kill Jesus. But He slips away and leaves the town.

4:31–37. Jesus makes Capernaum in the region of Galilee His headquarters city. He heals a demon-possessed man in the synagogue on the Sabbath. His reputation grows as people express amazement at His power and authority (parallel passage: Mark 1:21–28).

4:38–41. Jesus heals Peter's mother-in-law in Capernaum (parallel passages: **Matt. 8:14–17,** see p. 192; Mark 1:29–34).

4:42–44. Jesus preaches and heals in other cities throughout the region of Galilee (parallel passages: **Matt. 4:23–25,** see p. 192; Mark 1:35–39).

5:1–11. Jesus astonishes Peter by producing a miraculous catch of fish after Peter and his partners had worked all night without catching anything. Then Jesus calls Peter and his partners, the brothers James and John, to leave their fishing nets and become His followers (parallel passages: Matt. 4:18–22; Mark 1:16–20).

5:12–16. Jesus heals a man with leprosy (parallel passages: Matt. 8:1–4; **Mark 1:40–45,** see p. 206).

5:17–26. Jesus heals a paralyzed man and forgives his sins (parallel passages: Matt. 9:1–8; **Mark 2:1–12,** see p. 206).

5:27–32. Jesus calls Matthew (also known as Levi), a tax collector, to become His disciple. Scribes and Pharisees criticize Him for associating with tax collectors and sinners. Jesus explains that His mission is "not to call the righteous, but sinners to repentance" (v. 32) (parallel passages: Matt. 9:9–13; Mark 2:13–17).

5:33–39. Jesus tells why He and His disciples do not fast (parallel passages: **Matt. 9:14–17,** see pp. 193–194; Mark 2:18–22).

6:1–5. Jesus answers the charge that He is desecrating the Sabbath; He claims to be "Lord also of the sabbath" (v. 5) (parallel passages: **Matt. 12:1–8,** see pp. 193–194; Mark 2:23–28).

6:6–11. The Pharisees are enraged because Jesus heals a man's withered hand on the Sabbath (parallel passages: **Matt. 12:9–14,** see p. 194; Mark 3:1–6).

6:12–16. After spending all night in prayer,

7:36–50; 8:1–3. Jesus had compassion on various sinful women throughout His ministry, including one woman with a bad reputation who anointed His feet, and Mary Magdalene, who was possessed by demons.

Jesus selects twelve men from among His followers to serve as His disciples, or apostles. He will train them to continue His work after His ministry on earth has ended (parallel passages: Matt. 10:1–4; Mark 3:13–19). See Acts 1:13.

6:17–49. These verses contain Luke's version of Jesus' teachings known as the Sermon on the Mount. A longer and more complete record of these teachings appears in Matthew 5:1–7:29 (see p. 192).

7:1–10. Jesus heals the servant of a centurion, a Roman military officer (parallel passage: Matt. 8:5–13).

7:11–17. Jesus has compassion on a widow in the city of Nain. He raises her only son from the dead.

7:18–35. Jesus answers a question from John the Baptist about whether He really is the Messiah (parallel passage: **Matt. 11:1–19,** see p. 193).

7:36–50. A sinful woman anoints Jesus with an expensive perfume while He is a dinner guest in the home of Simon the Pharisee. Jesus uses her actions to teach Simon a lesson in forgiveness and gratitude.

8:1–3. Jesus conducts another teaching and healing tour throughout the region of Galilee. Accompanying Him and His disciples are several women followers, including Mary Magdalene, whom He had healed of demon possession.

8:4–8. Jesus teaches the crowds with the parable of the sower (parallel passages: **Matt. 13:1–9,** see p. 194; Mark 4:1–9).

8:9–10. Jesus explains why He teaches in parables (parallel passages: **Matt. 13:10–17,** see p. 194; Mark 4:10–12).

8:11–15. Jesus reveals the meaning of the parable of the sower to His disciples (parallel passages: **Matt. 13:18–23,** see p. 194; Mark 4:13–20).

8:16–18. Jesus delivers the parable of the candle, or lamp stand (parallel passage: **Mark 4:21–25,** see p. 207).

8:19–21. Jesus identifies His true relatives as those who follow God (parallel passages: Matt. 12:46–50; **Mark 3:31–35,** see p. 207).

8:22–25. Jesus calms a storm on the Sea of Galilee (parallel passages: Matt. 8:23–27; Mark 4:35–41).

8:26–39. Jesus heals a demon-possessed man who lives in a cemetery (parallel passages: Matt. 8:28–34; **Mark 5:1–20,** see p. 208).

8:40–56. Jesus heals a woman with a hemorrhage and raises the daughter of Jairus from the dead (parallel passages: Matt. 9:18–26; **Mark 5:21–43,** see p. 208).

9:1–6. Jesus gives His disciples power and authority and sends them out to teach and heal (parallel passages: **Matt. 10:5–42,** see p. 193; Mark 6:7–13).

9:7–9. Herod, the Roman ruler of Galilee, hears about Jesus and His miracles. He wonders if He could be John the Baptist returned from the dead.

9:10–17. Jesus performs a feeding miracle for more than 5,000 hungry people (parallel passages: Matt. 14:13–21; **Mark 6:30–44,** see p. 208; John 6:1–14).

9:18–20. Peter confesses Jesus as the Christ, the Anointed One sent from God (parallel passages: **Matt. 16:13–20,** see p. 197; Mark 8:27–30).

9:21–27. Jesus predicts that He will be killed by the religious leaders and then resurrected. He teaches His disciples about the high cost and rewards involved in following Him.

9:28–36. Jesus is transfigured before three of His disciples (parallel passages: **Matt. 17:1–13,** see p. 197; Mark 9:2–13).

9:37–42. Jesus heals a demon-possessed boy (parallel passages: **Matt. 17:14–21,** see p. 197; Mark 9:14–29).

9:43–45. Jesus again predicts His death and resurrection (parallel passages: Matt. 17:22–23; Mark 9:30–32).

9:46–50. Jesus teaches His disciples that true greatness consists of rendering service to others (parallel passages: Matt. 18:1–10; Mark 9:33–50).

9:51–56. Jesus is rejected by the citizens of a Samaritan village. He rebukes His disciples James and John because they want to destroy the village.

9:57–62. Jesus declares that people must count the cost of full commitment before they agree to become His followers (parallel passage: Matt. 8:18–22).

10:1–24. Jesus sends seventy of His followers out after empowering them to teach and heal. They return with reports of great success among the people.

[10:1–24] DON'T WASTE TIME. *Salute [greet, NIV] no man by the way [on the road, NIV]* (Luke 10:4).

Jesus gave these instructions to seventy of His followers when He sent them out on a teaching and witnessing mission. It seems strange that He would forbid them from greeting the very people whom they were sent to reach.

But Jesus did not restrict them from greeting strangers with a friendly "hello." He was referring to the elaborate and drawn-out salutations with which the Jewish people sometimes greeted one another. They would bow again and again, ask about the health and welfare of all the members of their respective families, and repeat their wishes for the peace and prosperity of the other several times.

This type of greeting took a lot of time. "Greet people quickly, and be on your way," is what Jesus was saying. "Let's use every precious minute we have to bring people into God's kingdom."

10:25–37. Jesus uses the parable of the good Samaritan to teach an expert in the law what it means to be a compassionate neighbor to others.

10:38–42. Jesus visits the sisters Mary and Martha. He teaches Martha that she should be more concerned about learning from Him than she is about getting the housework done.

11:1–13. In response to a question from His disciples, Jesus teaches them how to pray. Verses 2–4, which parallel Matthew 6:9–13, are known as the Lord's Prayer, or the Model Prayer.

11:14–28. Jesus answers those who are accusing Him of casting demons out of people through the power of Beelzebub, the chief of demons. Jesus shows that the charge is ridiculous. To cast out evil spirits through the power of Satan would mean that Satan is divided against himself.

11:29–36. The scribes and Pharisees ask Jesus to show them some spectacular sign to prove that He is who He claims to be. He responds that the only sign they will be shown is the sign of the prophet Jonah. Just as Jonah was delivered by the Lord from the stomach of a great fish after three days (Jon. 1:17; 2:10), so Jesus will be killed and raised from the dead after three days.

11:37–54. Jesus criticizes the Pharisees because of their hypocrisy, legalism, and emphasis on external matters in religion.

12:1–12. Jesus warns His disciples to beware of the teachings and traditions of the Pharisees. He also warns that anyone who denies the works of God is guilty of the unforgivable sin of blasphemy against the Holy Spirit.

12:13–21. Through the parable of the rich fool, Jesus warns against misplaced priorities—considering possessions and material wealth more important than commitment to God.

12:22–34. Jesus teaches His disciples not to be

13:1–9. Green figs ripen on the tree. Jesus told a parable about a fig tree that didn't produce fruit, saying the farmer vowed to cut it down unless it started producing. The implication was that God's people should produce the fruit of godliness and behave as though they are citizens of God's kingdom.

overly concerned about their physical needs but to seek first "the kingdom of God; and all these things shall be added unto you" (v. 31).

12:35–48. Through the parable of the unfaithful servant, Jesus teaches His followers to be watchful and ready for His second coming (1 Thess. 5:1–11).

12:49–59. Jesus makes it clear that the time of His death is drawing near. People should be aware of this critical moment and turn to God in repentance and faith.

13:1–9. Jesus' parable of the barren fig tree teaches that the Jewish people have failed in their mission as God's special people. But He is giving them one last chance to show their obedience by accepting His Son Jesus

and becoming citizens of His kingdom.

13:10–17. A synagogue ruler criticizes Jesus after He heals a woman with a crooked back on the Sabbath. Jesus points out that the Jewish law allowed livestock to be led to water on the Sabbath. Wasn't this woman more important than an ox or a donkey?

13:18–21. The parables of the mustard seed and the leaven show that the kingdom of God will eventually become a strong force in the world (parallel passage: Matt. 13:31–35).

13:22–30. The Jewish people thought they had an exclusive claim on God's love and generosity and that all non-Jews were excluded. But Jesus declares that the kingdom of God belongs to those who turn to Him in repentance and faith.

13:31–33. Jesus ignores a warning from the Pharisees to leave Galilee because of a supposed threat from Herod, the Roman ruler in the region.

13:34–35. Jesus predicts that the city of Jerusalem will be punished by the Lord because it has refused to accept Him as the Messiah (parallel passage: Matt. 23:37–39).

14:1–6. Jesus defends His healing of a man with the dropsy (a condition that causes a buildup of fluid in the body) on the Sabbath.

[14:1–6] DINING WITH A PHARISEE. *He [Jesus] went into the house of one of the chief Pharisees to eat bread on the sabbath day* (Luke 14:1).

Jesus' clash with the Pharisees throughout the Gospels may lead us to believe that all Pharisees were bad or that Jesus condemned them all. But this verse shows us otherwise.

A leader among the Pharisees apparently invited Jesus to dine in his home on the Sabbath, and He accepted the invitation. Jesus used the occasion to teach this man and several other Pharisees about His healing mission and His superiority over the Sabbath (Luke 14:3–6).

Two other Pharisees in the Gospels are also worthy of commendation. Nicodemus was a Pharisee who was known for his inquiring mind and seach for truth (John 3:1–12). Joseph of Arimathea was probably a Pharisee since he was a member of the Sanhedrin. He claimed the body of Jesus and buried it in his own new tomb (Mark 15:43–46; Luke 23:53; John 19:38).

14:7–14. Citizens of the kingdom of God should not seek positions of glory and honor for themselves. Humble service to others should be their main concern.

14:15–24. This parable of the great supper shows that the nation of Israel has refused God's glorious invitation to enter His kingdom. Now God is establishing a covenant relationship with the Gentiles—those once considered outsiders and sinners. Any person who accepts God's invitation and turns to Him in repentance and faith is included in God's kingdom, no matter what his or her race or ethnic background (Acts 15:19).

14:25–35. Following Jesus involves sacrifice. A person should consider the cost before making a commitment to discipleship.

15:1–32. Two of the three parables in this chapter about something lost—a lost coin and a lost son—are unique to the Gospel of Luke. The parable of the lost sheep also appears in Matthew's Gospel (Matt. 18:11–14). These parables show that God's love has no limits. He is relentless in His efforts to seek and restore to His favor those who are lost.

16:1–18. The dishonest manager in this parable is shrewd enough to look ahead and prepare for his future security. Believers should show the same foresight in their preparation for eternal life in fellowship with God.

16:19–31. The parable of the rich man and Lazarus shows the tragedy of a life devoted to earthly pleasures with no concern for spiritual values. The rich man's lifestyle of indulgence shuts him off from fellowship with God—an eternal separation that continues in the afterlife.

17:1–10. Jesus teaches that the lives of those who are citizens of God's kingdom should be characterized by forgiveness and service (Eph. 6:7). We serve others not for reward or commendation but because service is what God has called us and equipped us to do.

17:11–19. Jesus heals ten men with leprosy while on His way to Jerusalem. He commends the one man among the ten—a Samaritan—who seeks Jesus out to express His gratitude.

17:20–37. Jesus tells the Pharisees that the kingdom of God is already present. He stands among them as God's Son, the Messiah, the personification of the kingdom that God is building in the hearts of those who believe in Him. He also discusses the final consummation of this kingdom in the future, when He will return as the victorious King over all creation in His second coming (1 Thess. 4:13–17).

18:1–8. This parable of the persistent widow teaches an important lesson about prayer: We should be consistent and persistent in the prayer requests we present to God.

18:9–14. Through this parable of the Pharisee and the publican (tax collector), Jesus teaches about humility in prayer. God rejects the self-righteous prayer of the proud Pharisee, but He accepts the prayer of the publican because he admits his sin and unworthiness.

[18:9–14] TWICE-A-WEEK FASTING. *I [self-righteous Pharisee] fast twice in the week, I give tithes of all that I possess* (Luke 18:12).

These are the words of the self-righteous Pharisee in Jesus' parable about the Pharisee and the tax collector. The Pharisee tried to justify himself in God's sight by claiming he had kept the letter of the law. But the tax collector realized he was a sinner and cast himself on God's mercy (Luke 18:9–14).

Fasting twice a week, as the Pharisee claimed to do, was not commanded in the Law of Moses. This was probably a custom instituted by the Pharisees as an addition to the law that they practiced scrupulously.

The message of this verse is that we can't buy our way into heaven by observing certain rituals. We are justified in God's sight only through faith in Jesus Christ and His atoning death on our behalf.

18:15–17. Jesus welcomes little children (parallel passages: Matt. 19:13–15; **Mark 10:13–16,** see p. 210).

18:18–30. Jesus challenges the rich young ruler to sell all his possessions and follow Him (parallel passages: **Matt. 19:16–30,** see p. 198; Mark 10:17–31).

18:31–34. Jesus again tells His disciples that He will be executed in Jerusalem, then resurrected (parallel passages: **Matt. 20:17–19,** see p. 198; Mark 10:32–34).

18:35–43. Jesus heals a blind man near Jericho (parallel passages: Matt. 20:29–34; Mark 10:46–52).

19:1–10. A tax collector named Zacchaeus climbs a tree to get a better look at Jesus as He passes through Jericho. Confronted by Jesus, he vows to give half of his possessions to the poor and to repay fourfold any excess taxes he has collected "by false accusation" (v. 8).

19:11–27. This passage is known as the parable of the pounds. Ten servants are given one pound (a sum of money) each to manage for their master while he is gone. The servant who plays it safe and fails to increase his pound is criticized by his master. This parable teaches that we are held accountable for our management of God's resources.

19:28–44. Jesus is greeted and praised by the crowds as He rides into Jerusalem (Zech. 9:9). He weeps over the city because of its unbelief (parallel passages: **Matt. 21:1–11,** see p. 198; Mark 11:1–11; John 12:12–19).

19:45–48. Jesus drives out the merchants who are buying and selling in the temple (parallel passages: **Matt. 21:12–22,** see p. 199; Mark 11:12–26).

20:1–8. Jesus responds to the charge of the Pharisees by claiming that He has authority over the temple (parallel passages: Matt. 21:23–27; Mark 11:27–33).

20:9–19. Jesus condemns the religious leaders of Israel by comparing them to wicked husbandmen, or tenant farmers (parallel

19:45–48. Swinging a whip, Jesus drives merchants out of the temple's main courtyard. This courtyard was as close to the sanctuary as non-Jewish worshipers could go—it was their sacred space to worship God.

passages: **Matt. 21:33–46,** see p. 199; Mark 12:1–12).

20:20–26. Jesus is questioned by His enemies about paying taxes to the Roman government (parallel passages: **Matt. 22:15–22,** see p. 199; Mark 12:13–17).

20:27–40. Jesus avoids a trick question from the Sadducees about the resurrection (parallel passages: **Matt. 22:23–33,** see p. 200; Mark 12:18–27).

20:41–44. Jesus uses Scripture to show the scribes that the Messiah from the line of David is more than an earthly king (parallel passages: **Matt. 22:41–46,** see p. 200; Mark 12:35–37).

20:45–47. Jesus condemns the Pharisees for their pride and dishonesty (parallel passages: **Matt. 23:1–36,** see p. 200; Mark 12:38–40).

21:1–4. A sacrificial offering in the temple by a poor widow draws Jesus' praise (parallel passage: Mark 12:41–44).

21:5–38. Jesus discusses events that will occur in the end-time before His second coming (parallel passages: **Matt. 24:1–51,** see p. 200; Mark 13:1–37).

22:1–2. The Jewish Sanhedrin plots the death of Jesus (parallel passages: **Matt. 26:1–5,** see p. 200; Mark 14:1 2).

22:3–6. Judas makes a deal with the Sanhedrin to betray Jesus (parallel passages: **Matt. 26:14–16,** see p. 201; Mark 14:10–11).

22:7–13. Jesus sends Peter and John to find a room where He and His disciples can partake of the Passover meal together (parallel passages: Matt. 26:17–19; Mark 14:12–16).

22:14–20. Jesus turns the Passover meal with His disciples into a supper that memorializes His forthcoming sacrificial death (1 Cor. 11:23–26). He institutes the new covenant with all believers by declaring that the bread represents His broken body and the wine represents His blood, "which is

[21:5–38] HEROD'S TEMPLE IN JERUSALEM. *Some spoke of the temple, how it was adorned with goodly [beautiful, NIV] stones and gifts* (Luke 21:5).

When Jesus entered Jerusalem for the Passover celebration, His disciples were impressed with the Jewish temple that was being remodeled and expanded by Herod the Great, Roman ruler over Palestine. According to the Jewish historian Josephus, its white marble and gold-accented trim were dazzling to the eyes.

Herod began this building project about 15 B.C. in order to curry the favor of the Jews. It was still under construction about forty-five years later when Jesus and His disciples came to the holy city to observe the Passover. Finally completed in A.D. 64, the temple was destroyed—as Jesus predicted (Luke 21:6)—when the Roman army put down a rebellion by the Jewish people in A.D. 70.

The temple in Jerusalem has never been rebuilt. Today a Moslem mosque known as the Dome of the Rock occupies the site.

shed for you" (v. 20) (parallel passages: Matt. 26:26–30; Mark 14:22–26).

22:21–23. Jesus reveals to His disciples that one of them will betray Him (parallel passages: Matt. 26:20–25; Mark 14:17–21; **John 13:21–30,** see p. 233).

22:24–30. Jesus' disciples begin to argue over which of them is the most important. Jesus teaches them that the greatest citizen in the kingdom of God is the one who is self-giving in service to others.

22:31–38. Jesus tells Peter that he will face great temptation from Satan during the next several hours. He predicts that Peter will deny Him three times before the rooster crows at daybreak (parallel passages: Matt. 26:31–35; Mark 14:27–31; John 13:31–38).

22:39–46. Jesus pours out His heart to God in agonizing prayer in the Garden of Gethsemane (parallel passages: **Matt. 26:36–46,** see p. 201; Mark 14:32–42).

22:47–53. Jesus is betrayed by Judas and arrested by the Jewish Sanhedrin (parallel passages: **Matt. 26:47–56,** see p. 202; Mark 14:43–52; John 18:1–12).

22:54–62. Peter follows Jesus when He is led away to the house of the Jewish high priest for interrogation by the Sanhedrin. Questioned outside the house by three different people, he denies that he knows Jesus (parallel passages: **Matt. 26:69–75,** see p. 202; Mark 14:66–72; John 18:15–27).

22:63–71. Jesus is found guilty of blasphemy by the Jewish Sanhedrin when He admits He is the Son of God (parallel passages: Matt. 26:57–68; Mark 14:53–65).

23:1. Determined to have Jesus executed, the Sanhedrin delivers Him to Pontius Pilate, the Roman governor of Judea (parallel passages: **Matt. 27:1–2,** see p. 202; Mark 15:1).

23:2–12. After questioning Jesus, Pilate is convinced He is innocent. Trying to shift responsibility for a ruling in His case, Pilate sends Jesus to Herod, the Roman governor of Galilee, who is visiting Jerusalem during the Passover celebration. Herod refuses to get involved and sends Jesus back to Pilate.

23:13–25. Pilate finally gives in to the cries of the crowd and sentences Jesus to death by crucifixion (parallel passages: **Matt. 27:11–26,** see p. 202; Mark 15:2–15; John 18:28–19:16).

23:26–31. A citizen of Cyrene named Simon carries Jesus' cross to the crucifixion site. Addressing a group of women in the crowd, Jesus prophesies that great calamity will fall upon the nation of Israel in the future. He may have been referring to the destruction of Jerusalem by the Roman army in A.D. 70 (parallel passages: Matt. 27:32; Mark 15:21).

23:32–38. Jesus is crucified at a site known as Calvary (Latin for "Golgotha") (parallel passages: **Matt. 27:33–37**, see p. 202; Mark 15:22–26; John 19:17–24).

23:39–43. Jesus is crucified between two criminals. One of these men ridicules Jesus, but the other turns to Him in repentance and faith and is assured that he will be with Jesus in paradise (parallel passages: Matt. 27:38–44; Mark 15:27–32).

23:44–48. Jesus' suffering and death are accompanied by several supernatural events that can only be explained as acts of God (parallel passages: Matt. 27:45–54; **Mark 15:33–39**, see p. 213).

23:49. Several women from Galilee watch from a distance as Jesus is crucified (parallel passages: Matt. 27:55–56; Mark 15:40–41; John 19:25–27).

23:50–54. A wealthy man from Arimathea named Joseph claims the body of Jesus and buries it in his own tomb (parallel passages: Matt. 27:57–60; Mark 15:42–46; **John 19:38–42**, see p. 235).

23:55–56. Women followers from Galilee note the tomb where Jesus is buried so they can anoint His body with spices after the Sabbath is over (parallel passages: Matt. 27:61; Mark 15:47).

24:1–8. Several women visit the tomb on

23:55–56. Women followers of Jesus mourn His death, which took place as Friday evening approached, the beginning of the Sabbath. Jews were forbidden to work on the Sabbath—even to prepare a body for burial. By the time the women returned to the tomb on Sunday morning, Jesus was once again alive.

[24:44–49] **THE JEWISH SCRIPTURES.** *All things must be fulfilled, which were written in the law of Moses, and in the prophets, and in the psalms, concerning me [Jesus]* (Luke 24:44).

Jesus spoke these words to His disciples when He appeared among them in Jerusalem after His resurrection. He declared that He had fulfilled all the things foretold about the Messiah in the Jewish Scriptures.

The Scriptures used by the Jews in Jesus' time included the books in our present Old Testament, but they were arranged differently than in our modern Bibles. Jesus mentioned the three major divisions of the Jewish Scriptures.

1. The Law of Moses. This is what we refer to today as the Pentateuch—Genesis, Exodus, Leviticus, Numbers, and Deuteronomy.

2. The Prophets. This section included Joshua, Judges, 1 and 2 Samuel, 1 and 2 Kings, and all the prophets except Daniel.

3. The Psalms. Included in this section were the Psalms, the book for which the entire section was named, as well as Proverbs, Job, Song of Solomon, Ruth, Lamentations, Ecclesiastes, Esther, Daniel, Ezra, Nehemiah, and 1 and 2 Chronicles.

raised from the dead (parallel passages: Matt. 28:1–10; Mark 16:1–8; John 20:1–2).

24:9–12. The disciples are skeptical when informed by these women that Jesus has been resurrected. Peter runs to the tomb to check out their story. But he is not certain what to believe when he finds the tomb empty (parallel passage: John 20:3–10).

24:13–35. The risen Christ talks with two of His followers as they walk along the road to the village of Emmaus. He vanishes as they prepare to have a meal together, and they realize this was the resurrected Lord. They report this appearance of Jesus to His disciples in Jerusalem (parallel passage: Mark 16:12–13).

24:36–43. Jesus appears among His disciples. He convinces them they are not seeing a vision or a ghost by showing them His hands and feet and eating a meal in their presence.

24:44–49. Jesus charges His disciples to continue His mission by preaching "repentance and remission of sins...among all nations" (v. 47) (parallel passages: **Matt. 28:16–20,** see p. 204; Mark 16:14–18).

24:50–53. Jesus blesses His disciples and ascends to His Father (parallel passage: Mark 16:19–20).

Sunday morning to anoint Jesus' body. Two angels inform them that Jesus has been

OVERVIEW: Presents Jesus as the divine Son of God who came to earth in human form.

Introduction to John

John was the last of the Gospels to be written, probably as late as about A.D. 90. The author of this Gospel had probably studied Matthew, Mark, and Luke, so he chose to write a different type of Gospel. Rather than just reporting on events in Jesus' life and ministry, John's Gospel majors on the theological meaning of these events. In John, Jesus is portrayed as the eternal Word of God who existed before the world was created (1:1), as the divine Son of God who came to earth in human form.

The author of this Gospel was the apostle John, the son of Zebedee and the brother of James. These two brothers left their fishing business with their father to become two of the twelve disciples of Jesus (Matt. 4:18–22). Along with Peter, John and James developed an "inner circle" relationship with Jesus. They were often involved in important events in the ministry of Jesus when none of the other disciples were present (Matt. 17:1–2; 26:37; Mark 5:37).

Beyond this, John described himself in his Gospel as "the disciple whom Jesus loved" (21:20). He was the only one of the Twelve who dared to follow Jesus to the cross and witness the crucifixion. Jesus committed His mother, Mary, to the care of John just before He died (19:25–27).

In contrast to the other Gospels, John contains little of the teachings of Jesus on such subjects as prayer, the kingdom of God, and how to treat others. Instead, Jesus gives extended monologues about His reason for coming into the world and His inevitable return to the Father. A full five chapters (13:1–17:26) are devoted to Jesus' farewell discourses to His disciples. These reveal the inner mind of Jesus and His own conception of His mission and destiny more clearly than the material in any of the other Gospels.

John's Gospel is also unique because it tells us why it was written. John declared, "These [things] are written, that ye might believe that Jesus is the Christ, the Son of God; and that believing ye might have life through his name" (20:31). Clearly, John wanted to do more than give his readers the facts about Jesus. His goal was to lead us to acknowledge Jesus as the Messiah sent from God and to accept His offer of forgiveness of sin and His gift of eternal life.

Some accounts of Jesus' life and ministry in John also parallel events reported in Matthew, Mark, and Luke. These parallel passages are identified in the following summary of John. The parallel passages in bold type with "see" references refer to pages in this book where expanded summaries of specific Gospel accounts may be found.

Summary of John

1:1–5. John begins his Gospel with the creation, affirming that Christ, God's Son ("the Word," v. 1), participated with the

1:19–34. John the Baptist, a distant relative of Jesus, baptizes Him in the Jordan River. Several weeks later, after spending time alone in the barren wilderness, Jesus started His ministry.

Father in the creation of the world (Gen. 1:1, 26).

1:6–8. John the Baptist was sent to prepare the way for Jesus and to announce His coming into the world (Mark 1:1–8).

1:9–18. Christ left His place of honor with the Father and was born into the world in the form of a man in order to bring people to God (Phil. 2:5–8).

1:19–34. Jesus meets John the Baptist at the place where he is preaching and baptizing. John identifies Him clearly as the long-expected Messiah.

1:35–42. Andrew, a disciple of John the Baptist, follows Jesus. Andrew brings his brother Simon Peter and introduces him to Jesus.

1:43–51. Jesus calls Philip and his friend Nathanael to become His disciples.

2:1–11. Jesus performs His first miracle by turning water into wine at a wedding cel-

---

[1:19–34] HUMILITY OF JOHN THE BAPTIST. *He [Jesus] it is…whose shoe's latchet [thongs, NIV] I [John the Baptist] am not worthy to unloose* (John 1:27).

Although John the Baptist was divinely selected to serve as the forerunner of Jesus (Luke 1:76), he was aware of his unworthiness of such an honor. He declared in this verse that he was not even worthy to bend down and untie the leather thongs that held Jesus' sandals on His feet.

But Jesus recognized John's greatness and commended him for his faithfulness: "Among them that are born of women there hath not risen a greater than John the Baptist" (Matt. 11:11).

ebration in the town of Cana in the region of Galilee.

2:12. Accompanied by His mother and His brothers, Jesus visits the city of Capernaum in the region of Galilee.

2:13–25. Jesus drives out merchants who are conducting business in the temple during the Passover celebration. He charges them with desecrating the house of His Father.

3:1–21. Jesus explains the meaning of the new birth to Nicodemus, a ruler of the Pharisees.

3:22–24. Jesus and His disciples minister in the region of Judea, not far from the place where John the Baptist is preaching and baptizing.

3:25–36. John the Baptist points people to Jesus as the Messiah, the Son of God, who holds the keys to eternal life.

4:1–4. Jesus leaves the region of Judea in the south to travel to the region of Galilee in the north. During this journey He chooses deliberately to pass through the territory of the Samaritans.

4:5–44. Jesus stops at a well outside a Samaritan village and asks a woman for a drink of water. He talks with her about her life of sin and reveals to her that He is the long-expected Messiah. She brings many people from her village to meet Jesus, and they also become believers.

4:45. Jesus finds a receptive audience when He begins preaching in the region of Galilee (parallel passages: **Matt. 4:12–17,** see p. 190; Mark 1:14–15).

4:46–54. A nobleman, or royal official, from Capernaum seeks out Jesus in the town of Cana about twenty miles away. He begs Jesus to heal his sick son. Jesus heals the boy at a distance while his father is traveling back to Capernaum.

5:1–15. Jesus is criticized for healing a lame man on the Sabbath at the pool of Bethesda in Jerusalem.

5:16–47. Jesus defends His healing on the Sabbath by declaring that He has been given all authority as God's Son. Furthermore, He is doing the work that His Father has sent Him to do.

6:1–14. Jesus multiplies a boy's lunch of five pieces of bread and two fish to feed more than 5,000 hungry people (parallel passages: Matt. 14:13–21; **Mark 6:30–44,** see p. 208; Luke 9:10–17).

6:15–21. Jesus walks on the water to join His disciples in a boat on the Sea of Galilee (parallel passages: **Matt. 14:22–33,** see p. 196; Mark 6:45–52).

[6:15–21] SUDDEN STORMS ON LAKE GALILEE. *The sea arose by reason of a great wind that blew* (John 6:18).

Jesus' disciples were crossing the Sea of Galilee in a small fishing boat when they were caught in a sudden storm. This freshwater lake, about thirteen miles long by eight miles wide, is fed by the Jordan River. It sits about seven hundred feet below sea level in an area surrounded by high mountains. Cool winds frequently rush down from these mountains and mix with the warm air on the surface of the lake. The result is a sudden, violent storm such as that which overwhelmed the disciples.

6:22–65. Many people look for Jesus, expecting a handout because they hear He has fed more than 5,000 hungry people. He teaches them that He is God's Son, the true "bread of life" who offers eternal life to all who place their faith in Him.

6:66–71. Many of Jesus' followers turn away when He does not live up to their expectations of the Messiah. Peter, speaking for the other disciples, declares that they will continue to be His faithful followers. Jesus predicts that one of the Twelve will betray Him.

7:1–9. The brothers of Jesus do not believe that Jesus is the Messiah. In a mocking and skeptical tone, they urge Him to attend the Feast of Tabernacles in Jerusalem where He can declare openly that He is the Messiah.

7:10–52. Jesus decides to attend the celebration in Jerusalem without revealing that He is the Messiah. But His teachings and His reputation as a healer and miracle worker cause a division among the people. Some believe He is the Messiah, while others deny this possibility. Nicodemus, a Pharisees who had talked with Jesus earlier (John 3:1–21), urges his fellow Pharisees not to condemn Jesus for blasphemy until they have more solid evidence against Him.

7:53–8:11. Jesus forgives a woman who is accused of adultery and condemns the self-righteousness of her accusers: "He that is without sin among you, let him first cast a stone at her" (8:7).

8:12–30. Jesus angers the Pharisees by claiming

13:1–20. Though Peter doesn't feel worthy, Jesus takes on the role of a servant and washes Peter's feet. This took place at the Last Supper. Jesus washed the feet of each disciple and then urged them to become servants too.

to be the Son of God and the light that God has sent to deliver the world from darkness (1 John 1:7).

8:31–59. Jesus further angers the Pharisees by questioning their claim that they are "children of Abraham." If they were truly Abraham's descendants, He declares, they would be doing the works of Abraham rather than plotting to have Him killed. As the eternal, preexistent Son of God, He is superior to Abraham: "Before Abraham was, I am" (v. 58).

9:1–41. Jesus heals a man who had been blind all his life. The Pharisees question Jesus' credentials, since He had sinned, according to their legalistic laws, by performing this healing on the Sabbath. They question the man about this healing, and he stands his ground in defense of Jesus. After this healed man becomes a believer, Jesus declares that the Pharisees are the real blind people in this situation; they fail to see the truth because of their sin and prejudice.

10:1–21. This is one of Jesus' "I am" statements in the Gospel of John. He compares Himself with a shepherd who watches over his sheep. As the good shepherd, Jesus will make the ultimate sacrifice for those who follow Him: "The good shepherd giveth his life for the sheep" (v. 11).

10:22–42. Jesus declares to the religious leaders of Israel that He is the Christ, the Son of God. They accuse Him of blasphemy and try to execute Him by stoning. But He slips away to an isolated spot in the wilderness of Judea to rest and pray.

11:1–44. Jesus is informed that His friend Lazarus of Bethany has died. After two days He goes to Bethany, where He is met by Lazarus's sister Martha. He declares to Martha, "I am the resurrection, and the life" (v. 25), then raises Lazarus from the dead.

11:45–57. Jesus' raising of Lazarus and His claim to be God's Son drive the Pharisees and the Jewish Sanhedrin into a frenzy. They begin to plot how they can arrest Him and have Him executed.

12:1–8. Mary of Bethany, sister of Lazarus and Martha, anoints Jesus with an expensive perfume (parallel passages: **Matt. 26:6–13,** see pp. 200–201; Mark 14:3–9).

12:9–11. The religious leaders continue their plot against Jesus, even including Lazarus in their accusations because he is responsible for causing many people to believe in Jesus.

12:12–19. Jesus makes His triumphal entry into Jerusalem on a young donkey (parallel passages: **Matt. 21:1–11,** see p. 198; Mark 11:1–11; Luke 19:28–44).

12:20–50. A group of Greeks (Gentiles or non-Jews) ask to see Jesus. They had probably heard about His miracles and unique teachings in regions beyond the Jewish nation. Jesus takes this as a sign that the time of His death is drawing near. He declares that He is the light sent by God to provide salvation for Gentiles as well as Jews—that is, the entire world (Rom. 3:29).

13:1–20. Jesus and His disciples observe the Passover by eating a meal together. He teaches them the meaning of humble service by washing their feet. This was a menial chore that only the lowliest slave would perform for household guests.

13:21–30. During the Passover meal, Jesus predicts that one of His disciples will betray Him. He identifies this disciple by dipping a piece of bread in a bowl of food and giving the bread to Judas (parallel passages: Matt. 26:20–25; Mark 14:17–21; Luke 22:21–23).

13:31–38. Jesus gives His disciples a new commandment: "As I have loved you...ye also love one another" (v. 34). He also predicts

[13:21–30] **RECLINING WHILE EATING.** *There was leaning on Jesus' bosom [breast] one of his disciples, whom Jesus loved* (John 13:23).

This verse describes the time when Jesus was eating the Last Supper with His disciples on the night before He was crucified. They were not seated at a high table, as some popular paintings show, but they were reclining around a low table, in accordance with the custom of that time.

Each person thrust his legs out to the side and leaned on his elbow while taking food from the table. This is how it was possible for John, the "disciple whom Jesus loved," to be leaning back against the bosom, or breast, of Jesus, who was immediately behind him.

that Peter will deny Him three times (parallel passages: Matt. 26:31–35; Mark 14:27–31; **Luke 22:31–38,** see p. 226).

14:1–16:33. Jesus delivers an extended farewell to His disciples. He tells them He is going to prepare a place for them (14:3–4), promises to send the Holy Spirit to guide them after He is gone (14:16–18, 26; 16:7–13), encourages them to abide in Him as the true vine (15:1–8), and assures them that the persecution they will experience in the world will be bearable since He has overcome the world (16:32–33).

17:1–26. These verses are known as Jesus' High Priestly Prayer. He prays for Himself, that He will glorify the Father in His suffering and death that are now just a few hours away (vv. 1–5), for His disciples (vv. 6–19), and for all future believers (vv. 20–26).

18:1–12. Jesus is arrested by officers from the Jewish Sanhedrin after Judas leads them to the spot where He can be found—probably the Garden of Gethsemane (parallel passages: **Matt. 26:47–56,** see p. 202; Mark 14:43–52; Luke 22:47–53).

18:13–14. Jesus appears first before Annas, father-in-law of Caiaphas the high priest.

18:15–27. Jesus next appears before Caiaphas the high priest and the rest of the Jewish Sanhedrin (v. 24). Standing outside the house of the high priest, Peter denies that he knows Jesus (parallel passages: **Matt. 26:69–75,** see p. 202; Mark 14:66–72; Luke 22:54–62).

18:28–19:16. Jesus appears before the Roman governor Pontius Pilate, who sentences Him to death by crucifixion (parallel passages: **Matt. 27:11–26,** see p. 202; Mark 15:2–15; Luke 23:13–25).

19:17–24. Jesus is crucified at a site known as Golgotha (parallel passages: **Matt. 27:33–37,** see p. 202; Mark 15:22–26; Luke 23:32–38).

[19:17–24] **CARRYING THE CROSS.** *And he [Jesus] bearing his cross went forth* (John 19:17).

A cross strong enough to hold the weight of a man and long enough to be placed in the ground and have the victim elevated at the same time would probably be too heavy for a person to carry.

Thus, Jesus probably carried only the horizontal beam to the crucifixion site. Here he was stripped naked, laid on the ground, and nailed to the beam, which was then raised and attached to the upright post.

This form of execution was so cruel and degrading that it was never imposed by the Roman government against its own citizens.

19:25–27. Jesus' mother and two other women—Mary the wife of Cleophas and Mary Magdalene—look on as Jesus is crucified. Jesus commends His mother to the care of His disciple John ("the disciple standing by, whom he loved," v. 26) (parallel passages: Matt. 27:55–56; Mark 15:40–41; Luke 23:49).

19:28–30. Jesus dies on the cross after the soldiers give Him vinegar to drink as a painkiller.

20:26–31. Doubting Thomas touches the spear wound in Jesus' side. Thomas was gone when the resurrected Jesus appeared earlier to the disciples. Thomas told the men he wouldn't believe Jesus was alive again unless he saw it for himself.

19:31–37. After Jesus dies, soldiers pierce His side with a sword to make sure He is dead. Jesus had died quickly, so it was not necessary for the soldiers to break His legs to hasten His death. This fulfills the Scripture that no bones of the sacrificial lamb offered during Passover were to be broken (Exod. 12:46; Num. 9:12).

19:38–42. Joseph of Arimathea, a secret follower of Jesus, claims His body to give it an appropriate burial. Joseph is assisted by Nicodemus (John 3:1–21), who brings perfume and spices to anoint the body. They bury Jesus in a new tomb that has never been used (parallel passages: Matt. 27:57–60; Mark 15:42–46; Luke 23:50–54).

20:1–2. Mary Magdalene discovers the body of Jesus is missing when she visits the tomb on Sunday morning. She reports this to His disciples Peter and John (parallel passages: Matt. 28:1–10; Mark 16:1–8; Luke 24:1–8).

20:3–10. Peter and John rush to the tomb to check out Mary's report that Jesus' body has been taken away (parallel passage: Luke 24:9–12).

20:11–18. Mary Magdalene remains outside the tomb after Peter and John leave. Two angels tell her that Jesus has been resurrected from the dead. Then Jesus appears before Mary and reveals Himself clearly as the risen Christ. She reports this to His disciples (parallel passage: Mark 16:9–11).

20:19–25. The resurrected Jesus appears to His disciples in a place where they are hiding because of their fear of the Jewish religious leaders. He convinces them He is the risen Christ by showing them the wounds on His hands and side. Jesus' disciple Thomas is not present during this appearance. He refuses to believe that Jesus is alive until he can see Him with his own eyes.

20:26–31. Jesus appears among His disciples again—this time when Thomas is present. He deals with Thomas's skepticism by inviting Him to touch the wounds in His hands and side. Believing, Thomas declares, "My Lord and my God" (v. 28).

21:1–14. Jesus appears to seven of His disciples at the Sea of Galilee. He prepares and eats a meal with them to prove they are not seeing a ghost or a vision.

21:15–19. Jesus forgives Peter for his denials and reinstates him to full service as His disciple, charging him to "feed my sheep" (v. 17). He predicts that Peter will suffer persecution and death because of his faithfulness to the risen Lord.

21:20–23. Jesus deals with Peter's question about how long His disciple John ("the disciple whom Jesus loved," v. 20) will live.

21:24–25. Jesus' disciple John, the author of this Gospel, vows that the things he has written about Jesus are authentic eyewitness accounts. He also declares that Jesus did many things he has not included in this Gospel. If he had written about all these events, John says, "the world itself could not contain the books that should be written" (v. 25).

[20:19–25] SUPERNATURAL PEACE. *The same day at evening…came Jesus and stood in the midst, and saith unto them [His disciples], Peace be unto you* (John 20:19).

According to John's Gospel, this was Jesus' first appearance to His disciples after His resurrection. His first word to them was the common greeting used by the Jewish people of that day—a wish for their peace, wholeness, and well-being.

When Jesus greeted them with these words, perhaps the disciples remembered a promise of His supernatural peace and presence that He had made to them while training them for the task of carrying on His work: "Peace I leave with you, my peace I give unto you: not as the world giveth, give I unto you. Let not your heart be troubled, neither let it be afraid" (John 14:27).

CHAPTER 7
ACTS, A HISTORY OF THE EARLY CHURCH

Acts is a one-of-a-kind book in the New Testament. It is not a Gospel, since it contains only a few verses about the life and ministry of Jesus (Acts 1:1–10). Neither is Acts an epistle, or letter, to early Christians or churches, like the rest of the books in the New Testament canon. Acts is in a class by itself, and that is why it is treated here as a major section of God's Word.

The full title of Acts in the King James Version is "The Acts of the Apostles." But it could also be called "The Acts of the Holy Spirit," since it reports on the actions of the Spirit in the birth and development of the church. Jesus promised His followers that they would be empowered by His Spirit to carry on His work (Acts 1:8). This is exactly what happened as believers lived out their faith and shared the gospel in the pagan culture of their time.

ACTS

OVERVIEW: Traces the expansion of Christianity from a movement localized in Jerusalem that appealed mainly to Jews to a worldwide faith that included Gentiles.

Introduction to Acts

The book of Acts picks up where the Gospels end—with Jesus' ascension to the Father and His commission to his followers to take the gospel into all the world (Matt. 28:19; Luke 24:47). As the only book of history in the New Testament, Acts recounts how Jesus' commission was accomplished. In about thirty-five years (A.D. 33–68), the Christian faith spread from Jerusalem to the city of Rome, capital of the Roman Empire. More significantly, it grew from a movement that appealed mainly to Jews into a universal faith that included people of all ethnic backgrounds.

Acts was written by Luke, a physician and early church leader, as a sequel to the Gospel of Luke (see the introduction to Luke's Gospel on p. 214). Luke accompanied the apostle Paul on some of his missionary tours. Luke identified himself with the personal pronoun "we" when recounting some of Paul's experiences in which he was involved (16:10–17; 20:5–21:18; 27:1–28:16).

In addition to firsthand observation, Luke must have interviewed many of the people about whom he wrote and drawn on other reputable sources in order to compile his account of the spread of the church during its first thirty-five years. The book of Acts is known for its careful attention to detail and historical accuracy. It mentions ninety-five different people from thirty-two countries, fifty-four cities, and nine islands in the Mediterranean Sea.

The two dominant personalities of Acts are Peter and Paul. In chapters 1–12, Peter takes the lead in proclaiming the gospel to nonbelievers, mostly of Jewish background, in and around Jerusalem. But Paul becomes the leading witness in chapters 13–28, after his dramatic conversion in an encounter with the living Christ on the road to Damascus. As the "apostle to the Gentiles," he traveled throughout the Mediterranean world, calling people to faith in Christ and founding churches to serve as outposts of righteousness in a pagan world.

The book of Acts ends with Paul under house arrest by the Roman authorities in the city of Rome. But even his imprisonment fails to stop the advance of the gospel. He continues to witness for Christ "with all confidence, no man forbidding him" (28:31).

Summary of Acts

1:1–5. Luke, the author of Acts, reminds his friend Theophilus (v. 1) of the things he wrote about Jesus in his other book, the Gospel of Luke. Theophilus is also mentioned by Luke in the opening verses of his Gospel (Luke 1:3).

1:6–9. Jesus ascends to His Father after assuring His followers that they will receive power

[1:12–15] A SHORT WALK. *Then returned they [early Christian believers] unto Jerusalem from the mount called Olivet, which is from Jerusalem a sabbath day's journey* (Acts 1:12).

Jesus ascended to heaven from the Mount of Olives after delivering a farewell message to these believers (Acts 1:6–9). This hill east of Jerusalem is just a few minutes' walk from the city. This tells us that a "sabbath day's journey" was probably less than a mile.

The prohibition against working on the Sabbath (Exod. 20:8–11) led to this regulation about a Sabbath day's journey. Walking farther than this short distance permitted on the day of worship was considered work, and thus a violation of the Sabbath law.

Jesus may have had this regulation in mind when He told His followers they might have to flee to escape persecution in the end-time: "Pray ye that your flight be not…on the sabbath day" (Matt. 24:20).

from the Holy Spirit to witness for Him throughout the world (Mark 16:19–20).

1:10–11. Two angels tell His followers that Jesus will return to earth again someday.

1:12–15. About 120 followers of Jesus, including His disciples and several women, meet together in Jerusalem.

1:16–26. Under the leadership of the apostle Peter, also known as Simon (Mark 1:16–18), this group of followers selects Matthias to replace Judas as one of the twelve apostles.

2:1–13. While celebrating the festival of Pentecost (Lev. 23:15–21) in Jerusalem, Jesus' apostles are filled with the Holy Spirit. Their normal spoken language is either Aramaic or Greek. But these followers of Jesus begin to speak in several different languages that are recognized by Jews from different parts of the world who are gathered at Jerusalem for the Pentecost celebration. Some

of these Jews are amazed at this display, but others accuse the apostles of being drunk with "new wine" (Acts 2:13).

2:14–42. In a great speech known as his "Pentecost Sermon," the apostle Peter assures the crowd that their strange speech is a fulfillment of the ancient prophecy of Joel 2:28–32. He turns their attention to Jesus, who has empowered the apostles with the Holy Spirit. Then he declares, "Repent, and be baptized every one of you in the name of Jesus Christ for the remission of sins, and ye shall receive the gift of the Holy Ghost" (v. 38). Three thousand people turn to Jesus in repentance and are baptized.

2:43–47. The apostles perform wonders and signs among the people in Jerusalem. The followers of Jesus pool their resources to care for the needy among their fellowship.

3:1–11. Peter and John heal a lame man outside the temple in the name of Jesus.

3:12–26. Peter preaches another strong sermon to the people of Jerusalem. He urges them to repent and be baptized in the name of Jesus—the one whom they have rejected but whom God has raised and designated as the Prince of Life.

4:1–22. Peter and John are arrested and questioned by the Jewish Sanhedrin about their healing of the lame man outside the temple. They are released after they declare boldly that the man was healed through the power of Jesus. But the Sanhedrin warns them not to continue to speak or teach in the name of Jesus.

4:23–31. Peter and John meet with other believers. Together, they pray for strength and boldness to continue to preach about Jesus, in spite of the threats from the Jewish Sanhedrin. God honors their prayers by strengthening them again with the Holy Spirit (John 14:16–18; Acts 2:1–13).

2:1–13. The Holy Spirit descends on the followers of Jesus, giving them the boldness and miracle-working power to establish a new religious movement that eventually takes its name from Christ: Christianity.

4:32–37. These early believers continue their practice of pooling their resources in order to care for the needy among their fellowship (Acts 2:43–47). Barnabas sells his land and places the proceeds in the common treasury.

5:1–11. Ananias and his wife, Sapphira, sell a field and pretend to place all the proceeds in the common treasury of the church. But they actually keep part of the money for themselves. They pay with their lives for lying to God.

[5:1–11] **IMMEDIATE BURIAL.** *The young men arose, wound him [Ananias] up [wrapped up his body, NIV], and carried him out, and buried him* (Acts 5:6).

Ananias, an early Christian believer, was struck dead when he lied about his contribution to the church's common treasury. He was buried immediately by his fellow believers.

Burial on the day of death was the customary practice in Palestine in New Testament times. Embalming was not practiced by the Jews, and a body would deteriorate quickly in the sweltering climate.

Bodies were often prepared for burial by being wrapped with strips of cloth. This procedure is suggested by the NIV translation of this verse. Spices were sometimes placed among these layers of cloth. This is how Joseph of Arimathea and Nicodemus prepared the body of Jesus for burial (John 19:38–40).

5:12–16. The apostles perform signs and wonders, including healing the sick, among the people of Jerusalem. The church continues to grow with the addition of many believers (Acts 2:41).

5:17–32. The apostles are imprisoned by the Sanhedrin for continuing to preach about Jesus. Released by an angel, they go right back to bearing witness about Jesus and His resurrection. They are dragged before the Sanhedrin again, only to declare, "We ought to obey God rather than men" (v. 29).

5:33–42. Gamaliel advises the other members of the Sanhedrin to release the apostles, with the observation that their work will come to an end if it is not in God's will. After a beating, the apostles return to their preaching, "rejoicing that they were counted worthy to suffer shame for his name" (v. 41).

6:1–7. Greek-speaking members of the early church complain that their widows are not receiving their fair share in the church's food-distribution efforts. The church selects seven men of Greek-speaking background to coordinate this ministry.

6:8–15. Stephen, one of the seven men selected to coordinate food distribution for the church, speaks boldly for Jesus in a debate with a group of Jewish zealots. They accuse him of blasphemy and drag him before the Jewish Sanhedrin for trial.

7:1–53. In a long speech before the Sanhedrin, Stephen reviews the history of the Jewish people. He accuses the religious leaders of rejecting God's messengers and disobeying His commands at every turn. This includes their rejection of Jesus as the Messiah.

7:54–60. Enraged by these accusations, the Jewish leaders execute Stephen by stoning him to death.

8:1–4. A Pharisee named Saul (later known as the apostle Paul) is a consenting bystander when Stephen is killed. Stephen's death stirs open persecution from the Jewish religious leaders against the church in Jerusalem. Saul is one of the ringleaders in these efforts to stamp out the church. Many believers flee Jerusalem and carry the message of Jesus wherever they go.

8:5–17. Philip, one of the seven men selected to distribute food to the needy, preaches the gospel in the region of Samaria. Many Sa-

7:54–60. An angry mob prepares to stone Stephen for his vocal faith in Jesus. Stephen prays, "Lord, lay not this sin to their charge" (v. 60).

maritans believe on Jesus Christ and are baptized. Peter and John come to Samaria from Jerusalem to help Philip in this evangelism effort.

8:18–25. Peter condemns Simon the magician for trying to buy the power of the Holy Spirit with money.

8:26–40. Philip witnesses in the desert to a eunuch from Ethiopia, an official under Candace the queen. The eunuch is baptized by Philip on his testimony of faith that "Jesus Christ is the Son of God" (v. 37).

9:1–7. Saul the persecutor is converted to Christianity in a dramatic encounter with the risen Christ on the road to Damascus, Syria (Acts 22:4–10).

9:8–18. Saul is struck with blindness for three days following his conversion experience. God sends a believer named Ananias to find Saul in Damascus and to restore his sight. The Lord makes it clear that Saul is a part of His plan to reach the Gentiles with the gospel (Acts 13:44–50).

9:19–25. Saul angers the Jews in Damascus by preaching about Jesus in the synagogue. They attempt to kill him, but Saul escapes when his fellow believers let him down in a basket over the city wall.

9:26–31. Returning to Jerusalem, Saul attempts to join the Christian fellowship. But he is met with suspicion and distrust because of his previous persecution of the church. Barnabas speaks up for Saul and convinces them he is a genuine believer. Saul eventually returns to Tarsus, his hometown, because of threats against his life from the unbelieving Jews in Jerusalem.

9:32–35. In Lydda Peter heals a man named Aeneas of the palsy.

9:36–43. Peter raises Dorcas, a female believer who "was full of good works" (v. 36), from the dead, in Joppa.

10:1–8. Cornelius, a Roman centurion and thus a Gentile, is a godly man who worships the one true God. In a vision, God instructs Cornelius to send for the apostle Peter, who will tell him what he should do. Cornelius obeys and sends three servants to Joppa to find Peter at the house of Simon the tanner.

10:9–16. As Cornelius's servants draw near the city of Joppa, Peter is praying in the outdoor space on top of Simon's house. In a vision, Peter sees a group of unclean animals that are forbidden as food for the Jews (Lev. 11:1–47). But God instructs Peter to kill and eat these animals. When Peter protests, God declares, "What God hath cleansed, that call not thou common" (v. 15). This is God's way of telling Peter that Gentiles are included in God's plan of salvation. No one

is to be excluded from His love and grace.

10:17–23. Just then, Cornelius's three servants arrive. Peter learns they want him to go to Caesarea to talk with Cornelius. Then he invites them in to spend the night.

10:24–48. The next day Peter travels to the home of Cornelius and preaches the gospel to him and his entire household. They repent, turn to Jesus, receive the Holy Spirit, and are baptized. This is dramatic evidence of God's inclusion of the Gentiles in His redemptive plan (John 12:20–50).

11:1–18. Leaders of the church in Jerusalem question Peter about the conversion of Cornelius and other Gentiles. One faction in the church is upset that Peter associated with uncircumcised Gentiles. But when Peter explains what happened, most of the church leaders are pleased. They declare, "Then hath God also to the Gentiles granted repentance unto life" (v. 18).

11:19–24. God blesses the work of a new church that has been planted among the people of Greek-speaking background in the city of Antioch in Syria. The Jerusalem church sends Barnabas to guide this new work, and it grows dramatically under his leadership.

11:25–26. Barnabas travels to Tarsus (Acts 9:27–30) and enlists Saul/Paul to help him in the church at Antioch.

11:27–30. A severe famine strikes the Mediterranean area, as foretold by the prophet Agabus. Barnabas and Saul/Paul deliver a relief offering from their area to the suffering Christians in Judea around Jerusalem.

12:1–5. Herod Agrippa I, Roman ruler over Palestine, executes the apostle James (Mark 1:19–20) and imprisons the apostle Peter.

12:6–19. Peter is miraculously delivered from prison by an angel and reunited with believers who are praying for his release.

[10:9–16] PRAYING ON THE HOUSETOP. *Peter went up upon the housetop to pray about the sixth hour [about noon, NIV]* (Acts 10:9).

This may seem to us like a strange place to pray, but it made perfect sense to Peter.

The roofs of houses in Bible times might be compared to our modern patios. They were flat and easily accessible by an exterior stairway. People often went to the roof for rest and relaxation, particularly at night to catch a cooling breeze (see the note "Guardrails on the Roof" on p. 42).

Peter probably went to the roof so he could be alone in prayer, since he was a visitor in the house of Simon the tanner (Acts 10:5–6).

12:20–25. Herod is struck dead by the Lord for allowing himself to be elevated to the status of a god in the eyes of the people.

13:1–3. The Holy Spirit selects Barnabas and Saul/Paul for missionary work. The church at Antioch obeys the Spirit's leading by sending them out after praying and fasting and commissioning them to this task through the laying on of hands. The work of Barnabas and Paul described in Acts 13:4–14:28 is known as the apostle Paul's first missionary journey.

13:4–12. On the island of Cyprus, Paul and Barnabas witness to the governor of the region, and he becomes a believer. Paul rebukes a magician or sorcerer named Barjesus when he tries to hinder their work.

13:13. Leaving Cyprus, Paul and Barnabas stop at the city of Perga in the province of Pamphylia. John Mark, who has been accompanying them on the trip, decides to return to Jerusalem.

[13:14–43] THE SYNAGOGUE LEADER. *The rulers of the synagogue sent unto them [Paul and Barnabas], saying…if ye have any word of exhortation…say on (Acts 13:15).*

During Paul's first missionary journey, he and his associate, Barnabas, attended worship services at the local synagogue (see the note "Reading in a Synagogue" on p. 217) in Antioch of Pisidia. They were invited to speak to the other worshipers by the rulers or presiding officers of the synagogue.

A synagogue ruler was elected to his position by other members of the congregation. His responsibility was to plan the services, enlist readers and speakers, and preside at the worship proceedings.

Most mentions of this synagogue officer in the New Testament refer to only one ruler (Mark 5:36–38; Luke 13:14). But this passage in Acts mentions more than one ruler. Perhaps a division of responsibilities was required in larger synagogues.

13:14–43. Paul preaches about Jesus in the Jewish synagogue in the city of Antioch in the province of Pisidia. The staunch Jews are skeptical of his message, but it is well received by Gentiles (Acts 10:45) and religious proselytes.

13:44–50. On the next Sabbath a crowd gathers in the city to hear Paul speak again. This time the Jews openly condemn Paul and accuse him of blasphemy. They expel Paul and Barnabas from the city. The two missionaries declare: "It was necessary that the word of God should first have been spoken to you [Jews]: but seeing ye put it from you, and judge yourselves unworthy of everlasting life, lo, we turn to the Gentiles" (v. 46; see Rom. 3:29). This represents a turning point in the ministry of Paul. From now on he will direct most of his evangelistic efforts to the Gentiles because of their openness to the gospel message.

13:51–14:5. Many Gentiles and Jews of Greek-speaking background turn to the Lord in Iconium. But Paul and Barnabas are eventually forced to leave the city because of strong opposition from the Jews.

14:6–20. In the province of Lycaonia, Paul and Barnabas preach in the cities of Lystra and Derbe. When Paul heals a lame man, the superstitious citizens of Lystra think the missionaries are gods. At Lystra Paul is also delivered miraculously by the Lord from a mob of Jewish zealots who try to stone him to death.

14:21–28. Paul and Barnabas return to their sending church at Antioch of Syria. This brings Paul's first missionary journey to a close. On the return trip the missionaries stop at the places they had visited, "confirming the souls of the disciples, and exhorting them to continue in the faith" (v. 22). They also appoint elders (Acts 20:17) to lead the

16:1–3. Ruins of ancient Lystra, in modern-day Turkey, the city where Paul met Timothy, his "own son in the faith" (1 Timothy 1:2).

churches they had founded. The church at Antioch rejoices when they learn that God has "opened the door of faith unto the Gentiles" (v. 27) through the ministry of Paul and Barnabas.

15:1–6. A faction within the church insists that Gentiles must convert to Judaism and be circumcised in accordance with the Law of Moses before they can be saved. Leaders of the church meet at Jerusalem to consider the matter.

15:7–35. The apostle Peter, followed by Paul and Barnabas, speaks against circumcision as a requirement for Gentile believers. James, the half brother of Jesus and a leader in the church, issues the church's opinion that all persons, Jews and Gentiles alike, are saved through faith alone (Rom. 3:21–31). Paul and Barnabas deliver this good news to the church at Antioch.

15:36–41. Paul and Barnabas prepare to set out on a second missionary journey. But they disagree on whether to take John Mark, who had left them and returned home on their first trip (Acts 13:13). Finally, the two missionaries agree to go their separate ways. Barnabas takes John Mark and sails for the island of Cyprus. Paul travels north through the provinces of Syria and Cilicia, accompanied by Silas, a believer in the church at Antioch.

16:1–3. Paul and Silas strengthen believers in Derbe and Lystra, two cities where Paul had preached during his first missionary tour (Acts 14:6–20). This stop begins Paul's second missionary journey, which continues through Acts 18:22. At Lystra Paul meets a young believer named Timothy, whom he enlists as a helper in his missionary work (1 Tim. 1:1–2).

16:4–10. After traveling through several provinces, Paul and Silas are persuaded by the Holy Spirit not to enter the regions of Asia and Bithynia. Through a vision they are beckoned instead into the province of Macedonia.

16:11–15. In the city of Philippi (Phil. 1:1) in Macedonia, a businesswoman named Lydia and her entire household become believers.

16:16–24. Paul and Silas heal a demented slave girl. They are thrown into prison on charges from her master, who was profiting from her fortune-telling abilities.

16:25–40. As they sing praises to God, Paul and Silas are freed miraculously from prison by an earthquake. The jail keeper and his entire household are baptized by Paul after they turn to the Lord.

17:1–9. Unbelieving Jews create an uproar in the city of Thessalonica after Paul preaches in the Jewish synagogue. But several Gentiles become believers.

17:10–14. Paul finds an open and eager audience in the city of Berea: "They received the word with all readiness...and searched the scriptures daily, whether those things were so" (v. 11). But enraged Jews who have followed Paul and Silas from Thessalonica drive them out of the city.

17:15–34. While waiting for Silas and Timothy to join him in Athens, Paul preaches to the philosophers and intellectuals in this cultured Greek city. Most are skeptical, especially about the resurrection of Jesus (1 Cor. 15:1–11). But a few are receptive and turn to the Lord.

18:1–18. Paul travels from Athens to Corinth, where he joins forces with a Christian couple, Aquila and Priscilla. They support themselves as tentmakers for eighteen months while witnessing for Christ and establishing a church in this pagan city (1 Cor. 1:1–9).

18:19–22. After preaching for a while in the city of Ephesus, Paul returns to his home base—the church at Antioch. This brings to an end his second missionary journey.

18:23. Paul begins his third and final missionary journey by traveling through the provinces of Galatia and Phyrgia, encouraging new believers and strengthening their churches. This journey will end with his return to Jerusalem in Acts 21.

18:24–28. Apollos, a zealous new believer from Alexandria, Egypt, preaches in the church at Ephesus. After instructions in the faith

19:24–41. The many-breasted goddess Diana was the favorite deity of Ephesus. Craftsmen and merchants made a good living selling figurines of her—until Paul arrived and convinced many people to stop worshiping idols. With their livelihood threatened, the merchants responded with a riot.

from Aquila and Priscilla, he moves on to the province of Achaia to minister in the church at Corinth.

19:1–7. Paul arrives in Ephesus, where he finds several believers who were followers of John the Baptist (John 4:1). He instructs them about Jesus and baptizes them in His name.

19:8–23. Paul continues his work in Ephesus and the surrounding province of Asia. In addition to preaching and teaching, he performs miraculous healings among the people. Black magic and superstition yield to the power of the Word of God.

19:24–41. Believers in Ephesus are threatened by a mob under the leadership of Demetrius, a silversmith. The gospel was cutting into the profits of those who made and sold miniature replicas of the pagan goddess Diana. But the crowd disperses quietly when calmed down by the town clerk.

20:1–5. Paul takes several believers on a preaching and witnessing tour through the provinces of Macedonia, Greece (Achaia), and Asia.

20:6–12. In the city of Troas, Paul preaches late into the night in an upstairs room. A young man named Eutychus goes to sleep and falls from the window. Paul revives him and stays with him until he regains his strength.

20:13–16. Paul decides to go to Jerusalem in time to celebrate the feast of Pentecost. He catches a ship headed for Miletus, a seaport city not far from Ephesus.

20:17–38. Paul sends word for the elders of the church at Ephesus to meet him at Miletus. He delivers a tearful farewell address and predicts that this is the last time they will see one another. He encourages them to remain true to the gospel that he has planted in their midst. Paul also tells the church elders about his feeling that trouble awaits

[19:24–41] PAGAN CHARMS. *A certain man [of Ephesus] named Demetrius, a silversmith, which made silver shrines for Diana [Artemis, NIV], brought no small gain unto the craftsmen* (Acts 19:24).

Paul worked in the city of Ephesus for almost three years—longer than he stayed at any other one place. A city of about 300,000 people, it was a strategic center for the planting of the gospel in the Gentile world.

The pride of Ephesus was a large, ornate temple devoted to the worship of Diana, or Artemis, a pagan goddess. Demetrius and other craftsmen of the city made their living by making and selling miniature replicas of this pagan goddess. These were probably worn as charms on necklaces or bracelets by worshipers of this goddess.

When the citizens of Ephesus began turning to the Lord and quit buying these pagan charms, Demetrius incited a riot against Paul (Acts 19:24–29). Religious tolerance was out of the question when pagan profits were at stake.

him in Jerusalem: "I go...not knowing the things that shall befall me there" (v. 22).

21:1–9. After sailing across the Mediterranean Sea, Paul's ship docks at the coastal city of Tyre, about 100 miles north of Jerusalem. At Tyre he meets and encourages other believers, then travels south to the city of Caesarea, the home of Philip the evangelist (Acts 8:5–17, 26–40).

21:10–15. At Tyre Paul is warned by a prophet named Agabus that he will be arrested by the Jews if he goes to Jerusalem. But Paul pushes on and finally arrives in the city. This brings to an end Paul's third missionary journey.

21:16–26. Paul greets the leaders of the church at Jerusalem. They rejoice over the acceptance of the gospel by the Gentiles under his ministry. At their suggestion, Paul agrees to serve as sponsor for several men who are undergoing purification rituals in the Jewish temple.

21:27–36. Paul is grabbed by an angry mob of Jews. They jump to the conclusion that he has taken a Gentile into an area of the temple reserved only for Jews—and thus polluted the holy sanctuary. A quick-acting detachment of Roman soldiers rescues Paul from the angry crowd.

21:37–22:22. Paul addresses the crowd, telling them he was a zealous Jew just like them until he was converted in a dramatic encounter with Jesus Christ (Acts 9:1–7). But the crowd renews their cry that he deserves to die for his blasphemous actions.

22:23–29. The Roman soldiers take Paul away to one of their own prisons where he will be safe from the Jewish mob. They prepare to force him to talk by giving him a scourging (beating), but Paul reveals that he is a Roman citizen. This guarantees that he will be treated with respect and fairness while in Roman custody.

22:30–23:10. Paul appears before the Jewish Sanhedrin. He causes dissension among the members of this body when he declares that Jesus was resurrected from the dead. The Roman soldiers return Paul to their own prison for his protection.

23:11. The Lord appears to Paul and informs the apostle that he will bear witness of Him in Rome, capital city of the Roman Empire (Acts 28:17–31).

23:12–22. Paul's nephew warns the Roman commander of a plot by Jewish zealots to kill the apostle.

23:23–35. The Roman commander, Claudius Lysias, sends Paul to the seat of the Roman provincial government at Caesarea. Here Paul is to stand trial before Felix, governor of the province.

24:1–21. The Jews from Jerusalem present their charges of blasphemy against Paul before Felix. Speaking eloquently in his own defense, Paul shows the charges to be false.

24:22–27. Felix holds Paul in prison at Caesarea for two years, hoping the apostle will buy his freedom with a bribe.

25:1–12. Festus succeeds Felix as the Roman provincial governor over Judea. He asks Paul if he is willing to have his case heard before the Jewish Sanhedrin in Jerusalem. The apostle realizes he cannot receive a fair trial in such an arrangement, so he appeals his case to Rome—the right of every Roman citizen.

25:13–27. While Paul is waiting to go to Rome, Festus discusses Paul's case with Herod Agrippa II, another Roman ruler over the Jewish territories. Agrippa asks for Paul to be brought before him so he can hear his story firsthand. Festus is glad to comply. He hopes this appearance by Paul will give him some specific charge against the apostle that he can send with him to Rome.

26:1–32. Paul makes a passionate defense speech before Festus and Agrippa. He recounts his conversion experience and tells how he was called by the Lord to serve as an apostle

---

[25:1–12] PAUL'S RIGHT OF APPEAL. *Festus… answered, Hast thou [Paul] appealed unto Caesar? unto Caesar shalt thou go* (Acts 25:12).

Festus was the Roman governor of Judea who agreed to hear the charges against Paul brought by the Jewish leaders. When Festus suggested that the apostle be sent back to the Jewish court, Paul invoked his rights as a Roman citizen. He appealed his case to Rome, the capital city, where he would be assured of a fair trial (Acts 25:10–11).

In Paul's time, a person could become a Roman citizen by birth or by buying this special status. Roman officials often granted these rights to non-Romans who had rendered special service to the empire. Although Paul was a Jew, he had been born a Roman citizen (Acts 22:28). How his parents had obtained their citizenship rights is unknown.

> **[27:27–38] PERILS OF THE SEA.** *Fearing lest we [Paul and shipmates] should have fallen upon rocks, they [sailors] cast four anchors out of the stern, and wished for the day* (Acts 27:29).
>
> Acts 27 reports on the voyage of Paul to Rome and the wreck of his ship in a ferocious storm. Ancient sailing ships were at the mercy of the winds. This verse reports that the crew tossed out four anchors from the rear of the ship to keep it from being broken to pieces on the rocky shore.
>
> This chapter of Acts also tells us that the captain of this ship was pushing his luck by sailing to Rome so late in the year. Most ships that sailed the Mediterranean Sea apparently docked in a protected bay or inlet until the storms of winter were over (Acts 27:7–12).
>
> Several actions were taken to save the ship when the storm struck with its full fury. The crew pulled ropes or cables tightly around the hull to keep it from breaking apart (Acts 27:17). They also lightened the ship by throwing the cargo and even its pulleys and ropes for hoisting the sails into the sea (Acts 27:19, 38).

to the Gentiles (Acts 9:1–7). Agrippa is so moved by Paul's remarks that he declares, "Almost thou persuadest me to be a Christian" (v. 28). Both Festus and Agrippa agree that Paul is innocent of the charges against him. But since he has appealed his case to Caesar, to Rome he must go.

27:1–13. Paul sails for Rome as a prisoner of the Roman Empire. The first part of their journey takes them several hundred miles to an area near the island of Crete in the Mediterranean Sea. The captain of the ship plans to land at a port known as Phoenix to wait out the approaching winter storms.

27:14–20. But the ship never reaches Crete. Struck by a violent winter storm, it drifts off course as it is buffeted by the crashing waves. The crew throws part of the ship's tackle overboard to give it more stability in the rough seas.

27:21–26. Paul assures the crew and the other passengers that no lives will be lost in this storm. This has been revealed to him in a vision by a messenger from the Lord. But the ship will be wrecked and they will be "cast upon a certain island" (v. 26).

27:27–38. As the ship drifts into shallow water, Paul urges everyone to eat so they will have strength to escape when they run aground.

27:39–44. The ship is torn apart by the violent waves when it hits land. But everyone on board escapes to the shore, as Paul had predicted.

28:1–6. The passengers and crew find themselves on the island of Melita (now know as Malta). Paul impresses the native islanders by surviving a bite from a poisonous snake.

28:7–11. Paul conducts a healing ministry during his three months on the island.

28:12–16. Paul sets sail again, making several stops along the way before finally arriving at Rome, capital city of the Roman Empire.

28:17–29. Paul takes the initiative to meet with a group of Jews in Rome. His message about Jesus is received by some but rejected by others.

28:30–31. For two years, while under house arrest in Rome, Paul preaches the message of Christ to many people (Phil. 1:12–13). He witnesses "with all confidence, no man forbidding him" (v. 31).

CHAPTER 8
EPISTLES OF THE APOSTLE PAUL

As a proud Pharisee, the apostle Paul (also known as Saul) was a zealous persecutor of the Christian movement during its early years (Acts 7:58). But he was converted to Christianity in a dramatic encounter with the living Lord on the road to the city of Damascus about A.D. 35 (Acts 9:1–8). From then until his death about thirty years later, he preached the gospel and founded churches with a holy passion. His travels in the service of Christ took him hundreds of miles throughout the ancient world. Toward the end of his ministry, he even traveled by ship to the city of Rome, capital of the Roman Empire (Acts 28:14–16).

Because Paul's ministry covered such a large area, he used epistles, or letters, to communicate with the churches he founded as well as with the members of these new congregations. In these epistles he dealt with problems in the churches, instructed new believers in the essentials of the Christian faith, and encouraged local church leaders to remain faithful to their calling.

Thirteen of these Pauline letters are included in the New Testament. Nine were written to churches: Romans, 1 and 2 Corinthians, Galatians, Ephesians, Philippians, Colossians, and 1 and 2 Thessalonians. Four were written to individuals: 1 and 2 Timothy, Titus, and Philemon.

OVERVIEW: A thorough exploration of the doctrine of justification by faith alone.

Introduction to Romans

Most of Paul's letters were written to congregations that he had founded. But Paul had never visited the church at Rome. Indeed, one of his reasons for writing to this congregation may have been to pave the way for a personal visit to the believers in that city (1:11). Perhaps he wanted to generate their support for a missionary visit he hoped to make

A model of ancient Rome shows the circular Colosseum and the oblong chariot racecourse dominating the cityscape, alongside the Tiber River.

to Spain (15:20–24). Paul probably wrote this epistle about A.D. 57 near the end of his third missionary journey.

No matter why or when Paul wrote this epistle, all believers should be thankful that he did. It is his most important letter because it expounds on the concept of justification by faith alone. The apostle affirmed that Gentiles and Jews alike are forgiven of their sins and declared righteous in God's sight not on the basis of human achievement, but because of God's gift of grace bestowed on those who accept it by faith.

According to Paul, every person stands in need of God's grace. This was certainly true in the case of Gentiles, or non-Jews, because they worshiped created things rather than God the Creator (1:25). But the Jewish people were in the same situation, although they claimed to be superior to the Gentiles because they knew God's revealed will through His law. They were condemned by this very law because of their failure to keep it. Thus, Paul pointed out in Romans, there was no difference between Jews and Gentiles because "all have sinned, and come short of the glory of God" (3:23).

But the good news is that God reaches out to us, even in our sin. His love was expressed supremely through the death of His Son. Jesus, the Righteous One, died on behalf of the unrighteous. We can receive this grace through committing ourselves to Him in faith.

Throughout Christian history, Paul's epistle to the Romans has served as a catalyst for reform within the church. Martin Luther was transformed when he rediscovered the principle of salvation by grace through faith alone while studying Romans. This truth led to the greatest reform the church has ever experienced—the Protestant Reformation of the sixteenth century.

Summary of Romans

1:1–7. Paul identifies himself as an apostle and servant of Christ and extends greetings to believers in the city of Rome, capital of the Roman Empire.

1:8–13. Paul had never visited Rome, but he assures the Roman Christians that he has heard from others about their stalwart faith. He expresses his desire to visit them in the future.

1:14–16. The apostle feels he has a responsibility to present the gospel to people of all backgrounds and circumstances—the uncultured as well as the cultured and the foolish as well as the wise (Gal. 3:26–29). The gospel of Jesus Christ is a powerful force that brings salvation to all who believe.

[1:14–16] GREEKS AND BARBARIANS. *I [Paul] am debtor both to the Greeks, and to the Barbarians; both to the wise, and to the unwise* (Rom. 1:14).

Paul meant by these words that he was under obligation—by virtue of his call from God—to share the gospel with all types of people. This included the Greeks, a highly civilized and cultured people, as well as the barbarians—a general term for the unlearned and unsophisticated.

The Greeks referred to any person who was not a citizen of Greece as a "barbarian," just as the Jews thought of all non-Jewish people—no matter what their ethnic background—as "Gentiles."

1:17. Paul introduces the concept of the righteousness of God, a key idea in the book of Romans. Because God is righteous, He condemns sin and judges sinners. But He has provided a way by which people can fulfill the righteousness that He demands. All who believe in Christ are justified before God, and they receive power for victorious living as His disciples (Eph. 2:1–10).

1:18–32. These verses portray the plight of Gentiles, or non-Jews. God has revealed Himself to them through His creation. But they have ignored His message and worshiped false gods, pursuing their own evil desires. Apart from God and His righteousness, they stand condemned and hopeless because of their immoral and depraved behavior.

2:1–16. God is a righteous judge. He will not judge some people because of their sin and overlook others. All who sin can expect to reap the consequences of their sin when God calls them to account. He will judge them in accordance with their deeds, not on the basis of their knowledge or ethnic background.

2:17–29. The Jewish people thought of themselves as superior to others in a moral sense because they had received God's special revelation through the Law of Moses. But they had failed to obey the law. Therefore, Paul declares, being a Jew and having God's law do not make a person righteous in God's sight.

3:1–8. Paul admits that the Jewish people do have one significant difference that sets them apart from the Gentiles. Through the Jews God has revealed and preserved His written Word, the Scriptures. This is the standard by which all people—Jews as well as Gentiles—will be judged by the Lord.

3:9–20. Quoting from several Old Testament passages, the apostle shows that righteousness before God is not something that a person attains by his or her own moral goodness, by observing the law, or by being born a Jew. The truth is that "there is none righteous, no, not one" (v. 10; see Ps. 14:1–3).

3:21–31. How, then, are people made righteous before God? Through throwing themselves in faith upon the atoning death of Jesus Christ.

Jew and Gentile alike are justified not by their works but by their reliance on Jesus and His saving grace (Eph. 2:1–10).

4:1–25. In this chapter, Paul uses the example of Abraham from the Old Testament to show that God has always justified people on the basis of their faith. Abraham was childless, but he had faith that his descendants would become God's special people. The Lord declared Abraham righteous on the basis of his faith in this divine promise (James 2:23).

5:1–11. The fruits of justification by faith before God are many. The believer enjoys "peace with God" (v. 1) and is able to overcome trials and tribulations (v. 3).

5:12–21. All members of the human race are infected by Adam's sin of rebellion against God in the Garden of Eden (Gen. 3). The punishment for these sins is death. But we have been delivered from this death sentence by Jesus Christ, who laid down His life on our behalf. Just as Adam was the first member of a lost race, Jesus is the first member of a saved race, or the Second Adam. He brings release from the judgment that our sins deserve.

6:1–14. Receiving God's forgiveness through faith in Christ does not mean that we are set free to sin at will. Believers are united to Christ in such a way through their conversion experience that they want to please their Lord through holy and righteous living. The "old self" is no longer in control. We are set free from slavery to sin to service in God's kingdom.

6:15–23. Paul challenges his readers to reject the way of sin and death and to choose the path that leads to abundant living in the Lord: "For the wages of sin is death; but the gift of God is eternal life through Jesus Christ our Lord" (v. 23).

7:1–13. Keeping God's law was the criterion by which righteousness was measured in Old Testament times (Deut. 6:1–3). But the law had only succeeded in stimulating people to greater sin. Humanity's sinful nature has not been changed by the law.

7:14–25. Paul gives his own personal testimony to illustrate the stubbornness of man's sinful nature. In his own strength, he was unable to overcome the sins of the flesh. The harder he tried to keep the law, the lower his tendency to sin dragged him down.

8:1–27. But believers who have found new life in Christ have a different story to tell. Energized by the power of the Holy Spirit, they are not victimized by sin and death. God's indwelling presence strengthens Christians and enables them to walk in the path of holiness and righteousness.

[8:1–27] ADOPTION AND SALVATION. *Ye [believers in Christ] have received the Spirit of adoption [sonship, NIV], whereby we cry, Abba, Father* (Rom. 8:15).

Paul compared the process by which believers are justified to the process of adoption in Roman culture.

If a Roman man had no son by biological birth, he could adopt one. One of his slaves might even be adopted as a son. The adopted son took the name of the father and had all the rights that would have been extended to a biological child.

Paul also made this comparison between adoption and salvation in his letter to the Galatians. After being delivered from bondage to sin and adopted into God's family, the believer is "no more a servant, but a son; and if a son, then an heir of God through Christ" (Gal. 4:7).

8:28–39. Reflecting on God's goodness and the redemption provided in His Son causes Paul to break out in a glorious song of praise. In spite of all the testings and troubles that confront God's people, they can rest assured that they are "more than conquerors" (v. 37) through Christ who loves them.

9:1–11:36. In these three chapters, Paul addresses the question of why the Jews, his own people, have rejected the gospel. His conclusion is that they missed the mark by stubbornly seeking justification with God by keeping the law. But some among the Jews have seen the light and have accepted Jesus by faith as the only way to salvation. This remnant of the saved gives Paul hope for the future of the Jewish people.

12:1–2. Total commitment to the Lord leads believers to have a new outlook on life. Resisting the temptations of the world, we make doing God's will our main concern.

12:3–8. God has given different spiritual gifts to the members of His body, the church. We should use these gifts not to bring honor to ourselves but to glorify the Lord and to enrich and build up the congregation (1 Cor. 14).

12:9–21. Love toward others, particularly fellow church members, gives evidence of our new life in Christ. Christian love is such a powerful force that it enables us to "overcome evil with good" (v. 21; see 1 Cor. 13).

13:1–7. Paul encourages his readers to respect the civil authorities, to pay their taxes (Matt. 22:15–22), and to live as good citizens of their nation (Luke 20:20–26). He believes human government is used by the Lord as a restraining influence on sin and disorder.

13:8–14. All the commandments, Paul declares, are summed up in this: "Thou shalt love thy neighbour as thyself" (v. 9; see Matt. 22:35–40). He also encourages the Roman Christians to be on the watch for Christ's return.

14:1–23. Believers should live in harmony with one another. Apparently, some of the Roman Christians were critical of their fellow believers for eating certain food. Paul urges

12:3–8. According to Paul, God gives spiritual gifts to all believers. Some people may preach or teach, but giving and showing mercy are also on the list.

them not to judge one another on such trivial issues. "For the kingdom of God is not meat and drink," he declares, "but righteousness, and peace, and joy in the Holy Ghost" (v. 17).

15:1–13. The foundation of Christian unity consists of mutual respect and acceptance among all believers. Paul holds up Christ as an example because He "received us to the glory of God" (v. 7).

15:14–33. Paul is confident that his readers will continue to serve as faithful witnesses in the capital city of the Roman Empire, just as he has shared the gospel as a traveling missionary. He intends to make a missionary trip to Spain, and he will visit them in Rome when he passes through.

16:1–2. Paul commends Phebe to the church at Rome. She may have carried this letter from him to the Roman believers.

16:3–16. Paul extends personal greetings to several believers in the Roman church, including Priscilla and Aquila (v. 3; see Acts 18:1–3).

16:17–20. Some problem had caused divisions in the church at Rome. Paul urges the believers to deal decisively with the troublemakers.

16:21–27. Paul extends personal greetings to the church from several of his missionary associates. He concludes with a beautiful doxology of praise to God for His faithful love.

1 CORINTHIANS

OVERVIEW: God's guidance for various problems that plagued the church at Corinth.

Introduction to 1 Corinthians

Paul's first epistle to the church at Corinth gives us a realistic view of the early church. Just like churches today, this first-century congregation had its problems and shortcomings.

The apostle dealt with these problems head-on in an attempt to make the church a more effective witness for Jesus Christ.

The church at Corinth was a product of Paul's own missionary efforts. He spent about eighteen months in the city of Corinth in A.D. 50–52. During this time he gathered a large congregation of believers (Acts 18:1–8).

Ruins, such as these pillars from what was once the temple of Apollo, are all that remain of the ancient port city of Corinth.

Eventually he moved on to other fields of service, leaving this church under the direction of other leaders. About five years later he received word about difficulties in the Corinthian church. He wrote 1 Corinthians about A.D. 57 to address these problems.

Most of the believers at Corinth had been converted from a pagan background. They seemed to be struggling to leave their past behind and commit themselves totally to Christian ethical standards. They also had questions or misunderstandings about some of the doctrines of the faith, including marriage, the Lord's Supper, spiritual gifts, and the afterlife. These concerns were also dealt with by the apostle in 1 Corinthians.

Summary of 1 Corinthians

1:1–9. Paul opens his letter with traditional greetings to believers in the church at Corinth (Acts 18:1–11), wishing them grace and peace.

1:10–17. Strife and division marred the Corinthian church. Some claimed to be following Apollos, while others were loyal to Cephas (Peter) and Paul. Perhaps those of the "Christ" party (v. 12) were claiming to be "super Christians."

1:18–31. Paul declares that people who follow their own drives and desires will always end up at odds with one another. The Corinthians should seek God's wisdom to help them achieve unity and peace, because "the foolishness of God is wiser than men" (v. 25).

2:1–5. Paul declares that he preached the gospel with simplicity when he ministered among the Corinthians. The results prove that God's power energized his message.

2:6–16. Human beings cannot discover God's wisdom on their own. But God has given us His written Word that tells us about Him and His nature. The Holy Spirit enables us to interpret His written Word. These two gifts from God lead us to understand "the mind of Christ" (v. 16).

3:1–9. The quarreling of the Corinthians over human leadership shows they are immature in their spiritual development. God, not human leaders, is the source of wisdom and spiritual growth.

3:10–15. Jesus is the foundation on which every believer's life should be built. Anything less than Him and His divine purpose will not stand the test of time (Matt. 7:24–27).

3:16–23. Each believer is a temple of the Holy Spirit, a place where God dwells. Jesus should be the focus of our lives. In Him alone—not human leaders—should we place our trust.

4:1–7. Human leaders in the church should find their joy in serving as "ministers of Christ" (v. 1). The standard by which He will judge their work is whether they are faithful to Him. God has given us different gifts to be used in His service (Rom. 12:3–8). We should exercise these gifts to His glory.

[4:8–13] GLADIATOR APOSTLES. *I [Paul] think that God hath set forth us the apostles last, as it were appointed to death: for we are made a spectacle unto the world, and to angels, and to men* (1 Cor. 4:9).

In this verse Paul compares himself and the other apostles of the New Testament to the gladiators who were "set forth...last" in the Roman arena. These were slaves or criminals who were forced to fight experienced gladiators or wild animals without weapons and who were quickly "appointed to death."

Paul was saying that he and the other apostles of New Testament times had made sacrifices to advance the gospel—and the Corinthian believers had been blessed by their witnessing efforts.

Paul's words were prophetic. Most of the apostles of the early church, including this great missionary to the Gentiles, were eventually martyred for their faith.

4:8–13. Spiritual leaders should not build little empires for themselves. It is their duty to accept suffering, if necessary, in the service of God and His people (1 Pet. 2:18–25).

4:14–21. Paul makes a personal appeal for unity in the church at Corinth. He was a spiritual father to many of them because they had been converted under his ministry. He urges them to follow his example as a faithful disciple of Christ.

5:1–8. In these verses Paul deals with the problem of sexual sin. A believer in the church at Corinth was involved in a sexual relationship with his "father's wife" (v. 1)—probably his stepmother. The apostle criticizes the Corinthian Christians for ignoring the problem and allowing it to continue. He advises the church to exercise discipline by expelling the unrepentant sinner.

5:9–13. Paul makes a distinction between relating to nonbelievers and associating with fellow believers. We are not to judge nonbelievers and isolate ourselves from them. Rather, we are to bear our witness for Jesus before them. But we are called to withdraw from fellow believers who continue in willful sin. Church discipline is designed to reclaim and restore those who have wandered away from the Lord (Matt. 18:15–22).

6:1–11. The apostle expresses disappointment that some of the believers at Corinth are taking one another to civil courts, perhaps to settle financial claims. He urges them to settle their differences through committees of their fellow believers.

6:12–20. Paul declares that sexual relationships outside the bonds of marriage are a perversion of God's plan. Sexual immorality is actually a sin against one's own body because of the Bible's teaching on the one-flesh relationship (Gen. 2:24). Believers should view their bodies as a temple, or residence, for the Holy Spirit of the Lord.

7:1–40. In this chapter Paul answers questions from the Corinthians on the nature and meaning of marriage. The married state is the best option for most people, he declares, but singlehood also has advantages for those who can control their sexual passions. Believers who are married to unbelievers should remain married. But if the unbeliever should leave the relationship, the Christian is released from the bonds of marriage and is free to get married again (vv. 12–16). All believers should live with happiness and contentment in the lifestyle in which God has placed them (vv. 17–24).

8:1–13. In this chapter Paul addresses the problem of meat sacrificed to pagan gods in the city of Corinth. Some believers felt that eating this meat after it had been sacrificed was no problem for worshipers of Christ. But others thought this practice was an act of idolatry. The apostle agreed, in principle, that it was acceptable to eat this meat because all creation belongs to God (v. 6). But he urged believers to abstain from eating

---

[9:1–27] DISCIPLINE AND TRAINING. *Every man that striveth for the mastery is temperate in all things* (1 Cor. 9:25).

This is one of many references in Paul's writings to the Greek games that were similar to our modern Olympics. An athlete who expected to win at these games had to be "temperate in all things," or undergo a strict regimen of discipline and training.

Paul was comparing the Christian life to the discipline required of these Greek athletes. Believers are saved to a life of service in the cause of Christ. Every day should bring us closer to the goal of total commitment to Christ and His work: "That the man of God may be perfect, thoroughly furnished unto all good works" (2 Tim. 3:17).

10:1–22. The apostle Paul, surrounded by idols in Athens. He preached about Jesus to the people, using their altar to "The Unknown God" as a starting point (Acts 17:23).

such meat if the practice offended weaker Christians (vv. 9–11).

9:1–27. This chapter consists of Paul's testimony about his motivation for ministry. He was not just preaching about the principles of making personal sacrifices and living as an example for the Corinthians. He had given up his freedom to do as he pleased and had accommodated himself to the needs of others in order to bring them to the Lord: "I am made all things to all men, that I might by all means save some" (v. 22).

10:1–22. Paul warns the Corinthian believers to stay away from idol worship. He uses the example of the Israelites during the wilderness wandering years to show how easy it is to give in to the temptation to worship pagan gods (Num. 25:1–18).

10:23–11:1. Paul returns to the issue of meat sacrificed to idols (see 1 Cor. 8:1–13). Such meat is neither good nor bad in itself. But our freedom in the Lord should not blind us to the fact that we must avoid certain activities that hinder our Christian witness before others. We bring glory to God when we seek the good of others, not our individual rights.

11:2–16. According to Paul, female believers in Corinth were to cover their heads during public worship and men were to worship with their heads uncovered. This was apparently the accepted custom in Corinthian society. He saw no need for believers to reject these customs if they did not hinder the worship of Christ.

11:17–34. The Corinthians were desecrating the Lord's Supper by turning it into a feast. The rich were eating like gluttons while the poor were getting shoved aside because they had no food to bring. This added to the problem of factions in the church (see 1 Cor. 1:10–17). Paul exhorted the church to stop this feasting and to make the Lord's Supper an occasion for remembering the sacrificial death of Jesus Christ on their behalf (Luke 22:14–20).

12:1–31. In this chapter Paul addresses the issue of spiritual gifts. The more spectacular gifts—such as speaking in tongues, prophecy, and teaching—are not more important than the other, more subdued gifts. All work together to edify and build up the body of Christ. The apostle compares the church to a human body, pointing out that all parts of the body contribute to the healthy operation of the whole.

13:1–13. This is known as the "love chapter" of the Bible. No matter how gifted or talented a person may be, he is nothing but "sounding brass" or "a tinkling cymbal" (v. 1) if he

[13:1–13] SPEECH BASED ON LOVE. *Though I [Paul] speak with the tongues of men and of angels, and have not charity [love, NIV], I am become as sounding brass [a resounding gong, NIV], or a tinkling [clanging, NIV] cymbal* (1 Cor. 13:1).

The Greek word translated as "charity" or "love" in this verse is *agape*—self-giving love that asks for nothing in return. No matter how eloquent in speech a person may be—even if he speaks several languages—this amounts to nothing if his words are not spoken in love.

Pagan worship in Paul's time was often accompanied by strange noises, the clang of gongs and cymbals, and loud blasts on trumpets. Paul declared that the speech of the Corinthian believers was no better than these meaningless rituals unless spoken in love.

does not exercise these gifts in the spirit of love (Rom. 12:9–21).

14:1–40. Some believers in the Corinthian church were elevating the gift of speaking in tongues above all other gifts. Paul declares that prophecy is actually the most important gift because it builds up and edifies the church. Speaking in tongues should be practiced only if an interpreter is present to clarify the meaning of the message to others. Paul's concern was that everything should be done "decently and in order" (v. 40) in a public worship service.

15:1–11. Some Corinthian Christians had doubts about the bodily resurrection. Paul insists on the reality of the resurrection of Jesus because He was seen alive by several different groups after He was raised from the dead (Mark 16:9–11; Luke 24:13–43; John 20:19–29). To Paul, Jesus' resurrection—and its promise of the future resurrection of all believers—is one of the cornerstones of the Christian faith.

15:12–34. The offering of firstfruits was presented by worshipers to the Lord on the first day of the week following Passover. This offering guaranteed the coming harvest (Lev. 23:9–11). This was true of Christ's resurrection as well. His bodily resurrection guaranteed the resurrection of all believers.

15:35–58. Paul insists that believers will experience resurrection with a body that is suitable for its new spiritual environment in the world beyond (1 Thess. 4:13–18). The hope of a future resurrection gives believers the courage to bear up under hardship and suffering for the sake of Christ. In Him we experience victory over sin and death.

16:1–4. Paul encourages the Corinthian Christians to give to an offering he is receiving for the impoverished believers in Jerusalem.

16:5–20. The apostle tells about his plans for a future visit to Corinth. He instructs them to receive Timothy when he visits, and he commends Stephanas and his fellow workers. Paul also sends personal greetings from Aquila and Priscilla (Acts 18:1–3).

16:21–24. Paul closes the letter with a benediction of grace and love to the Corinthian believers.

2 CORINTHIANS

OVERVIEW: Paul gives a vigorous defense of his credentials as an apostle.

Introduction to 2 Corinthians

Paul's second letter to the Corinthians is a follow-up letter to his first Corinthian correspondence (see the introduction to 1 Corinthians on p. 256). Apparently the believers at Corinth had responded appropriately to some of his admonitions in the first letter, and he wrote to express his appreciation for their actions (2 Cor. 2:1–11; chap. 7). He probably wrote this epistle about A.D. 58.

But at several places in this letter, Paul reveals that all was still not well in the Corinthian church. His credentials as a minister were being questioned by some people in Corinth. Paul defended his calling and ministry, assuring the church that his work among them was motivated by love for Christ and his concern for their welfare.

Second Corinthians is one of the most personal and emotional writings of the apostle Paul. He admitted he suffered from some physical malady that he called his "thorn in the flesh" (12:7). He also cataloged the various sufferings he had endured as a traveling missionary in the cause of Christ (11:16–33). Although he was weak and imperfect, he rejoiced that his shortcomings revealed "that the excellency of the power may be of God, and not of us" (4:7).

Summary of 2 Corinthians

1:1–2. Paul begins his letter with greetings of grace and peace to the Corinthian church (Acts 18:1–13).

1:3–11. The apostle uses his experience of suffering to comfort the Corinthian believers. He had also experienced God as the source of comfort in his afflictions. He assures them that God will comfort them in their sufferings for the sake of the gospel.

1:12–24. Paul had promised to make a personal visit to the Corinthian church (1 Cor. 16:3–6). In these verses he explains why he has not yet fulfilled his promise: "To spare you I came not as yet unto Corinth" (v. 23). He apparently wanted to give them time to respond to the instructions he had given them in his previous letter—1 Corinthians.

2:1–4. Paul's love for the Corinthian believers was another factor in his delay of his visit. He hopes the church will respond positively to his previous letter so they can rejoice together when he finally visits them at Corinth.

2:5–11. In his previous letter, the apostle had instructed the church to deal with a man who was living in an immoral sexual relationship (1 Cor. 5). The church had apparently done so, and the man had repented. Now Paul encourages the church to forgive the man and restore him to full Christian fellowship.

[2:12–17] TRIUMPHANT IN CHRIST. *Thanks be unto God, which always causeth us to triumph [leads us in triumphal procession, NIV] in Christ* (2 Cor. 2:14).

In this verse Paul compares the victory of Christ over death to a Roman military procession. A victorious general and his army would return from a battle with captives and spoils of war in tow. The entire city of Rome would turn out to welcome the warriors with loud shouts and joyful music.

To Paul, Christ's victory over the grave was more impressive than Roman military triumphs that led to such lavish displays. And more significantly, all believers share in this victory procession of Christ.

2:12–17. To Paul, the favorable response of the Corinthians to his instructions was like a sweet fragrance. He expresses thanks to God for the victorious ministry that He gives to His servants.

3:1–3. Paul's credentials as a minister were apparently being questioned by some people in the Corinthian church. He insists that changed lives as a result of his work were all the endorsement his ministry required.

3:4–18. Paul claims to be a minister of the new covenant of grace, which is far superior to the old covenant of law (Heb. 8:1–10:18). Anyone who questions the apostle's ministry must take its superior nature into account.

4:1–18. Paul compares himself as a human minister to an earthen vessel (v. 7), or a clay pot. But God had filled this common, unworthy container with His treasure, or the glory of the gospel. The sufferings Paul faced in living out his calling were light when compared with the glory God was storing up for him as an eternal reward.

5:1–21. God sent His Son Jesus Christ to reconcile sinners to Himself through His atoning death on the cross. Paul sees his ministry as a part of this divine plan. He

serves as an ambassador for Christ, imploring others, "Be ye reconciled to God" (v. 20).

6:1–13. Paul reminds the Corinthians of the suffering he has endured as a minister of the gospel. He wants them to understand that troubles and tribulations are a natural result of serving Christ (1 Pet. 4:12–17).

6:14–18. The apostle makes an eloquent plea for the Corinthian believers to throw off evil and unbelief and to follow the commands of Christ. They are not to be "unequally yoked together with unbelievers" (v. 14).

7:1–16. Titus apparently brought a report to Paul that the Corinthians had responded favorably to his words of rebuke and instruction in his previous letter—1 Corinthians. Paul expresses his joy at the news of their repentance.

8:1–9:15. In these two chapters, Paul discusses in detail the offering he had mentioned in his previous letter (1 Cor. 16:1–4). This was an offering he was taking among the churches of the province of Macedonia to assist the Christians in Jerusalem who were suffering from a famine. To motivate the

[6:14–18] GIVE UP THE PAST. *Be ye [Corinthian believers] not unequally yoked together with unbelievers* (2 Cor. 6:14).

Paul was probably alluding in this verse to a familiar prohibition in the Mosaic Law: "Thou shalt not plow with an ox and an ass [donkey] together" (Deut. 22:10).

The reason for this law was that a donkey was an unclean animal, while the ox was among the clean animals that Jews were permitted to eat. What's more, they would have been out of step with each other in their pull against the plow.

Paul's point is that the believers of Corinth should leave the patterns and habits of their old life of unbelief behind. They should live in accordance with their new status as members of God's family.

Corinthian believers to give to this fund, Paul reminds them of Jesus' example of giving His life unselfishly on their behalf (Phil. 2:1–11). He also set before them the method by which they should give: "Every man according as he purposeth in his heart, so let him give; not grudgingly, or of necessity: for God loveth a cheerful giver" (9:7).

10:1–11. Apparently, a rebellious element in the Corinthian church was critical of Paul and resistant to his authority. In these verses Paul answers their charge that he is a weak and timid leader. He assures them that his leadership approach is consistent, whether addressing them by letter or speaking to them face-to-face.

10:12–18. Paul refuses to buy into the game of his opponents in Corinth. They were claiming to be superior to Paul in their leadership ability. Rather than arguing the point, Paul declares that God's assessment is the only thing that matters.

[11:16–33] PAUL'S ESCAPE IN A BASKET. *Through a window in a basket was I [Paul] let down by the wall* (2 Cor. 11:33).

The event to which Paul refers in this verse is reported in the book of Acts (9:22–25). Paul traveled to the city of Damascus to persecute Christians. But after his dramatic conversion, he witnessed for Christ among the Jews of the city. Other believers had to help him escape over the city wall when the Jews determined to kill him.

The window out of which Paul escaped may have been in a house that was built into or on top of the defensive wall of Damascus. Such "wall houses" were common in some cities. This was the type of house in which Rahab the prostitute lived. She helped several Israelite spies escape over the city wall from the window in her house in Jericho (Josh. 2:15).

11:1–6. Paul warns against deceitful teachers who would lead the Corinthian believers to follow them rather than point the church to Christ.

11:7–15. Paul had supported himself while preaching the gospel in the Corinthian church (Acts 18:1–3). He expresses his frustration that his enemies have criticized him even for this. He charges these critics with trying to undermine his leadership by using false and deceitful tactics.

11:16–33. In these verses the apostle lists the various troubles he has suffered as a minister of the gospel. This litany of tribulations proves that he is a true follower of Christ. The same cannot be said of those who are questioning his leadership.

12:1–10. This passage contains Paul's famous "thorn in the flesh" statement (v. 7). This disability, possibly an eye disease, helped the apostle to come to the realization that God's power is made perfect in human weakness. In their human frailties, servants of the Lord must depend on His never-failing strength.

12:11–21. Paul has spoken boldly to the Corinthians to build them up in their faith. He assures them that he is not interested in their money or possessions. He has poured himself out gladly on their behalf.

13:1–10. The apostle promises the Corinthian Christians that he will visit them soon. He warns them that he will deal forthrightly with any who are in willful rebellion against the Lord.

13:11–14. Paul closes his letter with a beautiful benediction, praying that God's love and grace will abide with the Corinthian believers.

OVERVIEW: Jesus sets believers free from bondage to the law by granting them salvation by grace through faith.

Introduction to Galatians

Paul's epistle to the Galatians was not written to a specific church but to the *"churches of Galatia"* (1:2, emphasis added). The apostle visited several cities of this region during his first missionary journey about A.D. 47, founding several churches. He wrote this letter to these young churches about two years later, in A.D. 49. Of Paul's thirteen letters that are preserved in the New Testament, Galatians was probably the first to be written.

After the Galatian churches had gotten off to such a good start, the apostle was saddened to learn "that ye are so soon removed from...the grace of Christ unto another gospel" (1:6). A group of false teachers known as the Judaizers had won them over to the view that faith in the grace of Christ was not sufficient for salvation. They taught that it was also necessary to obey the Jewish law, which involved submitting to circumcision and observing Jewish holy days.

Paul condemned these false teachers and informed the Galatians that they were foolish indeed if they returned to the bondage of the law from which the grace of Christ had set them free (3:1; 5:1).

Summary of Galatians

1:1–5. Paul opens his letter to the Galatian Christians with wishes for grace and peace in the name of Jesus Christ.

1:6–10. The apostle expresses his disappointment that the Galatians have turned away from the true gospel he has preached to them; they are now following a false gospel.

1:11–24. Apparently the Judaizers at Galatia were claiming that Paul had no authority to preach the gospel among them. In response to this charge, Paul reviews the facts about his conversion and call from God to serve as an apostle (Acts 9:1–20).

[1:11–24] "UP" TO JERUSALEM. *After three years I [Paul] went up to Jerusalem to see Peter* (Gal. 1:18).

Paul indicates in the previous verse that he was in Damascus, Syria (Gal. 1:17), when he traveled to Jerusalem to see Peter.

Damascus was north of Jerusalem. Why didn't Paul say that he went "down" to the city to see Peter? To most people today, "up" refers to northern locations and "down" to southern sites.

Jerusalem was built on high hills in a mountainous territory about 2,500 feet above sea level. To the Jews, whatever the direction from which they approached Jerusalem, it was always "up" (Luke 2:42).

2:1–10. At first, early leaders of the church, such as Peter, James, and John, were hesitant to accept Paul because he had been a persecutor of the church. But they eventually

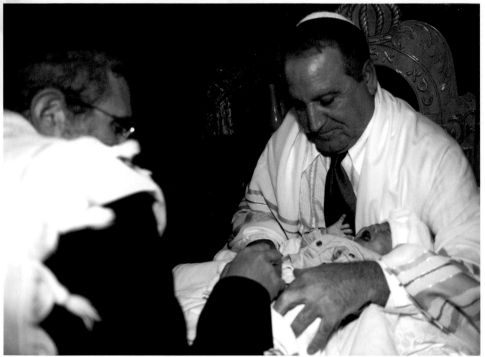

3:1–4:31. A baby boy is circumcised in Jerusalem. Though God demanded this ritual of the Israelites, the apostle Paul said it had no bearing on faith in Jesus Christ.

recognized his call from God and his apostleship (Acts 9:26–30).

2:11–14. Paul tells the Galatians how he rebuked Peter and Barnabas because they were led astray by a group of zealous Jews in the church at Antioch. Apparently Peter and Barnabas gave in to their demands that Gentiles had to be circumcised and keep the Jewish law before they could become Christians. On this issue, Paul declares, he "withstood him [Peter] to the face" (v. 11).

2:15–21. Paul declares that repentance and faith alone justify a person in God's sight. Nothing else is to be added to these basic requirements for salvation (Rom. 3:28).

3:1–4:31. In these two chapters, Paul contrasts the freedom that believers experience in Christ with the restrictions of the Jewish law. Anyone who would exchange the grace of Jesus Christ for keeping the Jewish law, as the Galatians were tempted to do, was foolish indeed. The Judaizers have been insisting on making Gentiles sons of Abraham through the rite of circumcision. But Paul declares that Gentile Christians are already Abraham's sons because they share the faith that he demonstrated (3:7, 29).

5:1–15. Freedom in Christ is not a license to live as one pleases. We are saved to a life of love and service toward others. Believers are compelled by God's grace to follow only one law—the royal law of love: "All the law is fulfilled in one word...Thou shalt love thy neighbour as thyself" (v. 14).

5:16–6:10. In these verses Paul gives some specific examples of behavior that should characterize the believer: "love, joy, peace, long-suffering, gentleness, goodness, faith, meekness, temperance" (5:22–23). These attitudes and characteristics are "the fruit of the Spirit" (5:22) in the believer's life— a natural result of God's grace and love in the human heart. Following a list of do's and don'ts in the law is a poor substitute for such a radiant pattern of life.

6:11–18. Paul closes his letter to the Galatians by reminding them that Jesus and His death on the cross are the central focus of the salvation story—not whether a person should be circumcised: "For in Christ Jesus neither circumcision availeth any thing, nor uncircumcision, but a new creature" (v. 15).

[6:11–18] MARKS OF PERSECUTION. *I [Paul] bear in my body the marks of the Lord Jesus* (Gal. 6:17).

In Paul's time slaves were branded with distinctive marks to show that they belonged to their masters, much as cattle are branded in modern times. Paul declared that his body bore marks from the persecution he had endured in Christ's service. These showed that he belonged to the Lord Jesus.

The apostle named some of these marks of persecution in 2 Corinthians 11:24–25: "Five times received I forty stripes save one. Thrice was I beaten with rods, once was I stoned."

6:11–18. The apostle Paul, who sacrificed much to follow his Lord, was often whipped and beaten like Jesus had been.

EPHESIANS

OVERVIEW: All who belong to Christ are bound together as one in His love and in His church.

Introduction to Ephesians

Ephesians, along with Philippians, Colossians, and Philemon, was written by the apostle Paul while he was in prison. Most scholars believe he wrote Ephesians near the end of his life, about A.D. 62, while he was under house arrest in Rome (Acts 28:16, 30).

Paul founded the church at Ephesus and spent three years among the believers in this city (Acts 19:1–41)—longer than he stayed at any other place during his ministry. He developed a close relationship with the Ephesian believers. The leaders of this church traveled to Miletus to greet him at the end of his third missionary journey. They sent the apostle away with sadness when they learned that he was determined to return to Jerusalem and face the dangers that awaited him there (Acts 20:17–38).

In this epistle Paul describes the exalted Christ, who is Lord of the church, the world, and the entire created order. As the living Lord, He is completing through His body—the church—what He began during His days on earth. Those who belong to Christ, both Jews and Gentiles, are united as one body in His church to serve as agents of reconciliation to a lost world.

Summary of Ephesians

1:1–2. Paul opens his letter by referring to the Ephesian Christians as "saints" (v. 1). This word as used in the New Testament means those who have been set aside for God's exclusive use (Rom. 1:7; Phil. 1:1).

1:3–14. God's redemptive plan for humankind from the beginning involved sending His Son to die for our sins. Paul marvels at such love and grace expressed in the life and sacrificial death of Jesus Christ.

1:15–23. The apostle expresses his thanks for these Ephesian Christians. He wants them to grow in their understanding of the riches of Christ's grace.

2:1–10. Paul reminds the Ephesian believers of the wonder of their salvation in Christ. They were dead in their "trespasses and sins" (v. 1), but God redeemed them and filled their lives with joy. This came about solely through God's grace, not because of any goodness or good works on their part: "By grace are ye saved through faith; and that not of yourselves: it is the gift of God: not of works, lest any man should boast" (vv. 8–9; see Rom. 3:21–31).

2:11–22. Jesus is the great equalizer who has broken down the barriers between different classes and ethnic groups in society (Rom. 1:14–16). All who belong to Him are bound together as one in His love and in His church.

3:1–13. Paul declares that in times past, God's promises have been interpreted as applying mainly to the Jewish people. But this

[1:3–14] SEALED BY THE SPIRIT. *After that ye [Ephesian Christians] believed, ye were sealed with that holy Spirit of promise* (Eph. 1:13).

Paul refers in this verse to the distinct mark of identification that was placed on a letter, contract, or other legal document in Bible times. This seal proved the document's authenticity.

Likewise, believers are sealed or authenticated by the Holy Spirit after their conversion. His mark in our lives results in holy and righteous living. God also gives us His spirit as His pledge of our future inheritance of eternal life (2 Cor. 1:22).

changed with the coming of Christ and His offer of salvation to the Gentiles, as well (Rom. 3:28–29). Paul is pleased that he was selected to help inaugurate this new phase of world redemption: "Unto me...is this grace given, that I should preach among the Gentiles the unsearchable riches of Christ" (v. 8).

3:14–21. Again, Paul prays for the Ephesian Christians—this time that they might be strengthened in their faith and in their commitment to Christ.

4:1–6. Paul encourages the Ephesian believers to express through their actions the underlying unity that exists in the body of Christ (1 Cor. 1:10). This calls for patience and humility on the part of all members of the body.

4:7–16. God in His wisdom has given many different gifts to the people in His church. They exercise their gifts as apostles, prophets, evangelists, pastors, and teachers. All these gifts are needed if the church is to function properly (Rom. 12:3–8).

4:17–5:20. This passage is known as the practical section of Ephesians because it deals with the way believers should live. Paul calls on the Ephesians to "put on the new man" (4:24) and to copy the character of God in their daily behavior.

5:21–6:9. Relationships should also reflect the lordship of Christ. Paul has advice on godly living for wives (5:22–24), husbands (5:25–33), children (6:1–3), fathers (6:4), servants (6:5–8), and masters (6:9).

6:10–20. Paul recognizes that living a godly life in a godless world is not an easy task. He urges the Ephesians to put on their spiritual battle gear and to get ready to "stand against the wiles of the devil" (v. 11).

6:21–24. Paul closes his letter with wishes of grace and peace for the Ephesian believers.

PHILIPPIANS

OVERVIEW: A joyful letter from prison in which Paul thanks God for the fellowship and support of the Christians at Philippi.

Introduction to Philippians

Paul's letter to the Philippians is one of his four "prison epistles" (see the introduction to Ephesians on p. 268). He sent it to the church at Philippi while he was being held a prisoner in Rome about A.D. 62 or 63.

Unlike most of Paul's other letters, this epistle was not written specifically to deal with a church problem, to warn against false teachers, or to correct the behavior of the recipients. He does make a passing reference to dangers from false teachers (3:1–11) and urges two church members to settle their differences (4:2–9). But Philippians is best characterized as a "friendship letter." Paul expressed his warm thoughts toward the Philippian believers and assured them of his appreciation for their support

Ruins of ancient Philippi, named for Philip II of Macedonia, the father of Alexander the Great.

of his ministry (1:3–11; 4:10–23).

The apostle founded the church at Philippi about A.D. 52, at the beginning of his second missionary journey. A businesswoman named Lydia became one of his first converts in this city (Acts 16:13–15). The keeper of the prison from which Paul and Silas were delivered at Philippi also came to faith in Christ, along with the members of his household (Acts 16:25–34).

Summary of Philippians

1:1–2. Paul begins his letter with greetings from himself and his helper, Timothy (Acts 16:1–3), to the church at Philippi (Acts 16:12–40).

1:3–11. Paul prays a beautiful prayer of thanksgiving for the Philippian believers. He remembers them with joy because of their kindness to him and their faithful support of the gospel.

1:12–26. Although Paul is in prison, he wants the Philippian Christians to realize that God has brought something good out of this experience (Rom. 8:28). It has actually

> **[2:12–30] POURED OUT FOR THE LORD.** *If I [Paul] be offered upon the sacrifice and service of your [Philippian believers'] faith, I joy, and rejoice with you all* (Phil. 2:17).
>
> The NIV translates this verse, "Even if I am being poured out like a drink offering on the sacrifice and service coming from your faith." Paul was comparing himself and his life to a sacrifice known as the drink offering.
>
> In this ceremony the worshiper poured wine on top of the animal that had been sacrificed as a burnt offering. The wine was vaporized as steam when it hit the hot carcass. This symbolized the rising of the offering to God (Exod. 29:38–41; Hosea 9:4).
>
> Paul viewed his life as a drink offering. He rejoiced that it was being poured out in sacrificial service on behalf of the Philippians and other early believers.

brought greater opportunity for the proclamation of the gospel and the growth of new believers. The apostle is content in this situation, whether he lives or dies: "To me to live is Christ, and to die is gain" (v. 21).

1:27–30. Paul encourages the believers at Philippi to remain loyal to Christ, even if they should be persecuted for their faith.

2:1–11. Paul uses the example of Christ to motivate the Philippians to live holy and righteous lives in the midst of a selfish world. Verses 6–11 are probably a hymn or confession of faith on the nature of Jesus used in worship services by early believers. Christ was God's Son—fully divine—but He came to earth in the form of a man—fully human—to bring salvation and eternal life to all who believe.

2:12–30. The Philippian believers are encouraged to continue the good work they have started. To help them, Paul promises to send two of his coworkers—Timothy and Epaphroditus.

3:1–11. Paul warns against the corrupting in-

12–4:1. Philippians contains one of Paul's references to the sporting world: "I press toward the mark for the prize of the high calling of God in Christ Jesus" (3:14).

fluence of the Judaizers. This group was teaching that Gentile converts must be circumcised and keep the Jewish law before they could become Christians. Paul declares that he was once a strict observer of all Jewish traditions, but he has learned that true righteousness comes only through faith in Jesus Christ.

3:12–4:1. Paul urges his fellow Christians at Philippi to "stand fast in the Lord" (4:1). He points to himself as the example they should follow, since he continues to "press toward the mark for the prize of the high calling of God in Christ Jesus" (3:14).

4:2–9. Apparently there was some problem with divisions in the church at Philippi (1 Cor. 1:11–13). Paul makes a personal appeal for unity to those who are causing trouble and urges the entire church to seek the guidance and counsel of the Lord.

4:10–23. Paul concludes by thanking his Christian brothers and sisters at Philippi for their generous support of him and his ministry. Their gifts had apparently been sent through Epaphroditus while the apostle was in prison (v. 18).

OVERVIEW: The salvation of believers is perfect and complete in Jesus Christ.

Introduction to Colossians

As one of Paul's four "prison epistles" (see the introduction to Ephesians on p. 268), Colossians was written to a church that the apostle had never visited. Epaphras, one of Paul's missionary associates, may have founded the church (1:7–8). He brought word to Paul about false teachers who had infiltrated the church at Colosse. To deal with this situation, the apostle sent this letter about A.D. 62 or 63, while he was imprisoned at Rome.

These false teachers were adding to the simple gospel that Paul and others had preached by claiming it was necessary to observe certain Jewish rules and regulations (2:16) and to assign a prominent role to angels in their worship (2:18). Paul corrected this misunderstanding by showing that Christ is the all-inclusive and all-sufficient Savior. He alone is the basis of our hope for salvation and eternal life.

Summary of Colossians

1:1–14. Paul opens his letter to the believers at Colosse with a prayer of thanksgiving for the faith and love of these brothers and sisters in the Lord. Paul had never visited this church, but he apparently knew about them through his missionary associate Epaphras (Philem. 23), who had ministered among them (v. 7).

1:15–23. The Colossian believers were being led astray by false teachers, who were challenging the divinity and supremacy of Jesus Christ. The apostle corrects this error by declaring that Jesus is the divine Son of God, the head of the church, and the one in whom God the Father is fully revealed.

1:24–29. Through the church as His body, Jesus is still at work in the world. Paul is pleased to be a minister who labors among the churches as a representative of the living Christ (2 Cor. 5:20).

2:1–23. Paul reminds the Colossian believers of the new life they have experienced as a result of their acceptance of Christ. He encourages them to continue their daily walk in obedience to His commands and to stay anchored to the truth in their doctrinal beliefs. They didn't need some mystical experience to per-

---

[2:1–23] SALVATION AND CIRCUMCISION. *In whom [Jesus] also ye [Colossian believers] are circumcised with the circumcision made without hands* (Col. 2:11).

Circumcision—the removal of the foreskin from the male sex organ—was a mark of the covenant between God and His people, the Israelites (Rom. 4:11).

In this verse Paul compares the death of Christ on the cross to this ritual. This "circumcision" of Jesus was the event that provided for the salvation of believers. We are also "circumcised" when we die to our sins by committing ourselves to Him as our Lord and Savior.

3:1–4:6. Though unmarried, Paul could instruct husbands and wives through the inspiration of God's Spirit: "Wives, submit yourselves unto your own husbands. . . . Husbands, love your wives, and be not bitter against them" (3:18–19).

fect their salvation, as the false teachers were claiming. Their deliverance from sin was "complete in him [Christ]" (v. 10).

3:1–4:6. In these verses Paul contrasts the old way of life with the new patterns of behavior that should characterize a person who has come to know Christ as Lord and Savior. The apostle has practical advice on Christian living for wives (3:18), husbands (3:19), children (3:20), fathers (3:21), servants (3:22), and masters (4:1).

4:7–9. Paul mentions his coworker Tychicus (v. 7), who may have delivered this letter to the Colossian Christians. Tychicus may have been accompanied by the runaway slave Onesimus (v. 9; see Philem. 10).

4:10–18. Paul closes his letter by sending greetings from several of his missionary associates and coworkers.

OVERVIEW: Answers to questions about the end times and the second coming of the Lord.

Introduction to 1 Thessalonians

Thessalonica was the capital city of the Roman province of Macedonia. Paul and his missionary associates witnessed in this city during his second missionary journey. Opposition from a group of fanatical Jews drove them out of Thessalonica after a short stay, but not before several Gentiles came to faith in Jesus Christ (Acts 17:1–9). These faithful few became the nucleus of the church to which the apostle wrote this letter.

First Thessalonians is one of Paul's earliest epistles, probably written about A.D. 51 or 52, while he was working at Corinth. Paul mentioned Silas (Silvanus) and Timothy (Timotheus) in the greeting of the letter (1:1). This suggests that these two missionary associates worked with Paul to encourage and strengthen this young congregation.

The theme of this epistle is the second coming of Christ. Every chapter contains some reference to this important future event (1:10; 2:19; 3:13; 4:13–18; 5:1–11, 23).

Summary of 1 Thessalonians

1:1–10. Paul commends the believers at Thessalonica (Acts 17:1, 11–13) for their faith and love, as well as their testimony to the power of the gospel. Because of Paul's work among them, they had "turned to God from idols to serve the living and true God" (v. 9).

2:1–16. Paul reminds these fellow believers of the time he had spent among them proclaiming the gospel. He had spoken the truth about Christ with all sincerity, not appealing to their pride or trying to win their favor with flattering words.

2:17–20. Paul has not forgotten these new believers, although he has not seen them for a while. He considers them his "glory and joy" (v. 20).

3:1–13. On a previous occasion while visiting Athens (Acts 17:13–15), Paul had sent his coworker Timothy to check on the new converts at Thessalonica. Timothy brought the apostle a good report about their growth in the Lord. Paul is grateful for this good news, and he offers a prayer of thanksgiving

---

[5:1–11] PROTECTED BY FAITH AND LOVE. *Let us…be sober [self-controlled, NIV], putting on the breastplate of faith and love* (1 Thess. 5:8).

In his letter to the Ephesian Christians, Paul instructed them to put on the "breastplate of righteousness" (see the note "Spiritual Battle Gear" on p. 269). Here he exhorts the Thessalonian believers to put on the "breastplate of faith and love."

The breastplate, or body armor, of a Roman soldier protected the vital organs of the upper body. Likewise, believers are protected from giving in to temptation when we focus on His love for us and exercise faith in His promises.

---

for the Thessalonian Christians.

4:1–12. The apostle reminds his fellow believers of the behavior expected of those who belong to Christ. They are to stay sexually pure, to practice justice, to love one another, and to bear their witness for Christ in a quiet and humble way.

4:13–18. In these verses Paul addresses a question that had been raised by some of the Thessalonian Christians. Apparently some of them expected Jesus to return during their lifetime. What would happen to those believers who had not lived to experience this great event? The apostle assured them that "the dead in Christ shall rise first: Then we which are alive and remain shall be caught up together with them in the clouds, to meet the Lord in the air" (vv. 16–17).

5:1–11. Paul described the returning Jesus as "a thief in the night"—someone w[ho] arrives unexpectedly.

5:1–11. Paul goes on to address the question of when the Lord will return. No one knows. But we can be sure He will return suddenly—and when we least expect it. We should be ready (Matt. 24:42–51).

5:12–24. With a series of short exhortations, Paul tells the Thessalonian believers how they should be living while waiting for the Lord's return.

5:25–28. Paul closes his letter by asking for the grace of the Lord to fill their lives and requesting that they continue to pray for him and his coworkers.

OVERVIEW: Believers should not be waiting in idleness for the Lord's second coming.

Introduction to 2 Thessalonians

This short letter of only three chapters is closely related to Paul's first letter to the believers at Thessalonica (see the introduction to 1 Thessalonians on p. 275). It was probably written within a few months of the first letter. Thus, the date for 2 Thessalonians is about A.D. 51 or 52, and the apostle wrote it while he was ministering among the believers in Corinth.

Second Thessalonians is a letter of encouragement as well as rebuke. Paul encouraged the believers in this church to remain faithful to the Lord in the midst of the persecution they were experiencing. He also exhorted those who were idly waiting for the return of the Lord to get back to work.

This epistle teaches us that idle speculation about the return of the Lord accomplishes nothing. We should be busy about His work while we wait for His return.

Summary of 2 Thessalonians

1:1–2. Paul opens his second letter to the Christians at Thessalonica (Acts 17:1, 11–13) with greetings from himself as well as Silas ("Silvanus," v. 1) and Timothy.

1:3–12. Paul thanks God that the Thessalonian Christians are continuing to grow and mature in their faith. This growth is helping them to endure the persecution they are experiencing. He reminds them that the roles of persecutor and persecuted will one day be reversed. In the final judgment, believers who have been persecuted in this life will be rewarded by the Lord with eternal life. But persecuting unbelievers will be punished "with everlasting destruction from the presence of the Lord" (v. 9).

2:1–2. Apparently the Thessalonians had been told by false teachers that the day of the Lord or the second coming of Christ had already occurred.

2:3–12. Paul corrects this falsehood. He assures the believers at Thessalonica that the second coming of Christ has not yet happened. This will not occur until after the appearance of "that man of sin...the son of perdition" (v. 3). Paul was referring to the Antichrist.

2:13–15. Paul exhorts the Thessalonians to "stand fast" (v. 15) and not be led astray by false teachings about the end times and their eternal inheritance. Their salvation has been purchased by Jesus Christ and sealed by the Holy Spirit because of their belief of the truth.

2:16–17. In a beautiful benediction, Paul prays that these believers will be strengthened in their faith and belief.

3:1–5. Paul urges the Thessalonian believers to pray for him in his work of planting and nurturing the gospel.

3:6–15. Jesus' return will be accompanied by "the voice of the archangel, and with the trump of God" (1 Thessalonians 4:16). Until that day, believers should stay busy with their jobs and witness.

3:6–15. Some of the Thessalonian Christians had apparently quit working to wait for the second coming of Christ. They may have been expecting others to support them as they waited for the Lord's return. Paul criticized such idleness and exhorted these people to get back to work. Christians are to share the gospel message with diligence until Jesus returns (Acts 1:8–11).

3:16–18. Paul closes with wishes of grace and peace for the believers at Thessalonica.

[3:16–18] PAUL'S OWN HANDWRITING. *The salutation of Paul with mine own hand, which is the token in every epistle: so I write (2 Thess. 3:17).*

In Bible times many people wrote letters by dictating them to a secretary—a professional amanuensis, or scribe. This apparently was done occasionally by Paul, the most prolific letter writer of the New Testament (see introduction to the epistles of Paul on p. 250).

To prove to the recipients of 2 Thessalonians that this letter was from him—even though it had been written by someone else—Paul wrote the final words in his own handwriting. He also closed 1 Corinthians (16:21) and Colossians (4:18) in the same way.

In Paul's letter to the Romans, his secretary identified himself and included his own greeting to the Roman Christians: "I Tertius, who wrote this epistle, salute you in the Lord" (Rom. 16:22).

1 TIMOTHY

OVERVIEW: A vigorous call for Timothy to be faithful to his calling as a church leader and to oppose false teachings in the church.

Introduction to 1 Timothy

First Timothy is one of three of Paul's letters classified as pastoral epistles (along with 2 Timothy and Titus). All three were written to individual church leaders rather than churches. They deal with issues of church leadership— thus the term "pastoral epistles." They show the apostle's concern for effective church organization and administration.

Paul met Timothy in the city of Lystra during his second missionary journey (Acts 16:1–3). Timothy may have been converted under Paul's ministry, since the apostle referred to him in later years as his "beloved son" (1 Cor. 4:17) and his "son in the faith" (1 Tim. 1:2). Timothy became one of Paul's missionary associates, accompanying him on his second and third missionary journeys (Acts 16:3–4; 19:22).

After establishing a church in the city of Ephesus and ministering there for about three years (Acts 20:31), Paul left Timothy in charge and moved on to other locations to preach the gospel and plant churches. He apparently wrote this letter to Timothy while Timothy was still working with the Ephesian church (1 Tim. 1:3). It was written about A.D. 63 or 64, near the end of Paul's life.

Timothy was a young and inexperienced church leader. Paul counseled him to do his job and act responsibly in spite of his immaturity ("Let no man despise thy youth," 4:12) and to deal forcefully with false teachers who were stirring up trouble in the church.

Summary of 1 Timothy

1:1–2. Paul opens this letter to Timothy (1 Cor. 4:17) by addressing him as his "own son in the faith" (v. 2).

1:3–11. Paul had left Timothy in the church at Ephesus while he moved on to preach the gospel at other places. The apostle urges Timothy to stay at Ephesus so he can oppose false teachings that are beginning to appear in the church.

1:12–20. Paul had once been a persecutor of the church (Acts 9:1–2). He expresses his amazement to Timothy that God is now using him to spread the gospel.

2:1–8. Prayer is one of the most important functions of the church. Prayers should be offered for kings and others in authority as well as a church's own members.

2:9–15. Paul reminds Timothy that a specific code of conduct is expected of female believers in the church.

3:1–7. Those believers who serve as bishops or elders in the church must meet certain qualifications (Titus 1:5–9).

3:8–13. High standards are also established for those who would serve as deacons.

3:14–16. Paul expresses his hope that he will soon be able to visit Timothy at Ephesus.

1:3–11. A cross-shaped baptismal pool in the ruins of a church in Ephesus. Many years before this church was built, Timothy pastored in the city.

4:1–16. With strong words, Paul condemns those in the church at Ephesus who are teaching false doctrine. He urges Timothy to stand firmly against these false teachings and to exercise discipline against the troublemakers. Although Timothy is young and inexperienced, he should exercise the authority that has been delegated to him by the Lord and officials of the church.

[5:1–16] ABOVE-AND-BEYOND HOSPITALITY. *If she [a widow] have lodged strangers, if she have washed the saints' feet* (1 Tim. 5:10).

In this verse Paul gave Timothy some criteria by which he could determine if a widow in the church was a sacrificial servant of the Lord who should receive financial assistance from her fellow believers.

One mark of her character was that she had shown hospitality to strangers. Throughout the New Testament the grace of welcoming strangers into one's home is commended (Rom. 12:13; 1 Pet. 4:9).

Another thing that Timothy should look for is whether a widow had gone beyond what was expected in the hosting of strangers. Washing a guest's feet was considered the job of a lowly slave.

5:1–16. The early church offered financial support to widows, many of whom were destitute (Acts 6:1–7). Paul instructs Timothy on how to conduct this ministry in the church at Ephesus. Older widows are more likely to need this assistance. The families of some widows can help their own. The church should make sure its resources go to those in dire need.

5:17–25. Elders, or pastors, should be selected by the church with great care. Once placed in positions of leadership, they should be treated with respect and compensated for their work.

6:1–10. Paul offers advice for masters and slaves and the rich and the poor. He warns against the blind pursuit of riches (Eccles. 2:8–11) and encourages believers to be content with what they have: "Godliness with contentment is great gain" (v. 6).

6:11–21. Paul closes this letter to Timothy with a charge to be faithful to his calling and to continue to oppose false teachings in the church.

OVERVIEW: A letter of love and affection to Paul's son in the ministry.

Introduction to 2 Timothy

Paul wrote this second letter to his young missionary associate Timothy in A.D. 66—about two years after he wrote 1 Timothy (see the introduction to 1 Timothy on p. 280).

Imprisoned for the second time in Rome, Paul expected to be executed at any time. He wrote to encourage Timothy to stand firm in his commitment to Christ in the midst of troubling times for the church.

This letter is classified as one of Paul's pastoral epistles (see the introduction to 1 Timothy on p. 280). But it is also one of his most personal letters. He expressed deep affection for Timothy and looked back with no regrets over his life that had been poured out for Christ.

Summary of 2 Timothy

1:1–7. Paul opens this letter by expressing deep love for Timothy, whom he calls "my dearly beloved son" (v. 2; see 1 Cor. 4:17). The apostle also remembers Timothy in his prayers and has a great desire to see his young coworker.

1:8–18. Although Paul is imprisoned in Rome, he has no regrets about the course his life has taken. He reflects on his years as a witness for Christ and rejoices in the assurance

of His presence in all of life's circumstances: "I know whom I have believed, and am persuaded that he is able to keep that which I have committed unto him against that day" (v. 12).

2:1–26. Paul knew better than anyone that staying the course as a Christian minister requires determination, prayer, and commitment to holiness and righteousness in one's daily walk. He counsels Timothy to "flee...

[2:1–26] HARDSHIP AND SACRIFICE. *Thou [Timothy] therefore endure hardness [hardship, NIV], as a good soldier of Jesus Christ. No man that warreth entangleth himself with the affairs of this life; that he may please him who hath chosen him to be a soldier [his commanding officer, NIV]* (2 Tim. 2:3–4).

Paul continues his imagery from the Roman military (see the notes "Spiritual Battle Gear" on p. 269 and "Protected by Faith and Love" on p. 275) by referring to the discipline and singleness of purpose required of a Roman soldier.

The ordinary foot soldier in the Roman military was loaded down with his armor and weapons, tools, and rations that would last him for several days. He was sworn through strict discipline and training to obey the orders of his commanding officer without question.

Paul was telling Timothy that the Christian life—while it has its rewards—is not an easy path. It requires discipline and sacrifice.

1:8–18. As his execution approached, Paul wrote Timothy one last letter. Paul wrote from a Roman prison, the building at right if an ancient tradition is correct. That tradition says Paul and Peter were both held in a dungeon below.

youthful lusts" and to "follow righteousness, faith, charity, peace" (v. 22).

3:1–13. According to Paul, perilous times are ahead for the church. As the time for Jesus' return draws near, evil will grow stronger, even within the fellowship of the church.

3:14–17. In the midst of such challenging times, Timothy is to stick to the truths revealed in God's written Word. It is a trustworthy and reliable guide for believers (Ps. 119:105).

4:1–8. Paul expects to be executed in Rome at any time. But he can look back over his life with the assurance that he has been faithful to his divine calling: "I have fought a good fight, I have finished my course, I have kept the faith" (v. 7).

4:9–22. Paul closes his second letter to Timothy by mentioning several coworkers who have supported him to the very end, as well as some who have let him down. He sends greetings to "Prisca [Priscilla] and Aquila, and the household of Onesiphorus" (v. 19).

OVERVIEW: Paul gives instructions for the way that church leaders, including Titus, should conduct themselves.

Introduction to Titus

Like the epistles of 1 and 2 Timothy, Titus was also written to a person, not a church, and it is also known as one of the apostle Paul's pastoral epistles (see the introduction to 1 Timothy on p. 280).

Paul wrote this epistle about A.D. 63 to his missionary associate Titus, whom he had sent to work with the church on the island of Crete in the Mediterranean Sea. This was a tough assignment, since the residents of Crete were known for their depraved behavior (1:12). But Paul had confidence that Titus could handle the situation. In his second letter to the Corinthians, the apostle described Titus as a reliable, hardworking, and dependable leader (2 Cor. 7:6; 8:16–17).

In his letter to Titus, Paul instructed him to appoint leaders for the Cretan church, to discipline those who were teaching false doctrine, and to lead the believers to practice godly behavior.

Summary of Titus

1:1–4. Paul greets Titus (Gal. 2:1–3) as "mine own son after the common faith" (v. 4) and wishes for him God's "grace, mercy, and peace" (v. 4).

1:5–9. Paul reminds Titus that he has given him the responsibility of appointing elders or pastors to serve the church on the island of Crete. Church leaders such as elders and bishops must be mature people of high moral character who are devoted to the Lord (1 Tim. 3:1–7).

1:10–16. Paul has harsh words for false teachers who are hindering the work of the Lord. His advice to Titus is to "rebuke them sharply" (v. 13) so they will be turned back to the truth.

2:1–10. Titus should overlook no segment of the church in his instructions on how to live the Christian life. Godly behavior is expected of aged men (v. 2), aged women (v. 3), young women (vv. 4–5), young men (vv. 6–8), and servants (vv. 9–10).

2:11–15. All believers are to live "soberly, righteously, and godly" (v. 12) in the world because of the example set for believers by Jesus Christ (Phil. 2:5–8).

3:1–8. What a difference Christ makes in the lives of believers, Paul declares. We who were "foolish, disobedient, deceived" (v. 3) have been delivered from our sin and filled with the "kindness and love of God" (v. 4). Good works are the outgrowth of this new life in Christ.

3:9–11. Paul warns Titus to shun those people who deal in foolish questions and argue about the merits of the Old Testament law. They condemn themselves by such vain and senseless behavior.

3:12–15. Paul plans to send someone to Crete as Titus's replacement. Then he wants Titus to join him.

PHILEMON

OVERVIEW: A plea for mercy and forgiveness for a runaway slave who has become a believer.

Introduction to Philemon

Paul's letter to Philemon, containing only twenty-five verses, is the shortest of his epistles. The apostle wrote it while in prison in Rome about A.D. 63. The purpose of the letter was to appeal to Philemon, a believer in the church at Colosse, to forgive and welcome back his runaway slave named Onesimus, who had been converted under Paul's ministry in Rome.

Philemon had the legal right as a slave owner in the ancient world to punish and even kill Onesimus for his act of betrayal. But Paul expressed confidence that he would welcome him back as a fellow believer, "a brother beloved" (v. 16) in the Lord.

This beautiful letter shows the warm and caring side of Paul's personality. It reminds us that Jesus Christ has the power to transform all human relationships.

[Verses 1–7] **PHILEMON'S HOUSE CHURCH.** *To the church in thy [Philemon's] house: Grace to you, and peace* (Philem. 2–3).

Paul sent greetings in this verse to the believers who met in Philemon's house. Groups of believers in New Testament times did not have church buildings, so they usually met in private homes. Priscilla and Aquila apparently made their home available as a meeting place in both Rome (Rom. 16:5) and Ephesus (1 Cor. 16:19). Early believers also met in the home of Nymphas (Col. 4:15–16).

Summary of Philemon

Verses 1–7. Paul, writing from prison in Rome (Acts 28:16, 30–31), greets his fellow believer Philemon in the church at Colosse. Philemon's home may have been the meeting place for the Colossian church, since Paul mentions "the church in thy house" (v. 2).

Verses 8–11. Paul begins his appeal on behalf of Philemon's runaway slave Onesimus by referring to Onesimus as "my son" (v. 10). Apparently Paul had led Onesimus to Christ, and he considered him a Christian brother who was as close to him as a son.

Verses 12–17. Although he preferred to keep Onesimus with him in Rome, Paul was sending him back to Philemon in Colosse. The apostle uses his influence and reputation to persuade Philemon to receive Onesimus back not as a slave but as a brother in Christ: "If thou count me therefore a partner, receive him as myself" (v. 17).

Verses 18–21. Paul even offers to repay Philemon for anything Onesimus might have taken from his master when he ran away. But the apostle also appeals to his spirit of forgiveness and generosity, confident that Philemon will "do more than I say" (v. 21).

Verses 22–25. Paul closes by sending greetings to Philemon from believers who had served as his helpers in the ministry. He also expresses hope that he might be released from prison and come to Colosse for a visit.

CHAPTER 9
THE GENERAL EPISTLES

The last nine books of the New Testament are known as the "general epistles" because they were addressed to broad, general audiences rather than to specific churches or individuals. The exceptions to this categorization are the letters of 2 and 3 John, which were addressed to specific people.

Most of these letters were written during the final years of the first Christian century, about A.D. 65–95. By this time false teachings had begun to creep into the Christian movement. Many of these epistles were written to correct or condemn these heretical doctrines.

These nine general letters—Hebrews; James; 1 and 2 Peter; 1, 2, and 3 John; Jude; and Revelation—are often called the "catholic (universal) epistles." They portray a Savior whose strength can sustain us in the midst of life's problems.

HEBREWS

OVERVIEW: Jesus Christ is superior to the Old Testament sacrificial system. He is the great High Priest, who sacrificed His life to atone for our sin.

Introduction to Hebrews

Hebrews is unique among the New Testament epistles because it does not give a single clue about its author. It omits the greeting and the conclusion that are typical of all the other letters contained in the New Testament, and it reads more like a sermon or an essay than a personal letter.

In the early years of the church, many people assumed that the apostle Paul wrote Hebrews. But this assumption has been rejected by modern scholarship because Hebrews does not fit the Pauline mold. Possible authors who have been suggested include several early believers mentioned in the book of Acts: Luke, Barnabas, or Apollos. But the bottom line is that no one knows who wrote the epistle to the Hebrews.

The date when this book was written is also a mystery, but we can assume that it was written before A.D. 70. In that year the Roman army destroyed the temple in Jerusalem during their campaign against a rebellion of the Jewish people. The author of Hebrews does not refer to this event, although he mentions Jewish temple sacrifices several times. It seems likely that he would have discussed the temple's destruction if he had written this epistle after A.D. 70.

While the author and date of Hebrews are a mystery, there is no doubt about the purpose of this epistle. It was written to people from a Jewish background who had become Christians. They were wavering in their commitment and were even considering returning to their former Jewish customs and beliefs. Hebrews declared to these weak believers that Jesus Christ had replaced Judaism as God's perfect revelation of Himself and that they should stand firm in their commitment to Him.

Summary of Hebrews

1:1–4. The epistle begins by affirming that God has spoken in the past, during Old Testament times, through the prophets. But He has revealed Himself supremely through the life and ministry of His Son, Jesus Christ.

1:5–14. Several Old Testament passages are quoted to show that Jesus is superior to all previous ways in which God has revealed Himself. He is especially superior to angels, messengers who often spoke for God in Old Testament times (Gen. 18:9–10; Exod. 14:19–20).

2:1–4. This is the first of four warning messages in the epistle to the Hebrews (see Heb. 5:11–6:12; 10:19–39; 12:12–29). This message warns believers to pay attention to the salvation offered by Jesus Christ.

2:5–18. Although Christ was God's Son, He was human and thus subject to all the temptations that people face. He is a Savior with whom we can identify: "In that he himself hath suffered being tempted, he is able to succour them that are tempted" (v. 18).

3:1–6. Moses was the great hero of the Jewish people. They considered him greater than the angels, since he had passed on God's law to His people. But Jesus is greater even than Moses. He is like the builder and owner of a house, while Moses is just a butler or servant in the house.

3:7–19. When the Jewish people were wandering in the wilderness, they rebelled against Moses and committed idolatry (Num. 14:1–35). This shows the danger of unbelief. It is an even more serious matter to reject Jesus, since He is superior to Moses.

4:1–13. The writer of Hebrews probably had Joshua in mind when he referred to the Israelites as failing to find rest in the land of promise (v. 1). The implication is that Jesus is superior to Joshua, because He provides rest for all who place their faith in Him.

4:14–16. Jesus Christ is the great High Priest for all believers. Although He was tempted just like we are, He never gave in to sin (Luke 4:1–13). He identifies with us in our temptations because He has experienced all the human emotions that we feel. When we commit ourselves to Him, we will be received with grace and mercy.

5:1–10. Jesus' comparison to Melchisedec (Gen. 14:17–20) is explained more fully in Hebrews 7. As our great High Priest, Jesus suffered on our behalf and became "the author of eternal salvation unto all them that obey him" (v. 9).

5:11–6:12. These verses contain the second warning to the readers of Hebrews (see also Heb. 2:1–4; 10:19–39; 12:12–29). This message cautions those who had professed faith in Christ to press on to maturity in their commitment. As new Christians, they were

[4:14–16] BOLD ACCESS TO THE KING. *Let us therefore come boldly unto the throne of grace, that we may obtain mercy, and find grace to help in time of need* (Heb. 4:16).

As a person becomes famous or rises to a high position, he limits his accessibility to others for his own protection. Many kings of Bible times, for example, could not be approached by anyone but their most trusted advisors. The Persians had a law that anyone who came into their king's presence without his permission could pay with their lives (see the note "Don't Bother the King" on p. 106).

This verse from Hebrews, when seen against the background of these "unapproachable" kings, makes us realize what a revolutionary Savior Jesus is. Although He is exalted to the highest position as God's Son, He is still as approachable to us as a member of the family or a close friend.

We can bring our needs boldly to Jesus and expect to be received joyfully into His presence.

in the elementary stages of their faith. But they should continue growing in their faith. A mature faith results in works of mercy and righteousness.

6:13–20. Abraham is an example of a person to whom God "made promise" (v. 13; Gen. 12:1–3). But Abraham had the responsibility to obey God in order to bring this promise to fruition. Human obedience is still a vital ingredient in God's plan for His people.

7:1–28. This entire chapter picks up on the topic of Melchisedec, first mentioned in Hebrews 5:6–10. Melchisedec was the mysterious priest and "king of Salem" who received tithes from Abraham (Gen. 14:17–20). The Bible gives no information about the genealolgy or death of Melchisedec. He simply appears out of nowhere, and this implies that his priesthood was eternal. But the priesthood of Christ is greater even

8:1–10:18. Though Jews no longer offer sacrifices, since they have no temple, a small community of Samaritans in Israel still sacrifices lambs at Passover. The writer of Hebrews, however, said Jesus was the sacrifice to end all sacrifices.

than that of Melchisedec. With His atoning death, the Old Testament sacrificial system was abolished. Human priests were no longer needed to offer animal sacrifices to atone for sin. Jesus took care of this "when he offered up himself" (v. 27).

8:1–10:18. This long passage describes the new covenant that was established by Christ. The old covenant between God and His people required them to offer animal sacrifices and to follow prescribed rituals to take away the stain of sin (Lev. 4:1–35). These rituals had to be repeated again and again. But under the new covenant, Jesus offered His own life as a permanent, once-for-all sacrifice for sin.

10:19–39. This is the third warning to the readers of Hebrews (see also Heb. 2:1–4; 5:11–6:12; 12:12–29). This message cautions them to persevere in the commitment they had made to follow Jesus Christ. The author of Hebrews also exhorts them to meet together for regular worship in order to encourage and strengthen one another in the faith. He uses the certainty of Jesus' second coming to motivate them to stand firm in their faith.

11:1–40. This is known as the great "faith chapter" of the Bible. Several heroes of the faith from the Old Testament are mentioned to encourage the readers of Hebrews to remain strong in their own faith. Personalities singled out for their faith include Noah (v. 7), Abraham (vv. 8–10, 17), Jacob (v. 21), Joseph (v. 22), and Moses (vv. 23–29).

12:1–2. Endurance and faithfulness are exemplified by Jesus, who followed the path of obedience all the way to the cross (Phil. 2:8). We as believers should also overcome every obstacle in our path in order to remain faithful to the Lord's call.

12:3–11. Chastening, or God's discipline, is something to be expected by all believers (1 Pet. 4:12–17). Trials and troubles teach us that we are not self-sufficient and that we should look to God for strength and guidance.

12:12–29. These verses contain the fourth and final warning to the readers of the book of Hebrews (see also Heb. 2:1–4; 5:11–6:12;

[11:1–40] EXECUTION BY SAWING. *They were stoned, they were sawn asunder [sawed in two, NIV], were tempted, were slain with the sword* (Heb. 11:37).

This verse appears in the famous "roll call of the faithful" chapter in Hebrews. The writer pays tribute to the people of past generations who remained faithful to God in spite of great persecution.

Execution by being sawed in two is cruel and inhumane by modern standards, but this form of capital punishment was apparently practiced in the ancient world. It was not out of character for the cruel Assyrians, who were known to cut off the ears and hands of their victims just for sport (see the note "Mutilation of Captives" on p. 50).

But even King David of Judah may have practiced this form of torture and execution against the Ammonites. After capturing their capital city, Rabbah, he "brought out the people that were in it, and cut them with saws, and with harrows of iron, and with axes" (1 Chron. 20:3).

10:19–39. Jews in Jerusalem gather for prayer at their most sacred site, the Western Wall. Once a retaining wall that held up the dirt sides of a hilltop on which the temple rested, this wall is all that remains of the temple. Hebrews was a book written for Jewish Christians who were leaving the faith because of persecution and returning to Judaism. The writer warned that there was nothing to return to because Jesus brought the prophesied new covenant between God and humanity.

[12:1–2] **A LIFETIME RACE.** *Let us [Christian believers] lay aside every weight, and the sin which doth so easily beset us, and let us run with patience [perseverance, NIV] the race that is set before us* (Heb. 12:1).

In this verse Paul compares the Christian life to the foot race in which Christians competed in the Greek games (see the note "Discipline and Training" on p. 258). The foot race was one of the most popular of the Greek games that were held every year in Athens.

To prepare themselves for these races, runners underwent rigorous training, trimming down their bodies to eliminate every ounce of excess fat. On race day they wore light clothing—perhaps no clothes at all—to give themselves every possible advantage in the competition against other runners. These races covered various distances—from short sprints where speed was called for, to longer runs where stamina and endurance were more important.

In Paul's thinking the Christian life is like a marathon. It's important for us to remain faithful to Christ during a lifetime of service so we can say with him at the end of the race, "I have finished my course, I have kept the faith" (2 Tim. 4:7).

10:19–39). This message cautions them against developing a stubborn attitude and disobeying the commands of Jesus. God has dealt forcefully with such sin and rebellion in the past, and He will do so again.

13:1–17. Believers are to demonstrate the character of Christ in their lives by loving one another, keeping themselves sexually pure, serving others, and praising and giving thanks to God.

13:18–25. The author of Hebrews closes with a benediction of God's grace and peace for his readers.

OVERVIEW: How genuine faith expresses itself in daily life.

Introduction to James

The epistle of James is one of the most practical books in the Bible. It shows there is a connection between what we believe and how we behave. Jesus summarized this principle in one succinct sentence: "The tree is known by his fruit" (Matt. 12:33).

The James who wrote this epistle was probably the half brother of Jesus, one of four sons born to Mary and Joseph after Jesus was born (Matt. 13:55; Mark 6:3). At first James was skeptical about Jesus and His claim to be the Messiah. But he apparently became a believer after the resurrection and ascension of the Lord. James eventually became a leader in the church at Jerusalem (Acts 15:2–21; 21:18).

The epistle of James is known for its direct and forthright declaration on the behavior expected of those who follow the Lord. For James the supreme test of religion is how we act rather than what we profess to believe.

Summary of James

1:1. The "twelve tribes...scattered abroad" to which James wrote this letter were probably Jewish Christians who were living outside Palestine.

1:2–18. James encourages these Christians of Jewish background who are being persecuted for their faith. He also cautions them

---

[1:2–18] AN ETERNAL CROWN. *Blessed is the man that endureth temptation: for...he shall receive the crown of life, which the Lord hath promised to them that love him* (James 1:12).

Crowns were worn by kings as symbols of authority and power (2 Sam. 1:10). James compared the believer's inheritance of eternal life through the atoning death of Jesus Christ to a crown.

This crown, unlike earthly and physical status symbols, will never grow tarnished or lose its luster because of changing cultural standards. It has an "eternal lifetime" warranty from the King of kings and Lord of lords (Rev. 21:5–7).

---

to remain faithful to God, even when they are tempted to do wrong.

1:19–27. The best way to stay true to God and to hold up under persecution is to live out one's faith: "Be ye doers of the word, and not hearers only" (v. 22).

2:1–13. The way of the world is to cater to rich people and to discriminate against the poor. But this is not how believers should relate to people. Everyone should be treated with equal respect, regardless of economic means, social status, or race (Rom. 1:14–16).

2:14–26. In these verses James is not teaching that a person is saved by his or her works. His point is that genuine faith will result in good works. If a person claims to be a believer but does not live righteously or perform acts of service toward others, we have

2:1–13. Claudius, Roman emperor around the time James likely wrote his epistle. James warned fellow Christians not to show favoritism to the rich and powerful. Instead, believers are to treat everyone with equal respect.

to question whether he or she has really experienced saving faith.

3:1–12. The greatest challenge any person faces is controlling the tongue (Prov. 21:23). Although it is one of the smallest organs of the body, it has the potential to build up as well as to destroy. Only God can give us the self-discipline it takes to tame the tongue.

3:13–4:10. Being wise in the ways of the Lord is different from being wise in the ways of the world. Worldly wisdom leads to strife, conflict, and ungodly lust. But seeking the Lord and His wisdom results in righteousness and treating others with justice and mercy (Zech. 7:9).

4:11–17. James warns his readers about the sin of presumption—making plans with no regard for God and assuming that we have unlimited time in this life. He reminds us that life is only a vapor or a cloud "that appeareth for a little time, and then vanisheth away" (v. 14).

5:1–6. Those who grow rich by cheating the poor will be judged harshly by the Lord. The accumulated riches that they thought would bring them pleasure will actually bring them misery and unhappiness.

5:7–12. James encourages his readers to display persistent devotion to the Lord in the midst of their persecution and suffering.

5:13–18. One key to bearing up under persecution is persistent prayer (Luke 18:1–8). This is one of the most eloquent passages in the Bible on the power of prayer: "The effectual fervent prayer of a righteous man availeth much" (v. 16).

5:19–20. James closes his letter with a plea to his readers to try to reclaim their fellow believers who have strayed from the truth.

[5:7–12] PATIENT WAITING. *The husbandman [farmer, NIV]. . .hath long patience for it [the harvest], until he receive the early and latter rain* (James 5:7).

The land of Palestine, known for its dry climate, had limited rainfall. Moisture for crop production was supplemented by heavy dews (Deut. 33:13).

But every farmer knew that at least two major rainfalls during the year were essential for crops to grow. The early rain in October and November softened the soil for planting. The latter rain of March and April brought a needed boost for the crops before they ripened fully for the harvest.

James declared that just as farmers waited patiently from the early rain to the latter rain for their crops to mature, so believers must wait patiently for the second coming of Jesus (2 Tim. 4:8).

1 PETER

OVERVIEW: Encouragement to believers who are suffering persecution because of their faith.

Introduction to 1 Peter

By about A.D. 65 the Christian faith had grown so dramatically that it was becoming a threat to the Roman Empire. Believers were feeling the first wave of persecution for their faith, and this seemed destined to grow stronger in the decades ahead. The first epistle of Peter was written to encourage Christians in these trying times.

This epistle was written by the apostle Peter, the disciple of Jesus who became the leader of the Christian movement during its early days in Jerusalem (Acts 2:14–41). Peter eventually traveled to Rome, capital city of the Roman Empire. From Rome, he addressed his letter to believers who had been "scattered throughout Pontus, Galatia, Cappadocia, Asia, and Bithynia" (1:1–2). Perhaps harassment from Roman officials had forced Christians to flee to these distant territories.

Peter encouraged these suffering believers to follow the example of Christ. His persecution and death—and subsequent resurrection—provided assurance and hope for the future.

Summary of 1 Peter

1:1–2. Peter addresses this letter to believers scattered throughout five distant regions of the Roman Empire.

1:3–25. The basis of the believer's hope is Jesus

[1:3–25] CLEAR THINKING. *Gird up the loins of your mind, be sober* (1 Pet. 1:13).

Both men and women of Bible times wore full-body outer robes that extended almost to the feet (see the note "Not Quite Naked" on p. 61). If a person needed to run or do strenuous work, he would tuck the bottom part of his robe into the belt or sash around his waist. This gave him greater freedom of movement.

This practice is described by the KJV as "girding up the loins." In this verse, Peter described the need for believers to do constructive thinking as girding up the "loins of your mind." The NIV translates it, "Prepare your minds for action." Peter means that believers should think clearly and reject the hindrances and temptations of the world by focusing on God and His grace.

Tucking the robe into the belt is sometimes referred to in the Bible in a figurative sense to denote strength and determination (Job 40:7; Pss. 65:6; 93:1).

Christ and His resurrection from the dead. He alone provides salvation and the promise of eternal life.

2:1–17. Jesus is the living stone who serves as the foundation for the faith of believers. Although He was rejected by His own people, God made Him the cornerstone of salvation for the world (Eph. 2:20). Those who place their faith in Him are delivered from their sins. They become part of God's "royal priesthood, an holy nation" (v. 9) that bears witness of Him and His kingdom to others.

4:12–19. Peter is crucified upside down in Rome. This story isn't in the Bible, but church leaders in the early centuries said Peter didn't feel worthy to be crucified the way Jesus was.

2:18–25. Peter uses the example of Jesus and His suffering to motivate believers. Just as He suffered to purchase salvation for them, they should endure persecution for His sake with a willing and joyous spirit.

3:1–7. Husbands and wives have a special responsibility to live in obedience to the commands of Christ. Husbands should love and honor their wives, and wives should "be in subjection to your own husbands" (v. 1; see Eph. 5:22–28). Such respectful and humble behavior by wives might lead their unbelieving husbands to the Lord.

3:8–17. Peter appeals to his readers to be united in the Lord, to practice humility and love, and to resist the temptation to seek revenge against those who are causing them pain and suffering.

3:18–22. Jesus was the ultimate sufferer—a case of the just suffering for the unjust "that he might bring us to God" (v. 18). After purchasing our salvation, He is now exalted at God's right hand. All earthly powers and authorities are subject to Him (Rev. 19:1–6).

4:1–11. Again, the example of Christ provides a demonstration of the way believers should live. Peter appeals to his readers to practice love and hospitality toward others, thus serving as "good stewards of the manifold grace of God" (v. 10).

4:12–19. It should not surprise Christians that they are called to suffer persecution for their faith. According to Peter, suffering is actually a badge of honor (Heb. 12:3–11). Just as Christ's suffering was the prelude to His glorification with the Father, so it will be for all believers.

5:1–4. Peter has a special word for the leaders ("elders," v. 1) of the churches to whom he is writing. The elders must have a loving, shepherd spirit and not a dominating attitude toward those whom they serve.

5:5–9. All the members of the churches are to respect their leaders and to show a kind and humble spirit. They should be on guard against the temptations of Satan (James 4:7).

5:10–14. Peter closes with a benediction, commending his readers to the grace of God. He also sends greetings from his coworkers Silvanus ("Silas," v. 12; see also Acts 15:40) and Marcus (v. 13; probably John Mark; see also Acts 13:13; 2 Tim. 4:11).

[5:1–4] JESUS THE CHIEF SHEPHERD. *When the chief Shepherd [Jesus] shall appear, ye shall receive a crown of glory that fadeth not away* (1 Pet. 5:4).

In Bible times wealth was often measured by the size of one's flocks and herds of livestock (see the note "A Man of Means" on p. 109). Some wealthy people had hundreds of sheep, and this required the services of several shepherds. These shepherds would be supervised by a chief shepherd or master shepherd (1 Sam. 21:7).

Peter compared Jesus Christ to a chief shepherd. This title is similar to His designation as "that great shepherd of the sheep" in Hebrews 13:20.

All ministers who lead God's people should remember that they are undershepherds who work under the supervision of the Great Shepherd or Chief Shepherd—Jesus Christ. He enables then to take care of God's people with wisdom and kindness.

OVERVIEW: A warning to be on guard against false teachers within the church.

Introduction to 2 Peter

This brief epistle of only three chapters was also written by the apostle Peter (see introduction to 1 Peter on p. 296). But unlike 1 Peter, the author named no audience for his second epistle. It was probably written from Rome just before Peter's martyrdom in that city about A.D. 68.

The problem that Peter addressed in this letter was not persecution from without but troubles from within. False teachers were leading people astray with their views of the nature of Christ and His second coming. Peter corrected these false views and advised the leaders of the church to deal firmly with these heretical teachers.

Summary of 2 Peter

1:1–2. Peter opens his letter with wishes for grace and peace to his readers.

1:3–11. These are some of the greatest verses in the New Testament on the need for growth in the Christian life. Growing more like Christ involves faith, temperance, patience, godliness, kindness, and love.

1:12–21. The Christian faith does not grow out of hearsay and myth. It is grounded in historical facts and the testimony of eyewitnesses who were with Jesus in the flesh (1 John 1:1–7). We can also trust God's revelation of truth through His written Word.

2:1–22. Peter warns that false teachers from within the church will rise up in the future to lead believers astray. The church should be on guard against such heresies. God will punish such false prophets, just as he has done in the past. They will "utterly perish in their own corruption" (v. 12).

3:1–10. These verses declare the certainty of the second coming of Jesus and the final judgment (1 Thess. 4:13–17). These will happen in God's own time. The fact that they haven't yet happened doesn't mean that God is slow or apathetic. Rather, He is loving and patient, waiting for others to respond to His offer of salvation. He is "not willing that any should perish, but that all should come to repentance" (v. 9).

3:11–18. While waiting for the Lord to return, how should believers conduct themselves? Peter declares that they should live as holy and godly people, continuing to "grow in grace, and in the knowledge of our Lord and Saviour Jesus Christ" (v. 18; see 2 Thess. 3:6–15).

1 JOHN

OVERVIEW: Jesus was fully human as well as fully divine.

Introduction to 1 John

The first epistle of John does not name an author, but there seems little doubt that it was written by the apostle John, the disciple of Jesus who also wrote the Gospel of John (see introduction to the Gospel of John on p. 229).

First John has many similarities to John's Gospel. Both contain numerous contrasts between "love" and "hate," "life" and "death," and "darkness" and "light." The opening verses of the Gospel and 1 John are also similar, and the author of 1 John claims that he was personally acquainted with Jesus during His earthly ministry (1 John 1:1–4).

John probably wrote his first epistle about A.D. 92, shortly after writing his Gospel. A leader in the church at Ephesus, he was in his eighties by this time. During this same general period, he also wrote 2 and 3 John and the book of Revelation.

One reason why John wrote his first epistle was to refute false teachers who were denying that Jesus had come to earth in human form. They believed that Jesus was a divine spirit who only seemed to exist in the flesh. But John affirmed that with his own eyes he had seen Jesus walk the earth as a man: "That which we have seen and heard declare we unto you" (1:3). This is a central doctrine of the Christian faith that the church has affirmed throughout

its history: Jesus was the God-man. In some mysterious way that the human mind cannot fully understand, Jesus was both fully human and fully divine.

Another important theme of 1 John is love. John declared that God is love (4:8, 16), and He acts in love on our behalf (4:9–10). We show our love for God by loving others (2:9–11; 3:10).

Summary of 1 John

1:1–7. John declares that he was an eyewitness of the earthly ministry of Jesus. As one of the Twelve, he saw Jesus' miracles with his own eyes and listened to His teachings with his own ears. Thus, John is qualified to bear witness about Christ to others (2 Pet. 1:12–21).

1:8–10. Even believers will fall into sin. Rather than denying our wrongdoings, we should confess them and bring them to Jesus for forgiveness.

2:1–6. True believers abide in Christ and keep His commandments.

2:7–17. Another characteristic of believers is love for others (1 Cor. 13). A person who harbors hate toward others is walking in darkness rather than in the light of God's salvation.

2:18–29. John declares that the Antichrist—the embodiment of evil and the archenemy of Christ—will appear during the last days when the return of Jesus draws near.

4:1–6. Jesus suffers through isolation and temptation during the several weeks He spent in the wilderness before starting His ministry. John warned believers not to listen to false teachers who said Jesus was just a spirit who only pretended to be human and to suffer.

Many false teachers ("many antichrists," v. 18) were denying that Jesus was the Messiah. John interprets this as a sign that the final judgment is close at hand.

3:1–10. John declares that true believers will not continue in a habitual state of sin. God's love guides believers to recognize their sins as soon as they are committed and to seek His forgiveness day by day.

3:11–24. John again encourages believers to love one another. This is the great lesson that Jesus taught His followers (John 13:34).

4:1–6. These verses refute the claim of some false teachers that Jesus did not come to earth in human form. They taught that Jesus was a spirit and that He only seemed to have a physical body. John declares, "Every spirit that confesseth not that Jesus Christ is come in the flesh is not of God" (v. 3).

4:7–21. These verses declare that God's essential character is love and that He is the author of all love (John 3:16). It is logical to John that if God loved us enough to grant us salvation and eternal life, then "we ought also to love one another" (v. 11).

5:1–12. The foundation of the Christian's hope for eternal life is faith in Jesus as God's Son. John boils it down to one simple statement:

"He that hath the Son hath life; and he that hath not the Son of God hath not life" (v. 12).

5:13–21. John closes his letter by assuring his readers that they can know with assurance that Jesus is who He claimed to be. They can also pray to Him with full confidence that He will hear and answer in accordance with their needs (James 5:16).

[3:11–24] BOWELS OF COMPASSION. *Whoso…seeth his brother have need, and shutteth up his bowels of compassion from him, how dwelleth the love of God in him?* (1 John 3:17).

In Bible times the bowels were considered the seat of emotions and feelings. According to the apostle John in this passage, a person who shuts his "bowels of compassion" has no pity or empathy toward those in need. In our modern figure of speech, we would probably say that a person like this does not have a compassionate heart.

The apostle John makes it clear throughout this epistle that love and compassion toward others is one of the marks of an authentic Christian believer: "This commandment have we from him, That he who loveth God love his brother also" (1 John 4:21).

5:13–21. During the Transfiguration, Jesus meets with Moses and Elijah while His body glows with the celestial radiance of divinity. John wanted his readers to believe that Jesus was both fully human and fully divine, even though it's impossible to comprehend how He could be both.

OVERVIEW: A warning to shun false teachers who deny that Jesus came in the flesh.

Introduction to 2 John

Like his first epistle, 2 John was also written by the apostle John about A.D. 92, when he was more than eighty years old (see introduction to 1 John on p. 300).

Second John is the shortest book in the New Testament, containing only thirteen verses. It was written to warn believers and churches against showing hospitality to false teachers (v. 10). John also encouraged Christians to obey the commandments of Jesus Christ and to love one another.

Summary of 2 John

Verses 1–3. The author of this letter refers to himself as "the elder" (v. 1). This was probably a title of authority or respect for the apostle John, one of the twelve disciples of Jesus. Nothing is known about the "elect lady" (v. 1) to whom this epistle is addressed. Was John referring to a church or a person? No one knows.

Verses 4–6. John is delighted to learn that the elect lady and her children are walking in love (1 Cor. 13). He repeats the commandment that he learned from Jesus: "Love one another" (v. 5; see John 13:34).

Verses 7–11. John warns the elect lady to shun false teachers who deny that Jesus Christ came in the flesh (1 John 4:1–6). These were probably members of a heretical sect known as the Gnostics. They taught that Jesus came to earth in spirit form and that He only seemed to suffer and die on the cross.

Verses 12–13. John extends closing greetings, with the hope that he will soon be able to make a personal visit.

3 JOHN

OVERVIEW: Words of criticism and commendation for early church leaders.

Introduction to 3 John

The third epistle of John was written by the apostle John about A.D. 92 (see introduction to 1 John on p. 300) to a believer named Gaius. John referred to himself as "the elder" (v. 1). This identified him as a leader in a local church, probably the church at Ephesus.

In this letter John has words of criticism for one prideful church leader but words of praise for Gaius and Demetrius, who were leading in the Spirit of Christ.

Summary of 3 John

Verses 1–8. John writes to a fellow believer named Gaius, who was probably a leader in one of the churches of Asia Minor. John commends Gaius for standing for the truth and for showing hospitality to evangelists who traveled from church to church preaching the gospel.

Verses 9–10. John has harsh words for Diotrephes, a believer who apparently had taken control of a local church and refused to receive the apostles and other traveling ministers.

Verses 11–12. John endorses a believer named Demetrius and assures Gaius that Demetrius can be trusted to follow the Lord and walk in the truth.

Verses 13–14. John extends personal greetings to other believers associated with Gaius and promises to visit him soon.

JUDE

OVERVIEW: A strong warning against false teachers in the church.

Introduction to Jude

The epistle of Jude addresses the same problem as 2 Peter: false teachers within the church who were leading believers astray (see introduction to 2 Peter on p. 299). The author probably wrote this letter about A.D. 82 to warn church leaders to beware of these heretical teachers and their dangerous doctrines.

Who was this Jude who wrote this brief epistle? The most likely candidate is one of the half brothers of Jesus who is mentioned in Matthew 13:55 ("Judas") and Mark 6:3 ("Juda"). Like Jesus' other half brothers, Jude was skeptical of Jesus and His mission while He was conducting His earthly ministry. But he apparently became a believer after Jesus' resurrection and ascension.

Jude identified himself in the opening verse of his

Some speculate that Joseph was much older than Mary, a widower who brought children into their marriage. In that case, Jesus' four brothers named in scripture—James, Joseph, Simon, and Judas (or Jude; Matthew 13:55)—may have been older than He was.

[Verses 3–16] **THE LOVE FEAST.** *These are spots in your feasts of charity, when they feast with you, feeding themselves without fear* (Jude 12).

The "feasts of charity" to which Jude refers in this verse was probably the love feast, a meal that early Christians ate together as part of their observance of the Lord's Supper. The purpose of this meal was to remember the sacrifice of Christ, since he was eating the Passover meal with His disciples when He turned it into a memorial of His sacrificial death (Luke 22:14–20).

In its early years, the love feast was also known as the agape meal. It became a charity meal for the poor in some Christian traditions. Most Christian groups today have dropped this communal meal from their observance of the Lord's Supper.

epistle as a "brother of James" (v. 1). This was probably another half brother of Jesus who wrote the epistle of James (see introduction to that epistle on p. 293).

Summary of Jude

Verses 1–2. Jude identifies himself as "the servant of Jesus Christ, and brother of James" (v. 1). His brother James, at first a skeptic like Jude, eventually became a believer and assumed a prominent leadership role in the early church at Jerusalem (Acts 15:13).

Verses 3–16. Jude urges his fellow believers to "earnestly contend for the faith" in opposition to certain people who were hindering the work of the church. These people were particularly dangerous because they were working from within the fellowship of the church (2 Pet. 2:1–3). Jude describes them as "murmurers, complainers" who were "walking after their own lusts" (v. 16). Apparently they were using the grace of God as a cover for their lifestyles of sin and wickedness.

Verses 17–23. Jude contrasts the ungodly behavior of these people with the characteristics of true believers. Those who truly know God reflect the love of Christ (1 John 3:11–24). They are strengthened for godly living through the power of prayer.

Verses 24–25. Jude closes with a beautiful benediction that should comfort and strengthen all believers. Jesus is able to keep us from falling and to present us justified before God.

OVERVIEW: A prophecy of the end times and God's ultimate triumph over the forces of evil.

Introduction to Revelation

Revelation is the only book of apocalyptic literature in the New Testament. This was a distinctive type of writing in biblical times that used symbols and numbers to depict the end of the present age and the coming of God's future kingdom. Revelation is similar to apocalyptic writings in several books of the Old Testament: Daniel (chaps. 7–12), Ezekiel (chaps. 37–41), and Zechariah (chaps. 9–12).

The book of Revelation was written about A.D. 95 by the apostle John, one of the twelve disciples of Jesus (see introduction to the

1:9–20. Modern-day Patmos. Exiled on this tiny island off the coast of Turkey, the apostle John wrote the last book in the Bible: Revelation.

1:1–3. John sees one of many visions he experienced on the island of Patmos. Revelation is a collection of those visions.

Gospel of John on p. 229). At this time he was imprisoned by the Roman authorities on Patmos (1:9), a rocky and barren island off the coast of Asia Minor (modern Turkey).

John wrote this book during a time of intense persecution of the Christian movement under the Roman emperor Domitian. The apostle probably used symbolism in his writing to hide the meaning of his message from the Roman enemies of the church. Christian "insiders" understood the images that John used, but the Roman persecutors did not have the "key" that enabled them to decode John's message.

The book of Revelation came to John under divine inspiration through a series of visions. In spite of the persecution that believers were experiencing, John affirmed that the all-powerful Lord would fulfill His promises and accomplish His purpose in history. Jesus Christ would be victorious over the forces of Satan, and He would reign forever as King of kings and Lord of lords.

Summary of Revelation

1:1–3. These verses indicate that the book of Revelation was revealed to the apostle John (Mark 1:17–20) through an angel. But it came directly from the Father through His Son, Jesus Christ. John chose to write this revelation down in the form of a letter. It was probably intended to be read publicly in local congregations.

1:4–8. John addresses this letter to the churches in seven cities that represent the major centers of Christianity in the region of Asia (modern-day Turkey). The theme of his letter is "victory in Jesus." God has guaranteed that His Son, Jesus Christ— "Alpha and Omega, the beginning and the ending" (v. 8)—will reign ultimately over the entire earth (Phil. 2:11).

1:9–20. While in exile on the island of Patmos, John had a vision of the risen Lord. He was told to write down what he saw and to send his message to the seven churches, represented by seven candlesticks. Jesus appeared among these candlesticks; this represented His presence with these congregations. In His hands Jesus held seven stars. These represented "the angels of the seven churches" (v. 20), perhaps angels with responsibility for and authority over these churches.

2:1–7. John writes a specific message to the believers in the church at Ephesus (Acts 19:1–40). Their initial love and enthusiasm for the Lord had cooled, and they needed to rekindle their zeal.

2:8–11. John encourages the church at Smyrna, which was undergoing great persecution. Their faithfulness would be richly rewarded by the Lord.

2:12–17. The church at Pergamos was accused of indulging in idol worship. Unless they repented immediately of their evil, the Lord promised to confront them and to fight against them with the sword of His mouth.

[2:12–17] A STONE FOR THE WINNER. *To him that overcometh will I give...a white stone* (Rev. 2:17).

This imagery of a white stone has been explained in various ways by interpreters: as a badge of acquittal in a legal case, as an expression of welcome by a host to his guests, or as a voting token used by a voter to indicate his choice of a candidate.

Perhaps the most believable explanation is that the apostle John, the author of Revelation, was referring to a white stone given to the winner of an athletic contest. This stone was an admission ticket to the winner's celebration at a later time. This may refer to the time when the faithful, persevering Christian believer will receive his ticket to eternal life and the Lord's great victory celebration in heaven.

2:18–29. Tolerating immorality and false teaching was the problem of the church at Thyatira. This congregation was exhorted to return to the truth.

3:1–6. The believers in the church at Sardis had lost their spiritual zeal. They needed to wake up and "strengthen the things…that are ready to die" (v. 2) so they could bring honor and glory to the Lord.

3:7–13. The church at Philadelphia is the only one of the seven churches that receives no rebuke. In spite of great persecution, this congregation remained faithful to the Lord.

3:14–22. The church at Laodicea is condemned more severely than all the other churches. The problem of these believers was spiritual apathy. They were "neither cold nor hot" (v. 16) about spiritual matters. God promised to deal with this church severely unless they repented of their waywardness.

4:1–11. This chapter describes a vision in which John saw the Lord in heaven, seated on a throne. Seated around the throne were twenty-four elders, representing angels who administered God's rule throughout the universe. The four creatures described as "beasts" (v. 6) were actually seraphim (Isa. 6:1–3), winged beings, or another order of angels who helped to administer the rule of God in the universe. God's unquestioned rule and authority are clear when these twenty-four elders and four seraphim fall down in worship before Him.

5:1–14. This chapter continues John's vision of God seated on a throne. In His hand God holds a book, or scroll, that is sealed with seven wax seals. One of the elders around the throne declares that only the risen Christ—represented by a Lamb—is worthy to remove the seven seals and open the scroll. God hands the scroll to Jesus. This symbolizes that He has delegated to His crucified and risen Son all authority in heaven and earth. The elders and angels who had previously bowed down to God now fall down in adoration and worship at the feet of Jesus.

6:1–8:1. This section of Revelation describes the events of God's judgment represented by the seven seals when Jesus removed them from the scroll. Seals 1 through 4 (6:2–8) show the horrors of war, including famine, devastation, and death. Seal 5 (6:9–11) represents the reward of believers who are martyred for their faith. Seal 6 (6:12–17) shows the earthshaking events that will happen before the second coming of Christ. The opening of the seventh seal (8:1) causes an eerie silence in heaven, as all the earth awaits the coming judgment of the Lord.

Chapter 7 of Revelation is inserted between the opening of seal 6 and seal 7. This chapter describes a great multitude of people who fall down before God and the Lamb in reverence and worship. These people have been redeemed by the Lamb, and they are in God's presence in heaven.

[Chapter 7] **SYMBOLS OF VICTORY AND JOY.** *A great multitude…stood before…the Lamb, clothed with white robes, and palms in their hands* (Rev. 7:9).

The "palms" held by this great multitude of believers were palm branches. These were considered symbols of victory and joy (Lev. 23:40; Neh. 8:15).

Jesus was welcomed on His triumphant entry into Jerusalem by the crowds waving palm branches (John 12:13). In the New Jerusalem, or heaven, believers will acclaim Jesus as the triumphant Lamb or Savior by waving these same symbols of victory and gladness.

8:2–11:19. This section describes the seven trumpet judgments, or God's judgment against the earth and those who have rejected Him. These trumpets are sounded by seven angels.

Trumpet 1 (8:7) brings hail and fire on the earth. Trumpet 2 (8:8–9) brings the destruction of sea life and ships. At the sound of trumpet 3 (8:10–11), a meteorite poisons earth's rivers and streams. Many of the heavenly bodies are darkened with the sounding of trumpet 4 (8:12). Trumpet 5 (9:1–12) brings torment and misery on earth's inhabitants. With trumpet 6 (9:13–21), widespread death occurs. The sounding of the seventh and final trumpet (11:15–19) indicates that the kingdoms of this world will become the kingdoms over which Christ will rule.

10:1–11:14 is inserted between the sounding of trumpets 6 and 7. Chapter 10 reaffirms the call of the apostle John. He is told to eat a book, or scroll. This recalls the experience of the prophet Ezekiel (Ezek. 2:1–3:11).

In Revelation 11:1–14, the apostle John sees the city of Jerusalem trampled for forty-two months. Two unnamed witnesses are raised up by the Lord to prophesy in His name. After their persecution and death, they are resurrected and called up to heaven. Faithfulness in God's service will be rewarded (Matt. 25:14–29).

12:1–17. John sees a vision of a woman who gives birth to a male child. Satan, represented by a red dragon, tries to kill the child. But the child is protected and delivered from harm by the Lord. The message of this chapter is that God will protect His church from Satan's threats.

13:1–18. The vision in this chapter shows that Satan continues his efforts to destroy the church. John sees a beast emerge from the sea. He is the Antichrist, the archenemy of Christ, who is determined to destroy the church and all who follow the risen Lord.

John also sees a second beast emerge from the earth. As a servant of the first beast, he uses miraculous signs and economic threats to try to turn believers away from loyalty to Christ and to convince them to worship the Antichrist. The symbol for this second beast is the number 666. Six was the number for evil, so triple sixes shows that this beast was thoroughly evil in his personality and intentions.

14:1–20. Several short visions of John are recorded in this chapter. He sees the Lamb, Jesus Christ (John 1:36), who has returned to earth and is standing with a multitude of the redeemed on Mount Zion. John also sees several angels, who deliver messages of encouragement to God's people in the midst of persecution and assure them that doom is coming for those who worship the beast.

15:1–16:21. Different aspects of God's judgment have already been revealed through the seven seals (6:1–8:1) and the seven trumpets (8:2–11:19). In this section, yet an-

---

[15:1–16:21] THE NUMBER SEVEN. *And I [John the apostle] saw another sign in heaven...seven angels having the seven last plagues* (Rev. 15:1).

The Jewish people thought of seven as a sacred number. It is used often in the Bible to show fullness, completion, and perfection (Gen. 2:2–3; Dan. 9:25).

The apostle John uses the number seven throughout the book of Revelation: seven churches (1:4), seven stars (2:1), seven lamps (4:5), seven seals (5:1), seven angels with seven trumpets (8:2), seven thunders (10:4), a beast with seven heads (13:1), seven vials, or bowls (17:1), and seven kings (17:10).

By using this number, John declared that God will bring about His perfect judgment in the end-time. All believers will participate in the full and complete victory of Christ over the forces of evil.

8:2–11:19. Most trumpet blasts that John wrote about in Revelation signaled monumental events, usually disasters and plagues. Christians, however, look forward to the day when "the Lord himself shall descend from heaven with a shout, with the voice of the archangel, and with the trump of God" (1 Thess. 4:16).

[19:11–21] A KING WITH MANY CROWNS. *His [the reigning Christ's] eyes were as a flame of fire, and on his head were many crowns* (Rev. 19:12).

John borrowed this imagery from the custom of kings who ruled over more than one country. They would wear several crowns to represent all the nations under their control. For example, the kings of Egypt wore a two-in-one crown to represent the unification of Upper and Lower Egypt under their rule.

To the apostle John in this verse, the many crowns worn by Jesus show His universal reign as Savior and Lord throughout the world. The hymn writer expressed it like this:

> Crown Him with many crowns,
>   The Lamb upon His throne;
> Hark! How the heavenly anthem drowns
>   All music but its own!
>
> Awake, my soul, and sing
>   Of Him who died for thee;
> And hail Him as thy matchless King
>   Thro all eternity.
>
> —Matthew Bridges, "Crown Him with Many Crowns"

other dimension of His judgment is communicated through John's vision of the seven vials (cups or bowls) of God's wrath poured out on the earth by seven angels. These events happen when the contents of the bowls are poured out: Sores break out on the followers of the beast (bowl 1; 16:2); all sea creatures die (bowl 2; 16:3); fresh waters of the earth turn to blood (bowl 3; 16:4–7); the sun scorches the earth (bowl 4; 16:8–9); darkness and suffering strike the earth (bowl 5; 16:10–11); the Euphrates River dries up (bowl 6; 16:12); and storms and a great earthquake devastate the land (bowl 7; 16:17–18). These bowl judgments give a graphic picture of the wrath of God poured out against unbelievers and an evil world.

17:1–18. In this vision John sees a despicable prostitute seated on a scarlet beast. Her name is Babylon, probably a code name symbolizing the forces of evil that are arrayed against God and the forces of righteousness. She was responsible for the continuing persecution of God's people. An angel explains to John that the beast on which she is seated is the Antichrist.

18:1–24. This vision is a continuation of John's vision in chapter 17. An angel appears and shouts, "Babylon the great is fallen" (v. 2). To John the term *Babylon* symbolized all the evil forces of the world that were allied against God. The Lord has won the victory over Babylon, but pride, idolatry, and immorality have also contributed to its downfall.

19:1–5. The twenty-four elders and the four seraphim around God's throne (see Rev. 4:1–11) fall down and worship God. Thanksgiving is offered for the destruction of Babylon.

19:6–10. John portrays the relationship with Christ that believers would soon begin to experience in terms of a marriage. Christ is the Lamb (Acts 8:32), and the church is His bride (Eph. 5:25–33), and "blessed are they which are called unto the marriage supper of the Lamb" (v. 9).

19:11–21. As "KING OF KINGS, AND LORD OF LORDS" (v. 16), Jesus will return to earth in victory. In a final battle against the forces of evil, He will defeat the Antichrist and the beast that worships him (see Rev. 13:1–18). Then He will cast them alive into "a lake of fire burning with brimstone" (v. 20).

20:1–15. Looking into the future, John predicts the events of the final days. Satan will be bound and sealed up in the bottomless pit for a period of one thousand years. Then he will be released to work his deception among the nations for a time. Finally, he will be defeated and cast into the lake of fire and brimstone to suffer eternally, along with the Antichrist and the beast. After this the great white throne judgment will occur. The unredeemed—those people whose names do not appear in the Book of Life—will also be cast into the lake of fire.

21:1–8. John foresees that believers will enter a final state of blessedness characterized by a new heaven and a new earth. Grief and pain will be no more. God will live among His people, and they will enjoy continuous fellowship with Him.

21:9–22:5. John's final vision is of the heavenly Jerusalem, where believers will live in the eternal state with God and His Son. No temple exists in this city, "for the Lord God Almighty and the Lamb are the temple of it" (21:22). Its gates are never shut at night as a security measure, because night and darkness do not exist. A river of pure water, representing the water of life (John 7:38), issues from God's throne. Along this river grows the tree of life. John is describing spiritual realities with physical metaphors that his readers could understand.

22:6–21. John concludes Revelation by stating that he has reported accurately the prophecies that God has revealed to him in a series of visions. He urges his readers to remain faithful to the One who is "Alpha and Omega, the beginning and the end, the first and the last" (v. 13; see Rev. 1:8). Thus, the Bible comes to a close with an affirmation of the supremacy of the Lord Jesus Christ.

Maps

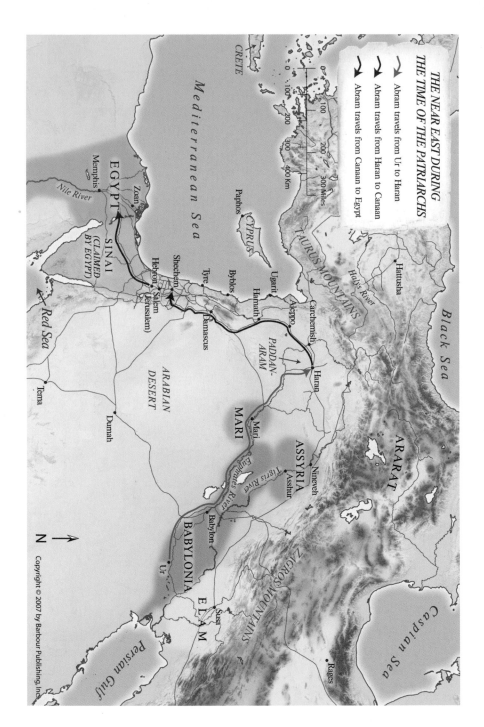

THE NEAR EAST DURING
THE TIME OF THE PATRIARCHS

Abram travels from Ur to Haran

Abram travels from Haran to Canaan

Abram travels from Canaan to Egypt

0   100   200   300   400 Km

0   100   200   300 Miles

N →

Copyright © 2007 by Barbour Publishing, Inc.

Mediterranean Sea

CRETE

CYPRUS

Paphos

Black Sea

Caspian Sea

TAURUS MOUNTAINS

Halys River

Hattusha

ARARAT

Nineveh

Asshur

ASSYRIA

ZAGROS MOUNTAINS

Raga

Susa

ELAM

Ur

Babylon

BABYLONIA

Euphrates River

Tigris River

Mari

MARI

Haran

PADDAN-
ARAM

Aleppo

Carchemish

Ugarit

Hamath

Byblos

Tyre

Damascus

Shechem

Hebron

Salem
(Jerusalem)

*ARABIAN
DESERT*

Dumah

Tema

Red Sea

Persian Gulf

SINAI
(CLAIMED
BY EGYPT)

Zoan

Nile River

Memphis

EGYPT

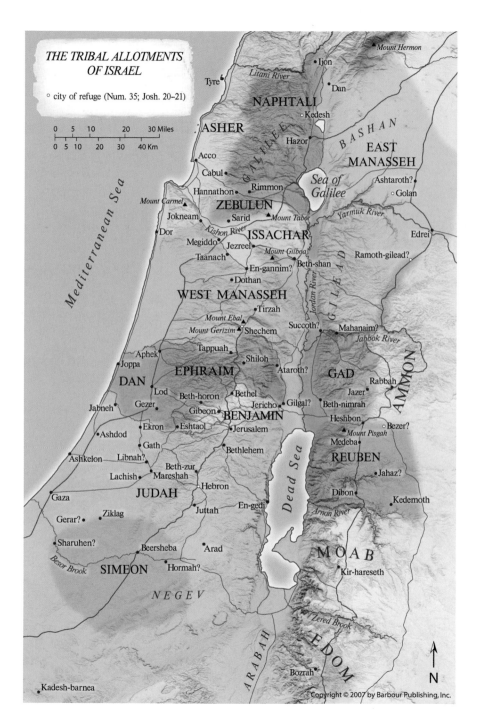

THE TRIBAL ALLOTMENTS
OF ISRAEL

○ city of refuge (Num. 35; Josh. 20–21)

0   5   10   20   30 Miles
0 5 10   20   30   40 Km

Mediterranean Sea

Mount Hermon

Ijon

Tyre

Litani River

Dan

NAPHTALI

Kedesh

ASHER

Hazor

B A S H A N

Acco

EAST
MANASSEH

Cabul

Ashtaroth?

Hannathon   Rimmon

*Sea of
Galilee*

Golan

Mount Carmel

ZEBULUN

Yarmuk River

Jokneam   Sarid   *Mount Tabor*

Kishon River

Edrei

Dor

ISSACHAR

Megiddo   Jezreel

Mount Gilboa

Ramoth-gilead?

Taanach

En-gannim?   Beth-shan

Dothan

G I L E A D

WEST MANASSEH

Tirzah

Jordan River

Mount Ebal

Succoth?

Mahanaim?

Mount Gerizim   Shechem

Jabbok River

Tappuah

Shiloh

Aphek

Joppa

EPHRAIM

Ataroth?

GAD

A M M O N

DAN

Lod

Bethel

Rabbah

Beth-horon

Jazer

Jabneh   Gezer   Gibeon

Jericho   Gilgal?   Beth-nimrah

Ekron   Eshtaol

BENJAMIN

Heshbon

Bezer?

Ashdod

Jerusalem

Mount Pisgah

Gath

Medeba

Ashkelon   Libnah?

Bethlehem

REUBEN

Lachish   Beth-zur

Mareshah

Dead Sea

Jahaz?

Gaza

Hebron

Dibon

Kedemoth

En-gedi

JUDAH

Juttah

Arnon River

Gerar?   Ziklag

Sharuhen?

M O A B

Besor Brook

Beersheba   Arad

SIMEON   Hormah?

Kir-hareseth

N E G E V

A R A B A H

Zered Brook

E D O M

Bozrah

↑
N

Kadesh-barnea

Copyright © 2007 by Barbour Publishing, Inc.

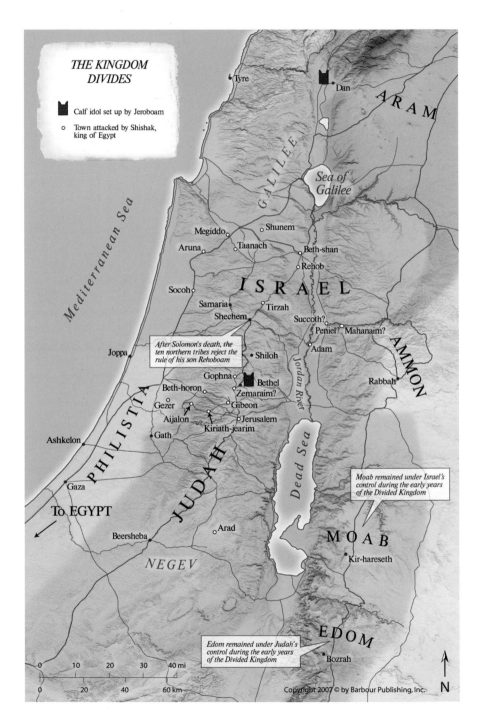

THE KINGDOM DIVIDES

■ Calf idol set up by Jeroboam

○ Town attacked by Shishak, king of Egypt

Tyre

Dan

A R A M

GALILEE

Sea of Galilee

Mediterranean Sea

Megiddo

Shunem

Aruna

Taanach

Beth-shan

Rehob

Socoh

I S R A E L

Samaria

Tirzah

Shechem

Succoth?

Peniel? Mahanaim?

Adam

After Solomon's death, the ten northern tribes reject the rule of his son Rehoboam

Joppa

Shiloh

Gophna

Bethel

Beth-horon

Zemaraim?

Gezer

Gibeon

AMMON

Rabbah

Aijalon

Jerusalem

Kiriath-jearim

Ashkelon

Gath

P H I L I S T I A

Jordan River

Gaza

J U D A H

Dead Sea

Moab remained under Israel's control during the early years of the Divided Kingdom

TO EGYPT

Arad

M O A B

Beersheba

N E G E V

Kir-hareseth

Edom remained under Judah's control during the early years of the Divided Kingdom

Bozrah

E D O M

0   10   20   30   40 mi

0   20   40   60 km

Copyright 2007 © by Barbour Publishing, Inc.

N

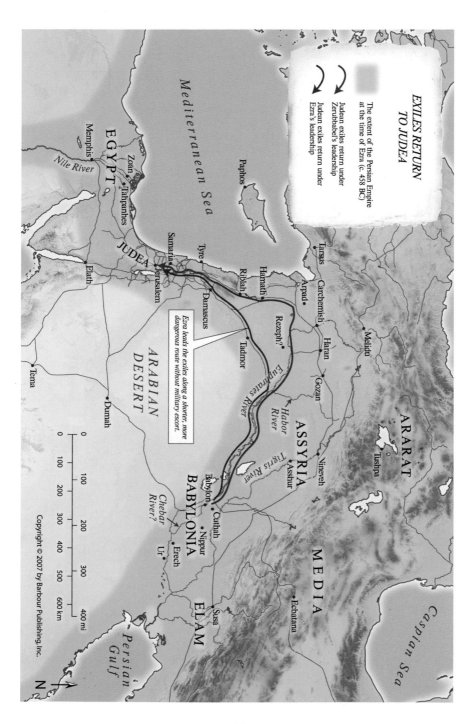

EXILES RETURN TO JUDEA

The extent of the Persian Empire at the time of Ezra (c. 458 BC)

Judean exiles return under Zerubbabel's leadership

Judean exiles return under Ezra's leadership

Ezra leads the exiles along a shorter, more dangerous route without military escort.

Mediterranean Sea

EGYPT
Memphis
Nile River
Zoan
Tahpanhes

JUDEA
Elath
Samaria
Jerusalem
Tyre
Paphos
Tarsus
Carchemish
Arpad
Hamath
Riblah
Damascus
Tadmor
Rezeph?
Haran
Gozan
Melidi

ARABIAN DESERT
Tema
Dumah

Euphrates River
Habor River
Tigris River
ASSYRIA
Asshur
Nineveh
Tushpa
ARARAT

BABYLONIA
Babylon
Cuthah
Nippur
Ur
Erech
Chebar River?

ELAM
Susa
Ecbatana
MEDIA

Caspian Sea

Persian Gulf

N

0   100   200   300   400   500   600 km
0   100   200   300   400 mi

Copyright © 2007 by Barbour Publishing, Inc.

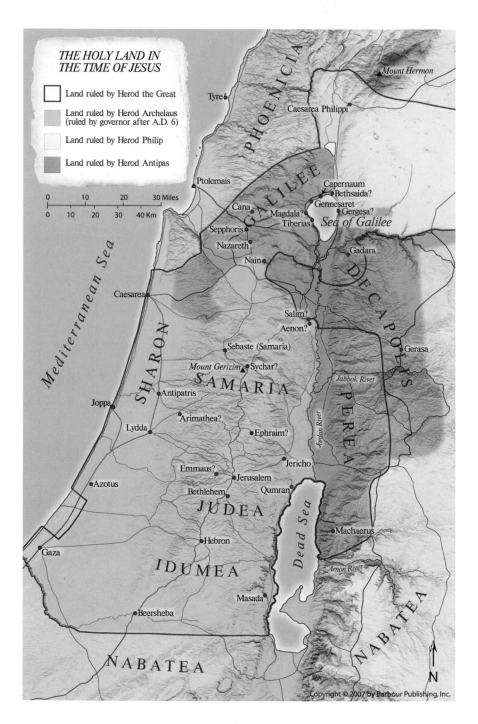

THE HOLY LAND IN
THE TIME OF JESUS

Land ruled by Herod the Great

Land ruled by Herod Archelaus
(ruled by governor after A.D. 6)

Land ruled by Herod Philip

Land ruled by Herod Antipas

0   10   20   30 Miles

0   10   20   30   40 Km

Mediterranean Sea

PHOENICIA

Tyre

Caesarea Philippi

Mount Hermon

Ptolemais

GALILEE

Cana

Magdala?

Sepphoris

Nazareth

Nain

Capernaum
Bethsaida?
Gennesaret
Gergesa?
Tiberias

Sea of Galilee

Gadara

DECAPOLIS

Caesarea

Salim?

Aenon?

Sebaste (Samaria)

Mount Gerizim Sychar?

SHARON

SAMARIA

Jabbok River

Gerasa

PEREA

Antipatris

Joppa

Arimathea?

Lydda

Ephraim?

Jordan River

Emmaus?

Jericho

Azotus

Jerusalem

Bethlehem

Qumran

JUDEA

Dead Sea

Hebron

Machaerus

Gaza

IDUMEA

Arnon River

Masada

Beersheba

NABATEA

NABATEA

N

Copyright © 2007 by Barbour Publishing, Inc.

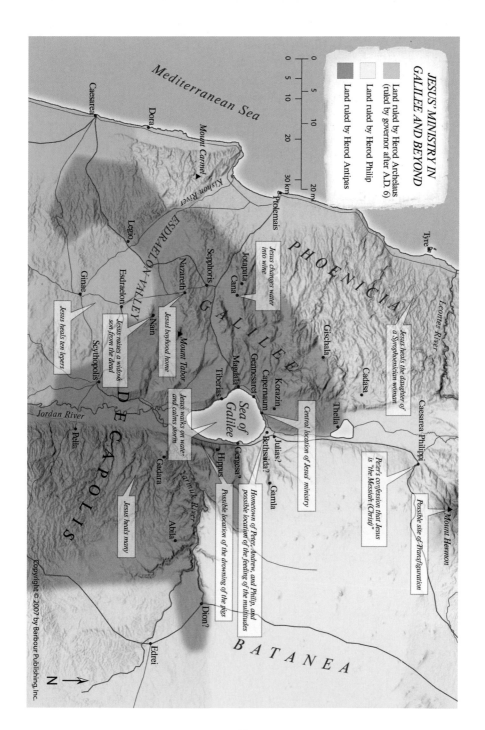

JESUS' MINISTRY IN GALILEE AND BEYOND

Land ruled by Herod Archelaus (ruled by governor after A.D. 6)
Land ruled by Herod Philip
Land ruled by Herod Antipas

Mediterranean Sea

Caesarea
Dora
Mount Carmel
Kishon River
Legio
ESDRAELON-VALLEY
Ginae
Esdraelon
Scythopolis
Jordan River
Pella
DECAPOLIS
Yarmuk River
Gadara
Abila
Edrei
BATANEA
Dion?

Nazareth
Nain
Mount Tabor
Sepphoris
Jotapata
Cana
Jesus changes water into wine
GALILEE
Gischala
PHOENICIA
Tyre
Ptolemais
Leontes River
Caesarea Philippi
Cadasa
Thella
Gamla
Julias?
Bethsaida?
Gergesa?
Hippus
Magdala
Gennesaret
Tiberias
Capernaum
Korazin
Sea of Galilee
Mount Hermon

Jesus heals the daughter of a Syrophoenician woman
Peter's confession that Jesus is "the Messiah (Christ)"
Possible site of Transfiguration
Central location of Jesus' ministry
Hometown of Peter, Andrew, and Philip, and possible location of the feeding of the multitudes
Possible location of the drowning of the pigs
Jesus walks on water and calms storm
Jesus boyhood home
Jesus raises a widow's son from the dead
Jesus heals ten lepers
Jesus heals many

N

321

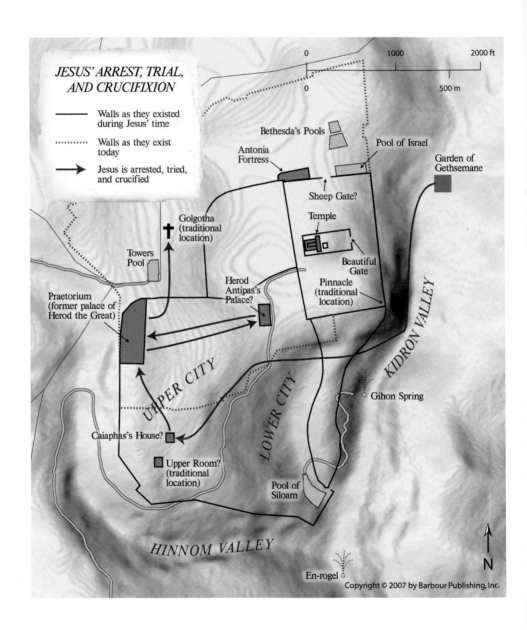

JESUS' ARREST, TRIAL, AND CRUCIFIXION

——— Walls as they existed during Jesus' time

·········· Walls as they exist today

⟶ Jesus is arrested, tried, and crucified

0   1000   2000 ft

0   500 m

Bethesda's Pools

Pool of Israel

Antonia Fortress

Garden of Gethsemane

Sheep Gate?

Golgotha (traditional location)

Temple

Towers Pool

Herod Antipas's Palace?

Beautiful Gate

Pinnacle (traditional location)

Praetorium (former palace of Herod the Great)

KIDRON VALLEY

UPPER CITY

Gihon Spring

LOWER CITY

Caiaphas's House?

Upper Room? (traditional location)

Pool of Siloam

HINNOM VALLEY

En-rogel

N

Copyright © 2007 by Barbour Publishing, Inc.

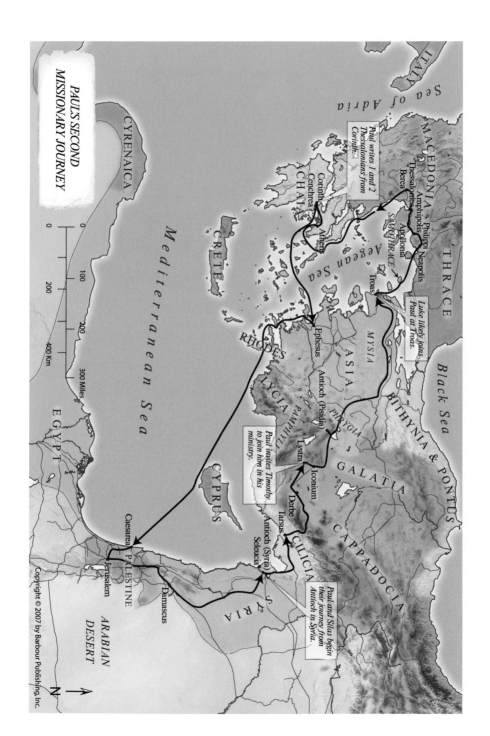

PAUL'S SECOND
MISSIONARY JOURNEY

CYRENAICA

Mediterranean Sea

CRETE

RHODES

LYCIA

CYPRUS

EGYPT

Caesarea

PALESTINE

Jerusalem

Damascus

ARABIAN
DESERT

SYRIA

Antioch (Syria)
Seleucia

Tarsus

CILICIA

Derbe

Iconium

Lystra

PHRYGIA

PAMPHYLIA

Antioch (Pisidia)

GALATIA

CAPPADOCIA

BITHYNIA & PONTUS

Black Sea

ASIA

MYSIA

Ephesus

Troas

Aegean Sea

SAMOTHRACE

ACHAIA

Corinth
Cenchrea

Athens

Berea

Thessalonica

Apollonia

Amphipolis

Philippi
Neapolis

MACEDONIA

THRACE

Sea of Adria

ITALY

N

Paul writes 1 and 2
Thessalonians from
Corinth.

Luke likely joins
Paul at Troas.

Paul invites Timothy
to join him in his
ministry.

Paul and Silas begin
their journey from
Antioch in Syria.

0   100   200   300 Miles
0   100   200   300   400 Km

Copyright © 2007 by Barbour Publishing, Inc.

323

Index

KEY:

Regular type—subject mentioned
Italic type—image

A

Aaron
  death of, 37; descendants of, 28, 30, 34, 37; appointed/consecrated, 27, 29, 30, 31, 36; lineage of, 35, 85; requirements for, 216; Moses' assistant, 24, 25, 26; sins of, 28, 35, 37
Abarim Mountains, 43
Abdon, 53
Abed-nego/Abednego/Azariah, 159, 160, *160,* 161
Abel, 18, 29
Abiathar, 63, 66, 71
Abigail, 61
Abihu, 30
Abijah/Abijam/Abia, 74, 91
Abimelech, king of Gerar, 20
Abimelech, son of Gideon, 52
Abinadab, 64, 86
Abiram, 36
Abishai, 67
Abner, 63, 64, 71
Abraham
  children, 19, 20; God's covenant with, 18, 19, 20, 21, 25, 26; and God's acts, 120; faith of, 189, 253, 266, 291; inferior to Jesus, 233; obedient to God, 19, 289; promises to, 173, 179, 185; wife Sarah, 19, 20
Abram. *See* Abraham
Absalom/Abishalom, 63, 66, 67, 68, 116
Achan, 46
Achish, 61, 62, 116
Acts of the Apostles, book of, 214, 215, 237, 238–249
Adam, 84. *See also* Eve
  creation of, *17,* 18, 66; in genealogy of Jesus, 218; sin of, 17–18, 253
Adar, 107
Adonijah, 70
Adoption, 254, *255*
Agabus, 243, 247
Agag, 59
Agrippa. *See* Herod
Agur, 124
Ahab, 75–76
  alliance with Jehoshaphat, 92; battles of, 76; death of, 93; end of dynasty, 79, *79;* and Naboth, 76; and pagan worship, 75
Ahasuerus, 105, 106, 107, 186
Ahaz, 77, 81, 94, 136, 173
Ahazariah. *See* Uzziah
Ahaziah, son of Ahab, 76, 77
Ahaziah, son of Jehoram, 79, 80, 93
Ahijah, 73

Ahimaaz, 67

Ahimelech, 61

Ahithophel, 116

Aholiab, 27

Ai, 46

Alexander the Great, 162

Alexandria, 246

Alphabet, 122

Amalekite(s), 27, 51, 59, 62, 65, 86

Amasa, 67, 68, 71

Amaziah, 80, 93, 169

Ammonite(s)
    oppose Israel, 52, 59, 65, 66, 86, 93;
    prophecies against, 150, 168

Amnon, 66

Amon, 82, 94

Amorite(s), 45

Amos, 91, 163, 168

Amos, book of, 168–169

Ananias, 241, 242

Anathoth, 144, 147

Andrew, disciple, 190, 206, 230

Angels
    at Ascension, 239; bring judgment,
    313; carry messages, 51, 309, 311,
    312; inferior to Jesus, 288, 289; not
    to be worshiped, 273; surround God's
    throne, 310, 313

Anna, 217

Annas, 234

Anointing, 60

Antichrist, 277, 300, 301, 313, 314

Antioch of Pisidia, 244

Antioch of Syria, 243, 245, 246, 266

Apis, 26

Apollos, 246, 257, 288

Apostle(s). *See also* Disciple(s)

Aquila, 246, 247, 255, 261, 284, 286

Arabia, 137

Ariel, 138

Ark, Noah's, 18, *19*

Ark of the covenant/Ark of the
    testimony
    crossing Jordan, 46, 58, 59; and
    Jerusalem, 64, 66, 85; places kept,
    86; in temple, 72, 90; and Ten
    Commandments, 40

Armor of God, 269

Artaxerxes 98, 99, 100

Asa, 74, 91, 92

Ascension of Christ. *See* Jesus Christ

Ashdod, 59

Asher, son of Jacob, 12, 34, 43, 48, 51, 85

Asia, 246, 247, 296

Asia Minor, 304, 309

Assyria, *119,* 135, 136, 137, 138, 163,
    165, 172
    cruelty in warfare 83, 175, *175,* 176;
    defeat of Northern Kingdom (Israel),
    44, 77, 81, 174; Nineveh, 171, *175;*
    prophecies concerning, 175, 176, 179

Astrologer, 140

Athaliah, 80, 92, 93
Athens, 246, 275, 292
Athletics, 258, 292, 309
Atonement 29, 30, 35
Atonement, Day of, 31
Azariah/Ahaziah, 80, 93

B
Baal, 51, 52, 70, 75, 79, 165
Baasha, 74, 92
Babel, Tower of, 12, 19
Babylon, 313
Babylonia/Babylonian Empire. *See also*
    Exile, Babylonian/Persian
    and astrology, 140; conquers Assyria,
    119, 175; conquers Egypt, 150;
    conquest/captivity of Judah (captives
    made, 83, 96; and Daniel, 159; as
    God's judgment, 142–143, 174,
    177–178; and Hezekiah, 82, 94,
    139; and Jeremiah; and Jerusalem,
    77, 100, 182; and Joel, 166; and
    Obadiah, 170; psalms of, 118, 119;
    return from, 44); judgment of, 137;
    prophecy concerning, 150, 161;
    tower of Babel, 19
Balaam, 37
Balak/Balac, 37
Barak, 50, 51
Barbarian, 252
Bar-jesus, 244

Barnabas, 205, 241, 242, 243, 244, 245,
    266, 288
Bartimaeus, 210
Baruch, 148, *149,* 150
Bashan, 40, 168
Bath-sheba/Bathsheba, 65, 66, 71, 117
Beatitudes, the, 192
Beer-sheba, 20, 21
Belial, 126
Belshazzar, 161
Benedictus, 216
Ben-hadad, 80
Ben-hadad I, 92
Ben-hadad II, 76, 79
Benjamin, 21, 22, 23, 34, 48, 54, 59, 60,
    85
Berea/Beroea, 246
Bethel, 21, 73, 74, 79
Beth-horon, 90
Bethlehem, 56, 173
    birthplace of Jesus, 173, 174, 189–
    190, 216
Bethsaida, 193, 208
Beth-shan, 119
Betrayal. *See* Judas Iscariot
Bezaleel, 27
Bildad, 110–112
Bithynia, 246, 296
Blasphemy, 31
Boanerges, 205
Boaz, 55, 56

Bride, 313
Burning bush, 24, 25

C

Caesar Augustus, 216
Caesarea, 247, 248
Caesarea-Philippi, 197
Caiaphas, 234
Cain, 18
Caleb, 33, 36, 47, 50
Calvary, 226
Cana, 231
Canaan, land of, 19, 23, 31, 33, 36, 38, 39, 40, 41, 42, 44, 45, 47, 49
Canaan, son of Ham, 19
Canaanites, 25, 33, 37, 38, 39, 43, 35, 45, 46, 47, 48, 49, 50, 51
Candace, 242
Capernaum, 190, 191, 193, 206, 218, 231
Cappadocia, 296
Captivity. *See* Exile, Babylonian/Persian; Israel, enslaved by Egypt
Carmel, Mount, 75, *75*
Cephas. *See* Peter
Cherith, 75
Children, training of, 127
Chorazin, 193
Christ. *See* Jesus Christ
Chronicles, books of, 44, 70, 84–88, 89–96
Chushan-Rishathaim, 50

Cilicia, 245
Circumcision, 19, 46, *267*
Claudius Lysias, 248
Coliseum, *251*
Colosse/Colossae, 273, 286
Colossians, epistle to the, 250, 273–274, 279
Commandment(s)/Commands. *See* Ten Commandments
Communion. *See* Lord's Supper
Coniah/Jehoiachin, 146
Corinth, 246, *256*, 257, 275, 277
Corinthians, epistles to the, 250, 256–261, 262–526, 279
Cornelius, 243
Covenant, new, 187
Creation, 16, 17, 18
Crete, 249, 285
Cross, 114, *212*
Crown, 293
Crucifixion, 182, 202, 203, *212*, 213, 234. *See also* Jesus Christ, crucifixion
Cymbals, 87, 88, 123
Cyprus, 244, 245
Cyrus, 96, 97, 140

D

Dagon, 54
Damascus, 46, 50, 137, 150, 168, 238, 242, 250, 264, 265
Dan, city of, 73, 79

Dan, tribe of. *See* Tribes of Israel, Dan

Daniel, 131, 161

Daniel, book of, 134, 159–162, 163, 307

Darius, 98, 161, 182

Dathan, 36

David

ancestry of, 56; anointed king, 116; and ark of the covenant, 86; battles of, 64, 65; city of, 138; death of, 70, 71; descendants of, 85; Doeg's betrayal of, 117; eternal kingdom promised, 63, 64, 84, 86, 90, 122, 147; family problems, 63, 65, 66, 67, 68, 115; God's covenant with, 120; kingdom of, 44, 57, 63, 64, 69, 153, 85, 221; "mighty men" of, 69, 85; as musician, 68, *87,* 113, 115; and Saul (pursuit by, 61, 62, 115, 118, 122, 232; service to, 60, 61); son, Solomon, 70, 84, 124; and torture, 291; wife, Bathsheba, 63, 65, 66, 117

Day of the Lord, 167, 179, 186, 277

Dead, treatment of the, 91, 119

Deborah, prophetess, 49, 50, 51

Decalogue. *See* Ten Commandments

Delilah, 53

Demetrius, church leader, 304

Demetrius, silversmith, 247

Derbe, 244, 245

Deuteronomy, book of, 39–43

Diana, 247

Dinah, 21

Diotrephes, 304

Disciple(s), 190, 192, 193, 206, 218, 229, 230. *See also* Apostle(s)

Dispersion. *See also* Exile, Babylonian/ Persian

Doeg, 117

Dome of the Rock, 226

Domitian, 309

Donkeys, 53, 59, 257

Dorcas, 243

Dreams/visions 22, 140, 161

Drought, 22, 75

E

Earthquake, 204, 246, 313

Ebed-melech, 148, 150

Ecclesiastes, book of, 124, 129–131

Eden, Garden of, 17, 18, 253

Edom/Esau. *See* Esau

Edomites

defeat of, 185; oppose Israel/Judah, 37, 65, 86, 93, 94; prophecies against, 137, 150, 152, 168, 170

Eglon, 50

Egypt

alliance with Israel 131, 138; enslaves Israel, 24, 25, 26, 27, 35, 40, 121, 143, 165, 167; holy family flees to, 190; opposes Judah, 83, 91, 95, 96; prophecies against, 137, 150

Ehud, 50

Elah, king of Israel, 74

Eleazar, 37, 38

Eli, 58, 126

Eliakim, 83, 96

Elihu, 112

Elijah, 70, 75, 76, 77, 78, 79, 89, 93, 186, 302

Elimelech, 55, 56

Eliphaz, 110–112

Elisabeth, 215, 216

Elisha, 75, 77, 78, 79, 80, 89

Emmaus, 213, 228

End-times, 158, 159, 310, 311

Epaphras, 273

Epaphroditus, 271, 272

Ephesians, epistle to the, 250, 268–269

Ephesus, 246, 247, 268, 281, 300, 304, 309

Ephraim, son of Joseph, 22, 23, 34, 48, 52, 85

Ephron, 20

Esau, 20, 21, 22, 84, 170

Esther, 104, *104,* 105, 106, 107

Esther, book of, 44, 104–107

Ethiopia, 92, 137, 179

Eunuch, 105, 347

Euphrates River, 72, 144, 313

Eutychus, 247

Eve, 17, 18. *See also* Adam

Evil, 109

Exile, Babylonian/Persian, 84, 104, 162, 170, 153

psalms of, 118, 120, 122; return from, 89, 163 (and book of Ezra, 97–98; and book of Haggai, 180; and book of Malachi, 185; and book of Zechariah, 182; and priests' duties, *103;* and restoration, 140)

Exodus, 27, 39, 120, 121

Exodus, book of, 24–28

Ezekiel, 311

Ezekiel, book of, 134, 153–158, 163, 307

Ezra, 84, 89, 97, 98, 99, *99,* 102

Ezra, book of, 44, 97–99, 100

F

Famine, 22, 23, 24, 55, 243, 263, 310

Fasting, 66, 99, 140, 162, 167, 174, 184 by Pharisees 224; Jesus' teaching on, 192–193, 206

Felix, 248

Festus, 248, 249

Fiery furnace, *160,* 161

Fig, 146, 169, 174, 199, 211, *222*

Flood, the, 18, 19

Fox, 152

Fruit of the Spirit, 267

G

Gabriel, 162, 215, 216

Gad, 34, 38, 40, 45, 47, 48, 85

Galatia, 246, 296

Galatians, epistle to, 250, 265–267

Galilee, Sea of, 194, 208, *209,* 231, 236

Gamaliel, 241

Gath, 61, 62

Gaza, 168

Gedaliah, 83, 150

Gehazi, 78

Genesis, book of, 17–23, 25, 82, 95, 102, 132

Gennesaret, 208

Gentile(s), 223, 244, 245, 268–269

Gershon, 34, 35, 48

Gethsemane, Garden of, 201, 212, 226, 234

Gibeah/Gibeath, 54

Gibeon, 71, 89

Gibeonites, 46, 68

Gideon, 51, 52

Gifts, spiritual, 254, 260, 269

Gihon, 71

Gilboa, Mount, 62, 85

Gilead, 53

Gilgal, 46, 59

Gleaning, 55

Gluttony, 260

Gnostics/Gnosticism, 303

God

covenant with, 16, 19, 20, 21, 25, 26; as Creator, 112, 123, 140, 253; and David, 64, 72, 86, 90; forgiveness of, 301; glory of, 115; laws of, 24, 27, 29, 30, 39, 40, 46; love of, 300, 301; and Moses, 24–28, 33, 34, 36, 37, 39, 40, 41, 45; omnipotence, 112; omnipresence, 234; omniscience, 109, 122; righteousness of, 253; as rock, 118; as Shepherd, 115, 132; as shield, 116; and Solomon, 71, 72, 90; source of comfort, 262; source of wisdom, 124; sovereignty of, 119; visions of, 131; and wisdom, 128, 257

Golden calf, 28, *28,* 79

Golgotha, 202, 213, 226, 234

Goliath, 60, 61, 86

Gomer, 164

Gomorrah/Gomorrha, 19, 136

Gospel, the, 117, 133, 142
Paul and, 262, 263, 264, 265, 269, 271, 273, 275, 277, 279, 280; preaching of, 136, 192, 193; rejected by Jews, 254

Gospels, 188, 189–204, 205–213, 214–228, 229–236. *See also* John, writings of; Luke, Gospel of; Mark, Gospel of; Matthew, Gospel of

Greece, 247

H

Habakkuk, book of, 177–178

Habakkuk, prophet, 163, 177

Hadad, 73

Hadarezer, 86

Hadassah, 105. *See also* Esther

Hadrian, 294

Haggai, book of, 180–181

Haggai, prophet, 98, 163, 180, 182, 185

Ham, son of Noah, 84

Haman, 105, 106, 107

Hanani, prophet, 92

Hananiah, false prophet, 147

Handwriting on the wall, 161

Hannah, 58

Hanun, 65

Harod Spring, *51*

Hazael, king of Syria, 79, 80

Hazor, city, 150

Healing, 333

Hebrews, epistle to the, 287, 288–292

Hebron, 47, 53, 63, 64, 66, 85

Heman, 88

Herod, Agrippa I 243, 244

Herod, Agrippa II 248, 249

Herod Philip, 193, 196, 226

Herod the Great, 190, 220, 223, 226

Herodians, 199, 211

Herodias, 196, 208

Hezekiah/Ezekias, 77, 81, 82, 94, 110, 138, 139, 173, 179

Hiddekel River, 162

Hiram of Tyre, 64, 72, 86, 89

Hizkiah, 179

Hobab. *See* Jethro

Holy Ghost. *See* Holy Spirit

Holy Spirit

    believers as temple of, 267, 258; in birth of Jesus, 190, 215; blasphemy against, 221; in early church, 237; empowers believers, 238–239; guides believers, 234, 246; in life of Jesus, 214; interprets scripture, 257; lives in believers, 257; at Pentecost, 167, 239, 240; received in salvation, 243, 269, 277

Hophni, 58

Hor, Mount, 37

Horeb, Mount, 75

Hosea/Osee, 163, 164, 168

Hosea, book of, 164–165

Hoshea, 81

Huldah, 82

Huram. *See* Hiram

Hushai, 66

I

Ibzan, 53

Ichabod, 58

Iconium, 244

Idol(s), 41, 50, 52, 258–259, 260, 275

Isaac, 84

Isaiah, book of, 134, *135,* 135–141

Isaiah, prophet, 61, 81, 135, 136, 142, 163

Ish-bosheth/Esh-Baal, 63, 64

Ishmael, 105, 84

Israel
    enslaved by Egypt, 24–27, 35, 40,
    121, 143, 165, 167; *See also* Exile;
    kings of, 57, 59; rules for, 24, 27, 29,
    30, 39, 40, 46; sins of, 37, 39, 50, 52,
    79, 81, 119; *See* Tribes of Israel; as
    vine, 119

Israel (Northern Kingdom), 63, 76, 78,
    79, 135, 164, 168, 169, 173
    falls to Assyria, 44, 77, 163, 164, 165,
    174; punishment foretold, 165, 174;
    sins of, 70, 74, 77, 139, 162, 168;
    splits from Judah, 70, 73, 80, 90, 94

Israelites. *See also* Israel; Israel (Northern
    Kingdom)

Issachar. *See* Tribes of Israel

Issachar, 48, 85

J

Jackal, 152

Jacob
    death of, 23, 67; descendants of,
    18, 21, 22, 24, 25, 84; and Esau/
    Edom, 20, 21, 22, 170; faith of, 290;
    renamed Israel, 21; wife, Leah, 21;
    wife, Rachel, 21

Jael, 51

Jair, 52

Jairus, 220

James, apostle, 190, 197, 198, 206, 210,

218, 220, 229, 243, 265

James, epistle of, 287, 293–295

James, half brother of Jesus, 245, 293,
    306

James, son of Alphaeus, 204

Japheth, 84

Jebus, 85

Jebusite(s), 64, 69, 85

Jeconiah/Coniah/Jehoiachm, 83, 96,
    146, 147

Jehoahaz, 79, 80

Jehoahaz. *See* Ahaziah

Jehoahaz/Shallum, 83, 95, 96

Jehoiachin. *See* Jeconiah

Jehoiada, 80, 93

Jehoiakim/Eliakim, 83, 96, 143, 146,
    147, 148

Jehoram/Joram, king of Israel, 76, 77,
    78, 79, 93

Jehoshaphat/Josaphat, 74, 76, 79, 92, 93

Jehu, king of Israel, 79, *79,* 80, 81, 93

Jehu, prophet, 74

Jephthah/Jephthae, 52, 53

Jeremiah/Jeremias/Jeremy, 91
    beaten, 146; forbidden to marry, 145;
    as prophet, 142–143, 163 (weeping
    prophet, 144, 151); threatened by
    the wicked, 144, 146

Jeremiah, book of, 134, 142–150

Jericho, 46, *47,* 210, 224

Jeroboam, 70, 73, 74, 77, 79, 90, 126

Jeroboam II, 80, 81, 171

Jerusalem, 81, 91, 94, 115, 121, 122, 136, 263, 266
  as Ariel, 138; arrival of Holy Spirit, 167, 239, *240;* capital of Judah, 80; and David's headquarters, 64, 67, 85; destruction of, 77, 96, 100, 137, 141, 150, 151, 152, 170, 288; future glory of, 141, 167, 174, 179, 314; and Jesus' triumphal entry, 183, 184, 198, 211, 224, 233; Paul's visits to, 247, 268; prophecies against, 173, 223, 226, 311; rebuilding of walls, 100, 101, 102; worship center, 91, 217, 218; as Zion, 117, 120, 136, 138

Jesse, 60, 137

Jesus Christ
  anointings of, 200, 211, 220, 233; ascension of, 213, 228, 238; baptism of, 190, 205, 218, *230;* betrayal of, 116, 200, 202, 225, 226; birth of, 305 (foretold, 136, 146, 174, 215; Luke's story of, 214, 215, *215*); calms storm, 192, 208, 220; cleanses temple, 199, 224, *225,* 231; Creator, 229–230; crucifixion, 204, 227, 234–235. *See also* Crucifixion; death of, (and atonement, 288, 290; burial of, *227*); deliverance through, 253; disagreements with Pharisees (on authority of Jesus, 211, 221, 223–224; on blasphemy, 232–233; on fasting, 206; on hypocrisy, 197, 200, 225; on ritual washing, 196, 208; on sabbath breaking, 193–194, 218; on traditions, 199, *210*); disagreements with Sadducees, 197, 225; disciples of. *See* Disciple(s); Apostle(s); early life of, 190; eternal life through, 301–302; eternal rule, 184, 309, 313; fulfills prophecies, 189; genealogy of, 189; Great Commission, 203, 204, 213, 238; headquarters in Capernaum, 190; and healing, (the blind, *195,* 198, 224; demon possession, 197, 210; in Gospel of Matthew, 192, 193, 194, 196; in Gospel of Mark, 206, 208; in Gospel of Luke, 218, 220, 223; in Gospel of John, 231; palsy, *193;* woman with crooked back, 222); as High Priest, 288, 289; "I am" statements, 233; as Lamb, 310, 311, 313; Last Supper, 201, *201;* Lord's Supper, 260; and love of God, 252; as Mediator, 121; as Messiah, (acclaimed as, 198, 224, 225; belief in, 229; David's descendant, 200; Peter's confession, 210; prophecies concerning, 162, *183;* recognized by John the Baptist, 230, 231; recognized by Stephen, 241; unbelief in, 232, 293); miracles

of, 194, 196, *196*, 197, 205, 208, 218, 220, 231, 233; Jesus Christ, as Savior; and Jesus Christ, as Redeemer (Word of God, 229); and new covenant, 187; parables of, 194, 196, 197, *198*, 198, 199, 200, 207, *207,* 211, 214, 220, 221, 222, 224 (Lazarus, 223); prayers of, 234; predicts own death and resurrection, 194, 197, 198, 210, 220, 221, 224; quotes Old Testament, 39, 115, 116; as Redeemer, 268; rejection of, 196, 208, 220, 231, 233, 239, 296; resurrection (apostles' witness to, 241, 260, 261; and authority, 310; Gospel accounts of, 204, 213, 228; and hope, 296; Jesus as, 233; in Psalms, 115; prophecies of, 197, 210, 221, as sign, 194; and Thomas, *235,* 236); return of (second coming), 275, 276, *276,* 277, *278,* 279, 290, 295, 299; sacrifice of, 29; and salvation, 267; Savior (death of, 189; and judgment, 167); servanthood of, *232,* 233; Shepherd, 233, 298; suffering of, 118, 139, 140, 194, 205, 298; superiority of, 288, 314; tempted by Satan, 190, 206, 217, 218, 288–289, 301; transfiguration/divine glory of, 197, 210, 220, *302;* triumphal entry, *183,* 184, 198, 211, 224, 233; as victor, 263

Jethro/Reuel/Hobab, 25, 27

Jezebel, queen of Israel, 70, 75, 76, 79, 126

Jezreel, city, 51

Jezreel valley, *75*

Joab, 64, 65, 66, 67, 68, 69, 71, 86

Joash/Jehoash, 80, 93

Job, book of, 109–112, 120, 124

Joel, book of, 166–167

Joel, prophet, 163

John
   as apostle, 188, 198, 206, 210, 220, 225, 236, 242, 265; arrested, 239; biblical author, 188, 229, 300, *308, 312;* called by Jesus, 190, 218; healings by, 239; at Jesus' tomb, 235; at Transfiguration, 197; writings of 205, 229–236, 287, 300–302, 303, 304, 307–314

John Mark. *See* Mark

John the Baptist, 138, 230, 231, 247
   baptizes Jesus, 190, 205–206, 218, 230; birth of, 215, 216; as Elijah, 186; execution of, 208; imprisoned, 193, 196; prepares way for Jesus, 186, 190, 205, 215, 218, 230

Jonah, book of, 171–172

Jonah/Jonas, prophet, 163

Jonathan, 59, 61, 63, 65, 67, 68

Joppa/Jaffa/Japho, 243

Jordan River, 39, 43, 45, 46, 47, 66, 68, 78, 85, 231

Joseph, earthly father of Jesus, 189, 190, 216, 217, 218, 293

Joseph of Arimathea, 204, 213, 223, 227, 235, 241

Joseph, son of Jacob, 22, 23, 24, 181, 290

Josephus, 226

Joshua/Oshea/Hoshea/Jehoshuah/Jeshua

    leader of Israel, 33, 36, 37, 38, 44, 45, 46, 47, 48, 50, 68, 289; priest, 182, 184

Joshua, book of, 45–48

Josiah/Josias, 73, 77, 82, 83, 95, 143, 179

Jotham/Joatham, 52, 80, 81, 93, 94

Jothan, 173

Jubile/Jubilee, 32

Judah/Juda, son of Jacob, 22, 23, 34, 47, 84, 85

Judah/Juda, Southern Kingdom, 55, 78, 79, 135, 168, 173

    captivity of, 83, 89, 84, 147, 151, 163. *See also* Babylonia; conquered by Babylon, 77, 137, 147, 148, 152, 159, 166; David as king, 63, 64; plagued by locusts 166, 167; punishment foretold, 82, 145, 146, 151, 168, 173, 174, 177, 179; sins of, 74, 77, 81, 82, 93, 94, 95, 100, 102, 136, 139, 142, 143, 151, 179, 185, 186; splits from Israel, 70, 73, 80, 90, 94

Judaizers, 265, 266, 272

Judas Iscariot, 116, 200, 202, 211, 225, 233, 234, 239

Jude, epistle of, 287, 305–306

Judea, 216

Judges, book of, 44, 49–54, 55

Justification, 224, 251, 252, 253, 254, 266, 306

K

Kedar, 150

Keturah, 84

Kings, books of, 44, 70–76, 77–83

Kirjath-jearim, 58

Kishon brook, 75

Kohath, 34, 35, 48

Korah, 36

L

Laban, 21

Laish, 53

Lamb of God. *See* Jesus Christ, as Lamb

Land of Promise. *See* Promised Land

Lamentations, book of, 134, 151–152, 163

Laodicea, 310

Last Supper, 201, 234. *See also* Lord's Supper

Law. *See* Law of Moses

Law of Moses, 15, 16, 82, 95, 102. *See also* Pentateuch

Lawsuits, 258

Lazarus of Bethany, 233
Lazarus, parable of, 223
Laziness, 126
Leah, 21
Leaven, 30
Lebanon, 28
Lemuel, 124
Leper/leprosy, 30, 35, 78, 93, 192, 206,
    218, 223
Levi, disciple Matthew, 189, 206, 218
Levi, Jacob's son, 26, 35
Levites, 34, 35, 37, 38, 41, 43, 47, 48, 53,
    54, 84, 85, 86, 88, 92, 94, 97, 98, 99,
    102, 103
Leviticus, book of, 29–32
Locust, 166, *166*, 167
Lord's Prayer, 221
Lord's Supper, the, 211, 260, 306
Lot, 19, 20
Lots, 102, 103, 106, 156, 171
Luke/Lucas, 188, 214, 238, 288
Luke, Gospel of, 205, 214–228, 238
Luther, Martin, 117, 252
Lycaonia, 244
Lydda, 243
Lydia, 246, 271
Lyre, 88
Lystra, 245

M

Macedonia, 246, 247, 263, 275

Machpelah, 20
Magic/Magicians, 41, 77
Magnificat, 216
Mahanaim, 67
Maher-shalal-hash-haz, 136
Malachi, book of, 185–186
Malachi, prophet, 163, 180, 185
Malta. *See* Melita
Manasseh/Manasees, king of Judah, 77,
    82, 94
Manna, 27, 35, 36
Manoah, 52
Marah, 26
Mark, Gospel of, 205–213
Mark, John/Marcus, 188, 205, 244, 298
Marriage
    betrothal, 190; Paul's teachings on,
    258; physical aspects, 132; sacred to
    God, 126, 132
Martha, 221, 233
Mary Magdalene, 204, 213, *219*, 220,
    234, 235
Mary, mother of Jesus
    betrothal of, 189, 190; children of,
    293; Luke's account, 215–217, 215;
    John (apostle) cares for, 229, 234
Mary of Bethany, 200, 221, 233
Mary, wife of Cleophas, 234
Masada, *114*
Mattaniah, 83, 96
Matthew, Gospel of, 189–204, 205, 214

Matthew/Levi, apostle, 188, 192, 206, 218; Gospel author, 188

Matthias, 239

Media, 137, 161, 162

Mediterranean Sea, 238, 243, 247, 249, 285

Megiddo/Megiddon, 216

Melchizedek/Melchisedec, 19, 121, 289

Melita/Malta, 249

Menahem, 81

Mephihosheth/Merib-Baal, 65, 66

Merari, 34, 35, 48

Meribah, 37

Meshach/Mishael, 159, 160, *160*, 161

Mesopotamia, 21, 50

Messiah/Messias, 141, 180
   ancestry of, 23; birth of, 173, 174, 216; Jesus as, 197, 200; as King, 138, 179, 224, 225; Lord of the Sabbath, 194; as Prince of Peace, 137; prophecies of, 114, 120–121, 135, 136, 146, 162, 182, 183, 186, 211, 215; as servant, 139, 140

Micah, book of, 173–174

Micah, priest, 53

Micah, prophet, 163, 173

Micaiah, 76, 92

Michal, 61, 64

Midian, 25

Midianites, 38, 49, 51, 52

Miletus/Miletum, 247, 268

Miracle(s). *See also* Healing
   of disciples, 239, 241; of Jesus, 194, 196, *196*, 197, 205, 208, 218, 220, 231, 233; of prophets, 25, 26, 75, 77, 78, 80, 82

Miriam, 35

Mizpeh, 58

Moabite(s), 78
   ancestry of, 20; judgments against, 137, 150; oppose Israel, 37, 49, 50, 65, 86, 93; prophecies against, 151, 168, 179; Ruth as, 55; worship of, 33

Mordecai, 105, 106, 107, 186

Mosaic Law. *See* Law of Moses

Moses, 186
   biblical writer, 24, 120; birth of, 25; death of, 39, 43; faith of, 290; and Jesus, 289; and Law, 16, 24; leads Israel, 25, 26, 30, 33, 36, 39, 45; miracles of, 25, 26; and Promised Land, 33, 37, 40; as teacher, 189; in Transfiguration, *302*

N

Naaman, 78

Nabal, 61

Naboth, 76, 126

Nadab, Aaron's son, 30

Nadab, Jeroboam's son, 74

Nahum, book of, 175–176

Nahum, prophet, 163, 175

Naomi, 55, 56

Naphtali, 34, 48, 85

Nathan, prophet, 65, 66, 71

Nathanael, 174, 230

Nazareth, 215, 216
  childhood home of Jesus, 190, 217;
  rejects Jesus, 196, 218, 340

Nazarite/Nazirite, 35, 52, 53

Nebo, Mount, 39, 43, *43*

Nebuchadnezzar/Nebuchadrezzar
  dreams of, 140, 160, 161; fiery
  furnace of, 160, 161; invades Judah,
  83, 96, 159; releases Jeremiah from
  prison, 148

Nehemiah, 100–103

Nehemiah, book of, 44, 100–103

Nicodemus, 223, 231, 232, 235, 241

Nile River, 25, 40

Nineveh/Nineve, 171, 172, 175, 176

Noah/Noe, 18, 19, *19*, 29, 84, 290–291

Nob, 61

Numbers, book of, 33–38

Nymphas, 286

O

Obadiah, book of, 152

Obadiah, prophet, 163, 170

Obed, 56

Obed-edom, 64, 86

Og, 37, 40

Olives, Mount of, 239

Olympics, 258

Omri, 75

Onesimus, 274, 286

Onesiphorus, 284

Ornan/Araunah, 69, 86

Othniel, 50

P

Palm, 310

Pamphylia, 244

Parable(s), 194, 196, 197, 198, *198*, 199,
  200, 207, *207*, 211, 214, 222, 223, 224

Pashur, 146

Passover
  observed by Jesus, 201, 211, 217, 225,
  233; in Old Testament times, 31, 35,
  41, 83, 94, 95, 98, 226, 261

Patmos, isle of, *307*, *308*, 309

Paul
  conversion of, 50, 241, 242, 248, 250;
  epistles of, 250, 288 (Colossians,
  273–274;Corinthians, 256–261,
  262–264; Ephesians, 268–269;
  Galatians, 265–267; Philippians,
  270–272; Romans, 251–255;
  Thessalonians, 275–276, 277–279;
  Timothy, 280–282, 283–284; Titus,
  285; Philemon, 286); healings by,
  244; imprisonment/trial (in Rome,
  238, 249; epistles written, 268, 270,
  273, 283, 284, 286); journeys of, 205,

238, 244, 245, 246, 280; letters from. *See* Paul, epistles of; preaching of, 238, 244, 252, 275, 280; teaching on women 260, 281, 282); as spiritual father, 280, 283, 285, 286; sufferings of, 46, 248, 249, 259, 262, 263, 267, 271, 283

Pekah, 81

Pekahiah, 81

Pentateuch, 16

Pentecost, day of, 167, 239

Pentecost, feast of, 31, 247

Perga, 244

Pergamos, 309

Pergamum. *See* Pergamos

Persecution, 236, 239, 241, 242, 267, 277, 291, 293, 295, 296, 298

Persia, 44, 83, 100, 104, 105, 106, 107, 140, 181, 186, 289
allows rebuilding of temple, 98, 101; defeats Babylonian Empire, 96, 97, 137, 159, 161; prophecies against, 162

Peter (Simon Peter), 191, 218, 225, 226, 228, 230, 235, 243, 257, 266
arrested, 239; called by Jesus, 190, 206, 218, 229; death of, 236, 297, 299; denial of Jesus, 211, 212, 226, 234; epistles of, 287, 296–298, 299; healings by, 193, 239, 243; and Jesus, 202; leader in early church, 239, 265, 296; and Mark, 205; at Pentecost, 167; preaching of, 197, 210, 220, 238, 239, 242, 243; reinstated by Jesus, 236; at Transfiguration, 197

Pharaoh, 167, 181. *See also* Egypt

Pharisee(s)
Jesus' disagreements with (on authority of Jesus, 211, 221, 223–224; on blasphemy, 232–233; on fasting, 206, 225; on hypocrisy, 197, 200; on ritual washing, 196, 208; on Sabbath breaking, 193–194, 218; on traditions, 199, 210); Paul's background as, 250

Phebe, 255

Philadelphia, 310

Philemon, 286

Philip, brother of King Herod, 196

Philip, disciple of Jesus, 174, 230, 241, 247

Philip II of Macedonia, 270

Philippi, 246, 270, 271

Philippians, epistle to, 250, 268–271

Philistine(s)
David lives among, 62; oppose Israelites, 21, 49, 50, 52, 53, *53*, 57, 58, 59, 60, 64, 65, 68, 83, 85, 86, 93, 94; prophecies against, 150, 179

Phinehas, 58

Phoenix, 249

Phrygia, 246

Phylactery, 200
Pilate, 202, 204, 212, 226, 234
Pisidia, 244
Plague, 26
Plumbline, 169
Pontus, 296
Potter, *145,* 146
Priscilla/Prisca, 246, 247, 255, 261, 284, 286
Prodigal Son, the, 214
Promised Land, the, 24, 33, 36, 37, 39, 44, 45, 143
Proverbs, book of, 124–128, 130
Psalms, book of, 113–123
Pul, 81
Purim, Feast of, 105, 106, 107

Q
Queen of Sheba, 73, 90, 125

R
Rabbah, 66, 86
Rahab, 46
Rain, 18, 26, 40, 75, 295
Ramah, 58, 61, 62
Ramoth-Gilead, 76, 79, 93
Reconciliation, 263, 268
Rehoboam, 70, 73, 90, 91
Rephaim, Valley of, 64, 86
Reuben, 26, 34, 38, 40, 45, 92, 48, 85
Reuel, 25

Revelation, book of, 287, 307–314
Romans, epistle to, 250, 251–255, 279
Rome, *251,* 252, 296, 299
    embraces Christianity, 238; Paul in, 248, 249, 250, 251, 286
Ruth, book of, 44, 55–56

S
Sabbath
    day of rest, 27, 31, 36; ignored by Judah, 103, 145; Jesus' teachings on, 193–194, 218
Sacrifice(s) 29, 290
Sadducees, 197, 199, 211, 225
Salt, 190, 192
Salvation, 135, 140, 182, 233, 243, 252, 254, 265, 266, 268, 269, 271, 273, 277, 270, 289, 296, 298, 299, 301
Samaria
    capital of Israel, 75, 76, 79, 80, 165; evangelized, 242; Jesus in, 221, 231; prophecies against, 173
Samaritan, Good, 214, 221
Samson, 52, 53, 54, 83
Samuel, 57, 58, 59, 40, 41, 42, 43; books of, 44, 57–62, 63–69
Sanballat, 101
Sanhedrin, 200, 202, 204, 211, 212, 223, 225, 226, 233, 234, 239, 241, 248
Sapphira, 241
Sarah, 20

Sarai. *See* Sarah

Sardis, 310

Satan

    afflicts Job, 109–110; battles Christ, 309, 311, 314; chief of demons, 221; tempts Jesus, 190, 206, 218

Saul, 85

    and David (pursues, 61, 62, 115, 117, 118, 122); death of, 58, 62, 63, 64, 91, 119; failures of, 57, 59, 60, 62, 63; king of Israel, 59, 68

Saul/Paul, 241, 242

Scribe(s), 210

Second Coming, the, 275, *276,* 277, 278, 279, 290, 295, 299

Sela, 170

Sennacherib, 81, 94, 138

Sermon on the Mount, the, 189, 192, 220

Serpent, 37

Sexual sins/purity, 31, 258, 262, 276, 292, 310

Shadrach, 159, 160, 161

Shallum, 81, 146

Shalmaneser, 79, 81

Shamgar, 50

Sheba, 68

Shechem, 52

Sheep, *186*

Shem, 84

Shemuel. *See* Samuel

Shiloh, 58

Shimei, 66, 67, 71

Shishak, 91

Shunem, 78, 79

Shushan, 105

Sihon, 40

Silas/Silvanus, 245, 246, 275, 277, 298

Silvanus. *See* Silas

Simeon, prophet, 216, 217

Simeon, son of Jacob, 21, 22, 26, 34, 48, 85

Simon, of Cyrene, 202, 213, 226

Simon, the Pharisee, 220

Simon, the sorcerer, 242

Simon, the tanner, 243

Sin, 345

Sinai, Mount, 27, 33, 35, 39, 40

Sion. *See* Zion

Sisera, 51

Skull, the. *See* Calvary

Slavery, 121, 143, 148, 164, 165, 167, 168, 169, 253, 254, 255, 257, 267, 274, 282, 286

Smyrna, 309

Sodom, 136

Solomon, 44, 65, 70, 71, 72, 73, 84, 89, 90, 124, *125,* 129, 130, 132, 210

Song of Solomon, book of, 132–133

Spain, 252, 255

Stephen, 241

Stephanas, 261

Suffering, 109–112, 118

Synoptic Gospels, 188

Syria, 65, 70, 76, 78, 80, 86, 92, 93, 94, 137, 245

T

Tabernacle, 24, 28, 29, 31, 33, 34, 35, 36, 71

Tabernacles, Feast of, 31, 41, 102

Tamar, daughter-in-law of Judah, 22

Tamar, daughter of David, 66

Tarshish, 171

Tarsus, 243

Taxes, 197, 225, 254

Teacher of the law. *See* Scribe(s)

Teacher, 346

Teachers/Teachings, false, 265, 270, 273, *274*, 277, 280, 282, 285, 287, 299, 300, 301, 303, 305

Tekoa, 168, 169

Temple

Jerusalem's destroyed, 77, 118, 119, 182, *291*; Jesus in, 216; looted by Nebuchadnezzar, 159; repaired, 82, 95; rebuilt, 97, 98,102, 180, 181; Solomon's, 72, 84, 89, 98

Temptation, 259, 298

of Jesus, 190, 206, 217, 218, 288–289, 301

Tent of Meeting. *See* Tabernacle

Ten Commandments, 24, 27, 40

Tertius, 279

Theophilus, 214, 215, 238

Thessalonians, epistles to, 250, 275–276, 277–279

Thessalonica, 246, 275

Thomas, *235,* 236

Thyatira, 310

Tiber River, *251*

Tiglath-pileser III, 81

Tilgath-Pilneser III. *See* Tiglath-Pileser III

Tigris River, 162

Timothy/Timotheus, 245, 246, 261, 271, 275, 277, 280, 281, 282, 283

Timothy, epistles to, 250, 280–282, 283–284, 285

Titus, epistle to, 250, 285

Tobiah, 101, 102

Tola, 52

Tongue(s), 239, 260, 295

Torah. *See* Pentateuch

Tribes of Israel

Dan, 34, 48, 53; Issachar, 34; Manasseh, 22, 23, 34, 38, 40, 45, 47, 48, 51, 85; Naphtali, 51

Troas, 247

Trumpet(s), 310, 311, 313

Turkey, *245,* 309

Tychicus, 274

Tyre, 64, 72, 247

prophecies against, 137, 168

U

Unity, 258, 269, 272, 298

Uriah, 65

Urijah, 147

Uzzah, 64, 86

Uzziah (Azariah), 80, 93, 94, 135

V

Vashti, 105

Virgin birth, 215

Vow, 130

W

Western Wall, *291*

Widow(s), 282

Wife/Wives, 128, *128,* 298

Wine, 31, 52, 100, 145, 148, 150, 151, 160, 165, 180, 225, 230, 239, 271

Winepress, 151, 180

Wise Men, 161, 189, 214

Word of God, 115, 177, 229, 247, 269, 257

Y

Yoke, 165

Z

Zacchaeus, 224

Zachariah, 81

Zacharias, 215, 216

Zadok, 66

Zalmunna, 52

Zebah, 52

Zebedee, 229

Zebulun, 34, 48, 51

Zechariah, book of, 182–184, 307

Zechariah, prophet, 98, 163, 180, 182, 183, 185

Zedekiah, 83, 96, 143, 146, 147

Zelophehad, 37, 38

Zephaniah, book of 163, 179

Zerah, 92

Zerubbabel, 97, 98, 102, 181, 183

Ziba, 66

Zidonians, 53

Ziklag, 62, 85

Zimri, 74

Zion, 117, 120, 122, 138

Mount, 152, 311

Zipporah, 25

Zophar, 110–111

Zorobabel. *See* Zerubbabel

Art Credits